CRAFTS
JAMBOREE

VNR VAN NOSTRAND REINHOLD COMPANY
NEW YORK   CINCINNATI   TORONTO   LONDON   MELBOURNE

Copyright © 1977 by Marshall Cavendish Limited
Library of Congress Catalog Card Number 77-6403
ISBN 0-442-21351-4

Published in 1977 by Van Nostrand Reinhold
Company
A division of Litton Educational Publishing, Inc.
450 West 33rd Street, New York, N.Y. 10001, U.S.A.

Van Nostrand Reinhold Limited
1410 Birchmount Road
Scarborough, Ontario MIP 2E7, Canada

16 15 14 13 12 11 10 9 8 7 6 5 4 3 2

Library of Congress Cataloging in Publication
Data
Main entry under title:

Crafts jamboree.

    Includes index.
    1. Handicraft. I. Deutch, Yvonne.
TT157.C685   745.5   77-6403
ISBN 0-442-21351-4

Introduction

Crafts are fun – and immensely satisfying too. **Crafts Jamboree** is the ideal introduction to a vast range of absorbing pastimes, ranging from basketry to preserving flowers. Whatever your age you'll find something here to appeal to your imagination. There are lots of super projects to try, all equally exciting and creative, which give really attractive results. In fact, even if you've never tried handicrafts before, you'll be amazed at how professional and stylish your work will appear.

Crafts Jamboree is delightfully easy to use – beautifully presented, packed with gorgeous illustrations, and backed up with the kind of expertise which combines clear, concise instructions with see-at-a-glance diagrams. Using step-by-step techniques for modeling, weaving, ropework, glass etching, lapidary, rugmaking, knitting, crochet, tatting and enameling, to name but a few, you'll be able to create both traditional and up-to-the-minute designs for yourself and for your home.

Remember that there are over 30 crafts to try, so you'll never be at a loss for ideas. You can make wonderful gifts for your friends too, for example a corn dolly makes an enchanting good luck symbol for a newly-wed couple. This is just one suggestion from a treasure trove of intriguing possibilities. Whatever project you choose to start off with, you'll be guaranteed hours of satisfaction.

Contents

Countrycrafts

From field and hedgerow generations have gathered the raw materials for country crafts such as basketry and rushwork. Here you can learn the basics of these skills, plus how to make enchanting corn dollies and corn shuck dolls.

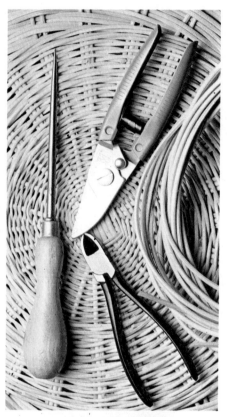

Simple corn dollies

Corn dollies were made as long ago as 5000 years. They are found in various forms all over the world. They were generally made as fertility symbols. After the last sheaf of the harvest was cut it would be made into a corn dolly and great feasting and celebration would take place. Ceres, the goddess of the harvest, was thought to live in the corn dollies which were kept indoors during winter to protect the goddess.

In the spring the corn dollies would be cast into the fields so that the goddess could help germinate the new corn.

Corn dollies were also used as sacrifices or in worship to a pagan god. Examples of corn dollies have been found in Mexico in the form of angels; Germany and Scandinavia also produced decorative objects made from corn and in Bulgaria they were made from maize. Corn dollies are not necessarily made in the form of 'dolls', but in a number of traditional, often symbolic shapes. The word doll or dolly is in fact a corruption of the word 'idol'.

In England different parts of the country made different types of corn dollies which have now become traditional. For example, a lantern is associated with Norfolk but a variation of it is also found in Hereford. A spiral is associated with Essex and fans are associated with Wales.

The plaiting and weaving techniques used to make corn dollies can be used to make all sorts of decorative objects for the home. The corn dollies in themselves are decorative but they can be combined to make mobiles, or stars can be made for seasonal decorations. Children as well as grown-ups will enjoy making them.

The straw most commonly used to make corn dollies is wheat. The straw should have a hollow centre. Oats, rye and maize [corn] can also be used. Cut the wheat when it is nearly ripe as it will give a longer length with which to work. The wheat is cut just above the first join or node and usually below the ear to remove the sheath. Do not remove all the ears as they are used as well. Keep the wheat with the more attractive ears whole and try to select them in similar sizes.

Fertilizer tends to make the wheat brittle so try to find wheat which has been grown with a minimum amount of fertilizer.

Cutting the wheat can be a problem as the modern combine harvester threshes and generally mangles the wheat, separating the grain, which makes it unsuitable. Cutting by hand is best but it can be tiresome if you want a great deal. A tractor-driven binder will provide suitable wheat as it cuts cleanly and ties the sheaves without too much damage to the ears.

Dry the straw by spreading it out on racks in the sun but if this is not possible bundles can be hung from rafters in a dry place or placed in an airing cupboard or in a slow oven with the door open. Once dry, straw can be stored for years.

Grade the straw before you work with

Red ribbons, symbolizing warmth, are tied to the Welsh fan to complete it. Made by Carolyn Tidmarsh.

it. Sort it out into two or three groups so that you have small and medium or large sizes. Compare the thickness of the wheat where it has been cut and the length of the stems and arrange them accordingly.

Storage must be in a dry atmosphere to prevent the straw from going mouldy. Other hazards are mice, rats and seed eating birds like sparrows—they can do a lot of damage in a very short space of time.

Working with straw

Damping. Once the straw has been dried it will split if it is plaited. To prevent this the straw must be soaked in water. The time taken to soften the wheat varies—depending on how dry it is. Test the wheat by pinching it, if it does not split it is ready to use. Do not oversoak the wheat as it becomes too soft to handle with ease.

Warm water will speed up the damping

A straw 'scythe'—a variation on a traditional corn dolly technique.

process. Do not let the ears get wet. Arrange a damp towel around the wheat while you are working—this prevents it from drying before you are ready to use it.

Paper straws

Getting hold of straw is not always easy as it is seasonal but if you stock up on it you will have plenty to keep you busy. If you are unable to obtain corn [wheat] you can use paper straws. Paper straws, similar to drinking straws, can be used in the same way as straw—the same techniques apply—but they do not require damping. The paper straws can be coloured to improve their appearance.

In the next two chapters the techniques involved in working with straw are explained.

Paper straw dollies

A good way to learn how to make corn dollies is to practise first with paper straws. These are more readily available from craft shops than are wheat straws and the weaving technique is very similar to that used in corn dolly weaving. Paper straws have added advantages in that they can be glued or threaded together and they can be coloured, thus extending the range of decorative objects it is possible to produce with them.

Drinking straws can also be used but because they are waxed they cannot be coloured or glued. Paper straws are available in two sizes; the standard size being similar to a drinking straw and the other size being slightly larger.

Colours

Several types of colour can be used for decorating paper straws.

Powder or poster colours are best applied to the finished object as the dry paint rubs off during the handling. Paint them as thickly as possible, so that the straws will not become soggy and unmanageable.

Aerosol paints, though more expensive, give a good all-over colour and help to make the finished model firmer. They also dry quickly.

Cold water dyes are an economical way to colour both finished objects and individual straws, but dip quickly to prevent the water softening the paper, then drain on newspaper. Handle wet objects with care to prevent them losing their shape.

Use dyes according to the manufacturer's instructions but with half the recommended quantity of water. Test dip straws in the dye before embarking on a project to ensure the right colour.

Wood stains can also be used. Colours are not limited to shades generally associated with timber. In powder form, you can mix the stain with water. Alternatively you can use methylated spirit [de-natured alcohol]. Test first.

Inks can be used for bright, fast colours and also for colouring individual straws before working with them, as they do not rub off in handling.

Joining

Both wheat and paper straws are plaited and woven the same way, but the joining methods are slightly different. Wheat tapers slightly along its length, so the smaller end is pushed into the hollow larger end of another straw, but paper straws all have the same diameter so cannot be joined like this.

To join paper straws, run your fingernail lengthways along the end of the straw that is to fit inside the other

Tractor made from paper straws.

straw and score it about 6mm (¼"). Squeeze the end lightly so that the indentation makes a heart shape on the cross-section. Push this end into the other straw as far as it will go without denting or creasing either of the two straws (fig.1). This makes a strong join.

Another method is to cut a slit 2cm (¾") down the length of the straw, squeeze the straw lightly so that the cut edges overlap, then push this end into the end of another straw (fig.2). Wheat straws of the same diameter are also joined together like this.

Try to join straws at a place where they will not have to be folded as it is difficult to bend a double thickness of straw. Bulky folds spoil the regularity of the weave.

Weaving

You can weave with any number of straws from four upwards. Two and three straws cannot be woven but can be plaited to make braids which were traditionally known as 'favours' and worn in the buttonhole. Braiding is simply the twisting together of straws of the same thickness.

To make a two-straw braid, tie two straws firmly together at the top, hold them in the left hand at the knot and fold the first straw over the second to form a right angle (fig.3a). Fold the second straw up and over to lie across the first straw at right angles. Continue like this until you have the length you want (fig.3b).

Using more than two straws. The shape of the objects being woven depends greatly on the number of straws used. Four straws, for example, produce a triangle in cross-section (fig.4), while five straws make a square (fig.5). The more straws you weave with, the rounder the shape will become and the firmer the finished object will be.

The five-straw weave is the basic weaving process for both corn dollies and paper straws. Once this has been mastered, it is fairly easy to tackle any number of straws up to about ten or twelve.

Weaving round a central core or 'former' is the easiest way to work because the former helps to shape the weaving as its grows. After this, you can progress to free weaving, working without a former.

Five-straw weave

☐ Tie the five straws together tightly about 2.5cm (1") from one end and again about half way along the length of the straws. The distance between ties makes the former. (When working a free weave, omit the second tie.)

☐ Hold the straws in your left hand with the fastened ends upwards, forming the core.

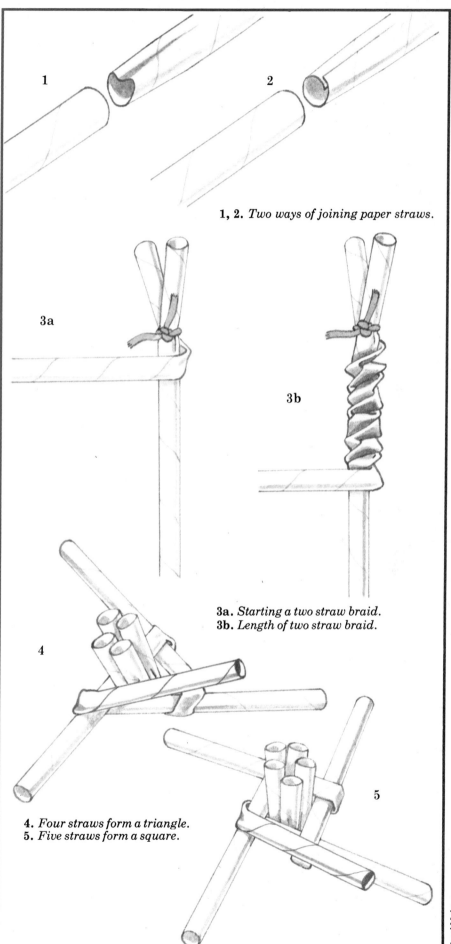

1, 2. *Two ways of joining paper straws.*

3a. *Starting a two straw braid.*
3b. *Length of two straw braid.*

4. *Four straws form a triangle.*
5. *Five straws form a square.*

Coral Mula

□ Fan out the straws below the second tie so that they make a square. Three corners have one straw each and the fourth corner has two (fig.6), which

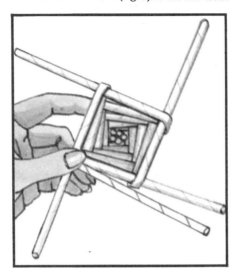

6. *Starting a five-straw weave.*

will be nearest to you. Bend the straw nearest you (A) and lay it anti-clockwise over the next two straws, close to the central former.

□ Move the work clockwise so that the last straw you went over (C) is nearest to you. Hold the work lightly, trying not to flatten the straws.

□ Take straw C up and over straws A

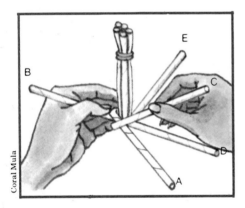

Coral Mula

7. *Working around the former.*

and D (fig.7), again holding it against the central former.

□ Continue like this always taking the last straw you passed over and moving it anti-clockwise over the next two straws to produce a spiral. Remember always to turn the work towards you in a clockwise direction each time you move a straw. The neatness of the work as it builds up round the former depends on the regular folds of the working straws.

Shaping is controlled by laying the straws in certain positions. To keep a straight shape, each straw must be placed exactly over the straws which are underneath it.

To increase the width, take the straw over the next two in the usual way but lay it slightly outside the straws underneath (fig.8). Pull the next

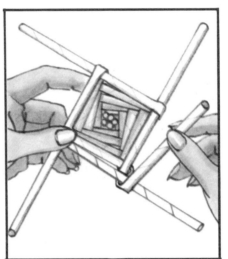

8. *First step to increase width.*

straw back under the overlying one, take it over and position it alongside the next straw (fig.9). Continue like this until you have the right size.

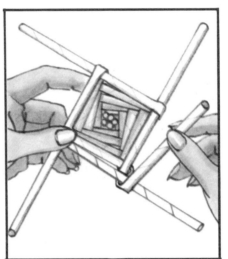

9. *Second step to increase width.*

To decrease the width lay the straw slightly inside one underneath (fig.10). Obviously, when working round a former, you cannot decrease width, so this applies only after increasing or in free weaving. Do not try to hurry the shaping process or it will spoil the finished result.

To finish off, tuck the ends of the straw into the weave. Glue is used on paper straws only when making pictures or collages or assembling woven pieces to complete an object. Use a quick-drying, clear adhesive so that the straws can be held in place while they dry.

Thread or thin wire may be used to tie

straws together and is especially useful when making mobiles. Pass thread or thin wire through the straws with a sewing needle.

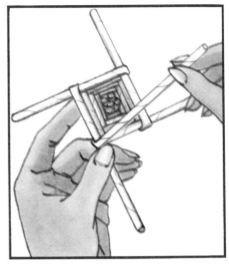

10. *Decreasing the width.*

Paper straw mice

These delightful little mice are made by free weaving without a central former. The largest mouse is about 10cm (4″) long excluding the tail.

The mice illustrated have been left white, but they can be coloured in various ways if you prefer.

Start a six-straw flat base weave without a former by taking three straws and placing them one on top of the other in a star shape.

Weave, but without a former, moving each straw over the next two (fig.11). Increase as soon as you can to make the

11. *Six straw weave.*

fat part of the mouse, then gradually decrease, ending by tying the six straws together with white cotton and trimming to a point for the nose.

For the tail, insert a flattened straw through the base weave. Use the two halves to make a two straw braid. Glue the two ends together and cut to a point. Two pieces of flattened straw are glued in place for the ears and another piece, fringed at both ends, is stuck in for whiskers.

Three white mice for the cat's delight. They are made from paper straws using corn dolly weaving techniques. Designed by Anne Stone.

Traditional corn dollies

Rupert Watts

Previous chapters contain information on how to cut, dry, store and dampen wheat straw and how to weave with paper straws when it is inconvenient for you to obtain the traditional dolly material. Having mastered these techniques, it is now possible to progress to making some of the traditional golden corn dollies that look so delightful hanging in a kitchen or serving as unusual table decorations. Another interesting use for them is to revive the old custom of making a baby rattle out of straw, enclosing inside either a small bell or a few beans to make an intriguing noise.

The materials for corn dolly making are simple enough: hollow-centred straw such as wheat, oats, rye or maize [corn]; raffia, a sharp pair of scissors, wire and ribbon.

The ribbons used to adorn traditional corn dollies have different meanings. Red stands for the poppy and for warmth, green for Spring and fertility, blue for the cornflower and Truth, yellow for the corn and the goddess Ceres, white for Purity and brown for the earth.

Remember it is essential to dampen the straw before working with it as dry straw will split when plaited.

Five straw favour

These were often made by farm hands as love tokens for their sweethearts.

☐ Take five straws with the ears still in place and, with raffia, tie them together firmly just below the ears.

☐ Spread out the straw and work a five straw weave (as previously shown on page 11) without a former and with the ears dangling from the weave. Do not increase the size of the work: keep it constant along its length.

☐ Leave a short length of unwoven straw at the end.

☐ Tie the straws where the weaving ends with raffia.

☐ Bend the plait into a loop and tie together above the ears.

☐ Trim off excess straw and decorate with ribbon bow.

Suffolk horseshoe

The 'horseshoe' is another five straw plait, like the 'favour' and the 'lantern' (described next).

You will need a former to work round and about twenty-five to thirty straws.

☐ For the former take about six 15cm (6″) long straws and a short length of wire. Bind the straws together with the wire.

☐ Tie five straws on to the end of the former with the straws pointing away from the former and spread the straws

Traditional corn dollies—Welsh fan, Hereford lantern and Suffolk horseshoe. Designed by Carolyn Tidmarsh.

Horseshoe and five straw favour.

into a five-pointed star (fig.1).

☐ With the former pointing upwards, plait round the core using the decreasing plait all the time.

1. *Working around the former.*

☐ Close the end and finish off by tucking one straw under the opposite one (fig.2).

2. *Straw tucked under to finish.*

☐ Trim straw ends close to the plait and bend into a horseshoe-shape.
☐ Trim with a spray of oats (as a compliment to the horse) and a ribbon. If you have some experience doing the five straw weave, you can bend the former into a horseshoe shape and then do the plaiting.

Yorkshire lantern

☐ Take five straws with the ears on them and about thirty without. Cut the ends at a slant to make joining easier.
☐ With raffia, tie five straws just below the ears.
☐ Work a five straw weave and increase the size on every round. Join in new straws as required.
☐ When the base of the lantern is the required size, start decreasing gradually, working until the work comes to a point and closes at the top.

The spiral effect will appear as you decrease. When the work has closed, make sure that you have five long straws joined in.

☐ Continue plaiting and make a loop to finish and tie with raffia. The addition of a coloured ribbon of your choice is optional.

Two traditional corn dolly lanterns, from Yorkshire and Hereford.

Short Welsh fan

☐ Prepare twenty-nine well-matched straws, each with ears the same size and colour.

☐ Tie three firmly together just below the ears.

☐ Lay them flat on a table with the ears facing away from you (fig.3).

Ears of wheat have two sides to them, a rough and a smooth, so make sure the ears are all facing smooth side up.

☐ Keeping the smooth side of the ear uppermost, take a straw and put it under the outside one of the pair so that it lies parallel to the single one (fig.4).

The straws added to the original three are not tied together but locked in position.

☐ Lift up the inside one of the two straws (the stem) and lock it in place by folding the outside straw under it and across to the left, then replace the inside straw (fig.5).

3. *Three straws tied together to start the Welsh fan.*

4. *Fourth straw positioned parallel to single straw.*

5. *Right-hand straw is folded under one and moved to the left.*

You now have one straw on the right side and three on the left.

☐ Insert another straw under the outside straw on the left-hand side (fig.6).

☐ Repeat the locking process (fig.7).

☐ Continue adding one straw on each

side until you have thirteen in all.

As the ears may now begin to crowd together, do an extra locking weave on each side after adding each pair of straws, to secure them.

☐ When all the straws have been used up, do five extra locking weaves

alternately on each side.

☐ Bunch the straws together at the ends, tie with raffia and cut off the surplus straw.

☐ Keep flat while drying.

☐ To decorate, tie ribbons on to each bunch of straws.

6. *Straw added to lie parallel to single one.*

7. *The locking process is repeated on the left.*

The red ribbons on the Welsh fan stand for warmth.

Corn shuck dollies

Making dolls from corn husks is an American craft originated by the colonists who made them to decorate their homes and as toys. Early settlers called their corn husks 'shucks', and so the craft has become known in America as 'cornshuckery'.

These dolls, made from corn husks, are fine examples of the American craft of cornshucking.

Chris Holland

Corn husks can be, and have been, used to make flowers, masks, birds, animals, insects, machines, baskets and place-mats, as well as dolls, so they can be both useful and ornamental about the home.

All kinds of corn provide the raw material for the craft, including field, indian and popcorn. Sweetcorn is probably the most readily obtainable and has the additional advantages of possessing whiter inner shucks and being softer and more pliable to work. Shucks can be mixed—use the sweet-corn for faces and hands of a doll, and the coarser, darker textures of other shucks to make interesting clothes and colour contrasts.

Save the silky strands inside the shuck, as they are used for dolls' hair. Each doll takes about five hours to make and two weeks to dry. You always work with wet shucks, which are blotted on a towel. If you are unable to complete the work in one sitting, the entire doll can be re-dampened and finished later.

Corn dolls are made entirely by rolling and tying. No glue is used except for the hair.

Preparing and selecting

Selecting the corn needs some care. Try to choose ears with as much silk as possible. Buy the ear unopened and avoid tearing down the shuck to look at the golden kernels inside. Remove the shuck very carefully with a knife—cutting round the corn at the top and the bottom, then slowly unravelling the shucks one at a time without tearing them.

This is the material from which the doll will be made and, as in sewing, you will need large pieces of material for sleeves and skirts. If you carelessly remove the shucks, you will have only strips with which to work. The cut at the top of the shuck should be high enough to give a long length and allow you to remove most of the silk in one clump, to dry separately and use for hair.

Drying and storing

When all the shucks have been cut, spread them individually in the sun to dry. Do not dry them in an oven, where even the lowest heat dries a shuck too quickly and makes it too brittle to use. On hot summer days, drying will take only a few days but in autumn it may take as long as a week. Make sure the shucks are completely dry before placing them in a plastic bag for later use, or some may mildew. When you have enough, store the bags in a dry place.

If you gather shucks at seasonal intervals, you will find that early corn has blond corn silk, mid-season corn

A family of dolls made from corn husks and dressed in period costume.

Transworld

has silk suitable for red-headed dolls and late corn silk makes beautiful brunettes. A bouffant hair-style will take the silk of about five ears of corn. Let the silk dry thoroughly in the sun for three to five days. Sort by colour and store in plastic bags separately from shucks.

Remove all silk from shucks, as, if it gets in between the ribbed surface of the shuck it will dry there like cement and if left on a finished doll it will spoil its clean and elegant look.

Colouring

The natural colours of shucks range from clear, pale greens to soft beiges and browns. However, they can also be coloured with dye (see box).

Cornshuck dolls

Instructions are given for a man and a woman doll, 18cm (7″) high.

You will need:
About 12 dried sweetcorn shucks per doll, plus 60 shucks to dress the pair.
Dried corn silk.
Sharp scissors and pinking shears.
Wire cutters.
Floral stem wires, 35cm (14″) long.
Strong, gold coloured thread.
12 coloured pins with heads.
Several sheets of white tissue paper.
Small, fine-pointed paintbrush.
Acrylic or water-colour paints for faces.
A large towel.
Plastic dish, big enough to soak shucks.
Cocktail stick or toothpick.

Clear-drying glue.
You will be making two dolls at the same time, up to the moment when the woman receives a skirt and the man legs and a coat.
☐ Soak 20 of the whitest shucks in the plastic dish and work on the towel.
☐ Cut two 9cm (3½″) pieces of stem wire, one each for the body of each doll.
☐ Cut two 15cm (6″) pieces of stem wire for arms, one for each doll.
☐ Cut one 28cm (11″) piece of stem

Dyeing grasses

Corn shucks and dried grasses, such as raffia, can be dyed very successfully.

Use a dye such as Dylon's Multi-Purpose dye, dissolved in half the recommended quantity of boiling water.

Test-dye a sample of the grass and check the results after half an hour: if too dark, add more water to dye bath; if too light leave the sample in the dye bath for a longer period of time—it is possible to obtain very intense colours.

Rinse carefully and allow to dry. As it is not possible to rinse grass as thoroughly as fabric after dyeing, care should be taken when combining dyed and undyed grasses (especially if they are damp) as the dye might run or smear.

wire for man's legs. (Woman has skirt, so no legs needed.)

☐ Cut about twenty pieces of thread, each 63cm (25″) long.

☐ Select two soaked shucks from the dish and gently blot them on towel. Use this blotting method throughout.

Bodies. Place one of the 9cm (3½″) wires lengthways on a shuck next to

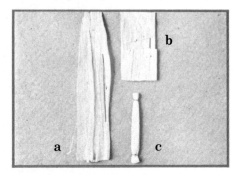

1. Making the body.

the edge (fig.1a). Fold top and bottom of shuck over ends of wire (fig.1b), then roll the wire up in the shuck.

☐ Using a piece of 63cm (25″) thread folded double, tie each end of the rolled shuck (fig.1c). To do this, place the middle of the double thread about 6mm (¼″) from the end of the rolled shuck, wrap it round twice and tie in a double knot (this knot is used throughout). Trim off excess ends of thread. Do the same thing at the other end of the shuck.

☐ Repeat this process for the second body.

Arms. Use two 15cm (6″) pieces of wire for the arms, one for each doll. Try to select shucks of even length, width and colour, then the dolls' hands at the end of the arms will be identical.

☐ Select four shucks. Using two shucks overlapped to extend the length to 20cm (8″), place one wire next to the edge of the overlapped shucks as for body, but this time without tucking in

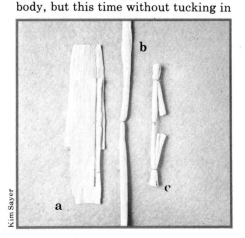

2. Assembling the arms.

ends (fig.2a). Roll and tie the centre tightly to hold wire and shucks in place (fig.2b).

☐ Find the one end of the wire amid the rolled shuck and place your thumb on it. Gently bring the end of the shuck over the wire and tie about 19mm (¾″) from the end to make a loop for the hand.

☐ Repeat at the opposite end of the wire. Do not cut off extra shuck past the wrist as this helps to fill the sleeves (fig.2c).

☐ Repeat with the second 15cm (6″) piece of wire. Use the cocktail stick to open the loop without tearing the shuck.

Man's legs. These are made from the 28cm (11″) wire. Use the same method as for bodies (see fig.1), since loops are not needed.

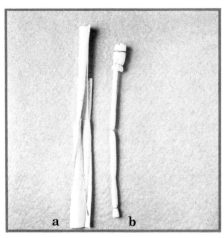

3. Making the man's legs.

☐ Roll legs from three shucks which have been overlapped to make up the extra length of 33cm (13″) as shown in fig.3a.

☐ Tie at each end, 2.5cm (1″) from the end. Mark the middle with a knot of thread, so legs will be equal.

Shoes. Use two shucks, one on top of the other, for each shoe.

☐ Fold both ends under towards the centre to make a piece 7.5cm (3″) wide.

☐ Roll the two pieces 3.75cm (1½″) on to the end of the made-up leg.

☐ Tie tightly at ankle and toe (fig.3b). Repeat for other shoe.

Heads. These must be as round as possible.

☐ Fold thread double, ready to tie and knot. Select two shucks and lay one on top of the other, making double thickness. (If only one shuck is used, it tends to split.)

☐ Select two extra shucks for filling. Holding one 9cm (3½″) rolled body, take the two filling shucks and tightly twist and wrap them round the top quarter of the body to make a ball (fig.4a).

☐ Place the double shucks over the front of the body holding the covering shucks in place with your thumb. At the top of the 'head', give the covering

shucks a full twist round (fig.4b) and bring them down behind the back of the head to produce a roundness.

☐ Tie twice with double thread tightly round neck below the ball and knot at the back (fig.4c). Make sure the front of the head is as smooth as possible.

Do not cut off the extra shucks below the neck knot unless they cover the

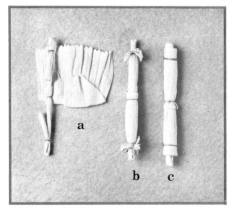

4. Shaping the head.

bottom knot on the body, as they will help fill the chest cavity.

☐ Repeat with other body piece.

Assembling and dressing. Soak about 60 more shucks and cut more lengths of thread. Make sleeves first, assembling them on arms before attaching to doll. One set of arms will be for the woman's fancy sleeves, the other for the man.

Woman's sleeves. Use eight shucks, four overlapping widths for each arm.

☐ With the widest part of the overlapping shucks towards the doll's hands, fold under the ends of the shucks about 2.5cm (1″) to meet at the centre of the arms. At the hand end of the arm, cut shuck edges with pinking

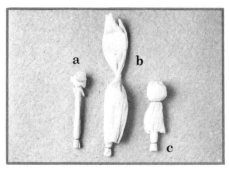

5. Sleeves for the arms.

shears (fig.5a).

☐ Roll all four shucks round arm, tie tightly at wrist and at centre arm. Make the other sleeve the same way (fig.5b).

Man's sleeves. Use eight shucks and proceed as for woman's sleeves except that at the hand end of the arm, fold the shucks under—just past the middle of the hand—to give the sleeves a hemmed look (fig.5c).

Trousers. Use four overlapping shucks for each trouser leg.

☐ Measure shucks from just past centre of leg to top of shoes. Fold under at both ends to give hemmed look. Do

6. Four shucks form a trouser leg.

not cover the top of the shoes as the foot will have to be bent later (fig.6). Tie tightly in centre and loosely at cuff.

Woman's chest. Lay sleeves horizontally across top of body, allowing a small space for the neck.

☐ Cut a 15cm (6″) piece of wire and, winding diagonally from waist to shoulder to waist again, wire arms to

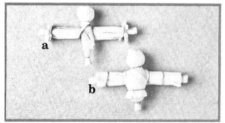

7. Arms are wired to body.

body securely (fig.7a).

☐ Fold one or more shucks in a 2.5cm (1″) square and lay it on the chest over the wire criss-cross.

☐ Take four shucks, two doubled from the front and two doubled from the back, and criss-cross them over the square to hold it in place. Tie tightly with thread at the waist.

(On both dolls, when you bring the shucks over the shoulder, push them into the neck to prevent a hunched appearance.)

☐ With pinking shears, cut two strips from a shuck and criss-cross these over the chest as a final touch for a woman's blouse. Wrap thread round waist twice and tie. Make sure you can see the bottom body tie. If you cannot, trim off excess shuck.

Man's body. Use same method as for woman but leave out the folded square on the chest and use only four shucks to make the chest (fig.7b).

Woman's skirt. Either overlap shucks round bundles of rolled shucks to make

a full skirt or, for a more economical method, wrap tissue paper round the centre body. Then apply about ten overlapping shucks to cover the tissue paper. Tie at the waist with thread, turn in the edges of the shucks at hemline and stuff with more tissue until dry. Tie three shucks together in a line and tie round bottom of skirt for decoration.

Man's legs. If you are unable to see the bottom of the body knot, trim shucks.

☐ Find the centre of the legs and bend them in half. Make a wire hook and insert it into the bottom of the body at the knot.

☐ Bending each shoe at the ankle, lay legs on top of the hook on the body and press hook tightly on to legs.

☐ Use five shucks, four to wrap round the legs, one for a good finish. Starting from the back, wrap between legs, round one leg and up round the waist.

☐ Repeat with second shuck on the same leg, then do the same thing with two more shucks for the second leg.

☐ Fold the fifth shuck under top and bottom and fold in half again lengthways. Place it between the legs with neat edges showing to give a finished look.

Man's jacket. Use eight shucks, four for the front and four for the back of the jacket.

☐ Spread out four overlapping shucks. Turn up about 19mm ($\frac{3}{4}$″) at the bottom edge of the shucks.

☐ Lay the man on top of the shucks so that the folded edge is just below the split in his legs.

☐ At the back of his neck, separate the four shucks and bring them in pairs

over the shoulders to the front. Pin all four where they cross at the centre of the chest with coloured pins.

☐ Take the other four shucks, overlap them, fold under as for back shoulders just below the split in the legs and pin at the middle of the waistline.

☐ Take two pairs of shucks and turn at an angle from the top of the waist, pin to make lapels, then pull the pairs of shucks over the shoulders and pin down at the back. Trim off excess shucks at the back.

☐ Pin all shucks under the sides of the arms. Tie jacket in place with sash made from two shucks knotted together.

Hair. Work clear-drying glue into a walnut-sized amount of corn silk until there is enough glue to hear it crunch between the fingers as you work it.

☐ Form it into a pancake and use fingers to mould the desired hair-style, bringing it in close to the head round the neck.

For extra curls, roll a small amount of well-pasted corn silk in a matching colour and add that. When the glue dries, the hair will keep in shape.

Finishing. Arrange the dolls' limbs into position while still wet and let the dolls dry for two weeks in an even temperature. Turn occasionally, so they dry thoroughly, inside and out.

When dolls are completely dry, paint on faces with acrylic or water-colour paints.

Dolls can be preserved by spraying them when dry with inexpensive hair spray (this contains lacquer), but do not spray too generously.

Dolls designed by Margo Daws Pontius.

Simple basketry

Basketry is one of the oldest crafts and has lasted since the beginning of history, adapting itself to various needs throughout the centuries.

It was Britain's first export industry, and the only one when the Romans first arrived. The ancient Britons were extremely good at basketry and made such articles as farm carts and wagons in wicker work. Many of the terms used in basketry even today are of Anglo-Saxon origin.

Many different materials, from cane to willow, are used for basketry and each material has its own particular techniques and adaptations.

Materials

Cane comes from the rattan family which is a creeper from SE Asia. It grows to enormous lengths and has sharp barbs. The outer layer is peeled off and discarded, while the bark is used for chair seating and handle wrapping. The inside pith or pulp is milled into canes of many thicknesses, from 000 (1mm) to 16 (5mm), and handle cane of 8mm or 10mm.

There are various qualities (all natural coloured, of course), 'blue tie' being the best, 'red' or 'green tie' and finally 'white tie' or bleached cane, which is rather poor in quality. Sea-grass, strawplait, raffia, enamelled cane or wrapping cane can all be used to add colour and interest; cane can also be dyed with fabric dye.

Preparation

Cane must be soaked in hot water for about 30 minutes before using. Once you start you will soon be able to gauge the soaking time. If it dries while you are working just re-soak it until it is easy to handle.

When you stop allow the work, plus all remaining cane, to dry before you put it away. Do not put damp cane into plastic bags as it will go mouldy.

Tools

The tools and equipment needed are inexpensive and some can be home-made and some improvised.

Side cutters, obtainable from tool shops, are useful but strong scissors, such as those used for flower arranging, or even garden secateurs will do.

A basket maker's bodkin is essential. It is used to form channels for canes to thread into or to split the cane. You can buy one from a craft supplier or improvise with an old, sharpened screwdriver or a medium-sized knitting needle.

Tape measure.

Clothes pegs [pins] are useful for temporarily holding the work in place.

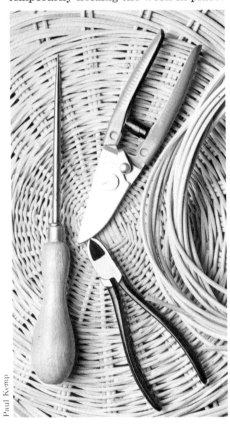

Tools and materials include cane, basket maker's bodkin, secateurs (top) and side cutters (bottom).

Techniques

There are various ways to begin a basket. Initially you can use a plastic or wooden base with holes in it made specially for basket making. You can use any base to suit your requirements as long as it has an odd number of holes.

However, as these bases limit the design potential, only use them in order to become familiar with the materials. The holes in the base are not always big enough to hold thick cane which means that you cannot make a large, sturdy basket. Bases also tend to make a basket heavy. However, the picnic basket illustrated is useful and makes an introduction to the various terms.

The picnic basket

The strong basket overleaf will give you years of use. It is designed to hold two flasks and a sandwich box in the middle.

You will need:

227gm (½lb) No.8 (3mm) cane.
113gm (¼lb) No.5 (2.5mm) cane.
3m (3yd) 10mm handle cane.
5.5m (6yd) glossy wrapping cane or 7.5m (8yd) No.6 (2.6mm) chair seating cane.
1m (1yd) enamelled cane—optional.
56gm (2oz) sea-grass—optional.
Oblong plywood or plastic base 15cm x 41cm (6"x16") with 49 holes.

☐ Prepare the cane by soaking it in hot water for 30 minutes.

For the ribs, ie the upright stakes; cut 49 stakes of No.8 (3mm) cane 51cm (20") long. Insert one stake into each hole allowing 10cm (4") to protrude on the wrong side of the base. If the cane is difficult to push through the holes you can widen them with the bodkin. Alternatively, as the cane swells when wet, insert the canes before soaking and soak them afterwards.

To make a foot border under the basket.

☐ Hold the base with the right side towards you and the short stake ends away from you. Starting with any stake end, bend it down to the right behind the next stake and back to the front. Then pass it in front of the next 2 stakes and tuck it to the back through the next space (fig.1).

☐ Repeat with each stake in turn. It will help if you say to yourself "Behind one, in front of two, and tuck it in". At the end of the round weave the stakes in and out of stakes that have already been turned down. You may have to push these stakes up a bit to get the others through. When they are all in place, give each stake a little pull to see that they are all tight and level.

☐ Place the basket right side up on the table. Put some sort of weight (a stone, flat iron) inside the basket to keep it steady. This will make it easier to hold the work and also to keep the shape you want.

Now you have to wale. Waling is a weave used for strength and is put on the bottom and the top of a basket. When a basket starts to lose its shape, a band of waling will help to retain it. It can be done with 3, 4, 5 or 6 weavers —for this basket use 3 weavers.

Paul Kemp

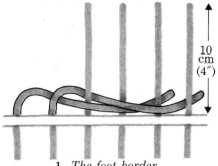

1. *The foot border.*

2. *The start of waling.*

3. *Starting the step-up.*

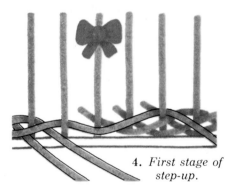

4. *First stage of step-up.*

5. *The step-up completed.*

☐ Insert 3 lengths of No.5 (2.5mm) cane, to be used as weavers, into any 3 consecutive spaces. Mark the stake immediately to the left of the first one in some way. Take the left hand weaver to the right in front of 2 stakes, over the top of the other 2 weavers and round the back of the next stake to the front again (fig.2).

☐ Now use the next left hand weaver and do exactly the same as before and then repeat with each weaver in turn all the way round the basket and back to the marked stake (fig.3).

Here you have to do a 'step-up'. If you don't, the work jumps up and spirals and the weave doesn't have the continuous rope effect that it should. You have to do this step-up at this spot on every round and then continue as you started.

☐ Take the right hand weaver in front of 2, behind one and through to the front again (fig.4).

☐ Take the middle one in front of 2 and behind one. Take the left one in front of 2 and behind one (fig.5).

All the weavers should now come out of the same 3 spaces you started with.

☐ Continue until you reach the marked stake again and step-up.

☐ Put on 5 rounds of waling, remembering to step-up at the marked stake, joining in new lengths when necessary.

Joining weavers. Join in when the cane which has run out is on the left of the other weavers. Pull it backwards slightly and insert the new cane into the hole beside, and to the right of, the old one. This means that the old and new weavers will lie side by side and the old end will be to the front and the new end will be inside the basket (fig.6). The ends are tidied later.

☐ To complete the 5 rounds of waling use the left hand weaver (not the right one this time), in front of 2, behind one and to the front again. This will go round the back of the marked stake. Cut it off to about 7.5cm (3″) (fig.7).

☐ Now use the next left hand weaver and pass it in front of 2, behind one and through to the front, but on its way to the front thread it under the top cane of the previous round. Cut this one off (fig.8).

☐ Use the last weaver now, in front of 2 and behind one, but thread it under the top 2 canes of the previous round, and cut it off (fig.9).

Bye-stakes are extra stakes that lie beside the main stakes to make the basket stronger.

☐ Cut one bye-stake for each stake, 41cm (16″) long of No.8 (3mm) cane. Make a point at one end of each and insert them into the waling, one on the right of each stake. They must lie in the same channel as the main stake. Use the bodkin to help form a passage for them to slip into (fig.10).

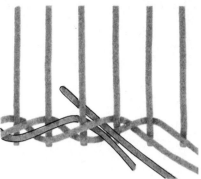

6. *Joining new cane in waling.*

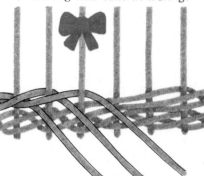

7. *The end of the waling.*

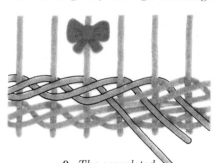

8. *Next stage in finishing the waling.*

9. *The completed waling before trimming the ends.*

10. *Inserting bye-stakes.*

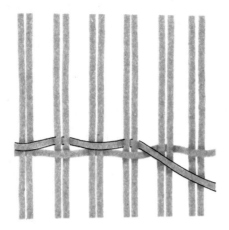

11. *Randing.*

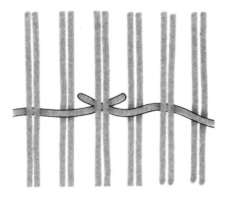

12a. *Front view of a new cane being joined in randing.*

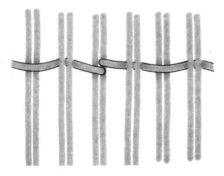

12b. *Back view of join with the ends trimmed back.*

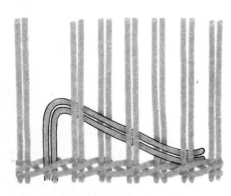

14. *Starting a trac border.*

Randing is a weave for economy and speed. It is very easy and only one weaver is used at a time.

☐ Put a weaver of No.5 (2.5mm) cane into any space and weave to the right, in front of one pair and behind one pair. Continue all the way round. There is no step-up in randing (fig.11).

Shaping. You must concentrate on the shaping. Every time a weaver goes round the front of a stake, hold that stake with the thumb and forefinger of the left hand. As you want the sides of the basket to go up straight you must hold the stake upright.

To join in a new weaver leave the old one at the back of a stake and place the new one against the same stake at the back (fig.12a).

Leave the ends until the siding is finished and then trim off with a slanting cut so that they won't catch on anything in the basket (fig.12b).

☐ Rand for 9cm (3½″) keeping the sides quite straight.

☐ Wale for 3 rounds with No.5 (2.5 mm) cane and step-up as before.

Preparing for the handles. At this point start making room for the handles to fit into later.

☐ Cut 4 pieces of the handle cane about 23cm (9″) long, for liners, and slype one end.

Slyping is a special way to cut cane to a point. It is done by making cuts on 2 consecutive quarters of the cane (fig.13).

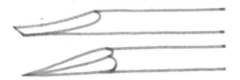

13. *A slype is made with two cuts.*

Slypes can be any length but start these 5cm (2″) from the end.

Insert 4 'handle liners' into the siding of the basket, beside 4 stakes and where you want your handle to be. Allow 8 stakes between the 2 liners on each side. Continue to weave round stake and liner together to form holes for the real handle.

☐ Rand for 2.5cm (1″) with sea-grass. You could substitute flat cane, raffia or No.5 (2.5mm) cane.

☐ Wale for 3 rounds with No.5(2.5mm) cane.

☐ Rand for 2.5cm (1″) with sea-grass.

☐ Wale for 3 rounds with No.5 (2.5mm) cane.

Trac border. The sides of this basket are finished with a trac border.

☐ Re-soak the stakes if necessary and start with any stake and refer to it as the 1st and the next one to the right as 2nd, and so on.

☐ Bend the first stake and bye-stake together, 4cm (1½″) up from the waling,

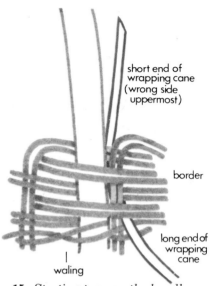

15. *Starting to wrap the handle.*

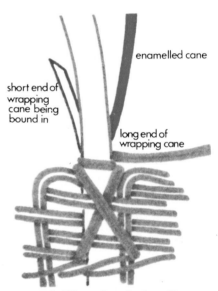

16. *Wrapping the handle.*

17. *Side view of handle wrapping showing the weaving over and under the enamelled cane.*

with quite a sharp bend. Pass this pair behind the 2nd pair, in front of the 3rd, behind the 4th, in front of the 5th and tuck them to the inside of the basket behind the 6th pair (fig.14).

☐ Now bend the 2nd pair down, making sure that the elbow of the bend is exactly the same height as the first bend. Repeat the weaving as for the previous pair and tuck them in behind the 7th pair.

☐ Repeat with each pair in turn and finish in exactly the same way, although you will weave the last few in front and behind stakes that have already been turned down. Be sure to keep them all in the correct order and don't let any cross over any others. Go in front of and behind the handle liners, together with the adjacent stake, and keep the pattern correct.

☐ Trim all ends of the weavers and the stakes with a diagonal cut so that they do not stick out. The border stake ends must lie against a stake or they will slip through to the front.

☐ Cut 2 pieces of prepared handle cane each 65cm (26″) long and slype all the ends. Bend into U-shapes. Remove the handle liners and keep them as they can be used again. Insert the handles well down into the spaces so the weaving grips them tightly. The handles should be about 13cm (5″) high.

☐ Insert a length of prepared wrapping cane, wrong side uppermost, into the siding, just under the border and to the immediate right of one of the handles. It should protrude 15cm (6″) to the inside (fig.15).

☐ Bring this short, protruding end up and over the top of the border, then down and across in front of the handle and the border. Re-insert it into the siding again just under the border, but this time to the left of the handle. Bring this same end up to lie behind the handle where it will be bound later.

☐ Cut a piece of enamelled cane (or wrapping cane), 41cm (16″) long, and insert it into the siding so that it lies against the outer curve of the handle, right side out. Use a peg to keep it in place temporarily (fig.16).

☐ Take the long end of the wrapping cane up and across the handle and the border so that a cross is formed in front of the border. Wrap this long end round the handle 4 times, binding in both the short end and the enamelled cane.

Continue to wrap the handle tightly but pass it over and under the enamelled cane to form a pattern (fig.17). This is not only decorative but helps to keep the wrapping tight. This handle was wrapped under twice and over twice but you can make any pattern you like.

☐ Continue wrapping handle, keeping

Jerry Tubby

the enamelled cane at the top and finish as you began with 4 plain wraps and a cross in front of the border to match the other end. Weave the end in and out of the waling to secure it.

☐ If you need to join in a new piece of cane lay the new cane, wrong side out, underneath the handle, when there is still enough of the old wrapping left to do another 5cm (2″). Continue to wrap with the old cane, binding the new cane in, until there is only 4cm (1½″) left of the old piece. Turn the new piece so that the right side is on the outside and commence wrapping with it. At the same time lay the old piece on the underside of the handle and bind it in with the wrapping.

☐ The handles need to be secured with a peg so that they will not slip out from the basket. While the handle cane is still wet, pierce it with a bodkin between the first and second rounds of the top waling.

☐ To make the peg point a short piece

The baskets are made using a plywood or laminated plastic base. The larger one is ideal for picnics and the smaller one is a child's basket.
Designed by Barbara Maynard.

of No.10 (3.35mm) cane, or a wedge of the handle cane, and insert it into the hole made by the bodkin. It must come right through to the inside. You may have to tap it in with a hammer.

Cut this peg off, on the inside and the outside of the basket, level with the waling. This forms a peg which prevents the handles from slipping out.

Repeat on the other 3 places where the handles enter the sides.

☐ Finish the basket by shaping the handles. Make them curve towards each other by tying them together at the top while they are still wet. At the same time keep the sides of the basket apart by placing a book or a block of wood inside at border level. Leave it in position until the handles are dry.

Rush work

Rush baskets and matting have been made for centuries. The ancient Egyptians used rushes a great deal and even made rush boats on which to live. In England, during Tudor times, rushes were used to make a tallow light by dipping rushes into wax. Rush was also used as a floor covering for those who could afford it. Only a wealthy family could have the rushes changed more than once a year. Later on rushes were plaited and sewn into mats which were longer lasting.

Rush work is quite easy, even if you have never done any before. The colour and texture of natural rushes make them a joy to handle. Nowadays many beautiful articles are made, both useful and decorative, that blend with perfect harmony to our modern way of living.

Rushes grow in still waters and slow moving rivers. Once harvested they are left to dry slowly. They are then tied into bolts and sold as such. The lengths of the rushes in a bolt vary—the average length is about 183cm (6′).

Storage

Rushes should be stored in a dry airy place, preferably in the dark, so that the colour does not fade. A loft is a good place because a layer of dust helps to protect them.

You can gather plants from the garden which are suitable for rush work. Irises, gladioli and montbretia, and

Left: some of the grasses suitable for rush work include montbretia, gladioli, irises and rushes. Rushes are found in still and slow moving water. Once harvested they must be left to dry slowly.

Melvin Grey

many grasses, dry into rich golden brown colours and many of the tall plants from ponds are also suitable. Cut the plants towards the end of summer and leave them to dry. Then prepare them in the same way as rushes when you are ready to use them.

Preparation

Be careful how you handle the rushes while they are dry because they are very brittle and damage easily.

Rushes must be wetted for about five minutes, either by sprinkling with a hose or watering-can in the garden, or by dipping the rushes in a bath of cold water. If you can put them out in the rain even better. The rushes are then wrapped up in a wet blanket, flannelette sheet or sacking for a further three hours to mellow. It is a good idea to leave the rushes overnight so that they have all night to mellow and are ready for working in the morning.

Before the rushes are used each rush must be prepared. The thin end must be tested for strength. Hold a rush in both hands about 15cm (6″) down from the brown flowery top (or thin end if it has lost its flower) and pull it apart with a gentle tug. Do not be too strong—just a little tug. Discard the broken end and try again another 15cm (6″) down until the rush is quite firm and does not snap. It is much less frustrating to get rid of the weak bits first, and so preventing the rushes from snapping when the weavers are pulled into place. You will soon get to know how much strength to use. If a rush snaps when weaving you will know you did not take enough away and if you chop it right up to the thick end, then you have been too heavy-handed.

Each rush must now be 'wiped'. This is partly to clean the rush and partly to

Three examples of flat rush work. Instructions are given for the round mat in the centre and the oval mat on the right. Designed by Barbara Maynard.

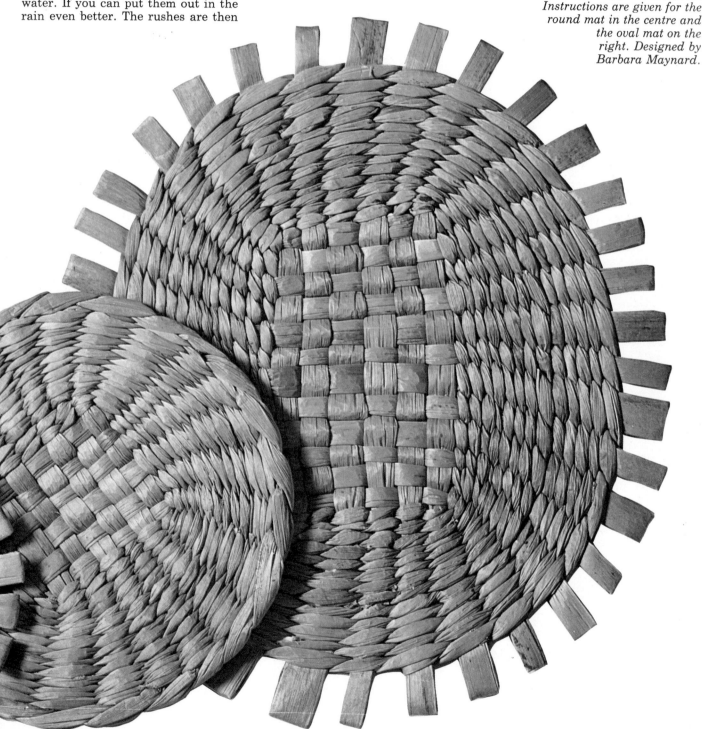

remove all the air and water from inside the stem. Hold the stem in one hand at the thin end and with a damp cloth in the other hand wipe along the rush, pressing it flat at the same time so that the water runs out of the thick end. If this is not done the work will shrink too much after weaving leaving it loose with gaps showing.

Tools and equipment

The tools and equipment for rush work are very few and inexpensive. Apart from the blanket to wrap the rushes in and the damp cloth to wipe them, you will need a pair of scissors and a rush threader. A rush threader (fig.1) can be obtained from craft shops but a football lacing awl is just as good.

1. A rush threader or football lacing awl is used to thread ends into work.

You will also need some form of frame or mould to build the baskets on—a block of wood, flower pots and biscuit tins all make good foundations for rush work. Later projects require string, or thread, both fine and coarse. Fine thread is used for sewing plaits together and coarse thread for tying the work on to the mould. A large-eyed needle is required for the sewing.

The round mat

Start working by making a table mat to familiarize yourself with the tools and materials before starting baskets.

The mat is about 20cm (8″) in diameter. When planning your own mats add 10cm (4″) extra to each end of each stake to allow for a border.

You will need:
12 thick rushes 12mm (½″) diameter, 41cm (16″) long. Cut them from the butt (thick end) of good quality rushes.
12-16 fine rushes for weaving.
Rush threader.

Check weave. Wipe the 12 thicker stakes to clean and flatten them. Lay 6 of them close together horizontally in front of you. Arrange the rushes with thick and thin ends alternating so that one side of the work does not finish more 'solid' than the other.

☐ Hold them on the table with your left hand to the left of the centre. Pick up, and hold in your left hand, the first (the one furthest away from you), third and fifth stakes.

☐ Lay another stake across the 2nd, 4th and 6th stakes close to your left hand as illustrated so that when the stakes in the left hand are returned to their starting position they form the first row of the check weave. Now the working order of the horizontal stakes will change and the 2nd, 4th and 6th stakes will come up. You will achieve better results if you start picking up the next row while putting down the stakes you have just worked. For example, the order will be: no.2 up, no.1 down; no.4 up, no.3 down;

The check weave is started with left hand in position illustrated with fingers holding alternate rushes making room for vertical stakes.

no.6 up, no.5 down. Pull the stakes as they are put down to keep the check tight.

☐ Continue until all six vertical stakes are in place and your check weave centre is complete.

Pairing is done in the same way as when working with cane.

☐ Bend one of the weaving rushes not quite in the middle and loop it round the first stake on any side. Pair all the way round twice—left-hand weaver in front of one, behind the next and return to the front. Pull each rush down well at each pairing stroke.

Joining in a new rush. When a weaver has about 7.5cm (3″) left to weave and is in the position to be used next, loop the thin end of the new rush round the stake in between the two weavers. Loop it about 7.5cm (3″) from the end (fig.2).

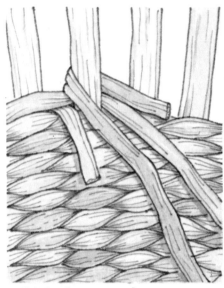

2. Joining in a new rush.

Now both weavers have a long rush and a short end. Continue to pair weaving in the short ends as you go.

If both ends run out together, loop the new one not quite in the middle and place it round the stake between the two short ends. Then once again you have two long ends. The two shorter ends are woven in together with the weaving.

☐ Pair for two rounds, then make sure that all the stakes are central and that they are tight. Pull them into position if necessary. Spread the stakes out like the spokes of a wheel after the second round.

☐ Pair until the mat is 19cm (7½″) across.

The ends of both weavers are finished off by threading them into the weaving. Push the rush threader through the last four rounds of pairing, just where the pairing finished. Thread the weaver into the eye of the threader and pull it back through the pairing (fig.3).

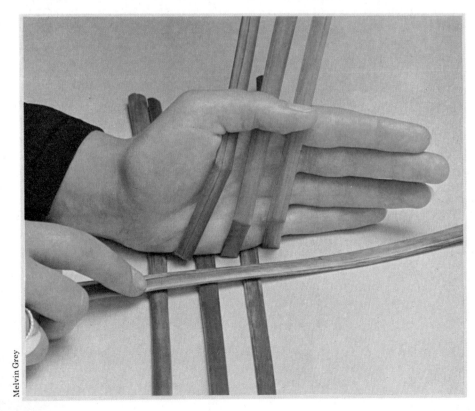

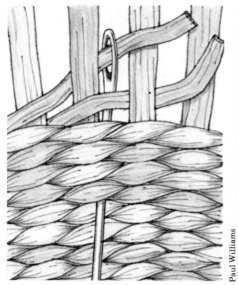

3. *Weaver end threaded into the work.*

Repeat with the other weaver. A border is now added to complete the mat. See 'Borders'.

The oval mat

Oval mats are made in the same way as round mats but the stakes are cut into two different lengths. There are fat ovals and long slim ovals—you can make whichever you prefer. In basketry an oval is merely an elongated circle. Some stakes will be longer than others. Allow for borders by adding an extra 10cm (4″) to each end of the stake. The mat measures 28cm x 23cm (11″x 9″) before putting on the border.

You will need:
6 thick stakes 48cm (19″) long.
12 thick stakes 43cm (17″) long.
14-18 weaving rushes.

☐ Place the long stakes close together horizontally on the table. Place your left hand in the centre and lift up the 1st, 3rd and 5th stakes. Place the 1st short rush across the remaining horizontal stakes. Continue to place five more of the short stakes into position to form a check weave.

☐ Turn the work round and place the remaining short stakes into position. This will ensure that the block of check weave is in the centre of the stakes.

☐ Pair for 5cm (2″) then, if you wish start Border no.3. Continue to pair for a further five rounds and finish off.

☐ If you wish to have one of the first two borders, pair for 7.5cm (3″) before bordering down.

Pressing

When you have completed the mat with its border, its appearance is improved if it is pressed flat.
Place the mat between a newspaper and put some heavy books on top. Leave it overnight. The newspaper will soak up any remaining moisture.

Borders

There are a number of simple borders that can be used in rush work and that are suitable for mats.
Make sure the stakes are damp enough before you start.

Border No.1
☐ Push the threader up through the last four rounds of pairing as you did to finish off the weaving. Thread the stake from the next channel to the left into the threader and pull it back through the pairing. Try to turn the stake over to the right before it is finally pulled down. Do not let it twist in various ways. If they are all turned down in the same way the border will look neat and tidy.
☐ Continue all the way round then give each one an extra pull to tighten the work.
☐ When you are satisfied that all the stakes are all in place, cut each one off at the point where it emerges from the pairing. If you pull the stake just a fraction before cutting the end will spring up a little and will be hidden in the weaving.

Border No.2
This border is exactly the same as the first border but the stake from the second channel to the left is threaded through the threader and pulled into the weaving. Finish as before.

Border No.3
When you have about five more rounds of pairing to do, flatten each stake in turn and bend it right up and over itself a set distance from the weaving. Allow for the five rounds of pairing—2.5cm (1″)—and the amount you want the stakes to protrude at the end. Devise some sort of gauge to make all the bends the same distance from the weaving. Pair round each stake as it is folded into position. Continue with the remaining rounds of pairing and cut off the ends of the stakes to finish.

Border No.3

Border No.1

Border No.2

Raffia coil work

Raffia comes from the leaf of a palm tree which grows in hot climates in Africa and Asia. Raffia is a versatile material—extremely tough and yet supple and easy to handle.

There are many ways of using raffia—it may be woven over a cardboard base by a child or stitched tightly into place to make beautiful bowls and urns. It may be used for embroidery on an existing basket or linen to make colourful beach bags and handbags. It can even be knitted or crocheted.

Although the basic techniques of raffia work are simple, they can be developed by the individual craftsman to produce articles of exceptional beauty. One has only to look at colourful North American Indian work or very fine African work to see this.

The type of raffia work described in this introductory chapter is called coiled work. It involves wrapping and stitching a material such as cane, into a coil. Raffia is used for the stitching and there are various stitches that can be used. Once the coil is started, it is just continued round and round until it is large enough for your design requirements.

To begin, we describe the start of the coil, the various stitches and joining new lengths. The stitches themselves have such fascinating names as Lazy Squaw and Mariposa. They all create the most exquisite patterns.

Buying raffia. Good quality raffia can be purchased by the hank from craft shops, either natural or in a variety of colours. It you cannot get the colour you want, however, raffia can be easily dyed with a common multi-purpose dye. Raffia of a poorer quality, though still quite usable, is available from some gardening stores.

Synthetic raffia can be used with equally good results and has two distinct advantages over the natural raffia. Firstly, the colours are much brighter and more vibrant and, secondly, it comes in continuous lengths of even thickness and is therefore easier to use.

Tools and technique

There are two necessary components in coiled work—the core and the wrapping material. Any round pliable material can be used for the core—cane, willow, straw, rushes or string. The choice of core will influence the firmness of the finished basket. The wrapping around the core is done with raffia.

The beginner will find that soft, pliable, thick string or fine rope (about 6mm ($\frac{1}{4}$″) in diameter) for the core and raffia (natural or synthetic) for the wrapping are the best materials with which to begin.

You will also need a pair of scissors and a needle. The needle must have a large enough eye through which to thread the raffia and it must be blunt. Special raffia needles which are flat and pass through the work easily can be purchased. A No.14 tapestry needle or a fine rugging needle will do just as well to start with.

Coiled work

Do not be too ambitious at the beginning. Stick to a flat shape and avoid fancy patterns at first. Be content with single bands of colour if you want any decorations.

It does not matter which way you work, either clockwise or anti-clockwise, or whether you are left or right handed. All coiled baskets are started in the middle of the base.

To start the coil shave the end of the core, whether it is cane or willow, rope or rush, down to a point. If using cane or willow, the start will be easier if you soak the material first.

☐ Place a piece of raffia along the end of the core so that the long end of the raffia sticks out beyond the pointed core end.

☐ Wrap the core with the long end of raffia starting 12mm ($\frac{1}{2}$″) from the point. Wrap about 25mm (1″) of the core binding in the short end of the raffia at the same time (fig.1). (There is no need to

Paul Williams

1. Securing raffia end.

Ethnic baskets in traditional designs made by the Washoe Indians. Courtesy of Heard Museum, Phoenix, Arizona.

Jerry D. Jacka

wrap right to the point—it is difficult to make the raffia stay on the core at the tip and, in any case, the end will be caught into the wrapping on the first round of coiling.)

☐ Twist the covered section of core into a tight circle—the smaller and closer the better although this is something that comes with practice.

☐ Thread the needle to the end of the raffia so that you can pass it through the centre of the ring to wrap the point in securely (fig.2).

Now you can start with any stitch you

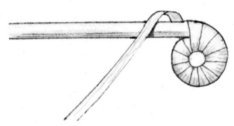

2. *Starting the coil.*

like, passing round and between the new section of the core you are covering and the previous round. The new core should fit closely next to the previous round or the work will be open and sloppy.

Joining raffia. When the old end has about 25cm (10″) left, lay the new end along the top of the outside coil and catch it in with the next few stitches.

Do not leave too long an end at the point where it is joined in—the end will be held firmly after only a few stitches. Continue to work with the old end until there is 5cm (2″) left, then pick up and use the new thread, binding the old end in as you go.

Joining the core. There are two methods of renewing the core.

The first method is to make a diagonal cut at the end of the old core and work until you have nearly reached the beginning of the cut. Cut the new end with a diagonal to match the one on the old end. When the two ends are placed together they should be the same thickness as the core. Holding them together stitch over both to secure the new end.

The second method is particularly suitable for cane but is no good for a rope core. Make a cut 7.5cm (3″) long to halve the old and the new end. Cut across one half on each end to remove half the cane. Fit the two ends together as shown in fig.3.

3. *Joining two cane ends.*

To finish off coiling, decide exactly where you want to stop—you may have to make the coil even, if you are working in bands of colour. Cut the core for the end and then shave the end to a point.

Continue to stitch in this end as far as possible and then bind in the short point with single whipping stitches. Thread the end of the raffia back into the work and cast off with a couple of stitches backwards and forwards.

The stitches

There are many different stitches—some are very simple and quick to do, others are more intricate. It is the choice of stitch with the core which determines whether the work is soft and flexible or so hard and rigid that it is almost waterproof. If a piece of work needs to be hard and rigid use a cane core and figure of eight stitch.

Lazy Squaw stitch

Beginners would be well advised to start off with Lazy Squaw stitch (fig.4).

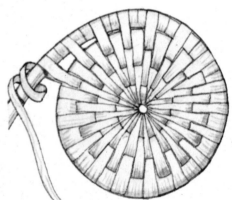

4. *Lazy Squaw stitch.*

As its name implies, this is a typical stitch from the North American Indian tribes and it is both easy and economical.

☐ After the cane has been wrapped and joined into a ring continue by wrapping the raffia round the new coil two or three times.

☐ Pass the needle through the centre of the ring and up over the new coil.

☐ Continue working in this way, always wrapping the raffia round the new coil before passing it once round the first coil.

☐ In the next round, the stitches will be taken round the new core and into the spaces formed by the second round. As the coil gets bigger, more stitches will be required. These can be added either by making an extra wrap round the new foundation, thus keeping all the long stitches in orderly lines, or by adding more long stitches between those of the previous round.

Straw forms the core of this base.

You can vary this stitch by passing the raffia into the previous round every other stitch. Alternatively, you can wrap the new coil for 5cm-7.5cm (2″-3″) and then make open-work patterns by looping the coil (fig.5) before stitching it to the previous round. Be careful always to keep the free loops exactly the same length. Catch the tops of the loops in with a straight round afterwards. This method can be used to make handles on baskets. To secure and strengthen the handle make additional stitches at the loops.

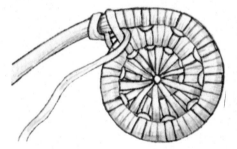

5. Looping the core forms open-work.

Mariposa or knot stitch

Many beautiful patterns can be built up using Mariposa or knot stitch (fig.6).

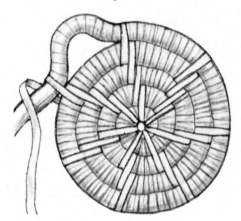

6. Mariposa or knot stitch.

☐ After the foundation ring, work one round of Lazy Squaw stitch.

☐ On the next round take the raffia into the previous round and up over the new coil. Bring the needle to the front, to the left of the long stitch just made, and down between previous round and the new round. Wrap the raffia two or three times round this 'shank', that is the long stitch, then continue wrapping the new coil. The shank can be pulled tight down to the previous round. or can be allowed to stand away for approximately 6mm (¼″) for open-work.

☐ On further rounds, the shank can be placed directly over the previous shank or may be put exactly in the centre of the space or, put slightly to one side, or each side of the previous shank.

West African stitch

West African stitch (fig.7) is a variation

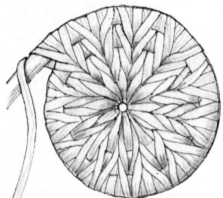

7. West African stitch.

on Lazy Squaw stitch.

☐ Start with a round of Lazy Squaw stitch that has every other stitch going into the previous round.

☐ Make the first stitch into the previous round and one wrap round the new coil. Then make a second long stitch into the previous round in the same place as the first one. This will form a V-shape.

☐ On the next round the points of Vs are worked into the centre of the previous Vs. Extra stitches are added if necessary by working a stitch between the Vs every so often, as well as in the centre.

Figure of eight stitch

This stitch (fig.8) gets its name from

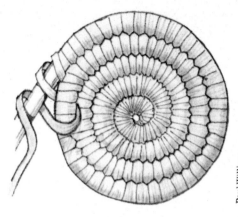

8. Figure of eight stitch.

the pattern of working which is in the form of a figure eight.

☐ Bring the raffia up through the foundation ring between the two cores and up behind the new coil. Pass it down and behind and through the ring again. This counts as one stitch.

☐ In the next round, the raffia is passed round the new coil and the previous round so that each coil is covered twice.

This method produces an extremely firm basket and, if worked with a cane or willow core, the work is very strong. This stitch is, however, much slower to work than Lazy Squaw stitch.

Colourful mats in Lazy Squaw stitch designed by Barbara Maynard.

Woodcrafts

With its beautiful colours and wide variety of textures wood
is a lovely natural material. Modelling is specially satisfying,
you can make all sorts of delightful shapes.

Simple wood modelling

Working with wood is not all practical carpentry. Often a piece of wood—a scrap or off-cut—shows a lovely range of colours and grain—the kind of piece a wood supplier would be happy to give you. Why not shape it with a file and polish it to show the surface at its best?

A large piece of wood may appear difficult to work with, as you have to imagine a three-dimensional shape emerging from it. So start on a small scale and become familiar with the tools, the texture of the wood and the way the grain runs. It will give you the confidence required to work with large pieces of wood. You can start with any odd pieces or use an old broom handle or piece of dowel.

The buttons illustrated were all made from pieces of scrap wood. You do not necessarily have to make buttons; using the same technique you can adapt the pieces to make counters for draughts [checkers] or backgammon. You could make chessmen in this way.

Tools

Bench clamp, vice or G[C]-clamp. You will need one of these tools to grip the wood while you are working with it. A bench clamp or vice is ideal. A G[C]-clamp is inexpensive but it can be a bit awkward if you want to grip the wood in a perpendicular position.

Hand drill with bit to drill holes.

Files are available in various sizes and shapes but start with a half-round file, size 150mm (6"), and add the others as you need them.

A saw for cutting the wood to the required size or thickness.

Materials for buttons

The wood can be any size or shape but start with small pieces that will not need too much cutting. Look for grain and colour as these features make the buttons very attractive.

It is best to shape as much of the object as possible before cutting it from a large piece—ie, if you use a piece of dowel, shape the flat surface first and then cut off the required thickness. This makes it easier to grip the wood while working.

To make a round button

Bought buttons are usually rather dreary or else extremely expensive. Wooden buttons look particularly handsome on coats and jackets made of tweed, linen or knitted yarn. A set of hand-made buttons will give an obviously store-bought coat a couture touch.

You will need:

A piece of dowel 3cm (1¼") diameter, 15cm (6") long. The number of buttons made will, of course, depend on the thickness of the buttons but you should be able to make at least 8 buttons.

Fine grade glasspaper [sandpaper].

Wax, paint or stain to finish.

Tools listed above.

Cushion the dowel with a piece of

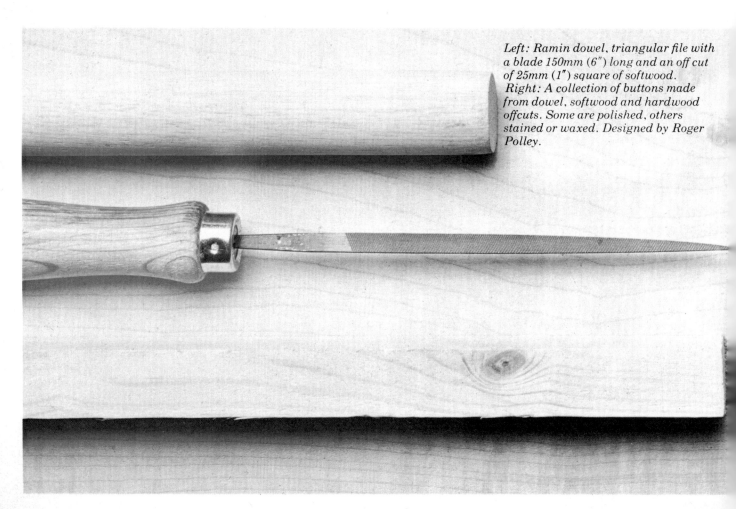

Left: Ramin dowel, triangular file with a blade 150mm (6") long and an off cut of 25mm (1") square of softwood.
Right: A collection of buttons made from dowel, softwood and hardwood offcuts. Some are polished, others stained or waxed. Designed by Roger Polley.

cardboard so that the bench clamp or G[C]-clamp does not mark the surface of the wood.

☐ Clamp the dowel to a working surface. Make sure that it is secure.

☐ Drill 2 or 3 holes in the round centre of the dowel (fig.1). You can make them

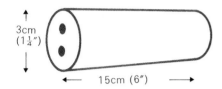

3cm (1¼")

15cm (6")

1. The holes can be drilled before actually cutting a section for a button from the length of dowel.

quite deep so that you will not have to drill holes for the next few buttons.

☐ Using the round file remove the wood to form a pattern. You can either make a corrugated surface or work at an angle towards the centre, depending entirely on the surface you want.

☐ Smooth the surface with a piece of fine glasspaper [sandpaper].

The buttons on this knitted cardigan are shaped from a piece of dowel and waxed to enhance the grain. Designed by Roger Polley.

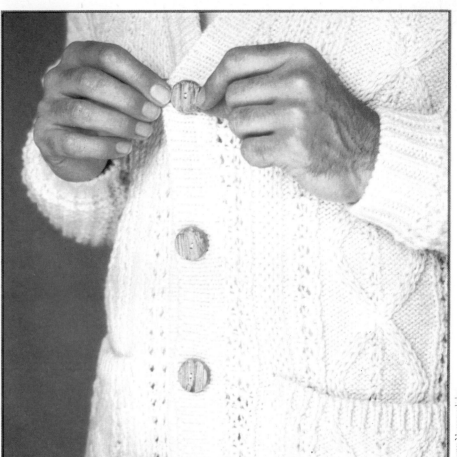

Tony Moussoulides

Roger Phillips

Tool box

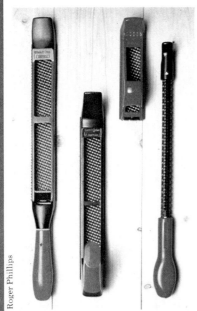

Surforms, above, are available in a variety of sizes and shapes. Flat Surforms are used in much the same way as large files and planes, while the round Surform, right, is perfect for shaping wood. They are similar to files but can be used on wood, plastic and some metals. Replaceable blades can be slotted into the handles. The blades do not clog as they are pierced like a cheese grater.
Files (below) are used for shaping in awkward corners, and come in a wide range of sizes. They can be flat, half rounded, or round. The files shown have 20cm (8″) blades and the three flat files, left, are about 19mm (¾″) wide.

☐ Saw off the thickness required for the button and sand the edge until it is smooth.
☐ Wax or stain the button to finish.

Varying the shape
You do not have to use a piece of dowel—a cross-section of softwood can also be used. Even if its shape is square you can file away until you have a bow shape or any irregular shape which you find interesting.

To make unusual shaped buttons, say in the form of a heart, cut the outline from a piece of paper and draw this on to the wood to get the buttons all the same size and shape.

It is not difficult to get the buttons similar and, if you use the grain running in the same direction for each button, it helps to achieve a uniform appearance.

Always make sure that the piece of wood is long or large enough to make the required number of buttons to complete the set. This is most important when waxing the buttons so that they will all have the same colour, whereas if you stain or paint them the applied colour will give them the required uniformity.

You can add to your collection of files as you progress. For grooves and flat surfaces you will need a triangular and a flat file and you can always use a saw to make a criss-cross pattern or a series of parallel grooves.

Once you have got the feel of shaping wood you can think in terms of larger items and any piece of wood then becomes an inspiration.

The sculptured box

This attractive plywood box can be used to hold trinkets and jewelry or, if the lid is close-fitting enough, cigarettes. The plywood can be shaped in a number of ways and its different layers can be used to break the straight lines of the box, giving it a softer, rounder appearance and interesting 'markings'. For a box 8cm x 10cm (3″x3¾″), 10cm 3¾″) deep:

You will need:
1cm (⅜″) thick plywood, 30cm x 20cm (12″x8″).
Wood glue.
2.5cm (1″) brass hinge and screws.
Brass hook fastening, eyelet, washer.
Masking tape.
Fine grade glasspaper [sandpaper].
Wax or wood stain for finishing.
Tools
Fine saw.
Hammer.
Flat file (or use the flat side of a half-round file).
Round Surform
Small screwdriver
Vice, bench clamp or G[C]-clamp
☐ Cut the plywood into 6 pieces:
4 to measure 8cm x 8cm (3″x3″) to make the sides, and 2 to measure 8cm x 10cm (3″x3¾″) for the lid and base.
☐ Glue the 4 sides together to form a bottomless box. Spread the glue evenly over the surfaces and secure the box in the vice or G[C]-clamp to hold it together until the glue is dry.
☐ Glue the base to the box. If the sides are uneven because of inaccurate sawing, don't worry as you can correct them when shaping the box.

Fitting the hinge. Decide on what is to be the back of your box and calculate the centre point of the upper edge. Find the corresponding point on the lid, using a side with the same length as the back.
☐ Measure 1.25cm (½″) on either side of the centre point and mark the box and the lid.
☐ File down 2mm (1/16″) between these two marks, along the top of the box, on the edge of the plywood side, as shown in the diagram below. Check the hinge fits snugly into each recess.
☐ Mark the position of the screws and tap a nail lightly in the marks to start

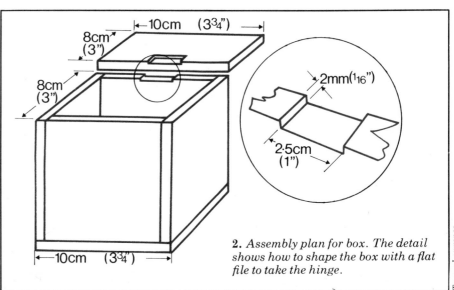

2. *Assembly plan for box. The detail shows how to shape the box with a flat file to take the hinge.*

Johnnie Ryan

The box is shaped with a Surform to create irregular hollows and to expose the layers of plywood.

the holes and to position the screws accurately.

☐ Screw the hinge to the top of the box and attach the lid to the hinge.

Shaping the box. You can stick down the lid with masking tape when you need to. Secure the box in the vice or G[C]-clamp.

☐ Mark the centre of the front of the lid, leaving this area flat when shaping to accommodate the hook at a later stage.

☐ Use the Surform to round the edges and to form curves. Even the corners can be rounded. Work diagonally downwards taking care not to remove too much of the plywood at any one particular point. Except when working

the join of the lid and the box, keep the lid open. Keep an eye on the thickness of the box when using the Surform— you don't want to file too far and wear right through the wood! Try to use the different layers of the plywood to form curves that are interesting.

Finishing. To finish the box rub it down with a fine grade glasspaper [sand-paper]. Wax or stain the entire surface. Natural wood stains will bring out the natural grain of the plywood.

☐ Place the washer underneath the hook and screw it to the centre of the front edge of the box lid.

☐ Screw in the eyelet. For a tight fastening, the hook must swing just under the top of the eye.

Hold the basic box securely in a G[C]-clamp, using the Surform at various angles to shape the plywood.

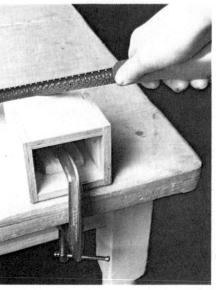

Roger Phillips

Wood sculpture

Carving and modelling is probably the most creative way of working with wood. These and the following chapters set out to give the beginner a step-by-step guide to sculpting and carving wood. However, it helps to get the basic terminology—low relief, high relief and three-dimensional work—clear at the outset.

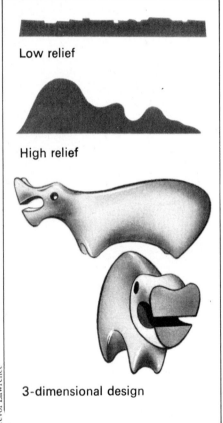

Low relief

High relief

3-dimensional design

Trevor Lawrence

Low and high relief are only worked on the front of the wood while the back is left flat. Low relief virtually interprets a 2-dimensional, linear design on the surface of the wood and is usually worked with gouges and chisels. In high relief, the contours are much more developed. In both cases, the design is only intended to be seen from the front.

Three-dimensional sculpture is made in the round. For this you have to consider how the piece will look from the other side, from above, below, end on.

It is easier to work up the three-dimensional sculpture via high relief so this chapter shows how to succeed with a simple, high relief crocodile design. Here are several tricks of the trade which should help you to be pleased with the outcome.

Good outline. A clear, well-drawn and easily recognizable outline is more than half the battle. Study silhouettes, outlines in photographs and drawings; analyse which shapes work as 'profiles', which ones are inexplicable unless they are filled in with detail.

Contour. To make high relief effective, you need to work out some simple contours, rather like the lines on a contour map. Plot out the 'hills' and 'valleys' that will indicate roundness and hollows on the model.

Appropriate tools. For most medium-scale high relief and three-dimensional work the Surform type of rasping-and-filing tools are excellent for beginners.

Clamping. It is essential to have work firmly anchored, either with a vice or clamp, so that it cannot wobble about.

Grain. Let the wood help you. Explore and exploit the beauty of the grain, use it to emphasize the contours and, if there are any knots or splits, try to incorporate them into the design.

Touchability. Finally, remember that any piece of carving or modelling should invite the viewer to touch it— either to stroke its smoothness or experience its jagged roughness. The designs in these chapters are most effective if polished to a silky smooth finish. The more care you use at this stage, the more pleasure your sculpture will give.

Wood. Some woods are easier to work than others so choose a mild working

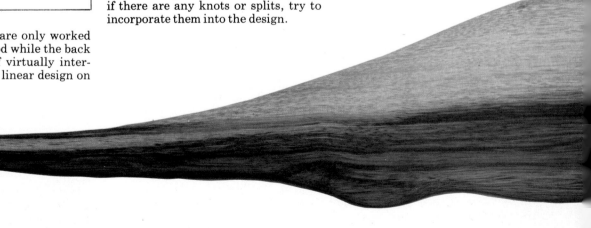

Alan Duns

40

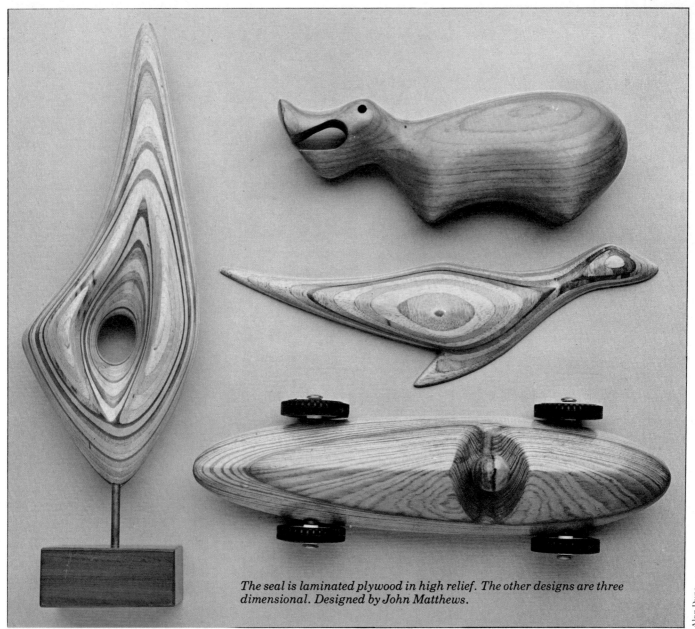

The seal is laminated plywood in high relief. The other designs are three dimensional. Designed by John Matthews.

hardwood such as sycamore, teak, walnut, African limba, African makore, or chestnut. If the wood is hard and close grained, you will have to work harder at removing the waste wood.

It is not always easy to obtain a specific type of hardwood so you may have to make do with what is available. If you have a piece of softwood you can use it to experiment on—parana pine is very attractive. Softwood, because of its grain is more difficult to finish so carefully choose a close-grained piece free of knots for the best finish.

Sculptured crocodile

The high relief sculptured crocodile is worked in a piece of hardwood. It is 47cm (18½″) long and can be attached to a wall with suction buttons, double-sided tape or metal clips etc. Alternatively you can use special sticky pads that will not mark the paint or paper on the wall.

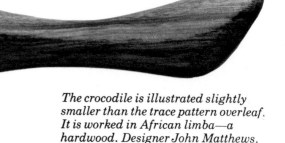

The crocodile is illustrated slightly smaller than the trace pattern overleaf. It is worked in African limba—a hardwood. Designer John Matthews.

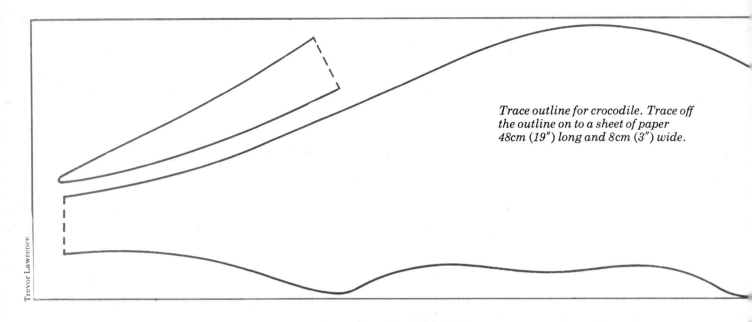

Trace outline for crocodile. Trace off the outline on to a sheet of paper 48cm (19") long and 8cm (3") wide.

Trevor Lawrence

To make the crocodile

You will need:

A piece of hardwood 75mm x 15mm (3"x⅝"), 51cm (20") long—the wood does not have to be planed smooth. Try to obtain an off-cut or experiment with a piece of close grained softwood, which is free of knots—with some experience knots can be incorporated into the design. Other suitable timbers include teak, walnut and chestnut.
Tools and equipment—see Tool Box.
Half-round wood file.
The design on tracing paper and a pencil. Carbon paper.
Medium and fine grade glasspaper [sandpaper] for polishing the crocodile to a smooth finish.
Wax or polyurethane varnish to finish.
☐ Transfer the design on to the piece of hardwood.

☐ Remove the waste with a coping saw by cutting out the outline of the crocodile.

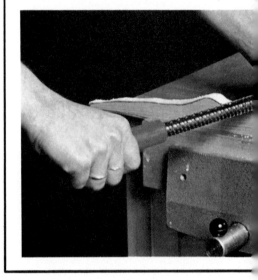

☐ Use the round Surform to tidy the edge and to remove any remaining waste.

Ray Duns

☐ Use the flat Surform and remove the waste down to the taper lines.

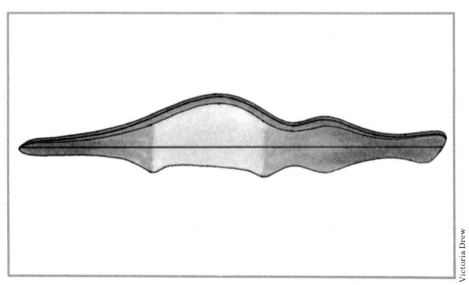

Victoria Drew

☐ Along the length, on the facing surface, draw a central line. Draw a line around the side edges 3mm (⅛") from the back.

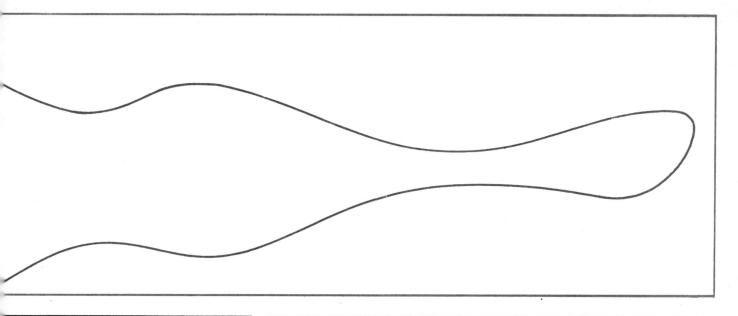

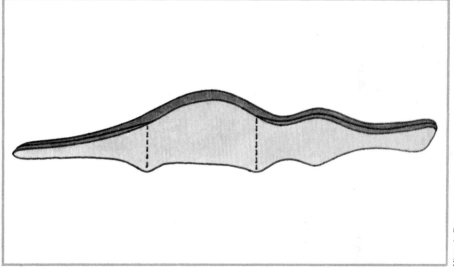

Victoria Drew

Work down to the outline and keep the side edge at right angles to the facing surface.

☐ Decide on the facing surface, ie which will be the front. Mark out where the head and tail taper along the side edge.

When marking the taper lines leave a minimum of 6mm (¼″) thickness to prevent the wood from becoming too thin and causing it to break.

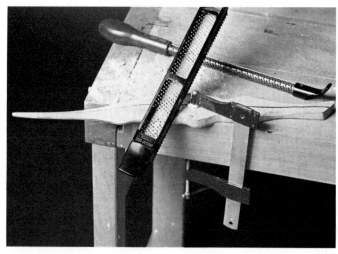

☐ Working from the front, round off the wood from the centre line towards the lines on the side edges. Continue working until all the edges are rounded, ie there must be no angles on the facing surface. Make sure you do not alter the outline of the crocodile while doing this.

☐ For a smooth finish, use the half-round wood file, followed by the medium and fine glasspapers [sandpapers].
☐ Polish or varnish the surface.

Carving
balsa wood

For all its softness balsa wood is a member of the hardwood family. The terms 'hardwood' and 'softwood' are confusing and it must be borne in mind that they are botanical terms.

Balsa wood comes from the tropical regions of America and is almost white in colour. It is very buoyant and is used extensively in the construction of rafts and lifebelts and in some parts of aircraft.

Once used as hunting lures, these picturesque balsa wood decoys are now popular as ornaments in the home.

1. *Laminating the pieces of balsa wood.*

2. *Cutting off waste with coping saw.*

3. *Whittling the decoy with a knife.*

Geoffrey Frosh

Many people will be familiar with model aeroplanes and boats which are constructed from balsa wood. The softness and close grained texture of the wood makes it ideal for modelling. Almost any sharp implement can be used to carve it and this chapter shows you how to carve decoy ducks with a simple household utensil such as a potato peeler or a sharp kitchen knife. The largest readily available pieces of balsa wood are in 90cm (3′) lengths, 50mm x 50mm (2″x 2″). You may find some pieces 100mm x 100mm (4″x 4″).

Decoys

The American Indian hunters were the first people to use decoys; a simple and ingenious device used to lure wildfowl into the range of concealed hunters. The early decoys were crudely made of mud and dried grass but these developed into closely simulated bird forms of stuffed skins and painted objects.

The colonists were quick to follow the example of the Indian and began carving their own decoys. Soon, professional decoy makers began to flourish and the craft has become a form of American folk art which still continues. The exquisitely carved and coloured decoys of these past masters is a legacy of the varied bird life that has vanished from the American skies. The decoy makers used well-aged pine or cedar and sometimes driftwood. Here, balsa wood is used because it is soft and easy to carve. Because of the sizes of balsa wood you will have to build up a suitably sized block by laminating layers of wood.

The decoys shown here are based on the shape of the Canada goose. A source for various bird shapes can be found in natural history books which should also provide you with a guide to the colourings of the birds.

The colouring of the decoys is a matter of debate. Some believe that the more 'realistic' the colouring, the more effective the decoy, while others hold that a more impressionistic

colouring should be used. It depends on your painting skill and personal preference.

You will need:
Four pieces 50mm x 50mm (2″x 2″) balsa wood 90cm (3′) long.
Potato peeler or kitchen knife.
Craft knife (optional).
Fret saw or coping saw with a fine blade.
Pencil, tracing paper and carbon paper.
Balsa wood sealer.
Enamel paints.
Glasspapers [sandpapers].
Balsa cement.
☐ Cut the pieces of balsa wood into 30cm (12″) lengths.
☐ Glue the pieces to form a laminated block 20cm (8″) high and 15cm (6″) wide (fig.1).
☐ Enlarge the pattern graph given and transfer the design to the laminated balsa wood. Be sure to transfer all three views of the duck correctly on to the wood surfaces.

☐ Cut off the larger pieces of waste with a fret saw or coping saw (fig.2).
☐ You can then begin whittling with the potato peeler or knife (fig.3). Work down to the basic outline, keeping the base flat.
☐ Working more carefully, add finer detail where necessary.
☐ The decoy is then smoothed down with fine grade glasspaper [sandpaper]. Where necessary use the medium grade glasspaper [sandpaper] to remove larger areas but remember that the wood is very soft.

Finish

The completed decoy is wiped with a damp cloth to remove any dust and then allowed to dry. Before painting, the decoy must be sealed with wood sealer. As it is very absorbent, the wood will probably need a couple of coats. The decoy is then painted using the enamel paints.

A graph pattern for the decoy ducks.

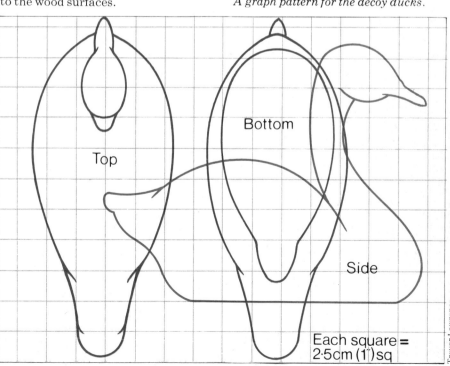

Top

Bottom

Side

Each square =
2·5cm (1″)sq

Trevor Lawrence

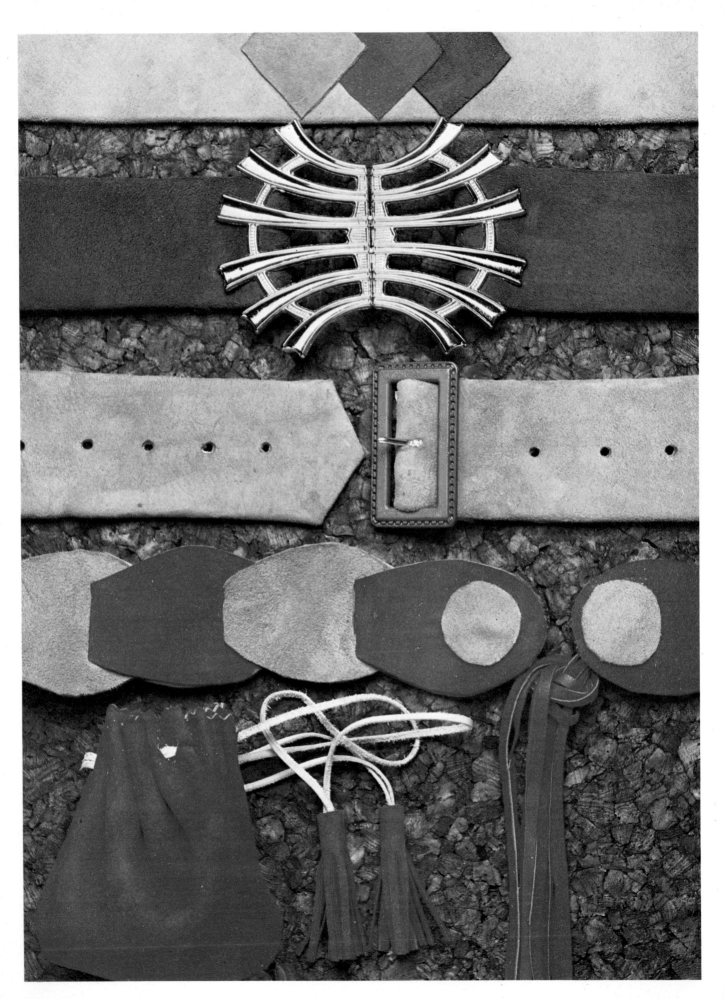

Leathercrafts

Leather is one of the most popular crafts materials, and is certainly versatile and fun to work. Learn the first steps in using thick leather hides for super belts. You could also try the complete wardrobe in supple chamois.

Simple leather projects

Revolving punch, edge shave, dividers [compasses], knife, rivet punch and rivets.

Thick leather or hide comes from large animals such as cows, oxen, horses and camels. The thickest types are used for footwear and the thinner varieties for lighter leather goods such as bags and belts. Although there is no need to be very expert in treating leather yourself, it is useful to have a working knowledge of the wide variety of skins available. Also you need to know the different weights.

Buying leather

Although the word 'hide' covers many types and qualities of leather, the most usual type of hide, and the one used in this chapter, is cow-hide.
Cow-hide is sold by leather suppliers and some craft shops. It comes in many thicknesses (usually measured in millimetres) so choose a suitable thickness according to what you want to make. It is sold by weight so the thicker the

leather, the more expensive it will be, so decide what you want.
When starting to work with cow-hide it is better to stick to the thinner types —about 2mm ($\frac{1}{16}$″) thick. Experienced leather workers can handle thicknesses of up to 6mm ($\frac{1}{4}$″).
The top of the leather is called the grain side, and the underside, which looks rather like suede, is called the flesh side.
Sometimes cow-hide is split into several layers to make a number of thin skins out of one thick skin. These 'splits' as they are called are used for lighter leather work, for example for gusset or lining leather. The top split will have the natural grain on one side and is the best to buy. The other splits will look like the flesh side on both sides, and are sometimes printed with a false grain by the tannery.
Cow-hide can be vegetable tanned

using natural tannin from tree bark which turns the leather a tan or brown colour; or it is chrome tanned using chromium salts and then dyed to any colour. Vegetable tanned hide usually wears better than chrome tanned—the vegetable tanned chestnut hide used in this chapter actually improves with age, wearing to a rich brown.
Cow-hide can be bought in different cuts coming from different parts of the body (fig.1). The butt is the prime cut

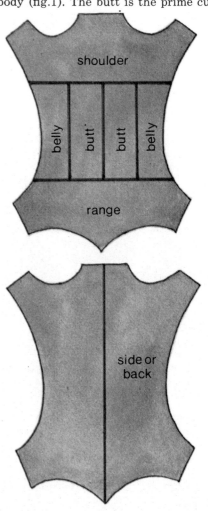

1. *The location and names of the different cuts of cow-hide.*

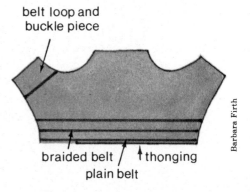

2. *Position pieces as shown here.*

of the hide and is used for top quality leather work. For longer pieces of leather a back or side is used. The shoulder is ideal for general leather work and is used in this chapter to make two belts. Cow-hide is usually sold in large pieces but offcuts and scraps are sometimes available.

Make sure that the piece of hide you buy is firm and well greased so that it will not crack when you start to work with it. Also look out for scars on the surface of the leather and see that the leather is the same thickness throughout. This is particularly important if you want a long piece for a belt, for example.

The plain belt

This is a very simple belt pattern which introduces some basic techniques for working with thick leather including cutting, punching and riveting the leather. The width of the belt can vary according to the size of buckle you buy. Cut the belt width equal to the inside width of the buckle.

You will need:
Tools
Steel rule at least 60cm (2′) long.
A very sharp knife for cutting the leather—special knives are sold for cutting leather but a sharp craft knife will do. If you intend doing much leatherwork it would be worth buying a proper knife for cutting leather. These and all leather-working tools mentioned here can be bought in leather tool shops and some craft shops.
A pair of dividers [compasses] with adjustable screw for scoring lines.
A revolving leather punch for punching holes for the buckle and rivets.
Hammer and rivet punch.
Medium grade glasspaper [sandpaper] or edge shave.

Materials
Three rivets 6mm ($\frac{1}{4}$″) diameter.
Buckle.
Piece of chestnut cow-hide 2mm ($\frac{1}{16}$″) thick: you can buy a piece large enough to take the two pieces or you could buy a shoulder from which you will be able to make all the items featured in this chapter plus spare leather for more. For the belt you will need two pieces: one piece the width of your buckle, and the length of your waist measurement plus 20cm (8″), and one scrap 1.25cm ($\frac{1}{2}$″) wide and as long as three times the width of the belt. If you buy the shoulder, follow instructions on how to position the belt pieces in fig. 2.
Sponge or rag for applying glue.
Scotch glue—this comes in small pellets which are dissolved in hot water.
Rag for polishing.

These two belts are ideal for wearing with denim. Designs by David Boot.

□ Find a firm hard surface to work on and lay out tools and materials.

Cutting. Cow-hide can be cut with a sharp knife or leather scissors. In this chapter, a sharp knife is used. A line is scored on the grain side with one point of a pair of dividers [compasses] or the point of a knife which is then run over the scored line several times until the leather is cut through. For cutting straight lines the knife is held against a steel rule.

□ If you are working from a shoulder you will have to straighten the bottom edge of the piece. To do this lay the steel rule along the bottom edge of the shoulder and score a line with the knife.

□ Keep on running the blade over the scored line against the steel rule until you have cut through the leather. Do not force the blade through the leather; cut gradually.

□ Set the dividers [compasses] to the required width for the belt, i.e. the inside width of the buckle.

□ Run one point of the dividers [compasses] along cut edge, scoring a line parallel to cut edge with other point.

□ Cut along the scored line using the sharp knife and steel rule as before.

□ Cut the strip of leather to the required length: your waist measurement plus 20cm (8″).

□ Round off one end of the belt by setting dividers [compasses] to the width of the belt and scoring two lines on the grain side as shown in fig. 3. Put one point of the dividers [compasses] on point A and score an arc, then put one point on point B, exactly opposite A, and score another arc.

□ Cut along the scored lines with a sharp knife.

□ Run the edge shave along the edges of the belt to trim off the sharp corners. This can also be done by rubbing with medium grade glasspaper [sandpaper].

Sealing the edges. The cut edges of the leather will be rough and fluffy and must be sealed. Sometimes the edges are stained to the colour of the leather by using a special process. In this case we shall use a glue mixture, one that results in a transparent finish.

□ Mix 2 teaspoons of Scotch glue in 6 teaspoons of boiling water and stir until the glue has dissolved.

□ Dip the sponge or rag into the mixture while it is still hot and rub along the cut edges of the leather.

□ When dry, rub the edges with a cloth to give a shine.

Attaching the buckle. Buckles can be sewn, thonged or riveted on to belts. For this belt, rivets are used to attach the buckle.

Rivets come in two halves. A hole is punched in the leather where each half of the rivet is to go, one half of the rivet is put into the top of the hole, and the other half of the rivet into the

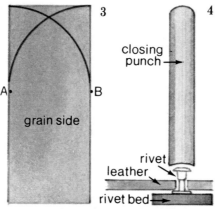

3. Scored lines for rounded end.
4. Rivet assembled for securing.

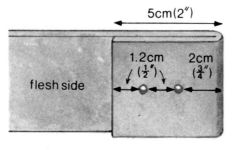

5. Punch these holes for the rivets.

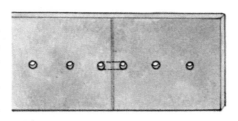

6. Cut out slot for buckle tongue.

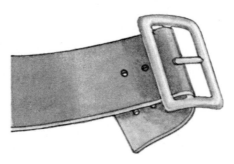

7. Fit the buckle into the belt.

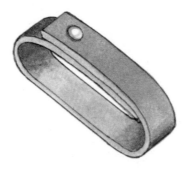

8. Belt loop secured with a rivet.

other side of the hole. The rivet is then fixed into a rivet punch. The rivet punch has two parts. One part, the bed, is placed underneath the rivet and the other half, the closing punch, is placed on the top of the rivet and the end hit with a hammer. This secures the two halves of the rivet (fig. 4).

□ Draw a line on the flesh side across the width of the belt, 5cm (2″) from the straight cut end of the belt.

□ Fold 5cm (2″) of the straight cut end of the belt, ie along the line, flesh sides together.

□ Using a revolving leather punch, punch two holes 3mm (⅛″) diameter through the double thickness of leather for the rivets (fig. 5). When punching holes in leather with a rivet punch, always put the cutting side of the punch in the side that will show so that the edges of the hole will curve inwards. Give the punch a little twist before removing it to make sure it has cut right through the leather.

□ To make a slot for the tongue of the belt, open out folded piece and punch one hole either side of the fold line, 3mm (⅛″) away from it.

□ Cut out the leather between these two holes (fig. 6).

□ Fit the buckle into the belt making sure it is the right way round (fig. 7).

□ Fold back 5cm (2″) of the belt, flesh sides together, so that the punched holes correspond.

□ Fit rivets into the two holes and secure with the rivet punch.

Fastening holes. These should be punched in the middle of the width of the belt, and should be large enough to take the buckle tongue. The distance between the holes should usually be equal to the width of the belt. Always punch one hole in the right place for your waist (or hips if the belt is to be worn on the hips) and measure the other holes from this point.

□ Measure your waist measurement from the buckle along the belt and punch one hole with the revolving punch at the required point.

□ Set dividers [compasses] to width of the belt, mark out the positions for two holes on either side of the first hole and punch the holes.

The belt loop. This is to hold in place the end that goes through the buckle (fig. 8).

Cut a piece of leather 1.25cm (½″) wide with length equal to three times the width of the belt.

□ Seal and polish the edges.

□ Fold the piece of leather into three, grain side outermost.

□ Check that the loop is big enough to take the double thickness of the belt.

□ Punch a hole in the double thickness, ie the back of the loop, fit in rivet and secure with rivet punch.

□ Slot the loop on to the belt.

Braided belt

This belt is made by braiding five strands of leather. If you are cutting your pieces from the shoulder of cow-hide used to make the plain belt, use the straight edge already cut on the shoulder for one edge of the braided belt.

You will need:
Tools as for the plain belt plus a G[C]-clamp and bulldog clip.

Materials
Buckle at least 2.5cm (1″) wide.
Three pieces of chestnut cow-hide all 2mm ($\frac{1}{16}$″) thick: one belt length at least 30cm (12″) longer than your waist measurement and as wide as your buckle—as the piece is to be cut into five strips, it should not be narrower than 2.5cm (1″); one piece 13cm (5″) long, the same width as the belt—this will be used to attach the buckle to the belt; one strip of thonging, 40cm (16″) long, 3mm ($\frac{1}{8}$″) wide.
Leather glue such as that supplied by Evo-Stik or Tandy.

☐ Cut out the pieces of cow-hide. If you are working from the previously used shoulder, follow instructions in fig.2.

☐ Round off one end of the belt length as for the plain belt.

☐ Trim, seal and polish edges of the rounded end of the belt, down to where the braiding is to start, ie (17cm 6$\frac{1}{2}$″) from the end.

☐ Divide the width of the belt into five equal widths and set the dividers [compasses] to this width.

☐ Starting 17cm (6$\frac{1}{2}$″) from the rounded end score four parallel lines along the length of the belt, dividing the belt into five equal strips (fig.9). Score the first line by running one point of dividers [compasses] along cut edge of the belt and scoring with other point. Score the second line by running one point along the scored line and scoring with the other point.

☐ Repeat this for the next two score lines.

☐ Using the sharp knife and steel rule, cut along the four scored lines to make five strips of leather.

☐ Secure the rounded end of the leather in a G[C]-clamp and start to braid. Work from alternate sides to the middle: take strip 1 over 2 and under 3 then strip 5 over 4 and under 1 and so on (fig.10).

☐ When you have finished braiding, secure the ends in a bulldog clip.

☐ Punch three fastening holes along the unbraided end of the belt for the tongue of the buckle.

☐ Measure your waist measurement from the centre fastening hole down the belt and cut off excess braiding.

☐ Unbraid about 4cm (1$\frac{1}{2}$″) at the end of the belt and trim the ends if they are not even.

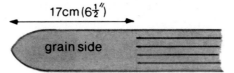

9. Leave part of the belt unbraided.

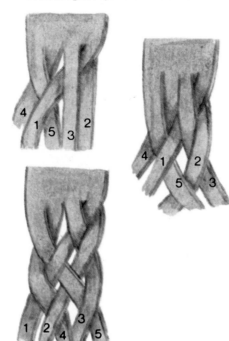

10. Start to braid belt as shown here.

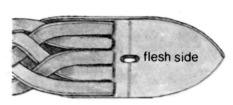

11. Stick end of belt on to buckle piece.

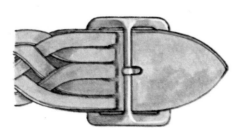

12. Fit buckle into buckle piece.

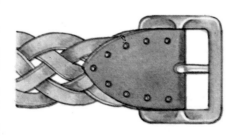

13. Fold buckle piece, punch holes.

☐ Secure the end in a bulldog clip.
To secure buckle. The buckle is fitted into the leather buckle piece which is attached to the braided end of the belt.

☐ Round off both ends of the buckle piece as for the belt end.

☐ Seal and polish the edges.

☐ Fold the buckle piece in half and mark the fold line on the flesh side.

☐ Make a slot for the buckle tongue across the fold line, as for the plain belt, see fig.6.

☐ Set the dividers [compasses] to 6mm ($\frac{1}{4}$″); score line round grain side of the buckle piece, scoring it 6mm ($\frac{1}{4}$″) in from the edge.

☐ Take the braided end of the belt out of the bulldog clip.

☐ Using leather glue, glue the buckle piece on to the end of the belt (fig.11).

☐ When dry, fit the buckle into the buckle piece (fig.12), and fold the buckle piece in half, ie along the line.

☐ Punch holes of about 3mm ($\frac{1}{8}$″) diameter at regular intervals, about 1.25cm ($\frac{1}{2}$″) apart, along the scored line on the buckle piece. These holes should go right through both sides of the buckle piece and through the braided belt (fig.13).

The buckle piece is now thonged on to the belt.

Thonging is a method of sewing leather using thin strips of leather woven in and out of punched holes, the method is simple and quick. Thonging is used on the braided belt to attach the buckle piece to the belt.

☐ Take the piece of thonging and cut one end to a point.

☐ Following fig.14, thread thonging in and out of punched holes keeping the grain side outermost all the time. Pass the centre thong through the middle of the braided belt.

☐ When you get to the last three laces leave them loose, pass the end of the thonging back through the three laces and pull tight.

☐ Trim off the end of the thonging and the belt is complete. Try on belt to check fit is correct. It looks super with denim and casual dress.

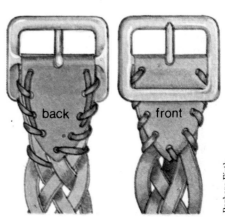

14. Thong buckle piece on to belt.

51

Chamois work

Making chamois clothes need not be difficult or complicated; the simple designs shown here involve no stitching—you simply punch holes and thong the pieces together. The moccasins and blouses are made very simply from your own measurements so will fit all sizes.

Animal skins like leather, suede, split sheepskin and chamois make perfect casual clothes—being supple, soft and extremely comfortable to wear. And now that other natural materials, such as cotton, wool and linen have increased so much in cost, there is no longer a great gap between the cost of natural fabrics and natural skins.

The loose fit of these designs makes them ideal projects for chamois but you could use other skins that are easier to get hold of or that you prefer. You will find all types of skin in markets and large department stores and there are also individual shops in many towns that deal in nothing but skins. It is best to shop personally for skins, especially chamois, as only you can decide whether the texture and colour is right for the object you want to make.

Sham chamois

Chamois used to be the skin of the mountain antelope of that name, but the large-scale sale of chamois as wash leathers as well as clothes would have meant the extinction of this animal years ago; so nowadays chamois is the softer side of the skin of a sheep or lamb, shaved away from the outer hide. It differs from split sheepskin only in the tanning process. Split sheepskin is tanned by formaldehyde, chamois by fish oils. Skins vary in size but an average chamois skin is 50cm (20″) square. Split sheepskins are usually larger—about 60cm (24″); they are more expensive than chamois but are much tougher in wear and they wash better too.

Choosing skins

Look at the skins carefully for blemishes, stains, holes or thin patches before you buy them. When you are buying a lot of skins for a garment, match them carefully in texture and colour.

Fashion designs

There are obviously limitations to the clothes you can successfully make from chamois. Because this skin does not hold its shape, you should only choose loose designs—those that do not require any fitting.

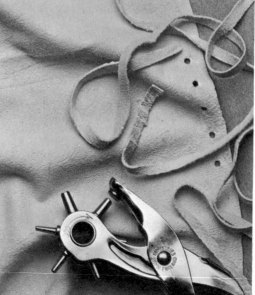

Far left (above): simple shoulder bag.
Far left (below): long-sleeved blouse.
Above left: short-sleeved blouse.
Centre left: comfortable moccasins.
Left: basic materials and equipment.

100 Idées de Marie Claire/Galand

Steve Bicknell

Washing and caring

Leather, suede and chamois all look just as good when they are old and worn but, whereas most leathers and suede need to be taken to a special dry-cleaner, you can wash chamois easily at home. Rub it with a pure, mild soap—not perfumed—and not a detergent. Rinse, but leave some soap in the skin at the end which will keep it supple. A drop of baby oil in the final rinsing water will also stop it drying out and becoming hard.

Pull it gently back into shape and dry it flat on a towel; don't hang it up or it will stretch. Dry it immediately after washing, away from direct heat.

Old spots can be rubbed off with a proprietary suede cleaner which is formulated, and contains nothing to damage the material.

Tools and equipment

None of the designs shown here is sewn so needles and thread are not necessary. You will need a leather punch, thonging (which you can buy in various thicknesses, either flat or rounded) and a pair of sharp scissors. A lacing needle or bodkin makes thonging easier.

Thonging

Punch holes to suit the thickness of the thonging you are using. The thonging in our designs is simply flat strips of chamois, about 6mm ($\frac{1}{4}$") wide. These are cut with sharp scissors or a Stanley knife or scalpel held against a steel rule.

There are three ways of using thonging in the designs shown here: criss-crossing (fig.1); straight overcast

1. Criss-cross thonging; start in the centre of one long thong and work with both ends.

2. Overcast thonging.

thonging (fig.2); and 'stitch' thonging, where the thong is simply threaded through two holes on one side then two holes on the other side (fig.3). This method is like sewing, pulling up the chamois, puckering it slightly.

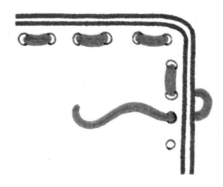

3. 'Stitch' thonging.

When calculating how much thonging you need, allow three times the overall length of the work for ordinary over-thonging and 'stitch' thonging and allow five times as much for criss-cross thonging.

Start and finish either by gluing the ends of the thong for about 2cm (1") to the inside of the skin or by tucking them away behind the first or last 'stitch'. Another method is to knot the ends inside the garment if this is not too uncomfortable. You can also leave long ends of the thonging hanging free outside the first and last holes (fig.4).

4. Leave long ends of thonging hanging for a casual finish.

Cutting out

Place the pattern on the wrong side of the chamois and hold in place with weights. Don't use pins. Mark out the pattern shape with chalk then cut out the chamois with sharp scissors or a Stanley knife.

100 Idées de Marie Claire/Galand

To make the bag

You will need:

One chamois skin, 50cm x 40cm (20"x 16"), or a piece of chamois **36cm** x 25cm (14"x10") for the back; a piece 25cm x 18cm (10"x7") for the front; a strip 120cm x 4cm (4'x1$\frac{1}{2}$") for a gusset between the front and back and to form the strap. (You will probably have to join strips for these.)
Thonging.

☐ Following fig.5 make paper patterns for the front and the back of the bag. The curves at lower edge of back, front and flap should be indentical. So cut out one curve and cut the others from it. Place them on the chamois in the best positions and cut out. Also cut out the strap 120cm x 4cm (4'x1$\frac{1}{2}$"), joining if necessary.

☐ At 13mm ($\frac{1}{2}$") intervals, punch holes all along the strip (or strips) 6mm ($\frac{1}{4}$") from the edge. If joining strips, punch holes across ends.
Punch holes all round the edges of the front, back and back flap pieces.

☐ Join strips into a ring with overcast thonging at narrow ends.

☐ Starting at one top edge of front of bag, join one long edge of gusset strip to front, down one side, along the

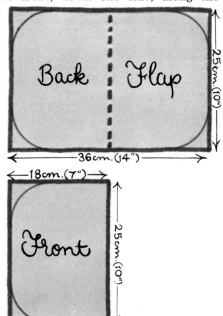

5. Patterns for bag back, flap and front.

bottom and up the other side, with overcast thonging.

☐ Matching the back to the front, join the other long edge of the gusset strip to the back in the same way. Leave the rest of the strip hanging to form the strap. Thread the thonging through each side of the strap and along the rest of the back of the bag which forms the front overlap. Also thread thonging along straight front edge to strengthen it.

☐ Punch two holes 25cm (1″) apart at centre front of bag just below where flap falls. Thread a few strips of chamois and knot loosely.

To make the moccasins

You will need:

A piece of chamois 50cm x 44cm (20″x 18″).

Thonging.

☐ Make patterns for base and uppers by drawing your foot outline on paper (fig.6). Make a base pattern by adding 6cm (2½″) all round foot and a further 6cm (2½″) for back flaps (a) and (b).

☐ Pierce holes with the punch at 13mm (½″) intervals all round each piece, 6mm (¼″) in from the edge, except where shown. The number of

holes punched round the outer edge of the uppers should be the same as the number round the corresponding edge of the base.

☐ Thong the upper to the base around the front using the 'stitch' method, threading through two holes on one side then through two holes on the other side. Pass another thong through the holes around the sides of the base, round the back and knot it at the front on the upper to act as a draw-string. Turn back the sides (a) and (b) to hide the thonging.

To make the blouses

You will need:

Two large skins for the sleeveless blouse; three large skins for the long-sleeved one. Thonging.

☐ Following fig.7 for long-sleeved blouse or fig.8 for short-sleeved blouse, make a front and back pattern and a sleeve if required.

As the patterns are made to your actual measurements it means they can be made to fit all sizes, adults and children alike.

☐ Cut pieces from chamois.

☐ Using a punch, punch holes all round pieces except at hem edge and

sleeve hem. Make the holes 13mm (½″) away from the edge and about 13mm (½″) apart. Make sure that the number of holes and their position on each side of a seam correspond.

Long-sleeved blouse. Work overcast thonging round the neck, leaving strips of thonging hanging loose at the bottom of the collar bones. Then criss-cross another thong at the lower edge of the V-neck, starting at the bottom.

☐ Thong the shoulders, side seams and the armholes as far as the side seams in overcast thonging. To finish ends of seams, knot the thonging and leave to hang as shown. Criss-cross the sleeve seam. At the wrist, thread another two strips through the last hole to hang as a trimming.

Short-sleeved blouse. Work overcast thonging around neck, leaving strips of thonging hanging loose at the bottom of the collar bones, then criss-cross another thong at the lower edge of the V-neck starting at the bottom.

☐ Thong armhole V as far as the side seams criss-cross fashion. To finish ends of seams, knot the thonging and leave to hang as shown. Join side seams and underarm sleeve seams with overcast thonging.

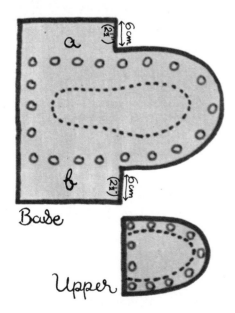

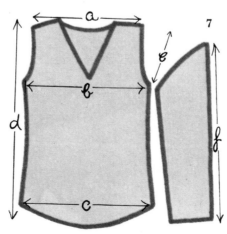

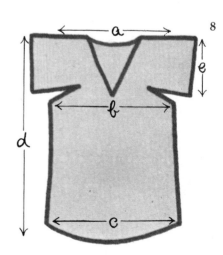

6. *Patterns for moccasins.*

7. *Patterns for long-sleeved blouse.*
8. *Patterns for short-sleeved blouse.*
a = *width from shoulder to shoulder.*
b = ½ *chest measurement plus 5cm (2″) for ease.*

c = ½ *hip measurement plus 5cm (2″) for ease.*
d = *length from shoulder to hip.*
e = *depth of armhole.*
f = *length from shoulder to wrist.*

Fabric crafts

Everyone loves the jewel colours of patchwork, and the inventiveness of appliqué. Here you can discover a wide range of ideas for these super fabric crafts, as well as some really beautiful beginners projects in quilting.

Simple hand stitched appliqué

Appliqué is very similar to collage, except that the shapes cut in one fabric are applied to another with stitches rather than glue. In its simplest form appliqué can be tackled by any beginner, results are quick and satisfactory and the easiest stitches can be used.

Appliqué can be left plain or richly decorated, worked in coarse or delicate fabrics. The more advanced methods for materials other than felt are discussed in later chapters.

Appliqué can be used to decorate clothes, curtains, bedspreads, cushions and, of course, to build up pictures.

Fabric choice

Choice of fabrics and surface decoration will depend upon whether or not the article is intended for hard wear and laundering. An appliqué motif on a baby's garment, for instance, is best made in a washable cotton.

It is easiest to begin with non-fraying fabrics. Felt is particularly easy to work with, is fun for quickly-made objects and ideal for creating pictures, when anything from string to sequins can be added.

Design inspiration

Start by thinking about pattern making and by working out designs with scissors and some folded paper, like those made by children.

Fold a piece of paper into quarters and then triangles, experiment with cutting out various shapes (fig.1a). then open out the paper to see the effect you have produced (fig.1b).

1a. *Cutting a shape in folded paper.*
1b. *The complete shape opened out.*

As you grow more skilled you can experiment with fruit shapes, stars, initials, the outlines of familiar domestic objects like a jug or teapot, or the silhouettes of flowers and leaves.

Remember when you draw a symmetrical shape to fold the pattern paper in half, so that both sides are exactly equal when you open the paper.

Appliqué waistcoat worked with embroidery stitches, including satin, buttonhole and running stitch. Designed by Susan's Cottage Industry.

Simple designing

Cut out small circles, squares or triangles from coloured, gummed paper and see how easy it is to arrange them into bold yet simple groups (fig.2).

2

K. Designs

Children's book illustrations are full of adaptable possibilities, from fairytale animals to supermen. Trace a favourite character and enlarge or reduce the scale to the size you need **with the aid of tracing paper and graph paper. Birds or animals, cars or trains, clowns, cartoons, even dinosaurs, can** all be adapted in this way as long as the basic shapes are sufficiently simple to be easily cut out and applied.

When you progress to more sophisticated designs, go to your local museum or library for inspiration. The flamboyant shapes used in Art Deco are ideal for appliqué, so are many oriental designs and the work of some primitive artists. Study the earliest forms of appliqué; you can find examples of the beautiful counterchanged designs that were used in ecclesiastical banners centuries ago, where two colours were intricately fitted together and used alternately for background and motif.

Linen pin cushions with felt motifs. Main motifs are built up of layers of felt applied one on top of the other.

PAF International

Left: felt motifs on corduroy squares; details in chain stitch and a French knot. Above: motif patterns.

Preparing felt motifs

Using thick paper, cut a template of the shape required. If there are several parts to the motif cut a template of the complete silhouette, then cut separate templates for each part of the motif you have designed.

Place the templates on the appropriate felt pieces and draw round them with a well-sharpened, soft pencil on the wrong side, so that pencil marks do not show on the finished work.

Cut out the motifs, using small, sharp scissors.

Positioning motifs

Carefully position the motifs on the right side of the background fabric, remembering to allow sufficient margin on the background fabric for any seaming required.

If the appliqué is to be centrally placed on a square of fabric, fold two diagonal lines from corner to corner of the square; the centre will be where they cross. Match this with the central point of the motif.

Joining methods

Bonding. For quick results appliqué shapes can be bonded to the background. The bonding material consists of a non-woven adhesive web which is sometimes prepared with a paper backing.

Cut a piece of bonding slightly larger shape required on to the paper backing and iron on to the wrong side of the motif material (fig.3a).

Allow to cool and cut out the motif shape. The non-woven adhesive web is now fused to the back of the motif.

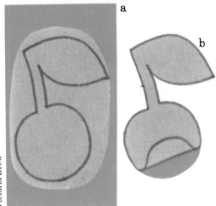

3a. *Bonding ironed on to motif fabric.*
3b. *Peeling the backing from motif.*

Peel off paper (fig.3b), place motif, right side up, on to the background fabric and iron into place. Use a steam iron or a dry iron and a damp cloth. Fabric bonded in this way can then have decorative stitching added around the edge.

This method is suitable for most fabrics except delicate ones and some, like velvet, which need special care.

Another simple technique is to use a little fabric adhesive, such as Copydex, on the back of the motif, taking care not to go right up to the edges, then add decorative hand or machine stitching.

Stitching felt motifs. Small motifs can be easily stitched in the hand so long as care is taken to keep the surface flat, but it is advisable to use an embroidery hoop or tapestry frame to hold the fabric taut on larger projects.

Tack [baste] the motif in place and sew to the background, making tiny stab stitches in matching thread. If this stitching is not intended to be part of the decoration it should be as unobtrusive as possible.

Alternatively, you can use a spaced blanket (simple buttonhole) stitch, worked with embroidery thread, to produce a strong, decorative edge on the motif.

Basic stitches

Stab stitch

Either: bring needle up through background fabric and motif, close to the edge of motif, then, making a very small stitch, take needle down again through the two thicknesses (fig.a) Or: bring needle up from background fabric immediately outside the edge of the motif, then take it down again a fraction inside the edge (fig.b).

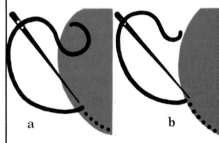

a   b

Blanket (simple buttonhole) stitch

This can be worked close for securing edges of motifs cut in woven fabrics, or spaced out for motifs cut in felt.

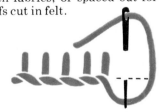

Outline stitching. Details can be picked out with simple embroidery stitches, such as satin stitch or French knots. If you wish to emphasize the outlines you can add couching or chain stitch in a contrasting embroidery thread.

Non-fraying woven fabrics

You can cut out motifs in most firmly woven fabrics and apply them successfully without turning under the edges. Choose a fabric of the same or a lighter weight than that used for the background and keep the shapes simple. When cutting the motif ensure, where possible, that the grain on the motif matches that of the background fabric. Cut out the motif and work oversewing close to the edge (fig. 4). Position the motif and tack [baste] it to the

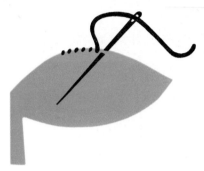

4. *Oversewing [overcasting] edges of a motif before applying buttonhole stitch.*

background fabric. Stitch into place with closely worked blanket stitch, covering the oversewing completely.

Using appliqué motifs

The patterns given in this chapter, enlarged if necessary, can be used in a number of ways.

Pot holder. Start with something small; make a pot holder for the kitchen from two squares of felt. Stab stitch the plump chicken motif to one square, place the two pieces of felt together with a piece of wadding [batting] in between, then machine stitch the layers together or pink the edges to finish.

Child's bed cover. Multiply the motifs to make a child's bed-cover. Alternate the colours of the background squares to make a chequerboard effect and join them together by hand or machine (see chapters discussing Patchwork on pages 66 to 73). Line the cover and interline it with synthetic wadding [batting] as in the section on Patchwork on page 70.

Patches for clothes. The apple motif, cut (without its stalk) in a tough non-fraying cotton, would make a fine patch for the knee of a child's jeans. It is essential, when cutting the motif, to make sure that the grains of motif and background fabric match, to avoid the motif splitting and puckering.

Girl's novelty apron. Any of the motifs cut in pretty printed cotton would add a charming individual touch to a little girl's apron or plain dress.

More hand stitched appliqué

The last chapter dealt fully with the methods of affixing appliqué motifs by hand, using felt and non-fraying woven fabrics, simple pattern making and sources for pattern inspiration. Some trace patterns for simple motifs were given, plus ideas for using them.

This chapter covers preparing a more complicated design and methods of hand stitching fabrics which fray. (The methods are also suitable for non-fraying fabrics.)

Preparing a design

You will need to work from a paper pattern unless you are sufficiently confident to cut out motifs directly from the fabric.

Make a full-scale drawing of the design on paper, marking in the various sections which are to be cut from different fabrics and noting where sections are to overlap. Ears, wings or paws, for instance, can be cut out separately and positioned with one edge under the main part of the motif, which makes sewing easier by avoiding difficult angles.

Trace the outlines of each section separately on to another piece of paper and cut them out to use as patterns.

Outline the complete design lightly in pencil on the background fabric or use dressmaker's carbon paper or a transfer pencil.

Bird motif tacked [basted] to interfacing with wings cut out separately and tacked [basted] under main motif.

Another method is to draw the design on tissue paper, pin this to the background, tack [baste] around the design lines, then tear away the paper.

Fabrics which fray

It is not difficult to apply motifs cut in fabrics which fray if a little extra time and trouble is taken in working with one of the methods described here.

Stitch and cut. This is a good method to use on thin fabrics. Cut out a larger area than required and mark in the shape the motif with a pencil. Tack [baste] motif to background fabric and work close blanket (simple buttonhole) stitch through both thicknesses around this outline (fig.1). Then carefully cut away the surplus motif fabric.

Interfaced method. Another method of dealing with fraying or flimsy fabrics is to reinforce them with iron-on, non-woven interfacing before cutting out the exact shape of the motif. This will provide a firm edge on which to work. The motif can then be tacked and closely blanket stitched to the background fabric.

Alternatively, cut out the exact shape in the interfacing. Iron it on to a larger piece of the motif fabric, cut out with seam allowance and apply as for turned under method.

Turned under method. Motifs cut from most woven fabrics can have their edges turned under before they are applied. Here are some techniques to help you achieve good results.

Closely woven cotton fabrics are the easiest to handle. Remnants of other dressmaking fabrics can also be used, but when selecting patterns bear in mind the purpose for which the design is intended and never add a non-washable fabric to a washable article. Careful cutting and placing ensures that the appliquéd design will lie flat. Find the straight of grain before **cutting each section if there is no selvedge to guide you. After this, you should match the straight of grain** of the applied fabric to the straight of grain of the background, except for small curved motifs which can be cut on the cross [bias].

Cut out each piece of the motif, adding a hem allowance of 6mm ($\frac{1}{4}''$) all round each section. Turn in and tack [baste] all raw edges except those which adjoin other parts of the motif, ie the pinafore and bonnet edges on the Polly Pinafore motif on the cushion. One edge

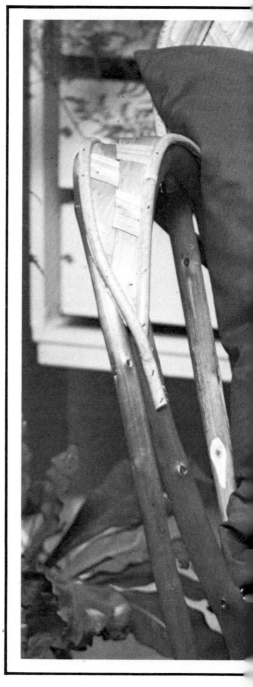

The edges of the Polly Pinafore motif on this cushion are turned under and then slip stitched into place.

(the pinafore edge) is left without its hem allowance turned in and the other has its allowance turned in.

If the shape is curved make snips in the hem allowance at frequent intervals, just less than 6mm ($\frac{1}{4}''$) deep, then turn in the edges. The snips will overlap on a convex curve and open out on a concave one.

To mitre a right-angled, or wider, corner, first fold in one edge (fig.2a), then fold over the other (fig.2b) and tack [baste]. For a sharper point, first fold in the point (fig. 3a), fold one side over this (fig. 3b), then the other (fig. 3c) and tack [baste] to secure.

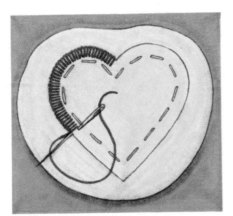

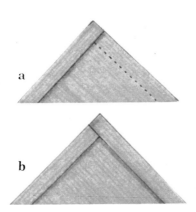

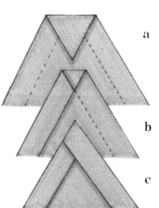

1. *Buttonhole stitching a motif to background before cutting away surplus.*

2. *Mitring a right-angled corner.*

3. *Mitring a corner of less than 90*

The edges can be pressed lightly before applying but take care to press only the edge so that the turnings [raw edges] do not mark the right side.

Or you can tack [baste] the shape to the paper pattern and then press the whole piece (the paper will prevent the turnings from marking the right side). Remove tacking [basting] and paper.

Position the motif on to the background fabric so that adjoining sections have the edge with hem allowance turned in placed over the one left raw (fig. 4). Tack [baste] and stitch the

4. *Turned in edge placed over raw one.*

motif in place with small slip stitches. You can either secure your motif with matching thread, or with neat running stitches worked in matching or contrasting thread.

Adjoining edges can be sewn on to the background in one operation.

Flowers in relief

A pretty variation of appliqué can be achieved by leaving the edges of motifs unattached to the background. Flower petals can be attached at the bottom only. Cover the stitches with a separate

Peter Heinz

Flower and leaf with edges unattached.

flower centre slip stitched in place. Edges can be either closely blanket stitched or the petals can be cut double, the edges stitched with right sides together, then turned to the outside through a small opening which is then stitched up. The second method takes a little longer to work, but results are sufficiently sturdy to be used on children's garments.

Leaves can be made in the same way, but stitch these in position with a stem stitched spine, to about two-thirds of the length of the leaf.

The petticoat frill of Polly Pinafore is attached in a similar way. In this case the frill is cut slightly wider than the bottom of the skirt and pinafore, and a small hem made on one long and the two short sides of the frill. The fourth side is then gathered and this edge is covered by the skirt and pinafore.

100 Idées de Marie Claire/Godeaux

On this cushion the edges of the motif are stitched down with open herring-bone stitch and embroidered flowers and hair added to the basic design.

Polly Pinafore cushion

The Polly Pinafore cushion is made in plain cotton with an appliqué motif made from printed cotton fabrics. The edges of the various parts of the motif

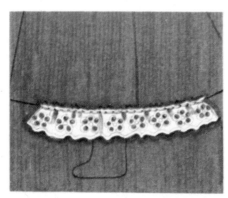

6. *The frill gathered and back stitched in position.*

are turned under and slip stitched into place. The finished cushion is 48cm (19″) square and the motif is 41cm (16″) high but the motif could be made to fit a cushion of any size.

You will need

For the cushion: 1.15m (1¼yd) of 90cm (36″) wide plain cotton fabric.

Cushion pad, 51cm (20″) square.

For the appliqué: bonnet and petticoat frill—20cm x 28cm (8″x11″) piece of broderie Anglaise; pinafore—26cm x 18cm (10″x7″) cotton fabric; dress—20cm x 10cm (8″x4″) piece of cotton fabric; scraps of cotton fabric for ribbons, hands, basket, sleeve, boot.

To make the cushion. Cut two pieces of plain fabric 51cm (20″) square and put one aside for the cushion back.

☐ Take the other square of fabric and find the centre by folding it diagonally and then diagonally the other way, locating the centre where the folds cross.

☐ Enlarge the motif (fig.5), make paper patterns and outline the design centrally on the cushion front as described in this chapter.

☐ Cut out the various parts of motif (except the petticoat frill) in appropriate fabrics, allowing 6mm (¼″) all round each piece for the hems.

☐ Cut a piece of broderie Anglaise for the petticoat frill, 28cm (11″) x 4cm (1⅝″).

☐ Narrowly hem one long edge and two short edges.

☐ Work a row of gathering 3mm (⅛″) from the fourth edge and pull up the gathers to fit the bottom of the skirt. Back stitch the frill into position on the cushion along the gathering line (fig.6).

☐ Work the rest of the appliqué by the slip stitch method as described in this chapter. Make sure that the bottoms of skirt and pinafore are slip stitched securely on the gathering line of the frill enclosing the raw edge (fig.7).

☐ Make up the cushion.

5. *Graph pattern for the Polly Pinafore motif. On this pattern each of the squares equals a 5cm (2″) sq.*

7. *Skirt slip stitched into position over the raw edge of the frill.*

Machined patchwork

Squares arranged diagonally make this attractive bag.

Development of patchwork

Patchwork is a truly sentimental craft which has always been connected with sharing and neighbourliness, particularly in America. It originated at a time when every scrap of material had a value and was saved to be sewn to one scrap and another to form fabric for clothing and covering. It is from these humble beginnings that real art emerged as women began to use their oddments of cloth to create rich and colourful designs.

Today the art of patchwork is having a great revival—not only because of the real practical need for re-cycling materials, but because it provides a means of relaxation and for exercising one's artistic talent in creating unique and exciting new patchwork designs. It can be worked in a wide variety of materials and has instant effect and is the ideal pastime while watching television or talking to friends.

Nowadays beautiful patchwork fabric can be made quite simply and quickly on any sewing machine. Oddments of material, which would otherwise be discarded, can be cut into squares or rectangles and joined together with straight machine stitching to form strong fabrics in a variety of patterns, colours and shades. Make them up into eye-catching clothing, soft furnishings for the home, children's toys etc. Patchwork can also be appliquéd on to plain fabrics to form striking decorations or borders for such things as skirts, curtains or bedspreads.

The fabric of patchwork will often conjure up a score of memories—a scrap of the first dress you ever sewed, a piece of the blouse that never looked right with anything—reminders of friends and family. Autographed patches can be turned into a cushion or wall-hanging to make a charming memento of a special occasion.

Choosing fabrics

The best fabrics for patchwork are those which do not fray or stretch and are firm in weave and texture. Good quality cottons head the list from all points of view. Man-made fibres are not so easy to use because of their crease-resisting qualities. Three important rules are: never mix silks with cottons, only combine materials of equal weight and thickness and never mix old and new fabrics—the stronger fabric will wear out the weaker one.

If in doubt always test materials for colour-fastness if the finished item is to be washed and, if using new cotton fabric, it is best to wash it first in case of shrinkage.

Gathering the scraps. The fabrics used in a patchwork can be gathered from many sources and it is useful to keep a bag or box in which to store

66

1. *Rectangles arranged in a 'brick wall' pattern.*

2. *Squares arranged diagonally with triangles at edges.*

3. *A border of diagonally arranged squares.*

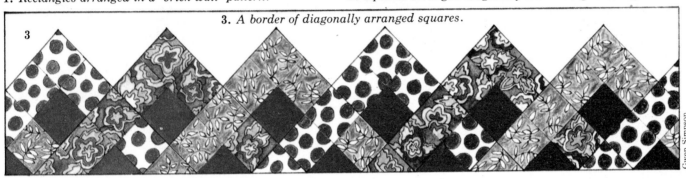

Gwen Simpson

them. Home dressmaking, either your own or a friend's, will yield a good supply of scraps: you can also use old clothes, providing the material is still strong, along with the laundered gleanings from second-hand sales. There is usually a remnant box in any shop selling fabric and these can provide useful offcuts at a reasonable price. The shopkeeper might also be willing to part with out-dated colour swatches of manufacturers' fabrics.

Part of the fun of patchwork is in collecting the right patterns and colours to create a design: and perhaps the sense of achievement is even greater when one knows that a skirt, shirt or bedspread was put together from scraps that cost next to nothing!

The design

When you have assembled your oddments of fabric, decide on the size of patches to be used in the patchwork, bearing in mind the size of the finished article and how it is to be used. It is pointless to use very large patches on a small item which will not show them off to advantage. When you have cut the patches, take time over planning the design—this can be an absorbing and enjoyable stage. A good design is generally a simple one and it's fun to work it out in shades and tints. Random schemes can be very pretty too, especially if some sort of colour grouping is attempted. If you are using a fabric with a nap or pile, the direction

of each patch should also be carefully considered.

Squares or rectangles can be sewn together in a 'hit and miss' pattern of alternating light and dark fabrics or in the rather more sophisticated 'brick wall' pattern (fig.1), which consists of rectangular patches of different shades sewn together like a brick wall. These designs are known as 'one patch'—ie an all-over design made from the same repeated unit.

With experience you can attempt more complicated patterns by dividing the basic square or rectangle in half diagonally (two-patch) or into four smaller squares or rectangles. Squares can also be used diagonally (fig.2) and look particularly effective as borders, appliqued directly on to a plain background (fig.3).

Two-patch patchwork and squares used diagonally require accuracy and are best worked by hand.

Machine worked patchwork

Equipment. The equipment needed for machining patchwork is probably already available in the home—a fine needle for the machine and a fairly fine thread for sewing, a ruler and pencil for drawing the patches on to the fabric and a sharp pair of scissors for cutting them out. You will also need an iron for pressing the seams.

A board or small table is useful for designing the arrangement of the patchwork. You can use it to lay out

the patches like a jigsaw, and the 'board' can be anything into which pins can be pushed to hold the patches in place—cork matting, thick cardboard, a card table or a carpeted floor.

Making the patchwork. First decide on the size of the squares or rectangles to be used, allowing 9mm ($\frac{3}{8}$") for seam allowances on all sides of the patch.

☐ Choose the fabric pieces to be used in the design and iron them. Then, working along the straight grain of the fabric, draw each patch accurately on to the wrong side of the fabric with a ruler and pencil (a sharp white crayon is best for darker fabrics).

☐ When cutting a large number of patches of equal size it may be a help to make a simple template from a piece of heavy cardboard or plastic. Draw the area of the patch, including seam allowances, on to the card with pencil and ruler and cut it out very accurately. This template can then be placed on to the fabric and used as a pattern for the patches. Card can wear quite quickly so you will need to keep checking that the template has not become inaccurate.

☐ Cut out all the patches carefully with a pair of sharp scissors.

☐ When you have cut out the required number of patches you can begin to plan the exact design of the patchwork by spreading out the patches and building up the required pattern.

☐ With right sides facing and taking 9mm ($\frac{3}{8}$") seam allowance, machine stitch the patches together into a strip the required length of the article you are making (fig.4). Use straight

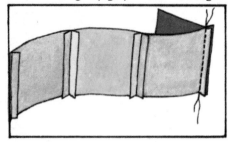

4. *Stitching squares into a strip.*

machine stitching and a toning cotton. If you want the seams to match later on make sure that you take exactly the same turnings for each join—you can use the foot on the sewing machine as a guide.

□ When you have enough strips to make the required width of fabric, press open all the seams.

□ Before machining the strips together it is advisable to check that all the corners of the patches match up, if it is accuracy you are after. It may be possible to ease the fabric slightly to ensure a match. If there is still a slight error it is possible to adjust this by re-stitching part of the seam that is inaccurate, gradually taking in or letting out the amount required. Unpick the old line of stitching.

□ Machine stitch the strips together, right sides facing, taking 9mm ($\frac{3}{8}''$) seam allowance.

□ When you have finished, press open the seams and tie off and cut the ends of thread.

Strengthening the fabric. To give extra strength to the patchwork you can carefully top-stitch up and down the lines of patches on the right side of the fabric, 3mm ($\frac{1}{8}''$) from either side of the seams (fig.5). This helps to keep the seam allowances in place and is

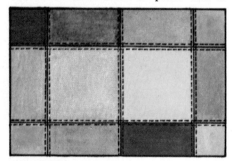

5. *Topstitched squares.*

particularly advisable for garments such as skirts and head scarves that will need regular washing.

Cut and stagger technique

Another way of joining machine patchwork is illustrated in figs.6 and 7. This method is extremely quick and

6. *First stage in cut and stagger technique: cutting and arranging strips.*

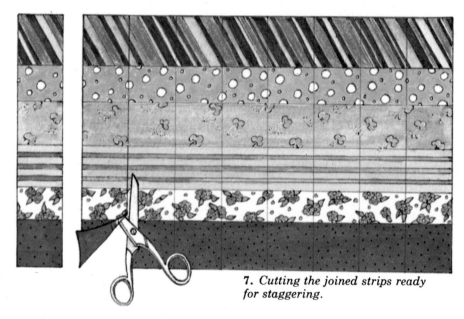

7. *Cutting the joined strips ready for staggering.*

A charming cushion made up in cottons using the cut and stagger technique.

Steve Bicknell

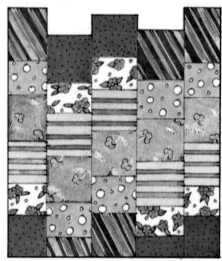

8. *Rearranging the strips to stagger the pattern.*

easy although the distribution of colour and design in the patchwork is fairly limited.

☐ Take strips of material of equal length and equal or varying width (fig.6) and machine them together, right sides facing, taking 9mm ($\frac{3}{8}''$) seams. The number and width of the strips, and their length, will be determined by the size of the patchwork required.

☐ Press open the seams, then cut across the fabric at intervals, in straight lines, allowing for seams on each side of the cutting line (fig.7).

☐ The resulting strips can be re-arranged in a variety of ways and machined together to form patchwork fabric in a random pattern of rectangles (fig.8).

If the strips are to be staggered they will have to be longer than the finished piece of work to allow for waste.

Squares. A patchwork of squares can also be made in this way but, in this case, the strips must be cut out accurately into equal widths and lengths, depending upon the size of square required. The seam allowance of 9mm ($\frac{3}{8}''$) must be accurately measured out all round the strips and they must be accurately sewn together.

Patchwork for clothes

Machine patchwork can be used in exactly the same way as any other fabric when making up clothes from a paper pattern.

To begin spread out all the pattern pieces needed to make up the garment, leaving those for facings to one side—these should be cut from a single piece of fabric rather than patchwork.

Cut out patches in squares or rectangles, allowing for 9mm ($\frac{3}{8}''$) seams all round, and lay them on a table until there are enough to make up each pattern piece—those pattern pieces that lie on a fold will, of course, need twice as much patchwork.

Make sure that the colours used in the patchwork are evenly distributed then, keeping the patches for each pattern piece separate, make up each section of patchwork as explained earlier.

The cut and stagger method for patchwork can also be used—just make sure that the strips are the right length and that the width will be enough to make up each pattern piece. Alternatively make up a long length and lay out pattern pieces as on ordinary fabric. Do top-stitch the patchwork fabric if the garment you are making is to be washed frequently.

Pin each pattern piece on to the patchwork (fig.9) and cut them out, then cut a lining from lining fabric. You can tack [baste] this to the patchwork pieces and make them up together following the pattern instructions, or you can make a loose lining.

Femina

Above: the simple lines of this blouse make it an ideal style for machine-worked squares.

9. *Below: pattern positioned on a piece of cut and stagger patchwork which has been made up to accommodate the pattern.*

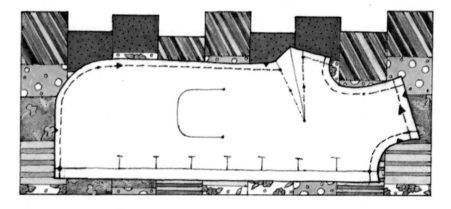

Gwen Simpson

Hand sewn patchwork

The last chapter showed you how to make patchwork fabric from squares and rectangles joined together with straight machine stitching. This method is both quick and effective in producing bright and colourful patchwork fabrics and is particularly suited to making patchwork fabrics which are to be used in dressmaking.

Even today, however, the art of patchwork relies very much on the traditional method of hand sewing, and for the majority of people who want to do patchwork this is the most convenient and pleasurable method. It is extremely relaxing and its great advantages are that you can pick it up at any time, work a few patches or do a little planning, and, like knitting, you can do it while sitting in an easy chair in the company of friends and still take an active part in the conversation.

Hand sewn patchwork can be handled by anyone who can oversew [overcast] and tack [baste] neatly. Why not start with a piece of hand sewn patchwork made up from odd squares and rectangles and see just how relaxing and rewarding it can be.

Equipment

The stitches in a patchwork must be fine and close together and a needle size 9 or 10 is best. For sewing the patches you will need a fine thread in a colour which blends with the patchwork.

Use fine pins for the patchwork. Dressmakers' pins will do, but tiny pins like 'lillikins' or 'lills' are better because they do not get in the way and are less likely to damage fine fabrics.

You will also need two pairs of scissors —one very sharp pair for cutting the patches and another for paper cutting as paper will quickly blunt a sharp pair of scissors.

Paper. The patches in hand sewn patchwork are generally constructed over paper shapes which are cut from templates. The papers ensure that the patches are exact and hold them firm— a help when joining them together. The paper from a glossy magazine is the ideal weight. Standard weight notepaper will also do as it is firm enough for the edges to be felt within the folds when the edges of the patches are turned. Paper which is too thick will make the work heavy and difficult to handle although it is necessary for heavier materials.

Non-woven interfacing, such as Vilene or Pellon, can be used as an alternative to paper and is left in when the work is finished to add firmness.

Templates are the patterns for the papers and patches, and metal and plastic templates can be bought from craft shops. As the square and rectangle are very simple shapes you can easily make your own from cardboard. They must be accurate, however, or the patches will not fit together properly.

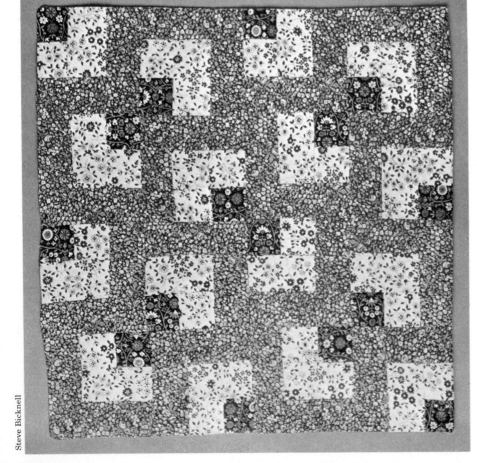

This patchwork cushion cover is made from squares and rectangles arranged in a regular, geometric pattern. Designed by Heather Mingay.

Steve Bicknell

A gorgeous patchwork evening skirt made from squares of printed velvet.

sewing [overcasting]. Start 6mm ($\frac{1}{4}''$) from the corner, make a stitch, take thread to corner, oversewing with small, even stitches along the whole edge, taking in the thread and the first stitch (fig.2). The stitches should be even and at right angles to the join. Take up two or three threads only from each fold into every stitch and do not take in the paper inside. To finish the seam sew back for three or four stitches, then cut the thread.

When you have completed the join flatten the seam and carry on sewing the other patches together by making up groups or units, then join these together. Repeat the process until the required area is completed.

When all the patches are sewn together, press the patchwork on the wrong side with a warm iron. If the front of the work needs pressing too, remove the tacking [basting] but leave in the papers to prevent the seams from making a mark.

Finally, when you are ready to line the work, remove all the papers. You may be able to use these several times if they are undamaged.

Method B. Square and rectangular patches can be joined, without papers,

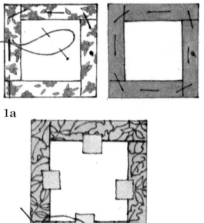

1a

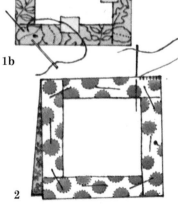

1b

2

1a. *Tacking [basting] patch to paper.*
1b. *On fine fabrics, stick edges with masking tape and tack [baste]. corners through seam allowance only.*
2. *Oversewing [overcasting] patches.*

To make the template for the papers draw the exact area of the patch, without allowance for turnings [seams] on a piece of cardboard with ruler and pencil. Then cut out the shape.

For the patch template draw a larger replica of this same shape, allowing 6mm-9mm ($\frac{1}{4}''$-$\frac{3}{8}''$) all round for the seam allowance and cut out this shape. Cardboard can wear quickly so you will need to keep checking the templates for accuracy.

Fabrics

As hand sewn patchwork is likely to take some time to make it is worth checking that you have enough patchwork pieces to complete a design before beginning the work — it may not be easy to come by a similar piece of fabric later on.

Because of the time and patience involved in making hand sewn patchwork the item produced may be of some sentimental value and you may wish to mix different fabrics in it which are of personal significance. It is possible to mix fabrics in a patchwork but, as the stronger fabrics will tend to pull out the weaker ones, it is better to confine these mixtures to items which will not receive hard wear.

Making patchwork

Size. With hand sewn patchwork it is a good idea to consider the size of the patch in relation to the work involved, using larger patches for big items such as quilts. Squares about 6cm-10cm ($2\frac{1}{2}''$-$4''$) are suitable for large pieces, 4cm-6cm ($1\frac{1}{2}''$-$2\frac{1}{2}''$) for medium pieces and 2.5cm-4cm ($1''$-$1\frac{1}{2}''$) for small pieces.

Method A. Cut out the papers two at a time by holding the smaller template firmly in position on a double thickness of paper. Keep the scissor blades close to the template for accuracy whilst cutting. Alternatively you can cut them out with a scalpel, cutting through several layers of paper.

Cut the patches singly by placing the larger template on the wrong side of the fabric, along the straight of grain. Pin the paper shape to the centre of the wrong side of the patch. Fold over the turnings [seam allowances] all round and tack [baste] down. To start first knot the thread. Start tacking [basting] in the middle of one side, work round the patch and finish off with an extra stitch over the first one (fig.1a). When turning the corners feel the fold edges to make sure the material fits the paper lining exactly.

Silks and some cottons can be permanently marked by pins and needles. On these fabrics it is best to stick down the seam allowance with masking tape and to sew the corners through the seam allowances only (fig.1b).

To join the patches take two, and with rights sides together begin the over-in the same way as machine patchwork. Cut the patches then take two and, with right sides facing, join them carefully with a small running stitch (fig. 3). Join the patches into strips, making sure that the seams are all the same width. Press the seam allowances to one side and join the strips together. Do not press the seams open as with oversewing [overcasting] or machine stitching as this will put too much strain on the running stitch.

Method C. As in the previous method, papers are unnecessary. Cut the patches, then make a 6mm-9mm ($\frac{1}{4}''$-$\frac{3}{8}''$) turning all round and tack [baste]. Oversew [overcast] the patches together. In both methods B and C the turnings taken must be exact to ensure that the squares fit together.

Lining and interlining

Patchwork, unless it is to be used for appliqué, should always be lined. If the piece of patchwork is to be made into a bedcover it is advisable to place a piece of interlining between the patchwork and the lining.

Lining. Use a firmly-woven cotton or other lining material. If edges are not bound with lining the work can be bagged. Trim the lining to 6mm-9mm ($\frac{1}{4}''$-$\frac{3}{8}''$) (the width of the patchwork turnings) larger all round than the patchwork. Unfold the turning on the edges of the patchwork. Place the lining and patchwork right sides together, tack [baste] three sides and part of the fourth, the width of the patch turning from the edge. Machine or hand sew along tacking [basting]. Clip the corners, then turn the 'bag' right side out. Slip stitch the opening. Make a line of neat running stitches all round the 'bag', 3mm ($\frac{1}{8}''$) from the edge, to hold the edges firm. If the patchwork is fairly large, knot it to the lining at regular intervals, placing each knot in the centre of a patch. Alternatively the lining and patchwork can be knotted together as for interlined patchwork and the edges finished as mentioned below.

Interlining. Synthetic wadding [batting] is ideal for interlining as it is washable, as well as quick-drying and available in a variety of weights. It is possible to use flannelette as interlining but this is not quick-drying like synthetic wadding [batting] and gives a much flatter result.

Lay a piece of lining fabric, 5cm (2") larger all round than the patchwork, wrong side up on a large flat surface. Place the wadding on top and then the patchwork, right side up, on top of that.

Tack [baste] the three layers together with regular parallel lines of stitches worked from side to side and from top to bottom. It is important that all the

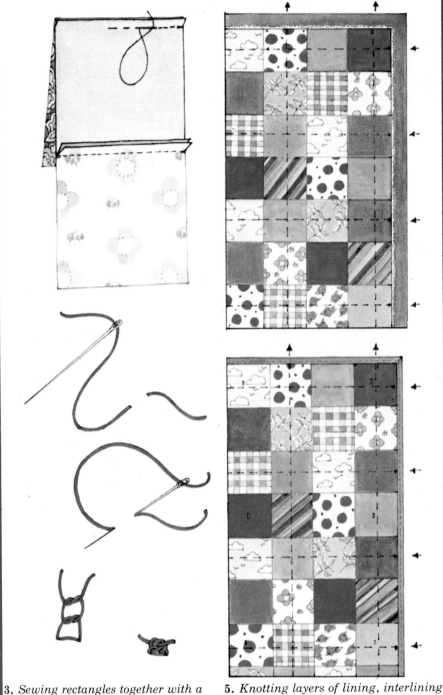

3. *Sewing rectangles together with a running stitch.*
4. *Tacking [basting] lining, interlining and patchwork together.*
5. *Knotting layers of lining, interlining and patchwork together.*
6. *The patchwork has been knotted in the centre of every third square.*

lines of tacking [basting] parallel to each other, are worked in the same direction (fig.4). This avoids wrinkles. Work knots as shown (fig.5) through all thicknesses at regular intervals across the whole piece of work (fig.6). The knots should be made on the lining side in the centre of every 4th patch, when small patches are used, and every 3rd patch, when larger patches are used. Trim lining 6mm-9mm ($\frac{1}{4}''$-$\frac{3}{8}''$) larger all round the patchwork, unless the edges are bound with lining. Remove tacking [basting].

The edges can be finished off in one of the ways mentioned below.

Alternative finishes for edges. The interlined or lined work can be finished with piping, bound with bias strips or mitred in the way described for the child's quilt at the end of this chapter. Or, trim interlining, if used, to 3mm ($\frac{1}{8}''$) less all round than the finished size of work. Turn in 6mm-9mm ($\frac{1}{4}''$-$\frac{3}{8}''$) all round the edge of the lining and press the turnings [hem allowances]. Oversew [overcast] the lining to the patchwork with small stitches.

Baby's quilt made up of hand sewn squares.

patchwork squares of cotton fabric joined together in a random pattern. It is lined with gingham cotton which also forms a narrow border round the edge. The same material is also used for some of the squares.

You will need:
300 fabric patches of similar weight measuring 5cm sq (2″sq) plus seam allowance all round.
Lightweight synthetic wadding [batting] 80cm × 105cm (32″ × 42″).
1.2m (1⅜ yd) gingham for lining. 90cm (36″) wide (this allows enough fabric for the lining and some patches).
☐ Make up the patchwork with 20 rows of 15 squares. Press on wrong side.
☐ Remove tacking [basting] and paper.
☐ Cut a rectangle 85cm × 110cm (34″ × 44″) from the gingham lining fabric. Place the gingham, wrong side up, on a flat surface.
☐ Place the interfacing and then the patchwork, right side up, centrally to the gingham. Tack [baste] the layers together and knot in the way described earlier in this chapter.

Finishing the edge. Trim wadding [batting] to exact size of patchwork.
☐ Trim the gingham to 2.5cm (1″) larger all round than the patchwork. Turn in gingham edge 6mm (¼″) all round. Tack [baste] and press edges.

To mitre the corners. First turn down the corners of the gingham diagonally over the right side of the patchwork (fig. 7). Trim off about 9mm (⅜″) across this corner.

7. *Folding and trimming the border corner for mitring.*

Fold down the surrounding gingham edges on to the right side of the patchwork, making a neat mitre at each corner (fig. 8). Tack [baste] edges.
☐ Slip stitch the mitre and slip stitch or machine stitch the edges.
☐ Remove all tacking [basting].

8. *The border slip stitched in place on the right side.*

Making paper patterns

To make up clothes from hand sewn patchwork choose a simple pattern, then draw the pattern of the patches on to it. Use a felt tip pen to avoid tearing the paper. Make sure that the shapes will fit together well at the seams, allowing for turnings [seam allowances]. Note the colour scheme if you are working a specific design.

Make a duplicate pattern of the gar-ment on stiff paper, marking both shapes and colour. Cut out these 'stiff' shapes and use them as papers for the patches. The original pattern can be used as a guide for stitching the patches together in the right sequence. Cut a lining from the original paper pattern and make up the garment in the usual way.

To make a child's quilt

The gaily patterned quilt shown in the photograph is 75cm x 100cm (30″x40″) and is made from 5cm (2″) hand sewn

Hexagonal patchwork

The regular hexagon, known as the honeycomb, with all its sides equal in length, is probably the best known of all patchwork shapes. It is extremely simple to use and the wide angles at the corners mean that there is no difficulty in making a neat fold when turning the hem round the patchwork paper.

Seven hexagons joined together make a single rosette which can be used for a decorative motif. Or you could join several rosettes together to make up a larger piece.

When using a patchwork shape for the first time it is wise to choose something small and quick to make, and instructions are given at the end of this chapter for making a simple but pretty tea cosy with a hand sewn rosette of hexagons as a decoration. Instructions are given also for making a coffee cosy from patchwork fabric using larger hexagons which can be joined together by hand or machine.

Templates

You will need to use templates for the hexagons and these are obtainable prepackaged, in a wide range of sizes, from most good crafts shops. The package usually contains a solid metal template for cutting the papers and a larger window template which is used for cutting the patches. The window template has a clear centre panel which is the actual area of the finished patch and a solid band, approximately 6mm ($\frac{1}{4}$″) wide, around the edge which is the seam allowance. The window template is extremely useful when cutting the patches because, when it is laid on the fabric, you can see what the finished patch will look like and you can choose which part of a pattern you want to appear on the patch.

It is often possible to buy the solid metal templates separately and, in this case, you can make your own window template from heavy card (mounting board). Draw the solid shape very accurately with a sharp pencil on to the card. Measure 6mm ($\frac{1}{4}$″) all round the outline to make a larger replica of the shape, then carefully cut out both outlines with a scalpel or craft knife. The size of the hexagon is usually given as the length of one of its sides— a 4cm ($1\frac{1}{2}$″) hexagon has sides of that measurement. This is a good size for a beginner to use.

A trace pattern for hexagons is given on the opposite page and you can make your own template from this by carefully tracing the shape on to heavy card and cutting it out carefully.

Hand sewn hexagons

Begin the patchwork by planning the design you wish to use, then cut out the papers and patches. Patches should be cut with two of the parallel sides on the straight of grain. Decide whether they are to be cut along the warp or the weft and cut all patches similarly.

Make each patch by pinning the paper patch to the centre of the wrong side of the fabric patch, then fold over the turnings and tack [baste] one stitch in the centre of each side and one over the fold at each corner. Finish off with an extra stitch at the starting point (fig. 1a). Remove pin. Silks and some cottons can be permanently marked by pins and needles. On these fabrics it is best to stick down the seam allowances with masking tape and sew the corners through the seam allowances only (fig.1b).

Arrange the patches into a design, making sure that the warps or wefts run in the same direction. Then begin to join them. Place two with right sides together; with tiny stitches oversew [overcast] along the full length

An unusual use for patchwork: the back of this chair is made from a piece of patchwork fabric mounted on to strong canvas and the seat is covered with a cushion in the same fabric.

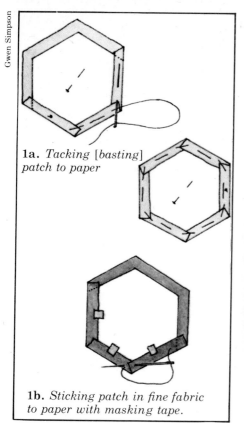

Gwen Simpson

1a. *Tacking [basting] patch to paper*

1b. *Sticking patch in fine fabric to paper with masking tape.*

Above: patchwork cushion made from a kit designed by Harriet Wincote.
Below: Trace pattern for hexagons.

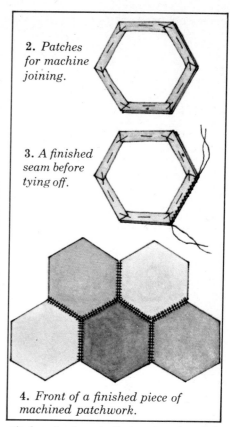

2. *Patches for machine joining.*

3. *A finished seam before tying off.*

4. *Front of a finished piece of machined patchwork.*

of one edge, as for squares and rectangles. Join a third patch into the angle made by the first two and continue sewing the patches together until you have completed a rosette, or the area of patchwork you need.

When all the patches have been sewn together press the patchwork on the wrong side with an iron. If the right side needs pressing, remove all tacking [basting] but leave in papers so the turnings do not leave a mark. Press gently on the right side. Remove papers. If you are mounting a rosette on to another fabric or adding a border to the edge of your patchwork, tack [baste] round the outside of the rosette to keep the turnings in place. Pin the patchwork into position and, using tiny stitches, slip stitch all round. Remove the tacking [basting] and press lightly.

Machine sewn hexagons

Hexagons can be joined together using a swing needle sewing machine and this is a speedy alternative to hand stitching, especially if you are working with patches of 4cm (1½″) or more. Smaller patches are better sewn by hand.

Many fabrics are suitable for machine patchwork, e.g. cottons and wools, silks, needlecord [fine corduroy], velvets and fine tweeds.

Prepare the patches as for hand sewing.

Needles and thread. Use a No. 14 machine needle (continental No.90). It will be necessary to renew the needle fairly frequently as patchwork papers tend to blunt the point. Use a fine

mercerised cotton, like Sylko, or synthetic thread, No.50 or 60, according to the fabric of the patchwork. Choose a thread of a suitable colour— white is good for lighter colours and black for darker shades. Black thread is better than white when joining light colours to dark ones as it does not show so much. Alternatively, you can match the thread to one of the basic colours in the patchwork.

It is important to use the same colour and type of thread throughout.

Stitches. On swing needle machines the 'swing' of the stitch (that is, the stitch width) can be adjusted in the same way as the stitch length. As a general guide for machine patchwork, select a swing of 1½-2 and a medium stitch length. Loosen the top tension a little.

It will be necessary to adjust the controls slightly according to the fabric and the length of the side of the patch. For instance, for a 7.5cm (3″) hexagon it may be necessary for the stitches to be further apart than for a 5cm (2″) hexagon, although the swing will remain the same. For the best results you should experiment with your machine, trying out the stitches on folded scraps of fabric.

Joining the patches. Plan your design and then begin to join the patches. Place two patches together with right sides facing. Make sure that they match evenly but allow the underneath patch to show just a fraction along the working edge (fig.2). You will then be able to see that the stitches are penetrating both patches.

A swing needle swings from left to right and back again. Left is the starting point and you must always start the needle ready to swing to the left.

Place the patches under the machine needle and turn the balance wheel towards you so that the needle pierces the top right hand corner of the pair of patches. Lower the presser foot and

stitch—slowly at first. At the left hand swing the needle should pierce the fabric and papers of the two patches and at the right hand swing the needle should pass just beyond the edges of the patches.

When you come to the end of the working edge, make sure that the needle swings to the right for the last stitch— you will then be ready to swing the needle back to the starting point when you begin the next seam. Give the balance wheel a half turn towards you, lift the presser foot and draw out the patch, leaving at least 5cm (2″) of thread before cutting off (fig.3). The long ends are essential as they must be tied off to secure the stitching. Use a double knot to tie off to prevent the threads becoming tangled.

It may be necessary with some fabrics to 'help' the machine over the corners as there are several thicknesses of fabric to penetrate.

Open out the seams and you will see that the patches are joined together with firm, even stitches—straight at the front (fig.4) and criss-crossed at the back. Add as many patches as you need, remembering to keep the straight of grain running in the same direction. When the work is large enough, take out the tacking [basting] threads. These may have been caught by the needle but will pull away easily.

Machine patchwork should be pressed well with a steam iron and pressing cloth.

If you are making a rosette for appliqué, slip stitch it in place.

Leather, suede and PVC coated fabrics are particularly good because they will not fray and so no turnings are needed. You can simply cut the patches to actual size without a seam allowance, butt the edges together and stitch them together on the right side using a swing stitch (fig.5).

Tea and coffee cosies

For the rosette on the tea cosy 3cm (1¼″) hand sewn hexagons were used and for the coffee cosy two pieces of machine sewn patchwork made up of 4cm (1½″) hexagons.

You will need:

For the coffee cosy:
45cm (½yd) heavily patterned floral cotton lawn (colour 1).
35cm (⅜yd) blue cotton lawn (colour 2).
45cm (½yd) lightly patterned floral cotton lawn (colour 3).
35cm (⅜yd) white cotton lawn for lining.
2 pieces of synthetic wadding [batting] 40cm×33cm (15″×13″).

For the tea cosy:
35cm (⅜yd) plain blue cotton lawn.
45cm (½yd) heavily patterned floral cotton lawn for frill and six patches
A 10cm (4″) square lightly patterned floral lawn for centre of rosette.
35cm (⅜yd) white cotton lawn for lining.
2 pieces of synthetic wadding [batting] 33cm×24cm (13″×9″).

Making the coffee cosy

☐ Make up 4cm (1½″) patches as follows: 28 colour 1; 24 colour 2;32 colour 3.
☐ Make a paper pattern for the cosy using fig.6 as a guide. Mark on the pattern the shape and colour of the patches.
☐ Arrange patches for the front of the cosy on this pattern, trimming patches to fit the outline and opening out the seam allowances on patches at the edge of the pattern.
☐ Stitch the patches together, then make a back section in the same way.
☐ Cut two sections of lining from the paper pattern, but make the lining 2.5cm (1″) shorter and then trim off 6mm (¼″) all round the outer edge (this ensures a smooth fit inside the outer cover).
☐ Cut the two sections of synthetic wadding [batting] same size as lining.
☐ Place the two patchwork sections of the cosy with right sides together. Tack [baste] around the outer edge. Machine stitch 1.5cm (½″) in from this edge. Trim turnings to 9mm (⅜″).
☐ Turn through to the right side, then

Pretty tea and coffee cosies—either would be an ideal first make in hexagon patchwork for a beginner. Designed by Heather Mingay.

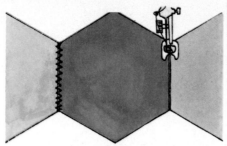

5. Joining non-fraying patches on the right side of the work.

1·5cm (½″) turning

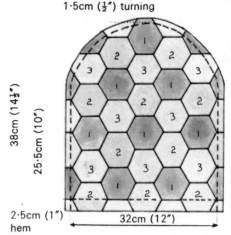

38cm (14½″)
25·5cm (10″)
2·5cm (1″) hem
32cm (12″)

6. Pattern for coffee cosy showing positioning of patches.

1·5cm (½″) turning

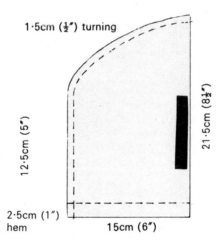

12·5cm (5″)
21·5cm (8½″)
2·5cm (1″) hem
15cm (6″)

7. Pattern for half of one side of tea cosy. Cut two.

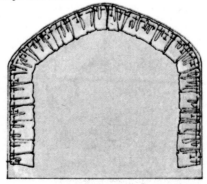

8. Gathering thread on frill pulled up to fit the tea cosy cover and pinned in position.

turn in a 9mm (⅜″) turning on the bottom edge and press the cover.
☐ Place lining sections with right sides together and place one piece of wadding [batting] outside lining. Tack [baste] and stitch four layers together around outer edge, 1.5cm (½″) from the edge. Do not turn through.
☐ Trim away edge of wadding [batting] as close as possible to the stitching and trim seam allowance on outer edge of lining to 6mm (¼″).
☐ Place lining inside outer cover, with wadding [batting] in between, so that bottom edge of lining and wadding [batting] is 1.6cm (⅝″) above bottom edge of the outer cover. Tack [baste] lining to cover.
☐ Finally turn 1.6cm (⅝″) along bottom of outer cover up on to lining and slip stitch into place.

Making the tea cosy

☐ Make up 3cm (1¼″) patches as follows: 6 heavily patterned floral and 1 lightly patterned floral.
☐ Make patches into a rosette with the lightly patterned one in the centre.
☐ Using fig.7 as a guide make a paper pattern for the tea cosy and cut out twice in blue fabric.
☐ Cut out two pieces of lining using the same pattern, but make the lining 2.5cm (1″) shorter and then trim off 6mm (¼″) all round the outer edge.
☐ Cut out two pieces of synthetic wadding [batting] from the pattern the same size as the lining.
☐ Cut two strips of heavily patterned fabric 15cm x 90cm (6″x36″) for frill.
☐ Place strips with right sides facing and stitch together along one short edge, taking a 6mm (¼″) turning. Press seam open.
☐ Fold strip in half lengthways, right sides together, to make a long strip 7.5cm (3″) wide.
☐ Stitch through the double thickness at each short end, making 6mm (¼″) seams. Trim corners, turn through and press.
☐ Run a gathering thread along the long raw edges of the strip, 1.5cm (½″) in from the edge, through both thicknesses.
☐ Place frill to right side of outer edge of one blue cosy piece, with raw edges together and folded edge of the frill towards the middle of cosy piece.
☐ Pull up gathering thread to fit the cover, leaving 2.5cm (1″) of the cover free at the bottom edge on either side. Pin into place (fig.8) and tack [baste].
☐ Place the other blue cover piece, right side down, on to the first piece, enclosing the frill. Tack [baste] and stitch cover sections together, 1.5cm (½″) from outer edge. Trim turnings [seam allowances] to 9mm (⅜″).
☐ Finish in same way as coffee cosy.
☐ Stitch rosette to centre of one side.

Machine quilting

Wadded, or English quilting, is probably the best known type of quilting and can be worked using either hand or machine stitches. This chapter covers fabrics and fillings and gives instructions for a set of bags machine quilted in a simple diamond design.

Wadded or English quilting
The decorative stitching on wadded quilting is worked through three layers of fabric—a top and a backing fabric enclosing a soft filling.

The resulting cloth has a variety of uses which will determine the choice of stitching worked. Fabrics and fillings are also dictated by the eventual purpose of the quilting.

Fabrics. The top fabric should be smooth and closely woven to show up the quilting effectively. Fine and medium weight cottons, silk, linen and fine wool are all suitable. The quilted pattern is more apparent on light-coloured fabrics.

The backing should be the same as the top fabric if it is to show when the article is completed. If the article is to be lined the backing can be of muslin or organdie.

Fillings. As the filling affects the finished look of the quilting, it is essential to choose the most suitable of the natural and synthetic fillings available. Some of the earliest quilting was padded with clean, carded sheep's wool laid evenly between the layers of fabric. The early settlers in America used or re-used any clean fabric: flannel, flannelette, even old blankets, to fill their elaborately stitched quilts. Domette, a wool and cotton mixture is often used in wadded quilting. This is available with either a flat or fluffy texture, the latter more suitable for quilting. It gives a slight padding and adds warmth without weight to clothes and small household articles. This material is not guaranteed for washing and should therefore be dry-cleaned.

Today, synthetic fillings are taking over from the natural ones as they are more readily available and often cheaper. They have the added advantage of being washable and quick drying.

Terylene, Tricel, Courtelle and polyester are all used quite frequently as fillings, the most popular weights of which are 55gm (2oz), 110gm (4oz) and 230gm (8oz). The lighter and thinner the wadding, the flatter and less distinctive the raised areas of the quilted pattern will be. The lightest weight is usually used for decorative purposes—on bags and cushions and on plain garments to create interesting textures and to add weight at hems and cuffs.

The slightly heavier weight fillings produce a more padded look and are used where warmth, as well as decoration is needed—for bed covers and on bedheads [headboards], cot covers and linings. The bulky and heavyweight fillings are ideal for bed covers.

The many different weights of wadding [batting] come in varying widths; the lighter ones range from 45cm-140cm (18″-54″) while the heaviest fillings are available in 205cm (80″) and 215cm (84″) widths.

Quilted bags made up in Brother Sun fabrics. From left to right: sewing pochette; handbag; dolly bag.

Simple machine quilting

When beginning machine quilting it is best to start by quilting a diamond or square pattern or simply to stitch in straight parallel lines. First tack [baste] the fabric, wadding and lining together with lines of tacking [basting]. For large items work a grid from side to side and from top to bottom (fig.1). On small items start by working from the centre to each of the four sides, then working outwards from these central lines, work lines parallel to them to form a grid.

Alternatively, the lines on small items can radiate from the centre outwards. When working machine quilting it is necessary to adjust the thread tension and reduce the pressure on the presser foot so that the fabric passes under it without fullness being pushed in front of it. It is always best to work a test sample.

A quilting attachment (gauge) is a useful and relatively inexpensive accessory. This is a guide which is used to quilt in straight, evenly-spaced lines.

Quilted bags

These bags are all quilted by machine in a simple, but effective, diamond pattern.

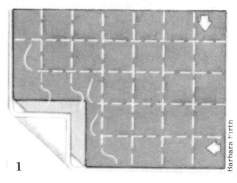

1

1. *Fabric, wadding [batting] and lining tacked [basted] with a grid of stitches.*

Drawstring dolly bag

The finished bag is approximately 20cm (8″) high and has a diameter of 14.5cm (5¾″).

You will need:

50cm (½yd) of 90cm (36″) printed cotton fabric.

30cm (¼yd) of 90cm (36″) muslin.

30cm (¼yd) of 90cm (36″) plain cotton lining.

30cm (¼yd) of 90cm (36″), 55gm (2oz) synthetic wadding [batting].

50cm (½yd) of 6.5cm (2½″) braid.

Note: seam allowance of 1.5cm (⅝″) included on all pieces unless otherwise stated.

☐ In printed cotton fabric cut pieces as follows:

Bag body, 1 piece 45.5cm x 28cm (18″x 11″).

Bag base, 1 circle, 16.5cm (6½″) in diameter.

Drawstrings, 2 pieces 61cm x 4cm (24″x 1½″).

☐ In lining fabric, cut pieces as follows:

Body, 1 piece 45.5cm x 16.5cm (18″x 6½″).

Base, 1 circle, 16.5cm (6½″) in diameter.

☐ Cut wadding [batting] and muslin as lining.

☐ Cut one piece of braid 45.5cm (18″).

☐ Lay printed fabric for bag body flat and work a line of straight stitching 11.5cm (4!″) from one long edge (the top).

☐ Tack [baste] wadding [batting] and muslin to wrong side of body between stitching and the lower edge and with bottom edges level. Quilt the three layers in a pattern of diamonds with 8.5cm (3¼″) sides, using the quilting attachment.

☐ On right side, tack [baste] braid 3.5cm (1⅜″) up from the lower edge of bag. Stitch in place with four rows of stitching.

☐ With right sides facing tack [baste] and stitch the side seam (fig.2). Press seam lightly open so as not to flatten the quilting.

☐ With right sides facing tack [baste] and stitch the side seam on the body lining piece. Press seam open and turn through to right side.

☐ Turn in 6mm (¼″) at top edge of lining.

☐ Tack [baste] bag and lining lower edges together, matching side seams and with wrong sides facing.

☐ Fold 6.5cm (2½″) at the top of bag to the wrong side and work two rows of stitching, the first on original line of stitching and the second 1.5cm (⅝″) above the first (this makes the casing for the drawstrings). Slip stitch lining over raw edge of bag top just below lower row of casing stitching (fig.3).

☐ Tack [baste] base fabric, wadding [batting] and muslin together; quilt. Tack [baste] base lining to base, wrong

sides facing.

☐ With right sides facing, tack [baste] and stitch base to bag, through all thicknesses (fig. 4). Neaten raw edges.

☐ Make four slits in the bag in top layer of fabric only, between rows of casing stitching, 2.5cm (1″) from each side of the seam and at corresponding points on the other side of bag, to insert the drawstrings.

☐ Blanket stitch the raw edges of slits.

☐ Fold one drawstring in half lengthwise, with wrong sides facing, and turn in 6mm (¼″) on all edges. Topstitch through all thicknesses close to the edge. Repeat with the other drawstring.

☐ Thread one drawstring through the casing from one side seam slit to the other. Thread the other drawstring through the casing using the other two slits. Knot ends of each pair of strings together.

2
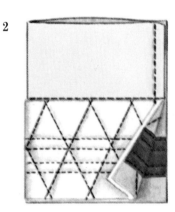

3
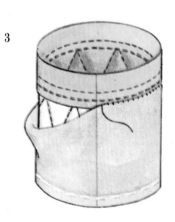

4
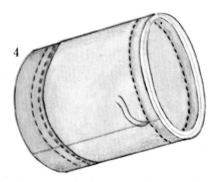

Sewing pochette

The finished bag is 37.5cm x 15.5cm (14¾″x6″) when opened out flat.

You will need:

50cm (½yd) of 90cm (36″) printed cotton fabric.

50cm (½yd) of 90cm (36″) plain cotton lining.

30cm (¼yd) of 90cm (36″), 55gm (2oz) synthetic wadding [batting].

13cm (5″) of 6mm (¼″) elastic.

Scrap of felt.

30cm (¼yd) of 6.5cm (2½″) braid.

Note: seam allowance of 1.5cm (⅝″) included on all pieces unless otherwise stated.

In printed cotton fabric cut pieces as follows:

Bag body, 1 piece 40.5cm x 18.5cm (16″x 7¼″).

Centre pocket, 1 piece 18.5cm x 11cm (7¼″x4¼″).

Lower pocket, 1 piece 21.5cm x 11cm (8½″x4¼″).

Ties, 2 pieces 23.5cm x 2.5cm (9¼″x1″).

☐ In lining fabric, cut body and pocket pieces as printed fabric.

☐ In wadding [batting], cut 1 piece 40.5cm x 18.5cm (16″x7¼″).

☐ Cut a piece of braid 18.5cm (7¼″) long.

☐ Tack [baste] to right side at one end of printed fabric body piece.

☐ Treating braid and printed fabric as one, trim the braided, short end of printed fabric body piece and one short end of lining to form top point as shown (fig.5).

☐ Trim wadding [batting] to 2cm (¾″) smaller all round than the fabric.

☐ Turn seam allowance on printed body piece and lining to wrong side and press.

☐ Unfold seam allowance on top fabric, place wadding [batting] on to wrong side and turn seam allowances over edges (fig. 6).

☐ With wrong sides together place lining and top fabric together to enclose wadding [batting] completely.

☐ Fold one tie in half lengthwise, with wrong sides facing, and turn in 6mm (¼″) on all edges. Topstitch through all thicknesses close to the edge. Repeat with the other tie.

☐ Insert one tie between the layers of pochette at point. Tack [baste] layers together. Quilt through all thicknesses using the quilting attachment and work three straight lines across braided section and a diamond design over the rest of the work, with the sides of the diamond 3cm (1¼″) long.

☐ Place centre pocket and lining with right sides facing, tack [baste] stitch along the long edges (fig. 7a). Turn through to right side, turn in the seam allowance on the remaining two edges and tack [baste] (fig.7b).

☐ Repeat with the lower pocket.

☐ Work two rows of stitching 1cm (⅜″).

apart on the lower pocket, the first 1.3cm ($\frac{1}{2}$″) from one long edge (the top). Thread elastic through this casing and secure the ends.

☐ Run a gathering thread along the other long edge of the lower pocket.

☐ Tack [baste] both pockets in position (fig. 8), pulling up the gathering thread on the lower one to fit. Work a line of machine stitching all round bag 1cm ($\frac{3}{8}$″) from the edge.

☐ Slip stitch the lower edge of the centre pocket to bag lining. Cut a scrap of felt with pinking shears 7.5cm x 6.5cm (3″x2$\frac{1}{2}$″) to make a needle holder and stitch this to lining along its top edge.

☐ Stitch remaining tie to centre of right side of bag (fig.9).

4cm ($1\frac{5}{8}$″)

5

6

7a

7b

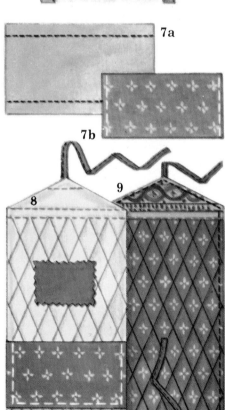

8   9

Handbag

The finished bag is approximately 20.5cm (8″) high, 25cm (10″) wide and 12cm (5″) deep.

You will need:

70cm ($\frac{3}{4}$yd) of 90cm (36″) printed cotton fabric.

70cm ($\frac{3}{4}$yd) of 90cm (36″) plain cotton lining.

70cm ($\frac{3}{4}$yd of 90cm (36″), 55gm (2oz) synthetic wadding [batting].

70cm ($\frac{3}{4}$yd) of 90cm (36″) muslin.

90cm (1yd) of 7.5cm (3″) braid.

Piece of cardboard, 24cm x 1.25cm (9$\frac{1}{2}$″x5″).

2 x 2.5cm (1″) button moulds (such as Trims).

Note: seam allowance of 1.5cm ($\frac{5}{8}$″) included on all pieces unless otherwise stated.

☐ In printed cotton fabric, cut pieces as follows:

Bag body, 1 piece 67cm x 28cm (26$\frac{1}{4}$″x 11″).

Side panels, 2 pieces 27.5cm x 15cm (10$\frac{3}{4}$″x6″″).

Handles, 2 pieces 48.5cm x 7cm (19″x 2$\frac{3}{4}$″).

☐ In lining fabric, cut pieces as follows:

Body, 1 piece 62cm x 28cm (24$\frac{1}{4}$″x11″).

Side panels, 2 pieces 27.5cm x 15cm (10$\frac{3}{4}$″x6″).

Tab, 1 piece 16cm x 7.5cm (6$\frac{1}{4}$″x3″).

☐ In wadding [batting], cut as follows:

Body, 1 piece 67cm x 28cm (26$\frac{1}{4}$″x 11″).

Side panels, 2 pieces 27.5cm x 15cm (10$\frac{3}{4}$″x6″).

Tab, 1 piece 14cm x 5.5cm (5$\frac{1}{2}$″x2$\frac{1}{4}$″).

Handles, 2 pieces 48.5cm x 2cm (19″x $\frac{3}{4}$″).

☐ Cut muslin as wadding [batting].

☐ Cut two pieces of braid 28cm (11″) long and a piece 16cm (6$\frac{1}{4}$″) long for tab.

☐ Round the corners of each tab piece.

☐ On body and side pieces tack [baste] wadding [batting] and muslin to fabric.

☐ Using the quilting attachment, quilt a diamond design, with the sides of the diamonds 8.5cm (3$\frac{1}{4}$″) long.

☐ Tack [baste] a piece of braid 5cm (2″) from each short edge on the right side of the body piece. Stitch into place with four rows of top stitching.

☐ With right sides together stitch the side panels to the bag body, enclosing the ends of the braid (fig. 10).

☐ Turn 3.8cm (1$\frac{1}{2}$″) along top edge to the inside. Press lightly to avoid flattening the quilting.

☐ Tack [baste] wadding [batting] and muslin to wrong side of braid tab.

☐ Make a 3.2cm (1$\frac{1}{4}$″) bound buttonhole at one end.

☐ Tack [baste] tab and tab lining together with wrong sides facing.

☐ Fold in a 1cm ($\frac{3}{8}$″) seam on lining and tab, tack [baste] and topstitch all round close to the edge.

☐ Work two lengthwise rows of tacking [basting] through all thicknesses.

☐ Make a slit in the lining to correspond with the buttonhole, turn in the edges and slip stitch to muslin (fig.11).

☐ With right sides facing, tack [baste] and stitch lining side panels to lining body. Press and turn right side out.

☐ Turn under 1.3cm ($\frac{1}{2}$″) at top of lining and press. Push card into base of lining.

Note: if you prefer, make a cover for the card from spare fabric and slip stitch covered card into lining. The stitches can be easily removed when the bag is washed.

☐ Take one handle strip, turn under seam allowance along each long edge and fold the strip in half lengthwise, wrong sides together.

☐ Cut a piece of wadding [batting] length of handle by the finished width. Place it inside the folded handle piece and tack [baste] layers together. Work four parallel lines of machine stitching along handle.

Repeat with the other handle strip.

☐ Stitch handles firmly to bag. Place bag inside lining, wrong sides facing, and slip stitch folded edge of lining to top of bag, enclosing the ends of the handles (fig. 12).

☐ Cover button moulds with braid. Attach plain end of the tab to the outside of the bag, and stitch a button to this end.

☐ Attach the other button to the other side of the bag and fasten tab.

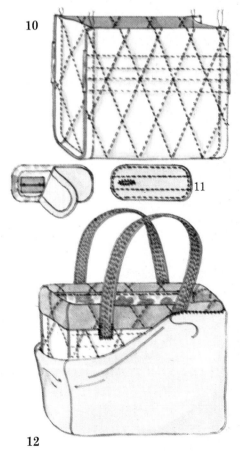

10

11

12

Quilted outline designs

Our discussion of quilting has covered fabrics, backings and types and weights of filling for wadded quilting. This chapter deals with quilting round a design on a printed fabric and with working quilting on a knitted garment.

Quilting a printed fabric

The easiest way of quilting a decorative pattern, other than a simple one based on straight lines, is to choose a fabric with a bold design and outline each shape with machine stitching. The swan fabric shown here is ideal for this purpose and would make a spectacular cover for a bed.

Tacking [Basting]. Cut the top and backing fabric to same size. Cut generously to allow for reduction in size during quilting. Press to remove all creases.

☐ Cut the wadding [batting] 2.5cm-5cm (1″-2″) smaller all round than fabrics.

☐ Lay the backing fabric right side downwards, then the wadding and then the top, printed fabric, right side upwards, on a flat surface.

☐ Tack [baste] three layers together as described in the previous chapter. This ensures that the layers do not move, causing the work to pucker or wrinkle, whilst stitching.

Working the quilting. Adjust the thread tension and reduce the pressure on the presser foot of the sewing machine. Work a test sample on some spare fabric and wadding [batting].

☐ Use contrasting or matching thread with a medium length stitch.

Work each motif in the same way.

☐ Starting at the innermost point of the design, and working outwards, stitch along the edge of each shape. Thus on the swan the blue diagonal line was stitched first, followed by the body, neck and beak shapes.

☐ Finally work details such as the swan's neck and eye.

☐ Take each thread through to the wrong side and finish off by working into the wadding [batting] by hand until the end is 'lost'.

Note: when quilting a large item such as a bed cover it may be easier to quilt in 'blocks'. (This technique involves working in separate sections).

Above left: a bold, swan-printed fabric, wadding [batting] and backing fabric tacked [basted] together before quilting with machine stitching. Tacking [basting] ensures the layers do not move whilst stitching.

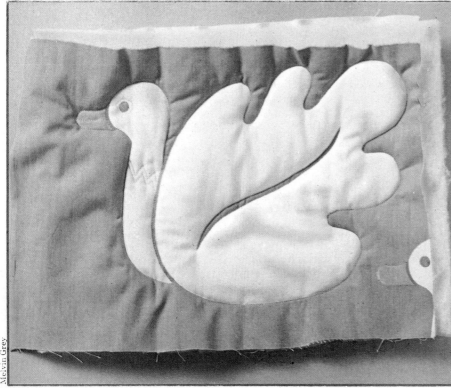

Below left: the machine quilted motif with tacking [basting] stitches removed
Right: choose a spectacular print to make a quilted bedspread for maximum impact. In this room, the same fabric quilted for the bedspread has been used to make large matching cushions

Quilting on plain fabrics

The cardigan shown here illustrates how quilting can be worked effectively on other than smooth and closely woven fabrics and it also demonstrates how to use a paper pattern when stitching by machine.

This type of quilting is equally suited to fine textured fabrics such as silk and looks particularly good on a simply designed garment. Try it round the hem of a plain linen or silk evening skirt, or decorate a round neckline or a collar. Test the tension and stitch length of your machine by working a sample pattern on a scrap of the same or similar fabric. The quilting is worked on the wrong side of the work so that the needle does not pull in the fabric, so ensure that the *back* of the stitch is perfect as this will be seen on the right side of the work.

Note: If you are using an electric machine it is often easier, when working difficult sections, to turn the wheel by hand so that you have greater control of the work.

Left: a simple knitted cardigan is given a whole new look of luxury by clever use of machine quilting.
Designer: Eleanor Harvey.

Melvin Grey

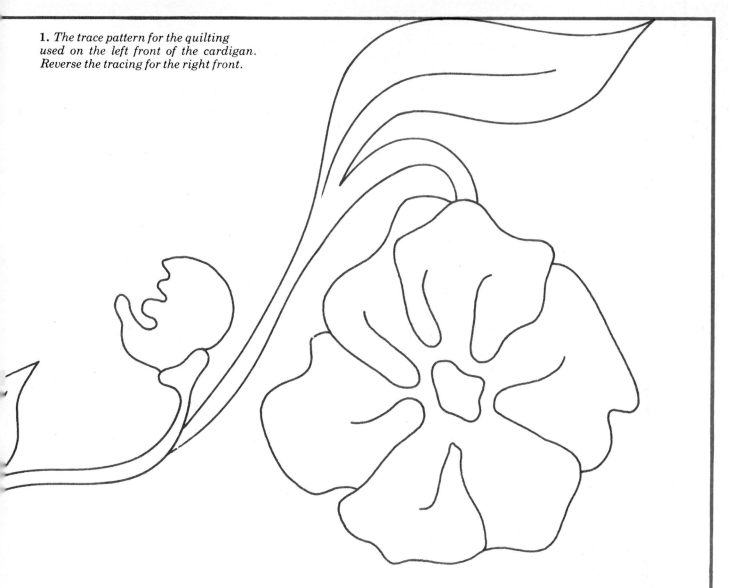

1. *The trace pattern for the quilting used on the left front of the cardigan. Reverse the tracing for the right front.*

Quilted cardigan

You will need:
A simply designed, stocking stitch cardigan.
Two 33cm × 23cm (13″ × 9″) pieces 55gm (2oz) synthetic wadding [batting].
Matching or contrasting thread.
Two 33cm × 23cm (13″ × 9″) pieces 55gm (2oz) synthetic wadding [batting].
Matching or contrasting thread.
Tracing paper and pencil.
Working the quilting. Make a tracing of the flower pattern (fig.1) for each side of the cardigan front (one will be reversed).
☐ Press the cardigan and lay the pieces of wadding [batting] on the wrong side of each front. Place the backing fabric on top, then pin and tack [baste] the three layers together, working from the centre outwards.
☐ Pin the pattern into place over the backing making sure the design is level on the two sides (fig. 2).
☐ Stitching through the tracing paper, work carefully round the flower first,

working the centre lines out to the edges.
☐ Stitch the leaves, stems and buds.
☐ Remove the work from the machine, tear away tracing paper, and finish off all threads by working them into the wadding [batting] by hand.
☐ Trim surplus wadding [batting] to within 6mm ($\frac{1}{4}$″) of the design.
☐ Neaten edges by hand.

Barbara Firth

2. *Pattern pinned on top of backing.*

Needlecrafts

Needles come in all sorts of shapes and sizes – for the
following projects you can choose embroidery, needlepoint,
knitting, crochet and tatting.

Straight stitch embroidery

Embroidery is as much a craft for today as it ever was. Modern dress designers now use stitchery both in lavish *haute couture* ways and in entertaining, charming motifs for everyday clothes. Modern embroidery designers continue to invent new and exciting combinations of colour, texture, stitch and pattern for panels which may be used decoratively or practically.

In addition, there is a re-appraisal of the traditional roots of embroidery in folk art throughout the world. Go into your local museum, seek out the rooms showing embroidery, costume and tapestry and you will discover a rich legacy of inspiration.

Fabrics

Any fabric can be used for embroidery, but for a novice fine evenweave fabric is the easiest to use. It has an even number of vertical and horizontal threads per square centimetre (inch) and, because the threads can be counted easily, each stitch can be made

All the simple motifs in this chapter are worked in two strands of six-stranded cotton.
For trace patterns see overleaf.

exactly the same size. Small motifs can be worked on any fabric because, as they are done quickly, the tension and size tend to be constant. However, you need not always use an evenweave fabric for embroidery—many linen, cotton and rayon dressmaking and furnishing fabrics are easy to use.

Needles

A basic range of needles will enable you to cope with any yarn or fabric.
Sharps needle, medium length, small eye—for sewing with sewing thread or a single strand of stranded cotton.
Crewel needle sizes 6-8, long and sharp, large eye—for stranded cotton, coton à broder, pearl cotton No. 5.
Tapestry needle, blunt end—for whipped and laced stitches, needlepoint, drawn fabric work as well as drawn threadwork.
Beading needle, fine—for sewing on beads.

Yarns

The yarns listed below are all fine to medium in thickness and are suitable for stitching on clothes and household linen.

All yarns which are used on fabric which will be washed must be fast-dye yarns. However, some yarns which are dye-fast are still not recommended for washing, so follow the manufacturer's instructions.

Different yarns can be effectively mixed together in the same work. Once you have worked a few stitches in one yarn it is fun to interpret them differently by using a finer or thicker yarn.
Soft Embroidery cotton, twisted, matt cotton.
Coton à broder, twisted, shiny cotton.
Stranded Cotton, 6-stranded, separable shiny cotton.
Pearl Cotton, twisted, shiny cotton, No.5—thick, No.8—thin.
Coats Drima, fine super-spun polyester, multi-purpose sewing thread.
Gütermann silk and silk buttonhole twist, both twisted, shiny silk sewing thread.
Button thread, twisted cotton.
Coats satinised machine twist, multi-purpose sewing thread.
Filo-Floss, six-strand embroidery silk.
Maltese silk, very fine sewing silk.

Frames

Embroidery can be worked successfully without a frame, but if you intend to do fine work or use long threads over the fabric then a frame is advisable. A square slate frame is the type recommended for needlepoint. For embroidery the tambour or round frame is the most popular and there are three types: a hand-held frame, a table frame with a clamp for attaching to a table or working surface and a floor frame supported on a stand. The one that clamps to the table is probably the most rigid and therefore the easiest to use. The sizes vary from about 10cm (4″) to 25cm (10″) in diameter. The size of frame chosen depends on the size of motifs and fabric most often worked, but one frame will do for all embroidery since the fabric can be moved to expose an unworked area.

Joy Simpson

1. *A tambour or round frame.*

To prepare a tambour frame. Remove the smaller of the two frames and wind bias binding evenly all round it, covering the wood completely. Place the fabric over the frame. Unwind the screw in the larger of the two frames so that it will fit over the smaller frame and the fabric fairly easily. Press the larger frame down over the small frame until it is enclosed.
Pull the fabric gently between the two frames until it is smooth and taut. Tighten the screw on the outside frame. The fabric is now ready to be embroidered.
If you are embroidering very fine fabric, or fabric that creases easily, first cover it with a layer of tissue paper before pressing down the larger frame. Cut away the tissue to within 12mm (½″) of the frame.

Transferring designs

There are several ways of transferring designs but, whichever you use, the idea is to mark the outlines clearly with the minimum number of marks.

Make a beautiful blouse unique by embroidering a profusion of flowers around the yoke and cuffs. Four strands are used to give extra body to the petals.

All smiles at bed-time with a beaming
Mister Moon nightdress.

A simple dress in a plain colour is made
demurely pretty with a few motifs.

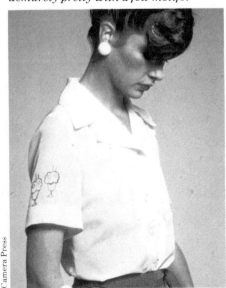

A subtle use of an ice-cream cone motif
gives this blouse a distinctive look.

For smooth fabrics use dressmakers'
carbon paper or a transfer pencil to
transfer the design.

Using dressmakers' carbon paper.
The carbon paper is used in conjunction with a tracing wheel. Use white
carbon on dark-coloured fabric and
yellow carbon on light-coloured fabric.
Place the fabric on a flat surface with
the warp at right angles to your body
(fig.2). Place the carbon, inky side

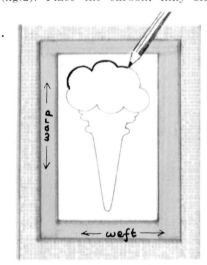

2. *Placing the design at right angles to
the warp and weft.*

downwards, on the fabric. Place the
paper with the design on it on the carbon. Using a tracing wheel, or a pencil
for small designs, follow the lines.
The points of the wheel press on the
carbon paper intermittently and give
little guiding points to follow when the
paper and carbon are lifted.

Using a transfer pencil. A transfer
pencil is perhaps simpler to use, especially for small designs. When using
the pencil use light pressure only.
Draw the design on tracing paper and,
on the other side, make small dots with
the transfer pencil. Place the fabric on
a flat surface. Lay the tracing paper
on top of the fabric and press it with a
warm iron. The heat of the iron transfers the pencilled dots to the fabric.

Use tissue paper for simple designs
only. For fine or light-coloured fabrics
it is a good idea to use tissue paper,
since this protects the fabric from becoming soiled while you are working.
Cut a piece of tissue paper slightly
larger than the size of the motif. Lay
the tissue paper over the motif and
trace it on to the paper with a soft
pencil which will not tear the paper.
Position the tissue paper on the
fabric and either pin it or tack
[baste] it down to prevent it slipping.
Embroider the motif by sewing through
and following the lines on the tissue
paper. Tear the tissue paper carefully from underneath the stitches and
throw it away.

Basic stitches

Running stitch. Make the stitches on the right side the same
length as those on the wrong side.

Running stitch.

Laced running stitch. This can
be effective using either the same
or contrasting yarn. Use a tapestry needle and thread it in and
out of the running stitches without catching in the cloth. This
lacing can be used with other
stitches.

Laced running stitch.

Back stitch. Bring the needle
through to the right side of the
fabric and make a small stitch
backwards. Bring the needle
through again a little in front of
the first stitch and make another
stitch backwards to make a
continuous line.

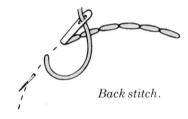

Back stitch.

Cable stitch. Work lower stitch A
on line of design, as shown; then
work upper stitch B in same way
with yarn above needle.

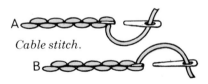

Cable stitch.

Stem stitch. Make a sloping
stitch along the line of the design,
and then take the needle back
and bring it through again about
halfway along the previous stitch.

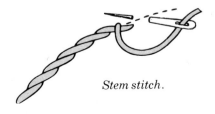

Stem stitch.

90

Motifs to use on their own or in groups. Trace the motifs off the page, transfer them to the fabric, then embroider them in pretty colours, using any of the straight stitches illustrated.

Continuous chain stitch

Chain stitch has no single origin but can be traced to all parts of the world where ancient fabrics have been found. Chain stitch was found on basketwork from pre-dynastic Egypt (c. 3500BC), on the earliest surviving Egyptian textiles, in graves in the Crimea dating from the 4th century BC and on some old textiles in China and Japan (7th-8th centuries AD).

The Chinese worked chain stitch with silk yarn on silk in a single line technique, widening or tightening the loop with a thread of uniform thickness to produce an effect of variable depths of colour and shadow. Some of the finest examples worked with chain stitch alone, using silk thread on satin, are 18th- and 19th- century Indian garments from Kutch.

In mediaeval western Europe the grandest embroidery used more elaborate stitches and chain stitch only appeared on more humble objects. In 18th-century England chain stitch was revived and widely used, often under Chinese influence, to decorate silk coats and satin bedspreads. It appears independently in peasant work throughout the world.

Using chain stitch

Chain stitch worked in lines and curves is very versatile. The stitch can be worked large or small to give a fine or a bold outline. For a regular appearance the proportions should remain the same; as a rough guide the width should be two-thirds of the length of the stitch.

Chain stitch adapts well to tight curves and can be worked round and round to partially fill in areas.

Chain stitch. When worked, this stitch makes a chain of loops on the right side of the fabric and a line of back stitches at the back. Bring the needle through on the line of the design, loop the yarn under the point of the needle and draw the needle through. Insert the needle close to where the yarn came out. Bring the needle through a little further along the line of the design, loop the yarn under the point of the needle and draw through. Continue in this way until the required length has been worked (fig. A).

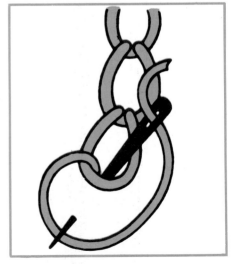

A. *Working a line of chain stitch.*

Don't turn your back on a design like this; copy it on to a jacket of your own.

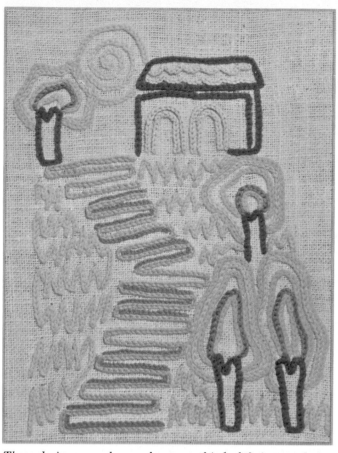

These designs are shown about one-third of their actual size, but they may be enlarged to the size you require.

This pretty butterfly picture would be ideal for a girl's bedspread or embroidered on to a dress or apron pocket.

An appropriate design for a beach bag or beach cover-up—a colourful landscape scene with rolling waves.

Brighten up plain table mats with this simple motif. All these designs are worked in Soft Embroidery Cotton.

Suitable yarns

Small stitches worked in a thick yarn give a solid line, while larger stitches in fine yarn give an open stitch. Use these characteristics to their fullest advantage.

Any of the finer yarns previously mentioned are suitable for chain stitch but for quickly worked chain stitch use a thick embroidery yarn such as:

2 ply Crewel wool: a twisted, matt wool. Use one or, more usually, several strands.

Persian wool: a three-strand wool, slightly thicker than Crewel wool.

Tapestry wool: a twisted, matt, separable wool.

Twilley's Lyscordet: a twisted knitting cotton.

Mercer Crochet Cotton: a fine knitting cotton.

Sudan Wool: a twisted, matt, separable wool.

Paton's Turkey Rug Wool: a twisted, matt wool for using on rug canvas.

To work the designs

Choose your fabric—perhaps a T-shirt, cotton jacket or whatever you wish to embroider on. Enlarge the design to the required size and transfer it to your material.

If you are using thick yarn you will need a chenille needle.

Follow the lines of the design with closely worked chain stitch until you have covered them all.

Flower bed cushion

You will need:

Single thread evenweave linen, 26 threads per 2.5cm (1″), 36.5cm x 36.5cm (14½″x14½″).

Soft Embroidery Cotton, 3 skeins purple, 4 skeins red, 4 skeins mauve, 5 skeins lilac, 6 skeins light green, 6

This flower bed design is set off well by a natural-coloured background.

skeins dark green, 6 skeins orange. Fabric for back of cushion 36.5cm x 36.5cm (14½″x14½″).

Square cushion pad 35cm x 35cm (14″x 14″).

☐ Transfer the pattern on facing page centrally to the linen.

☐ Lightly mark a square 2cm (¾″) in from outer edges with a transfer pencil.

☐ Work the design in fairly small chain stitch, working over 2 or 3 threads to make stitches uniform in length.

☐ Work around the edge of the square in chain stitch and work two more squares of chain stitch just inside the first.

☐ Make up into a cushion taking 1.25cm (½″) seams.

Jacobean crewel work

The lively designs of Jacobean crewel embroidery are fun to work. The motifs on these curtains were designed by Joan Cotton.

Jacobean crewel work is a lively style of pictorial embroidery which became popular in Britain in the 17th century. The inspiration for Jacobean work owes much to Eastern culture and the hangings, wallpapers and exotic fruits brought to Europe in the 16th and 17th centuries from India and later from China. This vivid eastern influence, combined with the delicate traceries and floral motifs of Tudor embroidery, produced designs of an enchanting if bewildering mixture of Christian, historical and oriental symbolism.

Typical Jacobean embroidery designs show a variety of colourful and stylized plants, animals and birds. These often 'grow' on one tree—the symbolic tree of life—which springs from a series of hillocks, known as *terra firma*.

The leaves and blossoms of the tree of life are heavy and out of proportion to each other, with thick and boldly embroidered stems. As a contrast some of the motifs are simply outlined and filled with openwork stitchery.

The animals, birds and plants are a mixture of the familiar and the exotic, and many have symbolic meanings. The acorn, for example, was associated with Charles II who hid in an oak tree in his flight through England in 1651. The English rose was a national emblem and the carnation was a symbol of the Stuart family. The lamb, the stag and the serpent all have religious connotations.

Colours on old pieces of Jacobean work were predominantly greens with blues, browns, yellows and some soft, dull reds. Green in several shades was used for the terra firma and brown for animals. Birds and flowers could be a combination of several colours with no regard to the true colours of nature.

You can copy the traditional motifs shown here and on page 101 by tracing the outlines and then enlarging them in scale to the desired size.

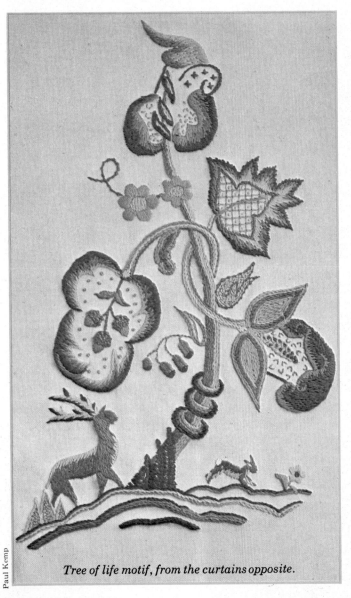

Tree of life motif, from the curtains opposite.

Paul Kemp

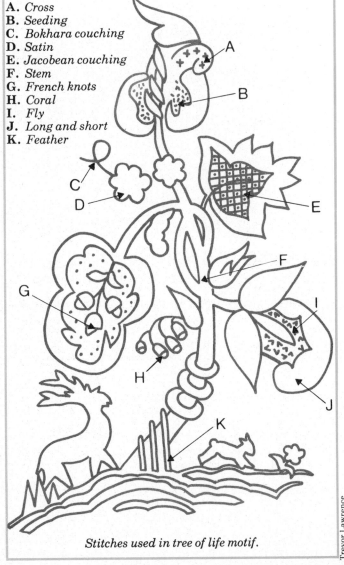

A. *Cross*
B. *Seeding*
C. *Bokhara couching*
D. *Satin*
E. *Jacobean couching*
F. *Stem*
G. *French knots*
H. *Coral*
I. *Fly*
J. *Long and short*
K. *Feather*

Stitches used in tree of life motif.

Trevor Lawrence

Some of the delicate motifs from an 18th century American bed-hanging.

Grapes are an unusual motif on this early 18th century bed-hanging.

Uses

Jacobean embroidery was originally used to decorate large items like wall- and bed-hangings where the heavy background fabric was needed. But it can successfully be worked on curtains and covers for beds, chairs and cushions. If you use a lighter weight fabric than twilled linen for the background, you could also make table linen and dress accessories.

Stitches

There are no rules about the stitches used for Jacobean work—it is a matter of personal choice. It is possible to work entirely in one stitch—such as chain stitch—throughout although the work is more interesting to do if several stitches are used. A leaf, for example, might be outlined with long and short stitch and have the centre filled with couching. A flower might have a couched outline with some petals filled with solid satin stitch and others with lines of stem stitch. An acorn could be

filled with closely worked French knots.
Starting stitching. Use lengths of yarn of approximately 50cm (20″) long. To start stitching, do not use a knot but bring the needle through the right side of the fabric on a line of the design. Work a couple of back stitches which will later be covered by the embroidery.
Finishing lengths. Turn the fabric to the wrong side and carefully weave the needle in and out of the backs of stitches so that the yarn does not show on the right side.

Basic stitches

Many of the stitches used in Jacobean work have been described in the previous Embroidery chapters. Some new ones are described below.

Cretan stitch

☐ To fill a shape like that in fig.1a, bring through the needle at point X. Take a small stitch on the upper line with the needle pointing inwards and over the thread.
☐ Repeat, taking a small stitch on the lower line (fig.1b).
☐ Continue working stitches alternately on the upper and lower lines in this way (fig.1c).

Fly stitch

☐ Bring through the needle and hold down the yarn with your thumb.
☐ Insert the needle to the right on the same level and take a small stitch downwards to the centre with the thread below the needle (fig. 2a). Pull through and insert the needle below the stitch at the centre to complete it.
Fig.2b shows completed stitches and how to begin subsequent ones.

Fern stitch

This stitch consists of three straight stitches of equal length radiating from the same point (fig.3).

Seeding

This simple stitch is made up from small straight stitches of equal length worked at random within the shape (fig.4).

Bokhara couching

For this filling stitch the thread is laid across the stitch from left to right (fig.5a) and tied down with small slanting stitches at regular intervals on the return journey (fig.5b). The tying stitches should be pulled tight, leaving the laid thread slightly loose between.

Coral stitch

☐ Bring the thread out at the right-hand end of the line to be worked, lay the thread along the line and hold down with the left thumb.
☐ Take a small stitch under the line and thread as shown in fig.6 and pull through, bringing the needle over the lower thread. Continue like this, working stitches at regular intervals.

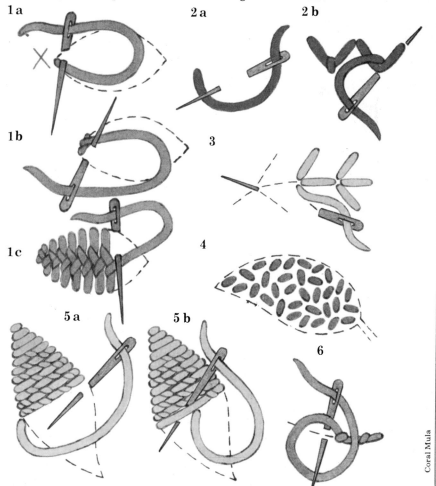

1a

2a

2b

1b

3

1c

4

5a

5b

6

Paul Kemp

Blocking

When the embroidery is finished, the fabric should be blocked to smooth it out and restore its shape. To do this, place a clean cloth on a piece of wood larger than the item to be blocked. Place the embroidery face down on it.

☐ Using tacks which will not rust, tack the top edge to the wood from left to right, pulling the edge taut. Tack the left-hand edge in the same way, then the bottom edge and then the right-hand edge. The fabric must be stretched tight enough to ensure that there are no wrinkles in it.

☐ Thoroughly wet the fabric by soaking it with water from a squeezed sponge. Mop up excess water with a towel and leave the fabric to dry.

Traditional Jacobean crewel design by Coats in typically soft colours and a variety of stitches which are shown in the diagram below.
A. *Satin*
B. *Jacobean couching*
C. *Fern*
D. *Daisy*
E. *Chain*
F. *French knots*
G. *Stem*
H. *Straight*
I. *Seeding*
J. *Back*
K. *Blanket*

The materials

The traditional materials help give Jacobean work its informal homely character. Use crewel wool for the stitchery unless a tapestry wool is required for a heavier effect.

Colours. Choose colours which are close to the old vegetable dyes of the Jacobean period. These hues blend exceptionally well and they give the work a pleasing softness.

Fabric. Jacobean colours look best on natural-coloured background and a particularly suitable fabric is twilled linen. This is close woven and firm enough to take large areas of heavy stitchery. Plain-weave linen or linen crash is suitable, as is unbleached calico [muslin], although care must be taken to avoid puckering.

Needles. Use crewel needles with an eye large enough for the wool to be threaded easily—a No.7 size is suitable for a single strand of crewel wool.

Frame. It is essential to use a frame of a suitable size for the major part of the embroidery, eg the couched open fillings and areas of long and short stitch. The fabric may be removed from the frame for stitches such as stem, chain and coral because these are awkward to work in a frame.

Left: a gay, modern Jacobean crewel design, worked entirely in chain stitch.

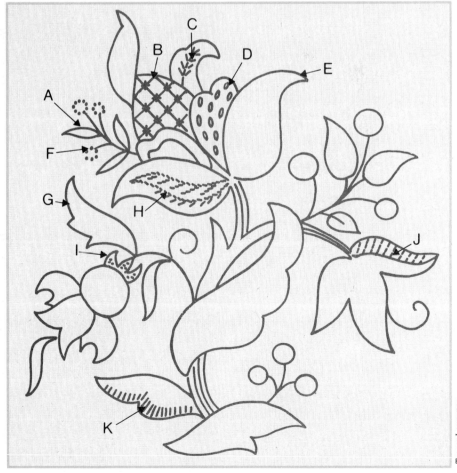

Trevor Lawrence

Straight stitch needlepoint

Tapestry, canvaswork and needlepoint are all words used to describe the art of building up a solid pattern of yarn on canvas. Usually this is presented as a specific pattern to be made up in a given yarn on a set size of canvas. But with an understanding of what yarns cover what canvas best, you can vary the scale and tailor designs to your own requirements.

You can achieve splendid, rich textures and original designs on canvas, working with any of a variety of yarns. Wool gives a beautifully firm, dense surface which is hardwearing and attractive. With silks and cottons you can work fine, detailed designs, and unusual yarns like raffia and metallic threads create interesting textures.

Canvas. There are 2 types: single thread, measured by the number of threads per 2.5cm (1″) and double thread, measured by the number of pairs of threads per 2.5cm (1″).

Single thread canvas is the best to begin on as you can try out a wide variety of stitches, whereas double thread is restricted to 4 or 5 only. The number of threads per 2.5cm (1″) can vary from 26 for fine work to 3 for very coarse work.

Needles. Use tapestry needles with large eyes and blunt ends. These are available in a variety of sizes, 18-21 being the most popular, but size 14 is better for very coarse canvas.

Yarns are available in many different thicknesses and some are made up of several individual strands twisted together, which can be separated as required. Use a length of yarn about 46cm (18″) long—if it is longer it will wear thin and become fluffy.

Straight stitch is used to work this bag and, as it does not distort the canvas, you don't need a frame. It can be worked over any number of threads, but large stitches are unsuitable for practical designs as they tend to get caught.

Satin stitch is usually worked over 4 threads to give a firm surface, and in this bag it is formed in steps of forward 4 and back 3.

Starting and finishing. Knot one end of the yarn. Put the needle in at the front of the canvas about 5cm (2″) from the position of the first stitch. Bring the needle up from the back and work the first few stitches. Cut off the knot, thread the end into a needle and slip the yarn through the back of the worked stitches, adding a small back stitch to secure. The next length of yarn can be threaded into the back of the previously worked stitches and finished off as before. Avoid fastening on and off in the same place. The extra-thick stitching may show through on the front of the canvas.

Satin stitch clutch bag in rainbow colours, designed and worked by Martyn Thomas.

To make the clutch bag

This neat envelope design is worked entirely in 'stepped' satin stitch blocks using rainbow colours, to create a fishscale effect. The finished bag measures 22.5cm x 15cm (9″ x 6″).

You will need:
Single canvas 14 threads per 2.5cm (1″), 50cm x 32cm (22″ x 13″)
Lining fabric, 48cm x 30cm (19″ x 12″)
Choose any yarn suitable for 14 threads per 2.5cm (1″) canvas. Calculate the number of skeins required from the total length of yarn given. Always round up to avoid the risk of running short, since everybody works to a slightly different tension.
Total length of yarn required:
Natural—55m (60yd)
Red—41m (45yd)
Orange—41m (45yd)
Yellow—28m (30yd)
Green—28m (30yd)
Turquoise—28m (30yd)
Blue—14m (15yd)
Violet—14m (15yd)
Tapestry needle No. 18
Snap fastener.
Sewing thread and medium-size sewing needle for making up.
☐Fold the canvas in half horizontally and vertically to find the centre.

Yarn	Length per skein or ball	Canvas size	Needle size
Anchor Tapisserie wool	13.7m (15yd)	14 threads per 2.5cm (1″)	18
DMC Laine Tapisserie	8m (8.8yd)		
Appleton's tapestry wool	13.7m (15yd)		
Appleton's crewel wool (4 strands)	27.5m (30yd)		

☐Following the design layout (fig.1), begin by working the natural yarn in diagonal lines of satin stitch, starting at the pointed end of the bag, which lies about 5cm (2″) in from the edge of the canvas.

Work the bottom right to top left diagonals in a continuous line. The opposite diagonals break at the intersections, where a small stitch worked over 2 threads fills in at the point where the diagonals cross.

☐Fill in the colour by following the chart given for the sequence of colours and stitches (fig.2). The filling-in stitches are worked over 2 threads at ends and apex of each colour block.
To make up. Pin the canvas to shape on an ironing board and press gently under a damp cloth. Leave to dry thoroughly. Trim the canvas to within 6 threads of the embroidery.

☐Mitre the centre of the bag flap by folding at A and turning under hems B and C (fig.3). Mitre other corners, turn under seam allowance and herringbone the canvas to the back of the embroidery.

☐Cut the lining to size, allowing an extra 1.5cm (½″) all round. Fold under this seam allowance and tack [baste] down. Fold the flap lining in the same way as for the mitred canvas.

☐ Slip stitch the lining to the embroidery neatly all round the edge and oversew [overcast] the sides of the bag.

☐Sew the snap fastener to the centre of the flap and on bag to correspond.

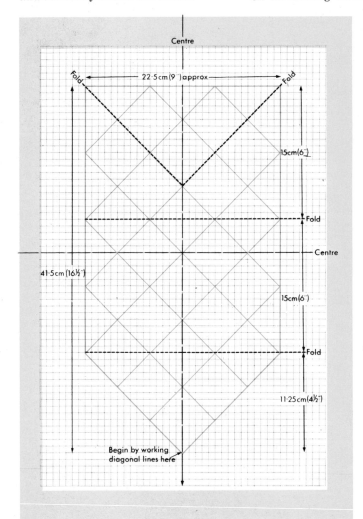

1. Design layout showing the position of the diagonals.

2. Colour and stitch chart, with stitch working detail.

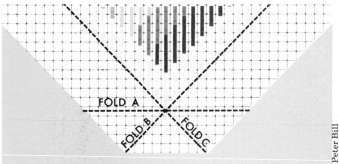

3. Folding the canvas to mitre the pointed flap.

Florentine needlepoint

104

Yarn	Length per skein or ball	Canvas size	Needle size
Anchor Tapisserie Wool DMC Laine Tapisserie Appleton's Tapestry Wool Appleton's Crewel Wool (4 strands)	13.7m (15yd) 8m (8yd) 13.7m (15yd) 27.5m (30yd)	14 threads per 2.5cm (1") single canvas	18
Anchor Tapisserie Wool DMC Laine Tapisserie Appleton's Tapestry Wool Appleton's Crewel Wool (3 strands)	13.7m (15yd) 8m (8yd) 13.7m (15yd) 27.5m (30yd)	16 threads per 2.5cm (1") single canvas	18
DMC Retours à Broder Coton de Pingouin	10m (11yd) 160m (175yd)	16 threads per 2.5cm (1") single canvas	18
Appleton's Crewel Wool (2 strands) Clarks Linen Embroidery Anchor Stranded Cotton	27.5m (30yd) 15.5m (17yd) 8m (8yd)	24 threads per 2.5cm (1") single canvas	22

Florentine embroidery is the name applied to a whole range of needlepoint designs which are worked in straight stitch. Also known as Hungarian Point or Bargello, most forms of Florentine stitch are worked over four or six threads in a variety of patterns, creating strong, geometrical shapes and striking visual effects. As straight stitch does not distort the canvas unduly, you will not require a frame when making small objects.

Although Florentine stitches can be used to create very elaborate and complicated designs, the simplest and two of the most characteristic patterns, zigzag and flame, look impressive but are very straightforward and quick to work. Each row of a separate colour is worked horizontally across the canvas, with either a step up or down from stitch to stitch. Once one line of colour has been worked, all the others will follow suit. If you have to join the yarn midway across a row, finish off the old thread by threading it through the back of the stitches and begin a new thread in the same way.

Zigzag is the simplest pattern of all. The zigzag base line forms regular peaks, which can be either very deep or fairly shallow. For small objects, a pattern that repeats about every ten stitches is suitable (fig.1). The stitches are usually worked over four threads and back two, which gives a pleasing regular pattern. Zigzag stitch looks good either in subtly shaded colours, or in vivid, contrasting colours.

Left: 18th-century American silk needlepoint shows the subtle shading of flame stitch. Also used here (section with flowers) is bricking stitch; this is very similar to Florentine but is worked horizontally instead of in a zigzag.

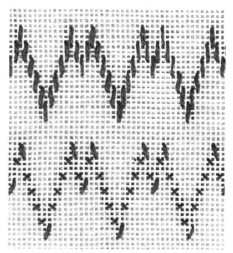

Steve Bicknell

1. Zigzag stitch, shown from the front (top) and the back (lower row).

Flame patterns are slightly more complicated, forming steep peaks of varying heights to give a variety of designs. This stitch is usually worked over four threads and back one (fig.2). Flame stitch looks best when worked in a range of toning colours for a subtly shaded effect.

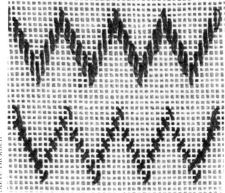

2. This sample of flame stitch shows how economical the use of yarn is.

Stitching notes. The easiest way to stitch Florentine is in two movements —put the needle in at the front and take it out from the back, putting it into the next position from the back. Repeat from the front. Working in this way it is easier to see the threads for counting. If you do make a mistake, cut it out rather than unpick it—the yarn gets so worn with unpicking it is impossible to use it again.

Base line. Most Florentine designs are begun with one row worked right across the width of the design—called the base line, although it is often worked in the centre of the canvas to keep the pattern symmetrical. Zigzag and flame can be started with a base line anywhere on the canvas and all other rows will follow automatically above and below.

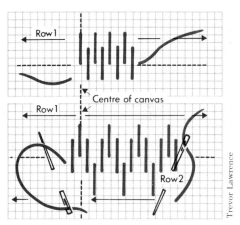

Trevor Lawrence

3. Above: the base line for bricking stitch, which is a very simplified version of Florentine stitch. Below: the base line for a simple zigzag pattern, showing how to start the second line.

Pattern repeats. An important aspect of all Florentine designs is to make sure that the base line consists of a complete number of pattern repeats and that each side of the design is symmetrical. Both zigzag and flame stitch build up their patterns from one base line in such a way that they can be started at any point on the canvas. Once the first row has been worked, the others follow almost automatically. The pattern is repeated above and below the base line. Where necessary, work ½-stitches at the edges to fill in the finished square or rectangle.

Estimating yarn length

As zigzag and flame stitch are always worked in horizontal rows, by calculating the amount of yarn needed to work one complete row it then becomes easy to estimate the total amount of yarn required to work a design of a given size. Working with a 46cm (18") length of yarn, stitch as much of the pattern repeat as this will work. Count the number of lengths needed to fill the row. Multiply again by the number of rows to be worked in each separate colour—each stitch covers four horizontal threads, so divide the total number of horizontal threads by four to get the number of complete rows. This gives the total amount of yarn required. The chart shown here gives the lengths of different manufacturers' skeins, so you can work out how many skeins you need.

Varying canvas sizes

A basic stitch like zigzag or flame can easily adapted for larger or smaller canvas, using the appropriate yarn (see chart on page 105).

The base line is worked as before, but the number of pattern repeats will be different if covering the same area on larger or smaller canvas. However, if working a pair of objects, one larger and one small, then the smaller object can be worked on a smaller size canvas with exactly the same design reduced in scale.

To calculate the pattern size on different sizes of canvas, count the number of threads covered by one pattern repeat. For example, in the patterns shown here the zigzag covers 10 threads and flame covers 14.

All canvas is measured by the number of threads per 2.5cm (1″), so divide the number of threads across the width you want to work by the number of threads covered by one pattern repeat. This will give the number of pattern repeats you can work in the base line. Remember to work an exact number of pattern repeats and to keep the base line symmetrical.

Pattern symmetry. If you are making a small object like a spectacles case, you can achieve stitch symmetry by counting how many pattern repeats can be worked in the base line, as described above. You can start at one side of the canvas and work in horizontal rows straight across. However, for larger objects like cushions this system is unsuitable because of the number of threads to be counted. So, for larger embroideries which need to be symmetrical, begin stitching at the marked centre lines of the canvas. Stitch the first row only from the centre outwards. Subsequent rows can be stitched straight across the whole width of the design, beginning at the point where the first row ends (fig.3).

Check carefully the number of stitches in the base line. A mistake is hard to spot in the early stages, but will ruin the completed embroidery.

If your base line is accurate there is no need to count stitches again.

Pretty presents to brighten any handbag — lighter and specs case in zigzag stitch, lighter and compact set in flame.

Steve Bicknell

106

Florentine designs

As an introduction to Florentine stitch these designs are small and manageable and can be made up in no time at all. Yet they show off well the characteristically subtle shading of Florentine embroidery. This stitch shows results quickly and you can produce a great variety of beautiful and practical objects—excellent for gifts. In the designs shown here the spectacles case and the compact case are worked on a medium canvas, while the two lighter cases show exactly the same designs scaled down on a fine canvas.

All these designs make excellent ways of using up scraps of yarn left over from other projects.

Zigzag specs case

Completed size: 15cm x 6.5cm (6"x2½")
You will need:
Canvas 16 threads per 2.5cm (1"), measuring 20cm x 13cm (8"x5").
Yarn (see chart) 24 pieces each 46cm (18") long. Shown here are 7 shades of browns and beiges — 3 pieces each of 4 shades and 4 pieces of the other 3 shades.
Lining fabric, 17.5cm x 9cm (7"x3½")
For back of case, 15cm x 6.5cm (6"x2½") of suede, leather or felt.
Matching sewing thread and needle.
☐ Mark the centre of the canvas horizontally and vertically and mark in the dimensions of the specs case. Fold masking tape over the edges of the canvas, or oversew [overcast] with wool. Trim away when making up.
☐ Following the diagram for zigzag stitch (fig.4), work one horizontal base

4. *Zigzag stitch detail.*

line anywhere across the narrow canvas width. This will comprise 4 zigzag pattern repeats and will use one 46cm (18") length of yarn.
☐ Using a different colour yarn for each row, build up the pattern in toning shades of brown.
To make up. Pin the canvas to shape on an ironing board and press under a damp cloth. Leave to dry thoroughly. Trim the canvas to within 1.5cm (½") of the worked area. Trim the lining fabric to the same size. Fold the canvas seam allowance to the back of the work, mitring the corners. Herringbone to

the back of the embroidery (fig.5). (fig.5).

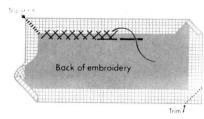

Back of embroidery

5. *Mitre corners and herringbone canvas to back of embroidery.*

☐ Turn under the lining fabric seam allowance and mitre the corners in the same way as the canvas. Slip stitch the lining to the back of the embroidery, wrong sides facing.
☐ Cut the back of the case to the completed size of the case, oversewing [overcasting] to canvas on 3 sides.

Zigzag lighter case

Completed size: 7.5cm x 4.5cm (3"x1¾").
You will need:
Canvas, 24 threads per 2.5cm (1"), measuring 13cm x 10cm (5x4"").
Yarn (see chart) 19 pieces each 30cm (12") long. Shown here are 7 shades of browns, beiges and pinks — 3 pieces each of 5 colours, 2 pieces of 2 colours.
Lining fabric, 10cm x 7cm (4"x2¾").
For back of case, 7.5cm x 4.5cm (3"x1¾") of suede, leather or felt
Matching sewing thread and needle
☐ Mark the centre of the canvas horizontally and vertically and mark in the dimensions of the lighter case. Either fold masking tape over edges of the canvas or oversew [overcast] with wool. Trim away when making up.
☐ Following the diagram for zigzag stitch (fig.4), work one horizontal base line anywhere across the narrow canvas width. This will comprise 4 zigzag pattern repeats.
☐ Continue to build up the pattern in rows of different coloured yarns.
☐ Make up the lighter case in the same was as for the specs case above.

Flame compact case

Completed size: 9.5cm x 9.5cm (3¾"x3¾")
You will need:
Canvas, 16 threads per 2.5cm (1"), measuring 14cm x 14cm (5½"x5½").
Yarn (see chart) 16 pieces each 46cm (18") long. Shown here are 6 shades of pink — 3 pieces each of 5 shades and one strand of the sixth shade.
Lining fabric, 12cm x 12cm (4¾"x4¾")
For back of case 9.5cm x 9.5cm (3¾"x 3¾") of suede, leather or felt
Matching sewing thread and needle 46cm (½yd) matching cord or braid (you can make handmande cords by plaiting together one or more of the yarns used in the embroidery).
☐ Mark the centre of the canvas horizontally and vertically and mark

in the dimensions of the compact case. Either fold masking tape over edges of canvas, or oversew [overcast) with wool. Trim away when making up.
☐ Following the diagram for flame stitch (fig.6), work one horizontal base

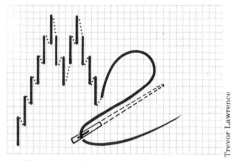

6. *Flame stitch detail.*

line anywhere within the marked outline. This will comprise 4 pattern repeats.
☐ Using a different shade of yarn for each row, build up the pattern in toning shades of pink.
☐ Make up the compact case in the same way as for the specs case above but, when attaching the back, leave 6mm (¼") open at one lower corner.
☐ Slip stitch the cord all round the edge of the canvas. Tuck in the ends and close the opening neatly.

Flame lighter case

Completed size: 6.5cm x 6.5cm (2½"x2½")

You will need:
Canvas 24 threads per 2.5cm (1"), measuring 11.5cm x 11.5cm (4½"x4½").
Yarn (see chart) 15 pieces each 30cm (12") long. Shown here are 5 shades of pinks and beiges — 3 pieces of each shade.
Lining fabric, 9cm x 9cm (3½"x3½")
For back of case 6.5cm x 6.5cm (2½"x 2½") of suede, leather or felt
30cm (12") matching cord or braid (bought or handmade from wool plaited by hand)
☐ Mark the centre of the canvas horizontally and vertically and mark in the dimensions of the lighter case. Either fold masking tape over edges of canvas, or oversew [overcast] with wool. Trim away when making up.
☐ Following the diagram for flame stitch (fig.6), work one horizontal base line anywhere within the marked outline. This will comprise 4 pattern repeats.
☐ Using a different shade of yarn for each row, build up the pattern in toning shades.
☐ Make up in the same way as for the specs case above but, when attaching the back, leave 6mm (¼") open at the lower corner.
☐ Slip stitch the cord all round the edge of the canvas. Tuck in the ends and close the opening neatly.

Basic knitting stitches

The aim of this course is to set you free from the limitations of any particular set of instructions. Here is a fresh approach to knitting—a new, simplified way to create effective patterns, textures and shapes. There are ideas on how to develop exciting, multi-coloured patterns and how to use them to make up beautiful, individual clothes and things for the home.

Casting on

There are various methods of doing this, but the one most commonly used in knitting terminology is known as casting on or knitting on.

It produces a strong, yet flexible, border which may seem tight at first, but can be stretched into shape. When completed the casting on looks equally good on both sides of the work.

Begin by holding one needle in each hand. Make a slip loop in the end of a ball of yarn and put this loop on the left hand needle (fig.1).

Hold the yarn in the right hand and insert the right hand needle point into the slip loop.

Wind the yarn under and over the point of the right hand needle and draw a new loop through the first loop (figs.2 and 3).

Put the newly made loop on to the left hand needle.

Insert the right hand needle point between the two loops (fig.4) on the left hand needle, wind yarn under and over point of right hand needle again and draw through a new loop.

Put the newly made loop on to the left hand needle.

Insert the right hand needle point between last two loops on the left hand needle and continue in the same way until the required number of stitches is formed.

Making basic stitches

Virtually every pattern is made up of knit or purl stitches, or combinations of both.

Knitting stitches

Hold the needle with the cast-on stitches in the left hand and the free needle in the right hand.

Insert right hand needle point into the first stitch on the left hand needle from left to right. Keeping the yarn at back of work, pass it under and over the top of the right hand needle and draw loop through the stitch on the left hand needle (figs.5 and 6).

Keep the new stitch on the right hand needle and allow the stitch on the left hand needle to drop off needle (fig.7). Repeat this series of actions until all the stitches are transferred to the right hand needle.

To work the next row, pass the needle holding the stitches to the left hand so that the yarn is again in position at the beginning of the row and repeat the first row.

Purling stitches

Hold the needle with the cast-on

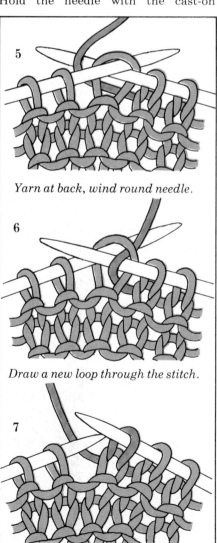

5 Yarn at back, wind round needle.

6 Draw a new loop through the stitch.

7 New knitted stitch is complete.

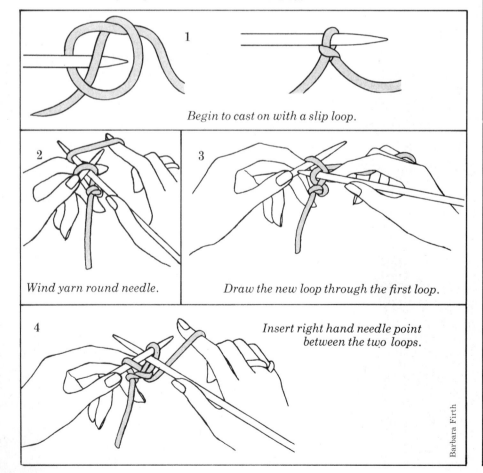

1 Begin to cast on with a slip loop.

2 Wind yarn round needle.

3 Draw the new loop through the first loop.

4 Insert right hand needle point between the two loops.

Barbara Firth

stitches in the left hand and the yarn and free needle in the right hand.

Insert point of the right hand needle into the first stitch on the left hand needle from right to left.

Starting with the yarn at the front of the work, pass it over and round the top of the right hand needle, bringing it out on the front of the work again, and draw loop through the stitch on the left hand needle (figs.8 and 9).

Keep the new stitch on the right hand needle and allow the stitch on the left hand needle to drop off needle (fig.10). Repeat this action until all stitches are transferred to the right hand needle. To work the next row, pass the needle holding the stitches to the left hand so that the yarn is again in position at the beginning of the row and repeat the first row.

Casting off

Having mastered the basic technique of knitting a fabric, it is vital to know how to securely fasten off stitches either at a given point for shaping or at the completion of a piece of work.

Hold the needle with the stitches in the left hand, with the yarn and free needle in the right hand.

Knit the first two stitches in the usual way and leave on the right hand

needle.

With the left hand needle point lift the first stitch on the right hand needle over the top of the second stitch and off the needle, leaving one stitch on the right hand needle, knit the next stitch and leave it on the right hand needle (figs.11 and 12).

Repeat the actions in the last paragraph until all stitches are cast off and one loop remains on the right hand needle.

Break off the yarn, draw through the last loop and pull firmly to make a tight knot.

Basic patterns

Practise the plain and textured fabrics shown here and then put your knowledge into practical use at an early stage by making a colourful bag with lots of interesting texture. Abbreviated forms are given in brackets.

Garter stitch (g st)

This is the result of knitting each stitch in every row. You will find that you will have a solid fabric where the stitches form neat rows of horizontal, wavy ridges. It looks the same on both sides, and is therefore reversible.

Stocking stitch (st st)

This is the most usual fabric in knitting and, because of its smooth, flat nature, it is an ideal background for knitted-in colour patterns.

The first and every following alternate row is knitted, whilst the rows in between are purled.

Each side looks completely different. The smooth side with the chain or knit appearance is the correct side for stocking stitch. However the reverse side is very attractive as it has a purled or ridged effect, similar to garter stitch. It is abbreviated as reversed st st and again it is a useful background for textured stitches or interesting ways with stripes of various colours.

Single rib (K1, P1 rib)

To produce a beautiful elastic fabric, knit and purl stitches are worked alternately along the first row, then on the second row the procedure is reversed so that each knitted stitch of the previous row is purled and each purled stitch is knitted. The fabric is reversible.

Single rib is normally found at any point on a garment where a close fit is necessary such as welt, cuffs and neckband, but it is extremely versatile and can be highly decorative.

Take care when alternating knit and purl stitches to see that the yarn is always on the correct side of the work for the stitch being worked.

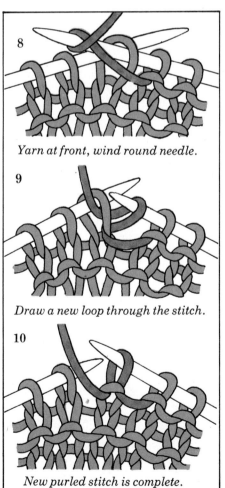

8
Yarn at front, wind round needle.

9
Draw a new loop through the stitch.

10
New purled stitch is complete.

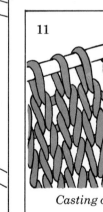

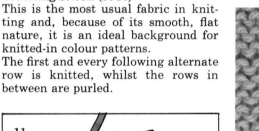

11
Casting off the first stitch.

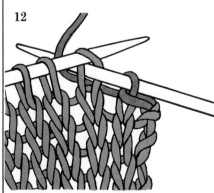

12
Knit next stitch ready to cast off.

Garter stitch—knit every row.

Stocking stitch—knit, then purl, a row.

Johnnie Ryan

Single rib—knit, then purl, a stitch.

Texture patterns

The next set of stitch patterns is basically made up of combinations of knit and purl stitches and they have decorative textures. There are many stitch patterns that may be substituted for each other within a piece of knitting as long as the number of stitches with which you are working is divisible by the number of stitches in one repeat of pattern so that the patterns are even at each end of the row plus any extra that may be needed.

Cane basket stitch—woven texture.

Cane basket stitch

Cast on a number of sts divisible by 6 plus 2.
1st row. (RS) K2, *P4, K2, rep from * to end.
2nd row. P2, *K4, P2, rep from * to end.
Rep 1st and 2nd rows once more.
5th row. P3, *K2, P4, rep from * to last 5 sts, K2, P3.
6th row. K3, *P2, K4, rep from * to last 5 sts, P2, K3.
Rep 5th and 6th rows once more.
These 8 rows form the pattern.

Tassel stitch—mock cable pattern.

Tassel stitch

Cast on a number of sts divisible by 6 plus 2.
1st row. (RS) P2, *K4, P2, rep from * to end.
2nd row. K2, *P4, K2, rep from * to end.
Rep 1st and 2nd rows once more.
5th row. K2, *insert right hand needle from front to back between 4th and 5th sts on left hand needle, take yarn across back of sts and draw through a loose loop across front of 4 sts and leave on right hand needle, K1, P2,

K3, rep from * to end.
6th row. *P3, K2, bring yarn forward to front of work (called byf), insert right hand needle through next st and loop on left hand needle from right to left and P these 2 sts tog to decrease one st—called P2 tog — rep from * to last 2 sts, P2.
7th row. K3, *P2, K4, rep from * to last 5 sts, P2, K3.
8th row. P3, *K2, P4, rep from * to last 5 sts, K2, P3.
Rep 7th and 8th rows once more.
11th row. P2, K3, *insert right hand needle from front to back between 4th and 5th sts on left hand needle, take yarn across back of sts and draw through a loose loop across front of 4 sts and leave on right hand needle, K1, P2, K3, rep from * to last 3 sts, K1, P2.
12th row. K2, P4, *K2, P2 tog, P3, rep from * to last 2 sts, K2.
These 12 rows form the pattern.

Bobble rib—highly textured design.

Bobble rib

Cast on a number of sts divisible by 6 plus 2.
1st row. (RS) P2, *K1, P2, rep from * to end.
2nd row. K2, *P1, K2, rep from * to end.
3rd row. P2, *K1, P2, (P1, K1, P1, K1) all into next st, this is done without removing the stitch you are working into until the 4 stitches have been made — called M4 — P2, rep from * to end. Note: try to make these stitches fairly loose.
4th row. K2, *K6, P1, K2, rep from * to end.
5th row. P2, *K1, P2, (P4 then turn both needles round as if you are starting a new row and K these 4 sts, turn both needles round and P these 4 sts— called B4 —), P2, rep from * to end.
6th row. K2, *byf, insert right hand needle through next 4 sts on left hand needle from right to left and P these 4 sts tog—called P4 tog — K2, P1, K2, rep from * to end.
Rep 1st and 2nd rows once more.
9th row. P2, *M4, P2, K1, P2, rep from * to end.
10th row. K2, *P1, K8, rep from * to end.
11th row. P2, *B4, P2, K1, P2, rep from * to end.

12th row. K2, *P1, K2, P4 tog, K2, rep from * to end.
These 12 rows form the pattern.

Striped bag (left)

For a bag 30cm (12″) wide by 25cm (10″) deep.
You will need:
200gm (7oz) of uncut rug yarn in main shade A.
100gm (3½oz) in contrast colour B.
One pair No.3 (US 10½) needles.
Optional: 30cm (12″) length of 90cm (36″) wide lining fabric.
2 wooden buttons or beads.
For the bag. Take a pair of No.3 needles and, using the main colour A, cast on 36 stitches.
☐ The bag is worked entirely in garter stitch, so begin by knitting just 2 rows.
☐ Now pick up your contrast colour B and *knit 2 rows with B, 2 rows with A, 2 rows with B, 6 rows with A, 2 rows with B, 4 rows with A, 2 rows with B and 2 rows with A, repeat from the point marked * 5 times altogether.
☐ Cast off all the stitches.
To make up. If you want to line the bag, cut lining to size of bag with 6mm (¼″) seam allowance.
☐ With right sides of bag facing each other, join the side seams. Join the lining side seams.
☐ Insert the lining and stitch round the top opening of bag.
☐ Cut 6 strands each of A and B into 178cm (70″) lengths. Divide the strands into 3 groups and plait together to form a handle, making an overhand knot at each end and leaving ends to form tassel.
☐ Stitch plait in position along side seams of bag, having a tassel at each lower edge and leaving remainder to form handle.
☐ Sew on one button to centre of each side of top edge of bag.
☐ Make a double figure of eight with yarn A large enough to fasten over both buttons and work round the figure with buttonhole stitch.

Carpet bag (centre)

This bag is worked in strips of knitting with 3 different stitch patterns in each one and incorporates all the patterns shown in this chapter. You will see that each strip needs 20 stitches which is a multiple of the pattern repeats given here plus the 2 extra stitches.
For a bag 45cm (18″) square.
You will need:
200gm (7oz) of uncut rug yarn in main shade A.
150gm (5¼oz) each of contrast colours B, C and D.
One pair No.3 (US 10½) needles.
Optional: one No.6.00 ISR (US K) crochet hook.

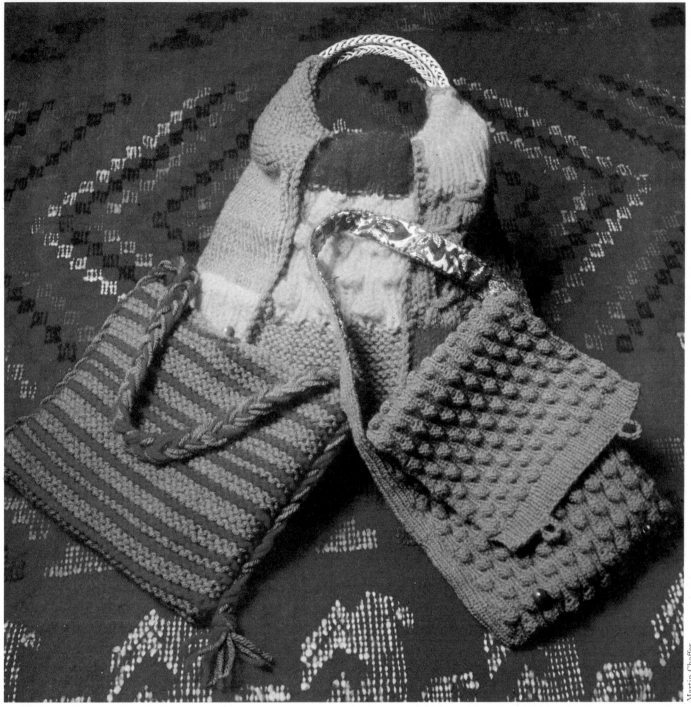

Striped, carpet and shoulder bags made up in Pingouin yarn from the Tapis rug and Europingouin ranges.

Pair of round wooden handles 20cm (8″) diameter.
☐ Take a pair of No.3 needles and colour A, and cast on 20 stitches.
☐ Work 15cm (6″) in garter stitch. Break off A.
☐ Join in colour B by inserting the needle into the next stitch and looping B over the right hand needle, then work next stitch only with 2 strands of yarn together.
☐ Work in cane basket stitch until the strip measures 30cm (12″) from the beginning. Break off B. Join in C.

☐ Continue this first strip by working 15cm (6″) each of bobble rib in C, stocking stitch in D, tassel stitch in A and single rib in B.
☐ Make 2 more strips in the same way, varying the colours and patterns.
To make up. Using No.6.00 ISR (US K) hook, colour A and with the wrong side of 2 strips facing, crochet them together. Otherwise sew them together with buttonhole stitch.
☐ Join all the strips in the same way.
☐ Fold the bag in half so that the right side is outside and join the first 30cm (12″) from lower edge as before.
☐ Neaten the open side edges with a row of buttonhole stitch.
☐ Fold each top edge over the handles

and sew down on the wrong side.

Shoulder bag (right)

Now experiment with Double Knitting yarn and any of the texture patterns. The bag shown is made from a strip worked in bobble stitch, 76cm (30″) long by 23cm (9″) wide. For this you will need about 200gm (7oz) of yarn and a pair of No.8 (US 6) needles. Cast on 62 stitches and start knitting.
For the strap, cast on 11 stitches and work 106cm (42″) in single rib. Sew together so that the strap makes a gusset at the sides of the bag. If you're handy with a sewing needle, you can line the bag with cotton lining or add a couple of buttons and loops.

111

Shaping and tension

Tension is the most important, yet often overlooked, principle in knitting. Learn the basic steps, then make a seeded rib jersey, shaped with different tensions, either from diagram (right) or instructions on page 115.

What is tension?

Tension is the number of stitches, and fractions of a stitch, that you achieve over a certain length, say 2.5cm (1"), with the yarn and needles you plan to use. In a pattern leaflet these numbers refer to the tension worked by the designer of the garment and all measurements for the design are based on these initial figures. They are used to calculate the total number of stitches and rows needed for the garment.

It is important to remember here that the metric and Imperial measurements are not equivalent. Therefore, you must work with one or the other set of figures entirely throughout any knitting instructions.

Tension samples. It is essential to make a tension sample before casting on every garment you make to see that you can obtain the correct number of stitches and rows to a given measurement. If this does not work out and you are even a fraction of a stitch out every 2.5cm (1"), then your garment will be loosely knitted and therefore too large,

or tightly knitted and therefore too small.

Checking tension on a pattern. At the beginning of most printed patterns a required tension is given, usually calculated to make a 10cm (4") square, using the correct yarn and appropriate needle size.

Work a sample in the stitch that you will be using and cast off. If the square is exactly the correct size you will be fortunate and it is safe for you to carry on with the pattern (fig.1).

If the tension square measures less than the given size, then your tension is too tight and you are working too many stitches and rows to 2.5cm (1"). Even half a stitch too many will result in an overall difference of about 5cm (2") on an 81cm (32") bust size and that means that your garment will be too tight.

Change to one size larger needles and try knitting the square again. It does not matter how many times you change needles as long as the final result is the correct tension.

If your tension sample is larger than the given size, then you are working too loosely and you will have too few stitches and rows to 2.5cm (1") (fig.2). In this case try using one size smaller needles and so on until you are satisfied that you have the correct tension.

Sometimes you will find that you can obtain the correct stitch tension, but not the right number of rows. Do not worry about this as the majority of patterns give a measurement that you have to work to, say 38cm (15") from cast on edge to underarm. Whether you have 14 or 18 rows to 5cm (2") it will have no effect on the 38cm (15") length that you have to work.

Designing and adapting patterns

Would you like to be able to adapt any pattern to fit your own personal measurements?
Choose any yarn you want?
Be able to use your own choice of stitch pattern?
If the answer to these questions is 'yes', then it is relatively simple to design or adapt existing patterns to suit you using a tension square as a basis. All you need is a certain amount of mathematical calculation and some idea of how dressmaking patterns work.

The European type of knitting instructions often show a scale drawing of the required shape with the points indicated where shaping is to be worked. Unlike the method used in most English-speaking countries, detailed row-by-row instructions are not given. Once you are accustomed to this method of working your scope becomes infinite as the same scale drawing can be adjusted to suit your own particular requirements.

Shaping with needles. The scale drawing illustrated (fig.3) shows a basic jersey which has been subtly shaped by using varying needle sizes. The main measurement is taken around the bust so most of the knitting is done on fairly large needles. Smaller ones are used for the waistband and yoke to make them fit snugly and still smaller

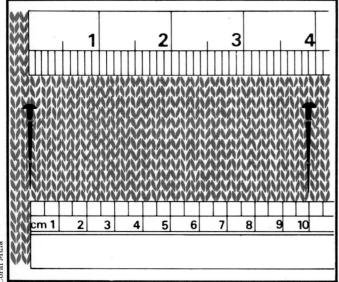

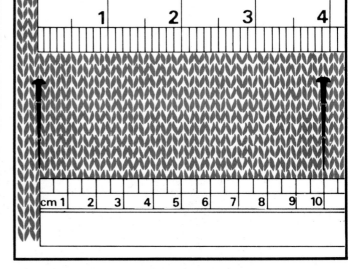

1. *Correct tension with 7 stitches to 2.5cm (1").*

2. *Tension too loose with only 6½ stitches to 2.5cm (1").*

Create your own jersey from this simple chart

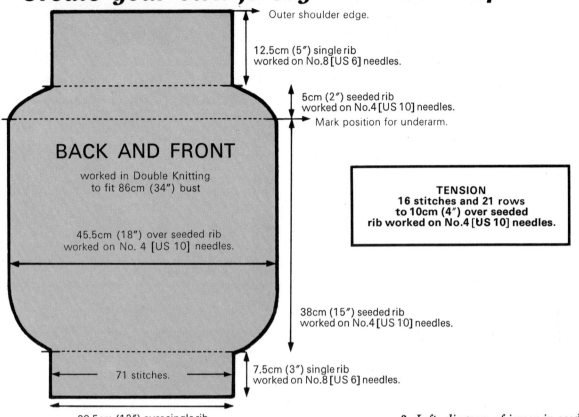

Outer shoulder edge.

12.5cm (5") single rib
worked on No.8 [US 6] needles.

5cm (2") seeded rib
worked on No.4 [US 10] needles.

Mark position for underarm.

BACK AND FRONT

worked in Double Knitting
to fit 86cm (34") bust

45.5cm (18") over seeded rib
worked on No. 4 [US 10] needles.

38cm (15") seeded rib
worked on No.4 [US 10] needles.

7.5cm (3") single rib
worked on No.8 [US 6] needles.

71 stitches.

30.5cm (12") over single rib
worked on No.8 [US 6] needles.

TENSION
16 stitches and 21 rows
to 10cm (4") over seeded
rib worked on No.4 [US 10] needles.

Cast off 2 stitches
12 times, 4 stitches
4 times and 11
stitches once.

Shape top of sleeve.

SLEEVE

worked in Double Knitting.

39.5cm (15½") seeded
rib worked on No.4
[US 10] needles.

33cm (13") over single rib
worked on No.4 [US 10] needles.

7.5cm (3") single rib
worked on No.9 [US 5] needles.

51 stitches.

20.5cm (8") over
single rib worked
on No.9 [US 5] needles.

*3. Left: diagram of jersey in seeded rib.
Below: seeded rib jersey made from
diagram in Mahony Claude.*

Steve Bicknell

Yarn quality	needle size	No. of stitches to 2.5cm (1")	No. of rows to 2.5cm (1")
Baby and 3 ply	11 (US 2)	8	10
4 ply	10 (US 3)	7½	9½
Double knitting	9 (US 4)	6	8
Aran and triple knitting	6 (US 8)	4½	5½
Chunky and other very bulky yarns	3 (US 10½)	3½	5

4. Sample tensions over stocking stitch.

needles for a tight, but elastic, cuff.
The calculations on the diagram are based on an 86cm (34") bust size where the jersey has been made in a seeded rib pattern using a double knitting yarn. However, you can adapt this diagram to fit your bust size. You can vary the length and use other stitches.
For example . . . the seeded rib jersey has been designed so that it is fairly long, it can be either pulled down over

Below: man's jersey in seeded rib and woman's jersey in striped garter stitch made up in Patons Purple Heather 4 ply.

trousers or, if worked in a soft enough yarn, pouched over at the waist.
Look at the instructions for this jersey to see how the theory works, then you will find it very rewarding to work out your own calculations.
To work out your own calculations, first make a tension sample using the chosen yarn, needles and stitch pattern. Generally the size of needles depends on the thickness of yarn so that you will need thicker needles for double knitting and Shetland yarns and smaller ones for finer yarns like 4-ply, 3-ply and baby qualities (fig.4). From the tension square you can establish the number of stitches and rows to 2.5cm (1").

Then halve your bust measurement and multiply this by the number of stitches to 2.5cm (1") plus about 2.5cm (1") extra for tolerance, or ease of movement, and seaming. The figure arrived at will give you the number of stitches to cast on for the back.
For instance, to calculate the number of cast on stitches needed for an 86cm (34") bust size with the tension worked out at 4 stitches to 2.5cm (1") follow the chart (fig.5). This has been filled in with these measurements, but you should substitute your own.
Back (and front) 43cm (17") multiplied by 4 = 68 stitches plus 3 stitches tolerance = total of 71 stitches.
Now that you have the right needle

No. of stitches to 2.5cm (1″)	=	4
½ bust chest measurement	=	17
½ bust chest measurement x no. of stitches to 2.5cm (1″)	=	17 x 4 = 68
Add extra stitches for tolerance (equal to about 2.5cm (1″)	=	+ 3
Total no. of stitches to cast on	=	71

5. *Chart showing the calculation of cast on stitches you need for a jersey.*

size to give your correct bust measurement, you can decide what needles you will need for the waistband, yoke and cuffs. The general rule is to work any ribbed waistbands, neckbands and cuffs on needles two sizes smaller than those used for the main pattern.

If you are working in a rib pattern, where the stitches tend to pull inwards instead of staying flat, then choose your needles in direct relationship to those quoted in the pattern.

In this case you will need needles four sizes smaller than those used for the main pattern for working the waistband and yoke, plus a pair, yet another size smaller, for the cuffs.

Bust chest needles	
Waistband and yoke needles	
Cuff needles	
No. of stitches to cast on	
Total length of jersey	
Length from underarm to wrist	

6. *Read the jersey instructions, then for easy reference, add the figures for your own jersey in the spaces above.*

To make a jersey

Read the instructions and then insert the appropriate figures in the box given below (fig.6). Allow about 28gm (1oz) more or less yarn for each bust/chest size larger or smaller than the one quoted.

For a jersey to fit an 86cm (34″) bust/chest size.

You will need:

Total of 700gm (25oz) of Double Knitting yarn.

One pair of No.4 (US 10) needles.

One pair of No.8 (US 6) needles.

One pair of No.9 (US 5) needles.

For the back, take a pair of No.8 needles and cast on 71 stitches.

☐ Work waistband for 7.5cm (3″) in single rib (as explained in the last chapter, on page 108) noting that, because there is an odd number of stitches, all right side rows will begin and end with a knit stitch and all wrong side rows will begin and end with a purl stitch.

☐ Change to No.4 needles and continue working in seeded rib.

☐ Now turn back to the chart to see where to mark the position of the underarm, change needles, work the yoke and cast off.

For the front, work in exactly the same way as the back.

For the sleeves, again follow the instructions given on the chart.

The sleeve top must be shaped so that it will fit neatly into the armhole.

☐ You will see that when you have knitted a total of 47cm (18½″) from the beginning, ie the length from underarm to wrist, you must cast off 2 stitches at the beginning of the next 12 rows and 4 stitches at the beginning of the following 4 rows.

☐ This will leave 11 stitches which are cast off on the next row and also form an integral part of the sleeve top shaping.

To make up. Do not press your work as this will spoil the elasticity of the rib pattern.

☐ You should use backstitch seams for sewing up a knitted garment, except for ribbed parts such as waistbands and cuffs which should be neatly oversewn [overcast].

☐ Join the shoulder seams for 7.5cm (3″) from the armhole edges.

☐ Sew the shaped sleeve top between the underarm markers on the front and back, then remove the markers.

☐ Join the side and sleeve seams.

Two alternative versions

A shorter jersey could be made by knitting a shorter length between the waistband and the underarm position, say, working 30cm (12″) between these points instead of 38cm (15″).

The striped jersey has been worked from the basic jersey shape, but in a finer yarn with smaller needles and it has been shortened to waist length. Perhaps the most interesting difference is the effect created by working entirely in multi-coloured stripes of garter stitch in a totally random sequence. Think of how creatively you could make up your own variations and at the same time use up any coloured oddments of yarn, if they are all of the same thickness.

The only thing that cannot be worked out accurately at this stage is the amount of yarn needed.

So look at the quantities of double knitting yarn used for the seeded rib jersey and remember that you will require less of a lighter weight yarn and more of a chunky yarn.

Stitch patterns

You might now be inspired to try out a more elaborate stitch pattern such as the bobble rib illustrated in the last chapter. Be careful when using stitch patterns to see you have enough stitches to repeat the pattern completely across the row, plus an extra stitch at each end which will be lost in the seamings. If you have worked out 71 stitches for the back, but your pattern repeats over 6 stitches, you will have to add another 3 stitches, so that you have 12 repeats of 6 stitches plus 2 extra for the seams.

Seeded rib stitch

Cast on a number of stitches divisible by 4, then add 3 more stitches.

1st row (RS) K1, *P1, K3, rep from * to last 2 sts, P1, K1.

2nd row K3, *P1, K3, rep from * to end.

Dick Miller

Knitted patchwork effects

Be your own designer with patchwork knitting—it is one of the most original ways of creating anything from shawls, jerseys and skirts to cushions, mats or bedspreads.

From simple patchwork squares to more challenging ones which give the effect of random shapes, the combinations of stitches and colours are endless. You can have hours of fun and interest, as well as using up your scraps of yarn economically.

The shawl shown here is based on a number of individual squares worked in stocking stitch (as previously shown on page 108) and three ends of yarn in various colours. These squares are joined together in such a way that a serrated effect is formed along two sides of the shawl. The gaps along the edge are then filled in with triangular shapes so that a final straight edge is made on to which the fringe is threaded. You can either follow the instructions for the shawl given below, or you can make your own using any yarn and size square that you want. All you will need to know is how to make a triangular shape for the edge of the shawl.

First you will need to complete a square in your chosen yarn. Measure this square diagonally across the centre from one point to another, marked A to A on the chart (fig.1), to

1. *Use the marked points on this square to calculate the number of cast on stitches and rows required to shape a triangle.*

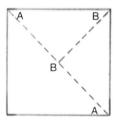

give the width of the base of the triangle. Use the stitch tension obtained on the square to calculate the number of stitches to be cast on for the triangle base.

Measure from B to B on the chart for the depth measurement, and using the row tension you can work out the number of rows needed to shape each side of the triangle up to a centre point. Calculate how many stitches need to be decreased in the given number of rows and keep the shaping even by working two stitches together at each end of every row, every alternate row, or at regular intervals until all the stitches are worked off.

Patchwork shawl

For a shawl that measures 137cm (54″) across the top and 68cm (27″) from top to point when each square measures 7.5cm (3″) square worked on No. 7 (US 7) needles with 3 strands of yarn.

Shawl made from square and triangular shapes in Pingouin Jericho cotton.

You will need:

Total of 400gm (14oz) of lightweight cotton yarn in 12 assorted colours or as required. You should choose a yarn which gives about 14 stitches to 7.5cm (3″) when using three strands.
One pair No.7 (US 7) needles.
One No.4.50 ISR (US I) crochet hook.

To make a square, use 1 strand of yarn in each of 3 colours together and cast on stitches to give 7.5cm (3″).

☐ Work 7.5cm (3″) in stocking stitch, then cast off.

Make 71 more squares, using colours according to taste and availability.

For a triangle, using 1 strand of yarn in each of 3 colours together, cast on stitches to give 10.5cm (4¼″).

☐ Work triangles in stocking stitch; shape the sides by decreasing one stitch at each end of the next and every following alternate row until 2 stitches remain. Cast off.

Make 17 more triangles.

To make up. Press the squares and triangles using a cool iron over a dry cloth.

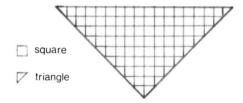

☐ square

▷ triangle

2. Join squares and triangles as shown.

☐ Join the pieces in the order shown in the diagram (fig.2), alternating the direction of the knitting on alternate squares as shown in the picture.
☐ Using the crochet hook and any 3 colours of yarn, work a row of double [single] crochet around the outer edge of the shawl.
☐ Cut yarn into 30cm (12″) lengths for the fringe.
☐ For each tassel take 2 strands of each of 3 colours and make a knotted fringe (see Crochet chapter 5, page 482) along both short sides of the shawl.
☐ Trim the ends of the fringe to an equal length.

Random patchwork

A simple but effective way to make random patchwork is to work out a series of square patterns, then combine any number in any order you fancy.

The exciting thing about this technique is the way in which the sequence of patches and colours is used. You will imprint your own individual personality on the work as no two knitters will work either the same patch or colour in identical order so that every sample of fabric will have a unique appearance.

Random patchwork patterns can be worked as separate squares and then joined together, as already described on page 110.

Otherwise, you can work an all-over fabric to the required size. This method means that you will be knitting small areas of stitches in different colours in the course of the same row. To do this, use a small, separate ball of yarn as it is needed instead of carrying the yarn across the back of the work until it is required again. Always twist the yarn you have just finished using around the yarn you are about to use on the wrong side of the work on every row, otherwise you will leave a gap between the colours.

In the following samples each colour has been coded alphabetically in the order in which it is used eg., A for the first colour, B for the second colour and so on. The five patches shown have been based on a combination of the eight colours used in the cot cover shown overleaf. However, you can of course knit each patch in any combination of colours you wish. *A represents the first colour you use in each patch but it does not represent a consistent colour from patch to patch.* For each patch you will need to cast on 28 stitches in Double Knitting yarn and the 36 rows in each pattern will form a square about 11cm (4½″) by 11cm (4½″).

First patch—a square based on a Greek key design and comprising three colours.

First patch

1st row. (RS) Using A, K14, using B, K14.
2nd row. Using B, P14, using A, K14.
3rd row. Using B, K6, slip 1 purlwise without working the stitch—called sl 1—, K5, sl 1, K1, K14.
4th row. Using B, P14, K1, yarn forward to the front of the work—called yfwd—, sl 1, yarn to the back of the work—called ybk—, K5, yfwd, sl 1, ybk, K6.
5th row. Using A, K1, sl 1, K3, sl 1, K1, sl 1, K3, sl 1, K2, using B, K14.
6th row. Using B, P14, using A, K2,

yfwd, sl 1, ybk, K3, yfwd, sl 1, ybk, K1, yfwd, sl 1, ybk, K3, yfwd, sl 1, ybk, K1.
7th row. Using B, K4, sl 1, K1, sl 1, K3, sl 1, K1, sl 1, K1, K14.
8th row. Using B, P14, K1, yfwd, sl 1, ybk, K1, yfwd, sl 1, ybk, K3, yfwd, sl 1, ybk, K1, yfwd, sl 1, ybk, K4.
9th row. Using A, K3, sl 1, K1, sl 1, K3, sl 1, K1, sl 1, K2, using B, K14.
10th row. Using B, P14, using A, K2, yfwd, sl 1, ybk, K1, yfwd, sl 1, ybk, K3, yfwd, sl 1, ybk, K1, yfwd, sl 1, ybk, K3.
11th row. Using B, K4, sl 1, K5, sl 1, K3, K14.
12th row. Using B, P14, K3, yfwd, sl 1, ybk, K5, yfwd, sl 1, ybk, K4.
Repeat 1st and 2nd rows once more.
15th row. Using C, K to end.
16th row. Using C, P to end.
Repeat last 2 rows 3 times more.
23rd row. Using B, K14, using A, K14.
24th row. Using A, K14, using B, P14.
25th row. Using B, K14, K6, sl 1, K5, sl 1, K1.
26th row. Using B, K1, yfwd, sl 1, ybk, K5, yfwd, sl 1, ybk, K6, P14.
27th row. Using B, K14, using A, K1, sl 1, K3, sl 1, K1, K3, sl 1, K2.
28th row. Using A, K2, yfwd, sl 1, ybk, K3, yfwd, sl 1, ybk, K1, yfwd, sl 1, ybk, K3, yfwd, sl 1, ybk, K1, using B, P14.
29th row. Using B, K14, K4, sl 1, K1, sl 1, K3, sl 1, K1, sl 1, K1.
30th row. Using B, K1, yfwd, sl 1, ybk, K1, yfwd, sl 1, ybk, K3, yfwd, sl 1, ybk, K1, yfwd, sl 1, ybk, K4, P14.
31st row. Using B, K14, using A, K3, sl 1, K1, sl 1, K3, sl 1, K1, sl 1, K2.
32nd row. Using A, K2, yfwd, sl 1, ybk, K1, yfwd, sl 1, ybk, K3, ywfd, sl 1, ybk, K1, sl 1, ybk, K3, using B, P14.
33rd row. Using B, K14, K4, sl 1, K5, sl 1, K3.
34th row. Using B, K3, yfwd, sl 1, ybk, K5, yfwd, sl 1, ybk, K4, P14.
Repeat 23rd and 24th rows once more—that makes 36 rows in all.

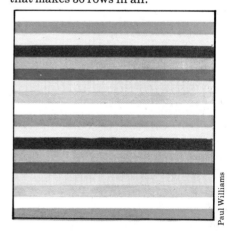

Second patch—striped in eight colours.

Second patch

1st row. (RS) Using A, K28.
2nd row. Using A, P28.

Repeat last 2 rows 17 times more, working in striped sequence of 2 rows each of A, B, C, D, E, F, G and H throughout —that makes 36 rows in all.

Third patch—four squares in one.

Third patch
1st row. (RS) Using A, K14, using B, K14.
2nd row. Using B, P14, using A, P14.
Repeat these 2 rows 8 times more.
19th row. Using C, K14, using D, K14.
20th row. Using D, P14, using C, P14.
Repeat last 2 rows 8 times more—that makes 36 rows in all.

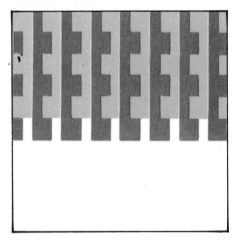

Fourth patch—plain and fancy.

Fourth patch
1st row. (RS) Using A, K28.
2nd row. Using A, P28.
Repeat last 2 rows 5 times more.
13th row. Using B, K2, *sl 1, K3, repeat from * to last 2 sts, sl 1, K1.
14th row. Using B, K1, *yfwd, sl 1, P1, K2, repeat from * to last 3 sts, yfwd, sl 1, P1, K1.
Repeat last 2 rows once more.
17th row. Using C, K1, *sl 1, K3, repeat from * to last 3 sts, sl 1, K2.
18th row. Using C, K1, *P1, sl 1, ybk, K2, repeat from * to last 3 sts, P1, sl 1, ybk, K1.
Repeat last 2 rows once more. Repeat last 8 rows twice more—that makes 36 rows in all.

Fifth patch
1st row. (RS) Using A, K28.
2nd row. Using A, P28.
Repeat these 2 rows 5 times more.
13th row. Using B, K7, using C, K7, using D, K7, using E, K7.
14th row. Using E, P7, using D, P7, using C, P7, using B, P7.
Repeat last 2 rows 11 times more—that makes 36 rows in all.

Fifth patch—striped in two directions.

Cot cover
For a cover 61cm (24″) wide by 81cm (32″) long.
You will need:
Total of 450gm (16oz) of Double Knitting in 8 contrasting colours.
One pair No.8 (US 6) needles.
For the cover. Take a pair of No.8 needles and cast on a total of 140 stitches if you are working the full width to give 5 patches, or 28 stitches if you are making 5 separate strips.
☐ Work in any pattern of patches and colours that you want until 7 complete rows of patterns have been worked— that makes a total of 252 rows in all. Cast off.

Patches worked in strips and joined.

For the fringe. Using No.8 needles and any colour, cast on 10 stitches.
☐ The first row is on the right side of the work and is formed by knitting 2

Fringe formed by unravelling stitches.

stitches, bring the yarn forward to the front between the needles, then carry it over the right hand needle so that an extra stitch is made, knit the next two stitches together, then knit the final 6 stitches.
☐ Purl 5 stitches at the beginning of the second row, knit 2 stitches, bring the yarn forward to the front between the needles, then knit the next two stitches together; knit the last stitch.
☐ Repeat the last 2 rows until the strip fits along all 4 edges of the cot cover centre, easing it in slightly at the corners.
☐ For the final row cast off 4 stitches and fasten off the 5th stitch, leaving 5 stitches on the left hand needle.
☐ Drop these 5 stitches off the needle and unravel them all the way down to the first row to form fringed loops.
☐ Join the cast on edge to the cast off edge by oversewing [overcasting] together.
To make up. Darn in all the ends on the back of the cover.
☐ Sew fringe in position all round the edges by backstitching it on top of the centre, about 0.5cm (¼″) in from the edge.

Right: cot cover designed by Pam Dawson in Madame Pingouin yarn. Back (below) is as neat as the front.

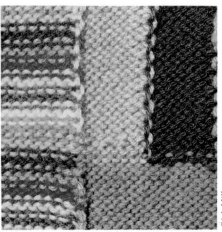

Dick Miller

Crocheted granny squares

Steve Bicknell

120

Crochet is quick and simple to work and, because it is so decorative, has become one of the most popular of all handicrafts. It is very adaptable and can be used in conjunction with many different fabrics and yarns. You can crochet borders, edgings and flower decorations which will enhance any garment; or you can create pictures, bedspreads and other home furnishings. The type of yarn used offers you as much scope as the articles you can make from it. Coarse wool or string can be made up into wall hangings or rugs while the finest yarns will make delicate table mats, fine curtains or gossamer-weight fabrics.

These chapters set out to explain the basic techniques so clearly that you will be able to make up any sort of

Bright and practical, this shoulder bag is just right for carrying those things a girl insists she cannot be without! The bandeau, which can be made in an evening even by a beginner, will keep your hair sleekly in place in most weathers and looks pretty too.

To make a chain

Make a slip loop at the end of your ball of yarn and place it on the hook.

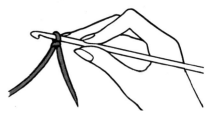

Hold the hook in your right hand...

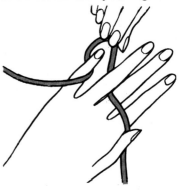

... and the yarn in your left hand, with the yarn looped round the little finger. This loop helps to control the flow of yarn.

pattern to the size you require—and then go on to make up your own designs with your choice of yarn. The easiest way to learn to crochet is to begin by making small, manageable shapes like granny squares. Practise a square first using scraps of double knitting yarn and a No. 4.00 ISR (U.S. size H) hook. These motifs are colourful and economical, since any odd scraps of the same thickness of yarn can be used and with the combination of half-squares, you can produce a variety of shapes.

This granny square uses three colours but when it gets bigger you can use more!

Slip stitch

Use it to join a new colour: insert hook into stitch in previous row, make a loop with the new yarn, catch it round hook, pull through stitch, wind yarn and end round hook and pull through.

To join crochet pieces, match edges, insert hook through both thicknesses, yarn round hook and draw loop through fabric and loop on hook in one movement.

Wind the yarn round the hook once..

... and draw the yarn through the slip loop. One chain stitch has been made, leaving one loop on the hook —this is not counted as a stitch.

Continue making chain stitches in this way.

Working a treble [double]

Make however many chain stitches you need and add 3 extra chain stitches. These make what is called a turning chain, which is required at the beginning of every row of treble to bring hook up to correct height to work the first stitch.

To work the first row, *wind the yarn round the hook, as shown for making a chain stitch and insert the hook from front to back into the fourth chain stitch from the hook, wind the yarn round the hook again ...

... and draw the loop through the chain stitch.

Wind the yarn round the hook ...

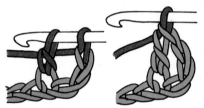

... and draw the yarn through 2 of the loops on the hook.

Wind the yarn round the hook and draw it through the remaining 2 loops on the hook.* One treble has been made, plus the first missed 3 chain stitches which count as the first treble, leaving one loop on the hook. Repeat from * to * into next and every chain stitch to the end of the row.

On the next and every following row, turn the work so that the yarn is again in position for the beginning of the row. Make 3 chain stitches to count as the first treble, miss the first treble of the previous row, work one treble into each treble to the end of the row inserting the hook ...

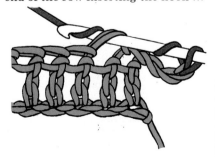

... under the top 2 loops of the treble in the previous row.

Chris Lewis

Barbara Firth

Granny square using one colour.

Making a granny square

Using one colour. Without breaking off yarn at end of each round. Make 6ch. Insert hook from front to back into first ch, yrh and draw loop through ch and loop on hook in one movement. One ss has been worked to join ch into a circle.

1st round. 3ch to count as first tr, 2tr into circle working under ch, 2ch, work (3tr into circle, 2ch) 3 times. Join with ss to third of first 3ch.

The beginning of the second row.

2nd round. 2ch, work (3tr, 2ch, 3tr) into first 2ch sp to form corner, *1ch, work (3tr, 2ch, 3tr) into next 2ch sp,

rep from * twice more. Join with ss to first of first 2ch.

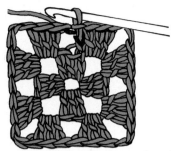

The beginning of the third row showing where the hook should be inserted.

3rd round. 3ch, 2tr into first ch sp to the left of ss join of previous round, 1ch, *work (3tr, 2ch, 3tr) into 2ch sp, 1ch, 3tr into 1ch sp, 1ch, rep from * twice more, (3tr, 2ch, 3tr) into last 2ch sp, 1ch. Join with ss to third of first 3ch.

Working under the top two loops of the treble in the previous row.

4th round. 2ch, 3tr into next 1ch sp, 1ch, *work (3tr, 2ch, 3tr) into 2ch sp, 1ch, (3tr into 1ch sp, 1ch) twice, rep from * twice more, (3tr, 2ch, 3tr) into last 2ch sp, 1ch, 3tr into last 1ch sp. Join with ss to first of first 2ch. Break off yarn, draw end through loop on hook and draw up tightly—called 'fasten off'.

To fasten off, break the yarn and pull the end through loop on hook.

Granny squares using 2 or more colours. Break off yarn at the end of each round. Make commencing ch and work first round as given for motif in one colour. Break off yarn and fasten off.

2nd round. Join next colour to any 2ch sp with ss, 3ch to count as first tr, work

2tr into same ch sp, *1ch, work (3tr, 2ch, 3tr) into next 2ch sp to form corner, rep from * twice more, 1ch, 3tr into same 2ch sp as beginning of round, 2ch. Join with ss to third of first 3ch. Break off yarn and fasten off.

3rd round. Join next colour to any 2ch sp with ss, 3ch to count as first tr, work 2tr into same ch sp, *1ch, 3tr into 1ch sp, 1ch, work (3tr, 2ch, 3tr) into 2ch sp, rep from * twice more, 1ch, 3tr into 1ch sp, 1ch, 3tr into same 2ch sp as beginning of round, 2ch. Join with ss to third of first 3ch. Break off yarn and fasten off.

4th round. Join next colour to any 2ch sp with ss, 3ch to count as first tr, work 2tr into same ch sp, *(1ch, 3tr into next 1ch sp) twice, 1ch, work (3tr, 2ch, 3tr) into 2ch sp, rep from * twice more, (1ch, 3tr into next 1ch sp) twice, 1ch, 3tr into same 2ch sp as beginning of round, 2ch. Join with ss to third of first 3ch. Break off yarn and fasten off. Darn in ends of yarn where colours were joined.

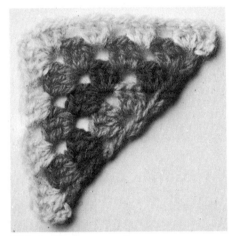

This half square makes granny squares even more versatile.

To make a half-square

Using one or more colours. Breaking off yarn at end of every row. Make 5ch. Join with ss to first ch to form a circle.

1st row. Using same colour, 4ch to count as first tr and 1ch sp, work (3tr, 2ch, 3tr) into circle, 1ch, 1tr into circle. Break off yarn and fasten off.

Each row must be started with a fresh strand of yarn from the same side at which the row was first begun.

2nd row. Join next colour to third of first 4ch with ss, 4ch, 3tr into first 1ch sp, 1ch, work (3tr, 2ch, 3tr) into 2ch sp, 1ch, 3tr into last 1ch sp, 1ch, 1tr into top of last tr in previous row. Break off yarn and fasten off.

3rd row. Join next colour to third of first 4ch with ss, 4ch, 3tr into first 1ch sp, 1ch, 3tr into next 1ch sp, 1ch, work (3tr, 2ch, 3tr) into 2ch sp, (1ch, 3tr into next 1ch sp) twice, 1ch, 1tr into top of last tr in previous row. Break off yarn and fasten off.

4th row. Join next colour to third of

first 4ch with ss, 4ch, 3tr into first 1ch sp, 1ch, (3tr into next 1ch sp, 1ch) twice, work (3tr, 2ch, 3tr) into 2 ch sp, (1ch, 3tr into next 1ch sp) 3 times, 1ch, 1tr into last tr. Break off yarn and fasten off.

Bandeau

For a bandeau 9cm (3½") deep by 50cm (20") long. Each motif measures 8cm (3¼") square.
You will need:
50gm (1¾oz) of 4-ply yarn in 6 contrasting colours, ABCDE and F. If you use scraps of yarn, the size of the bandeau may vary.
One No.3.00 ISR (US size F) crochet hook
To work granny squares
Make 6 granny squares, using one or more colours as required.
To make up
Sew squares tog and join into circle.
Edging. Using No.3.00 ISR (US size F)

hook, any colour and with RS of work facing, rejoin yarn with ss to any corner ch sp.
Next round. 3ch to count as first tr, (work 1tr into each tr and ch sp across top of first 3 squares), ss into same place as last tr, make 16ch, take ch down back of squares, round front to top again to gather the front, ss into next ch sp, 1tr into same place, work as given in brackets across next 3 squares. Join with ss to third of first 3ch. Fasten off.
Work along other edge in same way omitting the 16ch loop.

Handbag

For a handbag 27cm (11") square
Each motif measures 13cm (5½") square
You will need:
50gm (1¾oz) of 4-ply yarn in main colour and 100gm (3½oz) in 4 contrasting colours. If you use scraps of yarn, the size of the handbag may vary.

One No.3.00 ISR (US size F) crochet hook
To work granny squares
Make 10 granny squares using the colours as required.
To make up
Sew 4 squares together to make a square, and sew the remaining squares together to form an oblong 27cm x 40cm (11"x16½"). Place the square against the oblong, WS together, matching the squares exactly. Sew round the 3 sides of the square and oblong where they meet. This forms the body of the bag with a flap consisting of 2 squares.
To work the handle
Make 152ch, work 1tr into every ch and work 6 rows, varying the colours as necessary.
To complete the bag
Sew the right sides of the 2 ends of the handle to the back of the bag just where it joins the flap. Lining the bag will increase its durability and help keep its shape.

Cushion

For a cushion 40cm (16") square
You will need:
250gm (8¾oz) of yarn in one colour
50gm (1¾oz) of Double Knitting yarn in each of 7 contrasting colours, ABCDEF and G.
One No.4.00 ISR (US size H) crochet hook
Cushion pad 40cm (16") square
20cm (8") zip fastener [zipper]
To make large square
Using No.4.00 ISR (US size H) crochet hook and any colour, work first 4 rounds as given for granny square, changing colour for each round.
5th round. Join in any colour with ss to corner 2ch sp, 3ch to count as first tr, 2tr into same sp, *(1ch, 3tr into next 1ch sp) 3 times, 1ch, (3tr, 2ch, 3tr) into corner 2ch sp, rep from * twice more, (1ch, 3tr into next 1ch sp) 3 times, 1ch, 3tr into same sp as beg of round, 2ch. Join with ss to third of first 3ch. Break off yarn and fasten off.
Cont in this way changing the colour as shown and working one more group of 3tr and 1ch on each side on every round until work measures 40cm (16") across. Fasten off. Darn in all ends. Make another square in the same way.
To make up
With RS of squares tog, join 3 edges. Turn RS out. Insert cushion pad. Join rem seam, leaving sp to insert zip fastener in centre.
Edging. Using No.4.00 ISR (US size H) hook and any colour, rejoin yarn with ss to any corner sp through both thicknesses. Into each ch sp round all edges work (1ss, 4tr, 1ss) working through both thicknesses, except across zip fastener opening, where you only work through one thickness. Join with ss to first ss. Fasten off.
Sew in zip fastener.

Cushion made up in Jaeger Spiral-spun Double knitting. Designer Pam Dawson.

Rupert Watts

Simple crochet stitches

This chapter introduces two simple stitches—double crochet and half treble—which you can use to make up these pretty cushions and rag rug. Use heavy rayon, raffia or ribbon for effective cushions and oddments of cotton fabric for the rug.

Abbreviations
(for other abbreviations, see previous chapter, page 122)
dc double [US: single] crochet
htr half treble [US: half double]

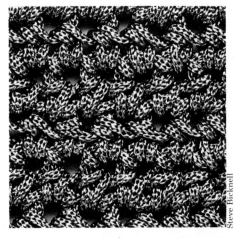

This close-up of a fabric worked in half trebles shows in detail the texture of the stitch. Yarn used: Atlas Novacord.

Double [US: single] crochet

Start by making the number of chain stitches you need, adding one extra chain stitch—this acts as a turning chain, which is needed at the beginning of every row of double crochet to bring the hook up to the right height for working the first stitch.

1st row. Insert the hook from front to back into the third chain stitch from the hook (fig.1).

*Wind the yarn round the hook (fig.2) . . .

. . . and draw the loop through the chain stitch (fig.3).

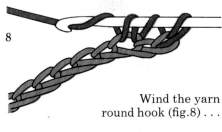

Wind the yarn round the hook and draw through both loops on the hook* (fig.4).
One double crochet has been made, plus first missed 2 chain stitches which count as first double crochet, leaving one loop on hook. Insert hook into next chain stitch and repeat from * to * into each chain stitch to end.

On next and every following row, turn the work so that the yarn is again in position at the beginning of the row, make one chain stitch to count as first double crochet, miss first double crochet of previous row, work one double crochet into next double crochet.

When working into a previous row, unless otherwise stated, insert hook under top 2 loops of double crochet (fig.5).
Continue working double crochet into each double crochet to end, working the last double crochet under the turning chain of the previous row.

To work a half treble

Make the number of chain stitches you need, then add one extra chain stitch to count as a turning chain.

1st row. Wind the yarn round hook, insert hook from front to back into third chain stitch from hook, *wind the yarn round hook (fig.6) . . .

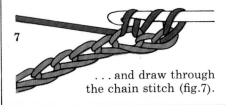

. . . and draw through the chain stitch (fig.7).

Wind the yarn round hook (fig.8) . . .

. . . and draw through all 3 loops on hook* (fig.9).

One half treble has been made plus first missed 2 chain stitches which count as first half treble, leaving one loop on hook. Wind the yarn round the hook, insert the hook into next chain stitch and repeat from * to * into each chain stitch to end.
On next and every following row, turn the work so that the yarn is again in position at the beginning of the row, make 2 chain stitches to count as first half treble, miss first half treble of previous row, work one half treble into each half treble to end, inserting hook under top 2 loops (fig.5) and working the last half treble under the turning chain in the previous row.

Mini cushions

For cushion about 23cm (9″) square worked in half trebles (you could also use trebles and double crochet).

You will need:

100gm (4oz) of tubular rayon macramé cord, raffia, or very narrow ribbon.

One No.7.00 ISR (US size K) crochet hook

23cm (9″) square cushion pad made from calico and stuffed

Using No.7.00 ISR (US size K) hook make enough ch to make 23cm (9″), about 22ch, which includes one extra ch to count as turning ch.

1st row. Into third ch from hook work 1htr, then 1htr into each ch to end. Turn. If you had 22ch to start with you should now have 21htr.

2nd row. 2ch to count as first htr, miss first htr, 1htr into each htr to end, working the last htr under the turning ch of the previous row. Rep second row until work measures 46cm (18″) from beg. Fasten off.

To make up

Fold work in half WS tog and join 2 side edges with a ss (see Crochet chapter 1, page 37). Insert cushion pad. Join rem edge.

Rag rug

This rug, measuring 2.6m x 1.3m (8′8″x 4′4″) is another example of using materials other than crochet wools. If you have a lot of scrap cotton fabric in a ragbag you can tear it up into strips about 2cm (¾″) wide. Wind up the strips into balls, separating the colours. Work two or three rows with one colour then change to another to build up a pleasing pattern.

Because the rug is worked in strips it is easy to handle while working.

If you don't feel like tackling a rug, use slightly thinner strips of fabric— say 1.5cm (½″)—to make country-style table mats.

You will need:

For rug 1.3m (4′4″) wide, lengths of cotton fabric in 4 colours. The total

This practical rag rug uses strips of colourful cotton material.

amount of material will depend on the length of rug required and the way which stripes of colours are arranged, 5.5m (6yd) of 90cm (36″) wide fabric will work out at about 76cm (30″) in length.

One No.7.00 ISR (US size K) crochet hook

Button thread

1st strip. Using No.7.00 ISR (US size K) hook and any colour, make enough ch to make 33cm (13″) width, about 27ch should be right, which includes one ch for turning.

1st row. Into third ch from hook work 1dc, then 1dc into each ch to end. Turn.

If you had 27ch to start with you should now have 26dc.

2nd row. 1ch to count as first dc, miss first dc, 1dc into each dc to end,

Lots of mini cushions make any chair comfortable. They are made in several yarns including Atlas Novacord.

working the last dc under the turning ch of the previous row. Turn.

Rep second row for required length, changing colours as required and working over the ends each time a new strip is joined in, to secure them.

2nd strip. Make enough ch (about 19 should be right including 1ch for turning) to make 23cm (9″) width.

3rd strip. Make enough ch (about 35 should be right including 1ch for turning) to make 43cm (17″) width.

4th strip. Work as given for first strip to make 33cm (13″) width.

To make up

Sew strips together with button thread.

Crocheted circular motifs

The beauty of circular motifs is that you just keep on working until they are the required size—as small as a coaster or as large as a rug. You can use any stitch and any yarn you choose. As in the two preceding chapters, U.S. readers should be using the U.S. equivalents for the stitches (pages 121 and 124).

To make a circular motif

Make 6ch. Join with ss to first ch to form a circle.

1st round. 2ch to count as first dc, work 7dc into circle. Do not join but cont working in rounds, working next 2dc into second of first 2ch.

2nd round. Work 2dc into each dc to end. 16dc.

3rd round. Work 1dc into each dc to end.

4th round. Work 2dc into each dc to end. 32dc.

5th round. Work 1dc into each dc to end.

6th round. 2dc into first dc, 1dc into next dc, *2dc into next dc, 1dc

Above: circular motif.
Below: belt made of circular motifs, made up in Atlas Raffene. Designed by Pam Dawson.

into next dc, rep from * to end. 48dc.

7th round. Work 1 round without shaping.

8th round. 2dc into first dc, 1dc into each of next 2dc, *2dc into next dc, 1dc into each of next 2dc, rep from * to end. 64dc.

Cont inc 16 dc on every other round until the motif is the required size.

To do this, the space between each 2dc into 1dc increases by one stitch every increasing round so, round 10, work 2dc into next dc, 1dc into next 3dc; round 12, work 2dc into next dc, 1dc into next 4dc.

Cont increasing 16dc on every alternate round in this way until circle is required size. Ss into first st of previous round and fasten off.

String place mat

For a place mat 30cm (12″) diameter
You will need:
1 ball of gardening twine (available from hardware and gardening stores)
No.4.00 ISR (US size H) crochet hook
To work place mat
Work as given for circular motif until 14 rounds have been worked, that is a total of 112dc, but do not fasten off.
To make scallop edging
Next round. 3ch to count as first dc and 1ch sp, miss first 2dc, 1dc into each of next 3dc, *1ch, miss 1dc, 1dc into each of next 3dc, rep from * to last 2dc, 1dc into each of last 2dc. Join with ss to second of first 3ch.
Next round. Into each 1ch sp work (1dc, 3tr, 1dc). Join with ss to first dc. Fasten off.

Raffia belt

Requirements to fit 58 (63:68)cm 23 (25:27)″ waist. Each motif measures 5.5cm (2¼″) diameter. The figures in () refer to the 63cm (25″) and 68cm (27″) sizes respectively.
You will need:
Total of 3 (3:4) hanks of raffia in one colour or oddments
No.3.00 ISR (US size F) crochet hook
To work belt
With No.3.00 (size F) hook and any colour work first 3 rounds as given for circular motif. Join next colour and work 2 more rounds as given for circular motif. Fasten off. Make 9 (10:11) more motifs in same way.
To make up
Join motifs tog where edges touch to form one row. Make 3 separate ch 122 (127:132)cm 48(50:52)″ long. Working on wrong side, stitch one ch across back of top edge of motifs, one across centre and one across lower edge, to tie at centre front. Trim each end of ch with wooden beads if required.

Right: circular string place mat, in double crochet with a shell edging. Designed by Pam Dawson.

Steve Bicknell

Simple tatting

Tatting is a simple form of lace making which is worked with one basic stitch throughout. It involves the use only of your fingers and—on large or fine pieces of work—a simple shuttle to hold the thread and a fine crochet hook to join the motifs.

At its simplest, tatting can be worked as a length of loops to form an edging or as individual circles to be mounted on to fabric. At its most elaborate,

it can be worked as beautiful gossamer-fine borders for fabric or as a piece of fabric itself.

Like macramé, tatting derives from the art of knotting which was popular throughout Europe in the 17th and 18th centuries. Rows of knots were worked with a shuttle and thread and the resultant cord was couched in various patterns on to fabric.

During the 18th century, when it was discovered how to form a fabric with this method, it evolved into what became known as tatting. Tatting became widespread as a pastime during the 19th century when caps, collars, cuffs, doilies and edgings for all kinds of things were made with it.

The yarn

Because it was intended to resemble other types of lace made by a more intricate method, tatting has traditionally been worked in fine threads such as linen or cotton. For delicate work these are still the best to use.

Linen lace threads are less readily available and are more expensive than cotton which is made in a variety of weights, colours and textures—both crochet cotton and pearl embroidery cotton may be used. Wool and other knitting yarns are not normally suitable for tatting, particularly for beginners, because they tend to stretch. String and cord such as used for macramé, however, are suitable for more chunky textures.

Amount of yarn. It is not usually easy to estimate the amount of yarn required for any particular project because this varies with the tension of the individual worker. When working a pattern in individual motifs, however, it is possible to calculate how much yarn will be required from the amount used for the first motif. To measure this, unravel several metres (yards) of yarn and make a note of the exact measurement. Work the motif and measure the amount of yarn left. This, subtracted from the total amount, gives the length used in the motif.

Double stitch

The stitch used throughout tatting, and the one from which all the intricate patterns evolve, is in fact a simple knot of the kind which many people use regularly about the house when tying on baggage or parcel labels without necessarily knowing the correct name: the double reverse half hitch or lark's head. When worked in tatting it is called double stitch.

This double stitch may be worked either to form a length, known as a

This pretty mat, designed by Coats, is worked in the basic double stitch which forms rings and chains with picots.

chain, or to form rings, and most tatting patterns combine the two methods. Although the basic principle in working the chains and rings is the same, it is easier to start with a chain and progress to rings when you have learnt the knack of forming the stitch. It is advisable to start in string rather than cotton so that you can see the formation of the stitch.

To make a practice length of about 7.5cm (3″), you will need:
One 60cm (24″) length of string and one 15cm (6″) length. You will find it easier to start with two different colours.

The basic knot. Double the shorter piece of string, loop it round the longer piece as shown in fig.1a and

1a. *Tying the basic knot*

pull the ends of the shorter piece through the loop. Tighten the resulting knot round the longer piece.

☐ Pick up the ends of the shorter piece and pull them straight out to the sides in opposite directions (fig.1b). Pull tightly allowing the ends of the longer piece to rise. As the length you are

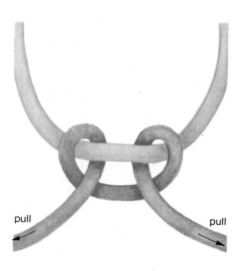

pull   pull

1b. *Pulling the ends of the knot.*

pulling straightens, the other length will form an identical knot, known as the double stitch, around it (fig.1c). This process shows what the basic knot looks like and how the loops are

1c. *The double stitch is formed.*

transferred. The next process shows how the knot is tied in two stages in tatting so that several stitches can be worked to form a chain.

Tying the knot in two stages. Undo the first knot and re-tie it by wrapping the shorter length over the longer one, thus forming the knot in two motions (fig.2).

1st stage   2nd stage

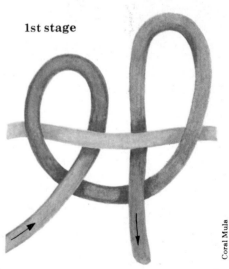

Coral Mula

2. *Tying the knot in two stages.*

Working over the hand. Undo this second knot and tie the lengths together at one end with a simple overhand knot. Hold the knot between the fingers and thumb of your left hand and wrap the two lengths over the back of the fingers with the shorter length on the right.

the loop so it is formed by the longer length (fig.3b). Keeping the shorter

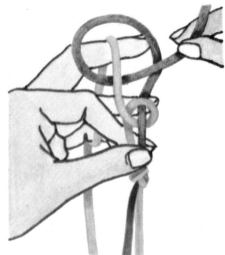

4a. *Forming the second loop.*

length on the right, work the second half of the stitch with it (fig.4a) and transfer the loop to the longer length

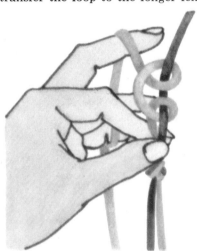

4b. *The second loop transferred.*

Tatted chains with large picots, worked in Twilleys Crysette crochet cotton, form this simple dress trimming designed by Mary Konior.

□ Work the first half of the double stitch with the shorter length (fig.3a).

Pull the shorter length, or push the loop with your fingers, to transfer

(fig.4b). Push the complete stitch along to the overhand knot.

□ Work another stitch in the same way and push along each loop when transferred to the first stitch. Continue like this for the whole chain.

Combining threads. When you are working a chain to form an edging it is usually better to use threads of the same colour because a different-coloured core would show through between the stitches. However, you could use a thicker thread for the core which would prevent confusion and would also give a thicker edge for stitching the chain to fabric.

Spirals. If you work chain using one half of the double stitch only, it will form an attractive spiral effect, as shown in part of the necklace in the photograph. It does not matter which half of the stitch you work as long as you are consistent.

3a. *Forming the first loop.*

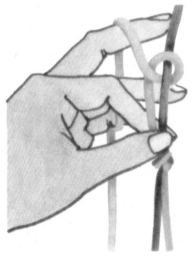

3b. *The first loop transferred.*

130

Picots

These make a very attractive addition to double stitches by forming loops between them. Make one double stitch in the normal way, then form the first half of a second stitch, pushing this one along to first stitch to leave a gap of 1.5cm (½") between the two (fig.5a). Complete the second half

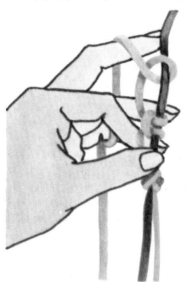

5a. *Leaving a gap between stitches.*

of the stitch and then push the whole stitch along to the first one (fig.5b).

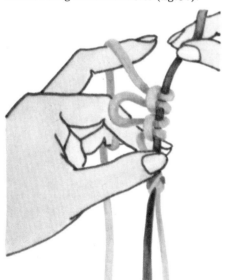

5b. *The picot is formed.*

You will then see that the gap left between the two stitches forms a small loop. The size of the loop can be varied by leaving a smaller or larger gap between the stitches. Any number of stitches may be worked between picots.
Adding beads. An unusual variation is to hang beads from the picots. To do

Necklace worked in macramé string is made with chain of double stitches and spirals, with beads hung from picots.

this, thread the beads on to the longer piece of yarn or ball thread (knot the end to prevent the beads from sliding off). Start tatting in the normal way and, when you form a picot, slide a bead along to the part of the yarn which forms the gap between the double stitches. Work the following stitch and push it along (fig.6).

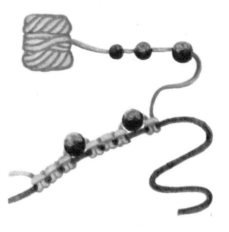

6. *Beads threaded on to the ball thread to be pushed along as required when forming a picot.*

Shuttles

When you develop the technique of tatting it is easier to wind the thread on to a shuttle and use this to pass the yarn which forms the loops initially (that is, before transferring them) over the other thread which can be taken direct from the ball. These are known respectively as the shuttle thread and the ball thread.

Most shuttles today are made from plastic and are about 5cm (2") long. It is worth looking out for old shuttles in antique shops because many of these were made from ivory or even silver, with interesting designs.

Preparing the shuttle. Place the end of the yarn into the notch at the centre of the shuttle and start winding the yarn round until the shuttle is full but not projecting beyond the edge. Cut the thread leaving a working length of about 40cm (16").

Heavier yarns. These are not suitable for winding on to standard-size shuttles because they may damage the opening. Instead, simply wind the yarn in a figure of eight round your fingers and secure with a rubber band. It is then easy to let out more yarn as you need it.

Tatted rings

Typical tatting designs resemble clusters of snowflakes and are formed by groups of rings arranged individually or joined by picots.

The rings are worked with the same basic double stitch as used for chain, and discussed in the previous chapter. Rings are always formed with one length of yarn instead of two (figs. 1-5). For joining rings you will also need a fine crochet hook.

Using a shuttle. When working several rings which are linked, it is advisable to wind the yarn on to a shuttle. For individual rings, however, you can wind the yarn in a figure of eight to form a 'butterfly' and secure it with a rubber band.

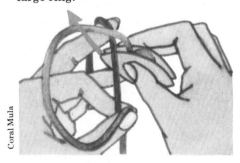

1. Hold the end of the yarn between the thumb and index finger of your left hand. Pass it over the other three fingers and back underneath to form a large ring.

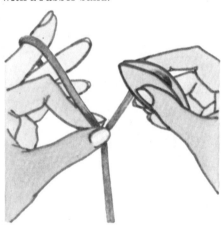

2. To make the first half of the stitch hold the shuttle or butterfly of yarn in your right hand and make a large loop over the top of the left hand. Pass

the shuttle or butterfly from underneath up and through both the ring and the loop from right to left.

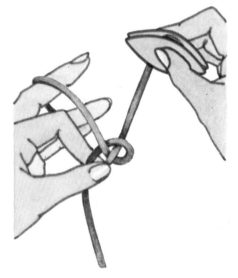

3. Transfer the loop thus formed to the ring round your hand by pulling the shuttle firmly to the right, and lowering the middle finger of the left hand. Tighten the stitch by raising the middle finger of the left hand again so that the stitch slides along the shuttle thread into position as shown. Then hold it between the thumb and index finger of the left hand.

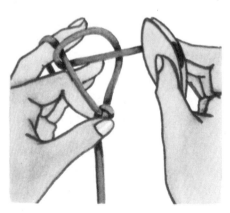

4. Work the second half of the stitch by passing the shuttle downwards from left to right through the ring round the left hand, and through the loop thus formed with the shuttle thread.

5. Pull the shuttle thread to the right as before to transfer the loop and draw up the stitch to the first half.

By forming more double stitches in this way you will form a ring. To complete the ring, release the thread from your left hand and gently pull up the shuttle thread to close it. Picots may be added between the double stitches as described in the previous Tatting chapter.

To complete the ring. If you are making individual rings knot the ends of the yarn together to secure the ring and cut off close to the knot.

Lampshade trimming

The lampshade in the photograph was trimmed with individually made tatted rings of varying sizes, some of which include picots to form daisy shapes. The lampshade can be of any size, and the rings made of any cotton crochet yarn of medium thickness. The rings and daisies are arranged to form a random pattern and stuck on to the lampshade with adhesive.

You will need:
Plain lampshade.
Cotton crochet yarn.
Tatting shuttle (optional)
Fabric adhesive.

☐ Wind several metres (yards) of the yarn on to the shuttle (or tie in a butterfly) and form the rings and daisies as described below.

Large rings (about 2cm (¾″) diameter). Make a ring of 20 double stitches and close it. Knot the ends of the yarn together to secure the ring and cut off close to the knot.

Medium rings (about 1.3cm (½″) diameter). Make a ring of 14 double stitches, finish as for the large rings.

Small rings (about 1cm (⅜″) diameter). Make a ring of 8 double stitches, finish as for the large rings.

Large daisies (about 2.5cm (1″) diameter). Make a ring as follows: 1 double stitch, (large picot, 2 double stitches) 6 times, large picot, 1 double stitch, close ring. Tie the ends and cut close to the knot.

Coral Mula

Lampshade trimming made from single rings and daisies, designed to form a random pattern by Mary Konior.

Small daisies (about 2cm (¾″) dia-meter). Make a ring as following: 1 double stitch, (large picot, 2 double stitches) four times, large picot, 1 double stitch, close ring. Tie the ends and cut close to the knot.

□ Arrange the rings and daisies at random round the lampshade. Affix each one with a dab of adhesive, making sure that the ends of yarn are tucked underneath.

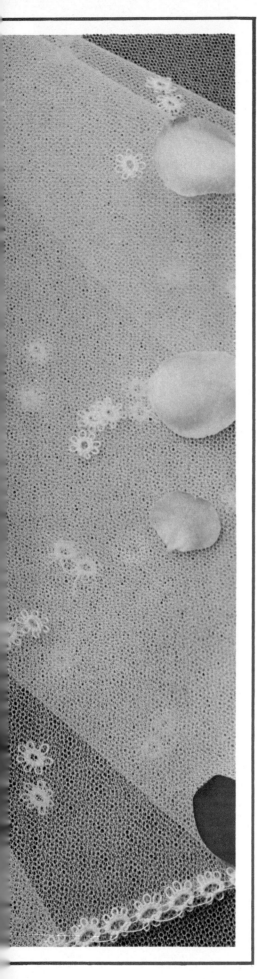

Decorated net

Fine nets look most attractive when decorated with tatted daisies. On the net in the photograph the daisies were made in a fairly fine crochet cotton and measure 1.3cm ($\frac{1}{2}$″) in diameter. They were attached to the net with adhesive.

You will need:

Net of required size.
Fine crochet cotton
Tatting shuttle (optional)
Fabric adhesive.

☐ Make each daisy as follows: 1 double stitch, (picot, 2 double stitches) 6 times, picot, 1 double stitch, close ring. Tie the ends and cut close to the knot.

☐ Arrange the daisies in an attractive random pattern over the net and stick on with a dab of adhesive, making sure that the ends of yarn are tucked underneath.

For the edging make a continuous length of daisies to the required length, joining them as described below. Fix in place with adhesive.

Joining rings

A row of rings can be formed without a break by joining them where they touch at corresponding picots. The best way of judging which picots to use for this is, when you have worked one ring, to draw a diagram of an identical ring and place the worked ring to the left hand side of the drawing with the ends of the yarn at the bottom. In this way one picot on the first ring will naturally touch a picot on the second ring, thus indicating which picots should be used for joining. You will also see how much yarn should be left to form the loop at the bottom between the rings (fig.6).

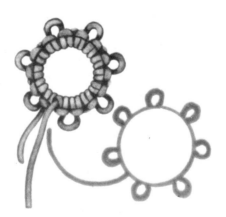

6. *Placing the ring to the side of the drawing so that the picots match.*

Tatted rings with picots make a charming trimming for a simple wedding veil, designed by Mary Konior. The rings were worked singly and in pairs for the main area of the veil and were joined to make a strip for the edging.

For example, if you are joining the daisy motifs previously described for decorating the net, the most suitable picots for joining would be the sixth one worked in the first daisy and the second picot worked in the second daisy.

☐ Work one daisy as described for the net; do not cut off the yarn but start the second daisy with the same thread. by working 1 double stitch. Draw up the stitch, leaving the required amount to form the loop at the bottom. Work a picot and 2 double stitches (fig.7).

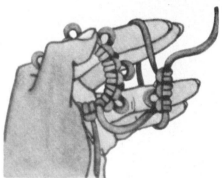

7. *Starting the second ring.*

☐ Insert the crochet hook through the sixth picot of the first ring, draw through the loop round your hand and hold in place. Thread the shuttle thread through the loop and draw up the thread (fig.8). This join stands for a picot and forms the first half of a double stitch. The second half of the stitch is then worked in the normal way.

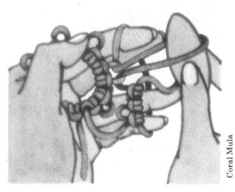

Coral Mula

8. *Joining the rings by threading the shuttle through the loop which has been pulled through the picot of the first ring.*

☐ To complete the second daisy so that it is like the first one, work 1 double stitch, (picot, 2 double stitches) 4 times, picot, 1 double stitch, close ring. It is at this point that you will see how essential it is that the loops are transferred from the shuttle thread on to the loop round your hand when you work each stitch—if you have not done this correctly, the stitches will lock and you will not be able to close the rings.

Yarncrafts

Yarn crafts such as weaving, ropework and macramé are becoming increasingly popular. Learn the basic skills in the following projects, and you'll be delighted with the results of your efforts.

Coiled ropework

One method of creating a shape from rope is by coiling and gluing each circuit as it is made. The easiest shape to make this way is a flat circle although it is not difficult to make ovals. With a little more skill you can make bowls, or lidded containers like those shown in the photograph.

The rope
The rope needs to be a fairly thick one so that it will hold the shape—a diameter of 8-10mm ($\frac{1}{4}$"-$\frac{3}{8}$") is suitable for most projects. A three-ply sisal can be used but if you prefer a less hairy texture, you could try hemp. Both these fibres are easy to handle and bond well.

The adhesive
Use a clear, general purpose adhesive (such as UHU) with a nozzle on the end of the tube so it is easy to apply.

Using a former
To help you make the correct shape, it is advisable to use a former or template. For a mat or the lid of a basket, a template can be made from cardboard with the required shape drawn on it—there is no need to cut out the shape. For a bowl you will need another bowl slightly smaller than the desired size so that the rope can be coiled round it.

Round mats
The instructions are for a round mat of 20cm (8") diameter, but you can make the mat any size you wish.

You will need:
2.70m (3yd) 8mm ($\frac{1}{3}$") diameter sisal or hemp rope. The rope should be three-ply or braided.
25cm (10") square cardboard.
Pair of compasses, pencil, general purpose adhesive and glass-headed pins.
☐ Draw a circle of 20cm (8") diameter on the cardboard and clearly mark the centre of the circle.
☐ Pin the end of the rope to the centre of the circle so that the pin can be used as a pivot. Hold the end of the rope in place with your left hand and rotate it from the centre in an anti-clockwise direction. Smear on a little adhesive to hold the centre together and place a couple of pins through the rope into the inner coil to hold it in place.
☐ Before you start the second circuit, smear a line of adhesive round the outside of the coiled section (fig.1). Coil the second circuit, pressing it firmly to the adhesive. Hold with pins through the first circuit (fig.2). This method of rotating the centre makes a firmer coil than if you try to wind the rope round.
☐ Apply more adhesive round the edge

of the second circuit and stick on the third circuit. Continue in this way until the mat is the required size. Cut off the excess rope at an angle and leave until the adhesive is dry. Remove the pins.

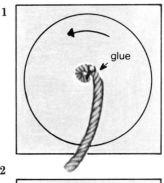
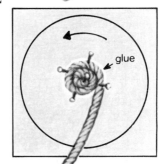

1, 2. Coiling and pinning the rope.

Oval mats
Oval mats are made in a similar way to round mats but they are started differently in order to produce an oval shape.
☐ Construct an oval from two adjacent circles drawn on a piece of cardboard and mark the centre line in both directions. Measure carefully the distance from the centre of the oval to the side along the shorter line X-A (fig.3). Mark off the same distance along the longer line from the edge of the oval in towards the centre B-Y (see fig.3). Do the same from the opposite end of the line.
☐ Place the end of the rope along the middle section of the longer line (Y-X-Y), so that one edge of the rope

is lying level with the line, and pin. Spread adhesive along this edge and double the rope back, pressing it

firmly together. Pin again (fig.4).
☐ Coil and glue the remaining rope round this section to complete the mat.

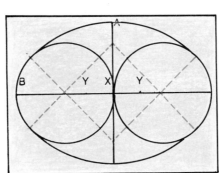

3. The marked oval template.

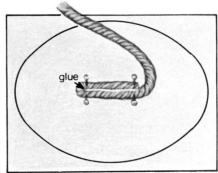

4. Starting to coil the oval.

Round containers
The instructions are for a medium-size bowl of 20cm (8") top diameter with lid.
You will need:
9m (10yd) 8mm ($\frac{1}{3}$") diameter sisal or hemp rope (three-ply or braided). Allow about 45cm (18") extra if you wish to make a knob.
Pair of compasses, pencil, general-purpose adhesive and pins.
Former (bowl slightly smaller than required size).

Chunky mats and containers made by the coiled and glued rope technique.

Piece of cardboard larger than base of former.
☐ Draw a circle round base of former on cardboard. Make base of rope container as for round mat but without cutting off the excess rope. Leave the adhesive to dry, then remove the pins.
☐ For the sides of the container, place the former centrally on the rope base and start coiling and gluing round it, forming each circuit above the previous one. Keep turning the former inside the ropework so that you cannot glue the rope to it.
☐ Trim off the excess rope at the top

of container and leave the adhesive to dry.
The lid. This is made in the same way as the round mat but with the addition of a knob in the centre. The knob can be made with a simple overhand knot in the end of the rope before you start coiling the lid or, if you want a more elaborate knob, it can be made separately and stuck on afterwards. In this case you could use either a miniature coil, as shown in the photograph, or a miniature of the container or you could make a small Turk's head knot and affix it with clear adhesive.

Star weaving

A primitive form of weaving—star weaving—has in recent years found its way into contemporary decor. These colourful stars are most commonly seen in Latin America though they are also found in Africa and the East. In Latin America they are known as Ojos de Dios—God's Eyes. In Mexico God's Eyes were made to symbolize the eye of a god and were a supplication for help or watchful care from the gods. If more than one God's Eye was woven on to the crossed sticks then it was primarily for the gods to look kindly upon a child. A God's Eye was made for each year of a child's life up to five years—after this the child was supposed to be able to make his own requests. The age of a child could also be represented by the number of colours used.

Today God's Eyes are enjoyed for their use of colour and texture and because they are easy and fun to make. The materials are inexpensive and readily available. This is an excellent opportunity to use up scraps of yarn.

Materials

You will need two straight sticks or dowels of about the same length and thickness. You can use sticks from the garden but straight, smooth sticks are the easiest to use to begin with.

When choosing yarn let your imagination run wild with colour combinations. The thickness of the yarn should be relative to the thickness of the sticks. 6mm ($\frac{1}{4}$") diameter sticks work best with double knitting weight. With practice you will be able to vary the yarn weights on each project.

The yarn may be of any material—wool, cotton or man-made fibres. It is best to use at least 2-ply on your first projects as you will be pulling on it to maintain the tension.

To make a star

You will need:
2 sticks, each 28cm (11") long and 6mm ($\frac{1}{4}$") thick
3-ply rug wool in following amounts:
orange — 15.5m (17yd)
purple — 14.5m (16yd)
red — 1m (1yd)
blue — 6.5m (7yd)
yellow — 2.75m (3yd)
rose — 14.5m (16yd)

Remember—it is always better to have too much yarn rather than not enough.
Lashing. Lay one stick on top of the other at right angles with centres matching.
☐ Lay one end of yarn (in this case orange) diagonally across the intersection of the two sticks.
☐ Hold the tail of yarn to the junction of the sticks with your thumb. At the same time, hold the junction of the sticks, on the side away from you, with the index and middle finger of the same hand.
☐ With your free hand begin winding the yarn away from you diagonally, holding it taut as you do so. In this way the yarn should cross the sticks diagonally at the junction, on one side and have parallel sides on the other.
☐ Wind the yarn diagonally around the crossing point of the sticks alternately to the right and to the left, thus forming an X over the centre of the sticks (fig.1). When the centre wood is

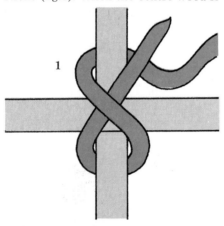

1. *Start the lashing by making a figure of eight around the two sticks.*

totally covered, you have lashed the sticks together.
Note: remember to pull the yarn taut as you wrap so sticks stay in place.
☐ Turn the sticks over and tie a small but tight knot at the centre of the back with the original tail of the yarn and the yarn you now hold in your hand. This secures the lashing. Do not cut the yarn. Turn the sticks over again so that the knot is at the back. The side facing you is from now on the 'right side' of the star. Always work with this side facing you.

Weaving. There are two basic methods of wrapping the yarn to make stars. One shows the shape of the sticks (fig.2), the other covers the shape of the sticks completely and is slightly raised (fig.3). In both cases, all wood is covered until the outer edge of the star is reached.

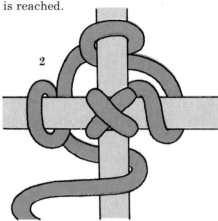

2. *The recessed method of wrapping.*

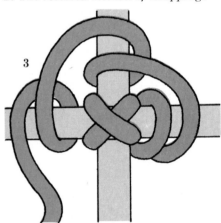

3. *This is the raised method of wrapping which covers the shape of the sticks.*

This example continues with the orange yarn that was used for the lashing, and begins with the method that covers the shape of the sticks completely.
☐ Begin by holding the star in one hand and the yarn in the other (with the right side of the star facing you).
☐ Carry the orange yarn over one stick so that the yarn lies just next to the last round of lashing.
☐ Bring the yarn under the stick and back around the top of the stick (fig. 3). (Keep the yarn taut throughout the entire procedure.) You have now completed one wrapping.
☐ Carry the yarn forward to the next arm of the star. Again, lay the yarn on top of the stick next to the last round of lashing. Wind the yarn under the stick and around the top of the stick. Don't forget to keep the yarn pulled taut.
☐ Continue on to the next arm of the star and finally the fourth arm and back to where you began. You have now completed one round. Repeat this round until you have woven about

2.5cm (1″) from the centre of the star in each direction.

Changing colours. You are now ready to change colours. This design changes from orange to purple.

☐ On the wrong side of the star stop at one arm and cut the yarn leaving a tail of about 5cm (2″).

☐ Loop the tail once round the arm and tuck the end under the loop. Pull the end tightly. (This will hold the tension of the yarn in place while you join the new colour.)

☐ Making a double knot, attach the purple yarn to the tail of orange yarn. Tie the knot as close as possible to the arm of the star (fig.4).

☐ Continue wrapping the purple yarn

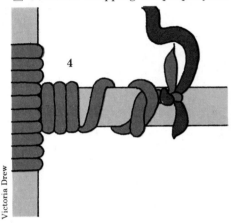

4. Join a new colour on the wrong side of the stick with a tight knot.

around the arms of the star just as you did with the orange yarn.

To follow the example shown, wrap the purple yarn until its width is 12mm (½″).

☐ Change to the red yarn, following the method for changing colours. After winding the red yarn for 6mm (¼″) in width, change to a blue yarn.

☐ With the blue yarn change to the other technique of wrapping the yarn (fig.2). You will note that the blue area appears to be recessed. This is due to the second wrapping technique which shows the shapes of the sticks.

☐ Begin by wrapping the blue yarn under the nearest arm of the star.

☐ Now bring the yarn around the top of the stick and around the underside again.

☐ Carry the yarn to the next arm and repeat the first two steps (fig.2). The blue yarn is wrapped for a width of 12mm (½″). Now, change back to the orange yarn and wrap it for a width of 6mm (¼″).

☐ Then change to a yellow yarn and resume the original method of wrapping (going over the stick, then under and back over). Continue this method to near the end of the sticks. The yellow yarn is wound for a width of 6mm (¼″). Then wind the rose yarn for 18mm (¾″); purple for 12mm (½″); orange for

This star uses the raised method of wrapping broken by just a small area of the recessed method. The lower end, being longer, is covered by winding the yarn round and round. The star is light enough to be hung from a panel pin hammered into a wall.

12mm (½″) and finally purple for 18mm (¾″).

Finally, on the wrong side, knot the purple yarn with an overhand knot.

If you wish to cover the longer bottom arm of the star, as has been done in this model, do not cut the purple yarn close to the knot after you have finished weaving the star, but instead wrap the yarn round and round the stick until you reach the end. Then make your overhand knot on the wrong side of the stick. This is a good method of covering the ends of the sticks that are longer than the others.

Finishing. Make certain that all knots are tight and cut tails close to the knots for a neat finish.

Decorating stars

You may leave your star as it is, or further embellish it with various orna-

141

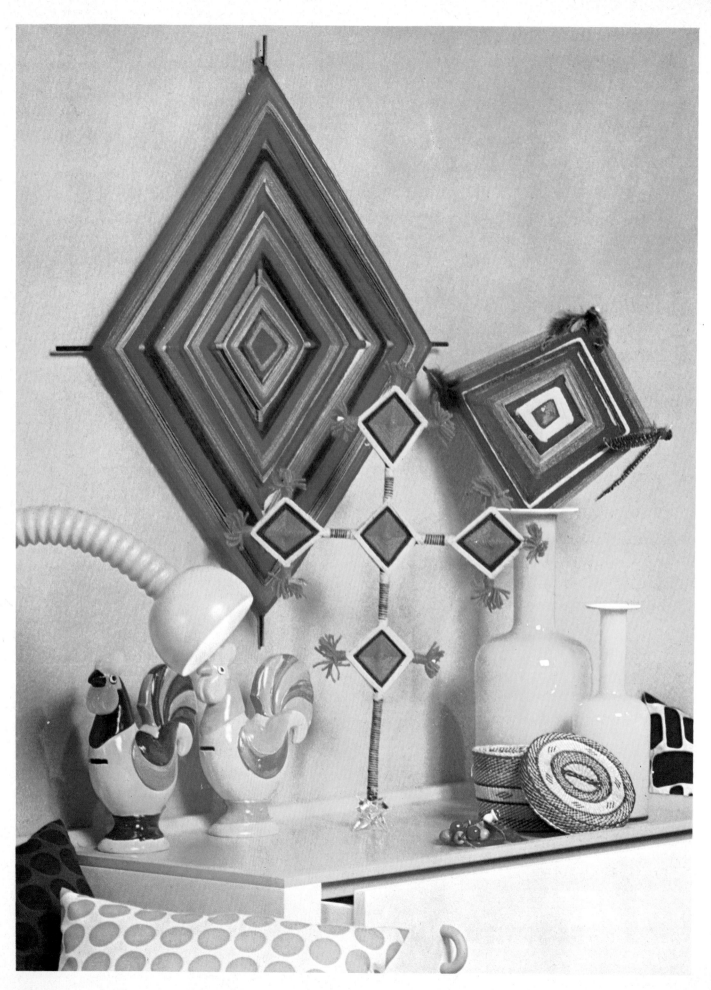

Left: stars are woven with 3-ply rug wool. The smaller star is based on curved twigs and the large star on green split bamboo garden stakes, which are available from hardware shops. The stars use both methods of winding— raised and recessed, and the smaller one is decorated with feathers. All God's Eyes illustrated (except five - starred one) were designed by Carol Packard. Right: group several stars together to make shapes like these traditional Mexican God's Eyes.

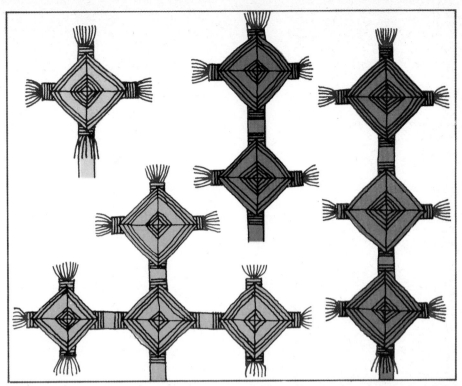

ments. The most common practice is to hang things from the exposed ends of the arms. You may, however, wish to sew or weave objects on to the face of the weaving. Tassels, pompons, feathers, bows, buttons, seashells and beads can all be used as ornaments.

As you become more proficient at making stars, you may want to try something more challenging. Some methods of varying stars are:

Irregular sticks will add bumps and concave areas to the wrapping. The sticks can be bumpy and/or curved to add interest. Just remember that these irregularities make it more difficult to maintain the tension and will require extra attention.

Very long, fat, short or thin sticks all give different looks to your stars. Remember that yarn thickness should be scaled up or down according to the size of the stick.

Besides changing colours with yarn, you may also like to try changing textures. There are all sorts of novelty yarns on the market, some giving a bumpy or looped effect. A smooth cotton followed by a bumpy, novelty yarn could give a dramatic effect.

God's Eyes

God's Eyes make a very effective hanging for a wall. Simply tie a string around the top arm, making a loop. Loop the string over a tack and you're all set. One star by itself looks good, or you may want to make a group of them, either all of one size or in a range of sizes.

Mobiles made with God's Eyes add a new dimension to a room. Children are attracted to them because of the lively colours.

You can even use very tiny stars (made with wooden tooth picks for the cross pieces and very fine wool or cotton) to hang on the Christmas tree. They add colour in an original way.

Right: the very small stars are woven with very thin wool on wooden tooth picks. The wool is wrapped in the recessed method of under-over-under, described above. One star has plastic sequin birds attached to the ends of the arms, while another has buttons attached to the points.

Finger weaving

Warp—a set of vertical yarns through which the weft is passed when forming a fabric.
Warp end—each warp length is called an end.
Weft—the yarn that is passed through the warp ends in a horizontal direction.

Finger weaving is a process of making woven cloth by using your fingers to guide the wefts through the warp ends. As well as being the simplest form of weaving it is also thought to be the oldest. Examples of ancient braids woven by this method have been found in almost every part of the world. People in places as far apart as Peru, Egypt and Scandinavia worked out patterns by manipulating various colours of yarn with their fingers.

Finger weaving travels well! Because you need no tools, it is the ideal pastime while travelling or sitting in the garden or on the beach.

The easiest patterns to make in finger weaving are diagonal bands of colour.

From this basic method wavy lines of colour can be woven as illustrated. Once the principle of separating the warp ends and inserting the wefts has been achieved, chevron and diamond patterns can be worked by grouping the yarn differently and weaving it in two directions. And so the progression, towards the complex grouping of yarns to produce double woven braids, is easy.

Uses for bands of finger weaving

Use the braids for decorating sweaters and woollen dresses, for making into belts, book markers, cuffs, napkin rings, watchstraps, chokers, bracelets, hatbands and sashes.

Braid widths

Although finger weaving is primarily useful for weaving narrow bands using about 16 strands, wider pieces can be made—with practice. The maximum number of strands which can be handled comfortably is about 48, however the width of the finished braid will depend on the thickness of the yarn. Narrow bands may be sewn together to make either wide bands of colour, wall hangings, place mats, cushions, hold-alls, shoulder- or handbags. Braids can also be joined by working several braids simultaneously and intertwining the outside strands of each set.

Materials

The materials needed for finger weaving are simple and inexpensive. All you need is yarn—rug wool, knitting wool or cotton or synthetic yarn—and a pencil to which to attach the yarn. Use double knitting yarn to begin with as this is the simplest to use. After learning the skill of finger weaving, interesting effects can be produced by using heavy wools and string or fine silks and cottons.

Colour

Colour is fundamental to weaving and the choice of colour combinations should be given some thought before a project is started. When choosing colour schemes for braids to decorate clothes, choose one colour which picks up or matches the colour of the garment. Experiment with colours and combinations of colour because the play of colour can be one of the most exciting parts of your work.

Finger weaving relies heavily on the use of colour contrasts. Strong contrasts produce a bold effect and accentuate the pattern, while subtle combinations create a softer mood and give a more subtle pattern which can be equally effective. Alternatively, use a small amount of a neutral colour to 'break up' bands of primary colours. Sections of 3 or 4 colours containing 6, 7 or 8 strands give an effective result although more or less can be used.

To make a belt or anything else which needs to have a fringe at either end, set up as follows:

An assortment of colourful braids.

Steve Bicknell

Chris Lewis

Bright hatband which is easy to make.

Preparation

Cutting the yarn. Cut the various coloured yarns into the required number of lengths. Each length of yarn should be two or three times as long as the finished length of the article, depending on how long you wish the fringe to be. If you wish to hem the ends, then twice the length is ample. For example, if you are weaving something 15cm (6″) long, cut the yarn 30cm (12″) long. The width of the finished braid will be about ½-¾ of the width of the yarn wound round the pencil and squeezed together.

First of all anchor the yarn firmly to some immovable object by tying an overhand knot at one end of the bunch of yarns and looping over a hook, door knob, chair or drawer handle (fig.1), or by pinning them securely to a cork board.

1. Loop yarn over an immovable object.

Wind each strand in turn around a pencil, about 5cm (2″) below the knot, (fig.2).

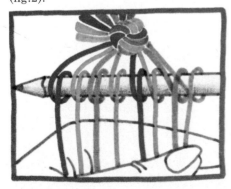

2. Winding strands round pencil.

Weaving

Set the strands on to the pencil in groups of colour, arranging them side by side. Hold the strands towards you about 8cm (3″) below the pencil in the right hand. (These lengths of yarn are called the warp ends.) As the threads are used, pass them to your left hand and hold taut.

☐ Working from left to right, pick up strand A and weave it under strand B, over strand C, under strand D and so on across all the strands (fig.3).

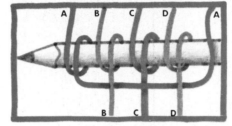

3. Weave A from left to right.

☐ Pull strand A parallel to the pencil and, using the forefinger of the left hand, push it up close to the pencil. Tuck strand A over the right end of the pencil.
☐ Pick up strand B and weave it under strand C, over strand D, under the next and so on across all the strands. (You may find it easier to think of the weaving movement as plaiting the travelling strand across.) (fig.4).
☐ Pull strand B parallel to the pencil and push it against the pencil. Remember to push up the strands after they have been carried through the warp ends. The pattern and tension can then be checked for evenness and corrected before the pattern has progressed too far.

To make a selvedge on the right hand side, bring strand A either under or over strand B (whichever completes the weaving sequence) and place it parallel to the other warp ends. Tuck strand B over the pencil. The method of making the selvedge is the same for whatever pattern you are weaving (fig.5).

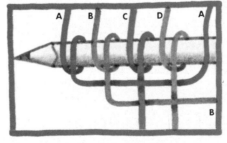

4. Weave B from left to right.

☐ Pick up strand C and weave it under the second warp end, over the third, under the fourth and so on across the warp ends.
☐ Continue weaving each warp end on

the far left, using it as a weft, through the warp ends, always reversing the sequence of the previous row and bringing every weft down over or under the lower one to complete the selvedge on the right hand side (fig.5).

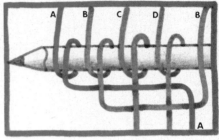

Victoria Drew

5. Bring A over B to make a selvedge.

Make sure the strands aren't getting tangled—sort them out as you go along. Pull each horizontal strand firmly but not too tightly and give the warp ends a gentle straightening pull after each movement. The horizontal strands should be completely covered by the warp ends.

For the first 5 or 10 minutes it will probably seem like an awful lot of strands and nothing effective happening. Then suddenly you begin to build up rhythm to achieve an even tension and the diagonal pattern starts to grow under your fingers. From that moment on you'll be hooked!

Make sure that you pull the right selvedge firmly, in a straight line. Otherwise the band will begin to curve. (Of course, you can turn this into a virtue when you are making a collar or a hatband.)

If you want a fringe at the end of the braid leave 20cm-25cm (8″-10″) of warp ends for finishing.

Diagonal stripes

For diagonal stripes, set the threads in groups. The 3-colour sample below has 8 orange, 8 pink and 8 yellow. Follow the weaving process, working always from left to right.

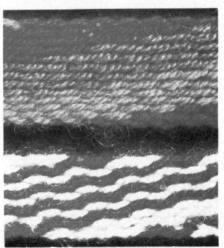

Three- and two-colour diagonal stripes.

Numerals on diagrams indicate number of strands needed to give patterns shown on left.

Red and white diagonal stripes.

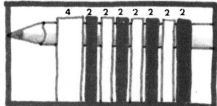

Wide diagonal, candy-coloured stripes.

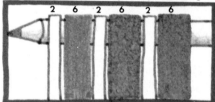

Wavy lines with single strands of white.

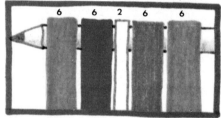

A wavy line on a yellow background.

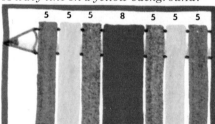

Chevron pattern in four colours.

Alternating chevron pattern.

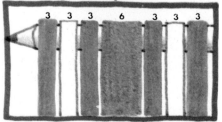

Chevrons make diamond patterns too.

Wavy line stripes

Arrange the strands as for diagonal stripes and follow the weaving process. The same method is followed as given for diagonal stripes, until all the warp ends have been used once as a weft.

☐ Then complete the selvedge on the right hand side and, with the last weft that you used, weave it in and out of the warp ends from right to left.

☐ Pick up the far right warp end and weave it in and out, working from right to left also.

☐ To make the selvedge on the left hand side, bring the upper weft either under or over the lower weft (whichever completes the sequence) and place it parallel to the warp ends.

☐ Continue in this way, working from right to left, until you want the bands of colour to curve in the reverse direction. If you wish, the change in direction may be made at any point, but the largest curves are achieved by using all the warp ends as wefts before changing direction.

Chevron pattern

Choose an even number of colours and strands. Divide each pile into two groups, with the same sequence of colours, and mount them on a pencil so that when the warp ends are divided in the middle the colour sequence of one group is reflected exactly in the other group (see opposite).

☐ Grip the left group of warp ends in your left hand and the right group in your right hand.

☐ Then, using the forefinger and thumb of your right hand, pick up the first warp end at the right edge of the left group.

☐ Weave this warp end (which is now the weft) over, under, over the warp ends in the right hand.

☐ Pull the weft parallel to the pencil. Grasp all the warp ends in the right group in your right hand except the one on the far left of this group.

☐ Pass this warp end (now the weft) over, under, over, working from right to left through the warp ends held in the left hand.

☐ Return to the right group of warp ends and pass the far right warp end from the left group over, under, over the warp ends held in the right hand.

☐ Repeat this movement with the left group, by passing the far left warp end from the right group over, under, over through the left group of warp ends.

☐ Form a selvedge on the right and left sides (fig.5) as you go.

☐ Continue weaving from the centre to the edges until the colour you started with on the far left and far right is positioned in the centre of the warp ends. You have now worked one chevron pattern. Continue in this way until you have worked the required length.

Chevron pattern with diamond shape

☐ Mount the strands of yarn on a pencil by tying them halfway along their length in the same sequence as for chevron pattern, (see opposite).

☐ Tie one lot of warp ends in a loose knot—to keep them out of the way while you are weaving the others.

☐ Using the free strands, work the required length in the chevron pattern. Untie the loose knot and the knots around the pencil. Turn the work around, but not over, so the unworked ends are towards you and weave chevron patterns as before. Because you are working in the opposite direction, a diamond shape is formed in the centre.

Finishing

A neat finish enhances any braid, so either knot, turn under and neatly hem or finish in one of the following ways to give a 'fringe' effect.

Even if you want a simple fringe, it will lie better if you start with a small amount of plaiting or ply before knotting. Knots straight after finger weaving tend to splay and look untidy.

Plaits. If the number of warp ends are multiples of three, plait sets of three warp ends. Knot the ends and trim them level or at an angle.

With a little practice even numbers of warps, if they are multiples of four, may be plaited using four strands.

Ply. Take a pair of warp ends. Twist one warp end between your thumb and forefinger to the right until it is very tightly twisted and begins to kink even when held fairly taut. Secure the end with a pin to a cushion or stick it to a table with sticky tape so that it can't unwind. Repeat the twisting with the other warp end and hold it firmly. Pick up the first twisted warp end and hold it firmly too. Hold both warp ends together between your thumb and forefinger and tug firmly while rolling the warp ends towards the left. Release the warp ends. They

Finishes: ply, and plait small knot.

should twist together, that is, form a ply. Knot the ends and trim them. Repeat with the remaining warp ends.

Knots. Finish plaits and ply by tying knots across the bottom of the sets of plaited and plied strands. To make a small knot, take only one of the

strands, wrap it round 2 strands, make a single knot and pull tight. Trim the strands either just below the knots, or leave a little tassel.

Hems. Tie strands in pairs with a double knot and trim ends as close as possible to the knots without weakening them. Turn the knotted ends in 6mm (¼") to the wrong side and fold again 2cm (¾") from the edge. Using the same coloured yarn, make neat stab stitches through the braid to prevent the ends from unfolding.

Decorative choker in diamond pattern.

To make the choker

The choker shown is about 2cm (¾") wide and 38cm (15") long, including 5cm (2") for finishing. Adjust the length according to your requirements by working a little more or a little less.

☐ Choose yarn in four colours and cut into 76cm (30") lengths, in the quantities given in the diagram at the bottom of the opposite page.

☐ Mount the centre of each length of yarn on a pencil in the sequence indicated and tie the warp ends that you are not working in a loose knot. Work 19cm (7½") in a chevron pattern. Untie the loose knot and the knots around the pencil. Turn the unworked warp ends around, but not over, and continue with the chevron pattern until the length is 38cm (15").

☐ Arrange warp ends at each end of the band in pairs and knot them. This prevents the work from unravelling.

☐ Turn each knotted end of the band 6mm (¼") to the wrong side. Turn each end 2cm (¾") under again and stitch the folded edges to the wrong side.

☐ Make a fastening by sewing a 12mm (½") button to the right side of the band near one edge. Make a loop at the other edge by passing a 10cm (4") strand of yarn through the folded hem. Knot the two ends together, adjusting to the right length. Trim the ends and thread the knot inside the hem so that it is hidden. The loop will then fasten over the button and secure the band.

Simple macramé

Macramé is essentially a free form craft because, once you have learnt a few basic knots, you will be able to experiment and build up your own designs. However, if you are trying new combinations of knots, be methodical and make sure that the pattern is balanced. In this chapter two knots and some of their variations are used to make two attractive, but totally different, hanging baskets.

Macramé can be worked in yarns of many different thicknesses, but parcel string is easy and economical to begin with. Synthetic string, rayon, cotton, silk, knitting and rug yarn, heavy string or thin rope—for really big projects — are all ideal. The yarn that you use for macramé often suggests what it should be used for: thick yarn which makes up into a chunky fabric is suitable for using around the home as pelmets, room dividers, lampshades, wall hangings, rugs and place mats; medium-weight yarns can be used for handbags, shopping bags, hammocks, luggage racks, cot covers, table mats, lampshades, chair backs and seats for folding chairs, and as seats for deckchairs; fine yarn makes lovely trimmings for dresses and blouses. Mac-

rame can be worked straight on to open weave material—and is suitable for tablecloths, small lampshades and for covering plain-coloured cushions.

Knotted hanging baskets

Made in 20 minutes these baskets are plain and simple, to set off an attractive plant to best advantage. The hanging basket can be made for a pot of any size.

You will need:
Twine; plant pot.

☐ Measure from the centre of the base of the pot to the height from which you intend to hang the pot, then add about 30cm (12″) to be sure of having enough yarn. Double this length — ie if the measurement from centre of base of pot to hanging point is 75cm (30″), add the 30cm (12″), multiply by two and the total length of yarn will be 210cm (84″).

For medium-weight yarn cut 5 lengths and for rope cut 4 lengths.

☐ Place all the lengths together, fold the bundle in half and make an overhand knot about 10cm (4″) from the fold (fig.A).

☐ To make the basket fit the pot, you have to actually work around it. So

work where the pot will be safe, possibly by sitting on a thickly carpeted floor if it is an expensive pot.

☐ Place the knot in the centre of the base of the pot. Make an overhand knot (fig.A) with two of the strands at the edge of the pot; if there is no edge, make the knot 7cm (3″) from the large knot. Repeat with the remaining strands (fig.B).

☐ Arrange the knots so that they are equal distances from each other around the edge of the base.

☐ Hold two of the knots in place and, using a strand from each pair of strands, pinch them together (fig.C). This gives the position of the next row of knots. Remove the pot from the basket. Make an overhand knot where your fingers pinch the strands. Split the other pairs of strands and make overhand knots at the same distance along the length of the strands (fig.D).

☐ Return the pot to the basket and repeat the pinching, taking two strands, one from each pair of neighbouring strands. Remove the pot and tie an overhand knot where your fingers pinch the strands. Split the other pairs and knot them at the same distance along the strands (fig.E).

☐ Lay the basket around the outside of the pot and measure to the top of the pot with a strand from each pair of strands. Remove pot from basket and make an overhand knot which should come just above the rim. Repeat with the other strands. Return the pot to the basket and check the position of all knots.

☐ Using all the strands, tie an overhand knot near the ends as shown. Trim the ends (fig.E).
The basket is now ready to hang.

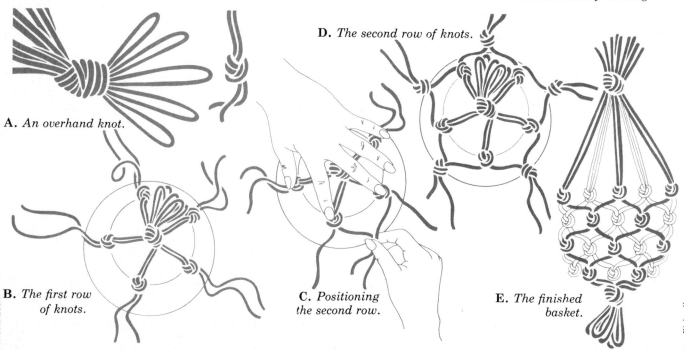

A. *An overhand knot.*

B. *The first row of knots.*

C. *Positioning the second row.*

D. *The second row of knots.*

E. *The finished basket.*

Quantities

The quantity of yarn required for making an article is difficult to judge accurately. A complex design obviously takes up more yarn than a simple one and thick yarn is used quicker than thin yarn. An approximate guide is 5 to 8 times the length of the finished article for each strand, depending on the type of design.

To mount the strands

Macrame needs a foundation on which it can be worked. This can be made from a dowel, a length of yarn or, if you are working in a circle, a curtain ring. Anything which is used for mounting the knots is called a knot bearer.

Fold each strand in half and attach to the knot bearer as shown (fig.1). These lengths of yarn are called knotting strands. When making any knot, pull it tight so that it feels firm.

1. Mounting strands on knot bearer.

Double [half hitch] cording

This cording [double half hitches] can follow the knotting strands or be used as part of a pattern. The cording has to be knotted around a knot bearer, which may be an additional dowel, piece of yarn, larger curtain ring or, if the cording is to form part of a pattern, one of the knotting strands is used as the knot bearer.

These simple knotted baskets may be decorated with beads.

Cording [double half hitching] is done from left to right. Bring up each strand in turn and wrap it round the knot bearer from front to back twice, threading the end between the two loops as shown (fig. 2).

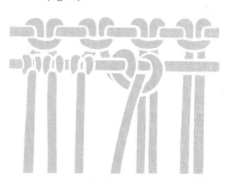

2. Cording knots [double half hitches]

149

Flat [square] knots

Before making these, the number of knotting strands must be in multiples of 4. Divide the pairs of strands into groups of 2. Pick up the left strand and make a loop, with the end passing under the centre 2 strands. Make a loop with the right strand and pass it under the end of the left strand, over the centre 2 strands and through the left loop (fig.3). Pull the ends to form a firm knot.

3. *The first stage of flat [square] knot.*

To complete the flat [square] knot, make a loop with the right strand with the end passing under the 2 centre strands. Make a loop with the left strand and pass it under the end of the right strand, over the 2 centre strands and through the right loop (fig.4). Pull

4. *Completing the flat [square] knot.*

the ends to form a firm knot. You have completed one flat [square] knot.
Continue in this way using first the left strand to make a loop and then the right strand.
A spiral with flat [square] knots always use the same strand, either the outer left or outer right one, to make the loop.

Knotted chain

Using 2 strands, bring the left one over the right and then thread it through the loop made by the 2 strands. Bring the right strand over the left and then thread it through the loop made by the 2 strands (fig.5).

5. *A knotted chain.*

One knotted chain has been made. Continue knotting with the left and then the right strands.

Single cording [half hitches]

This can be used to cover one or, when used for finishing or if a heavy cord is required, numerous strands (fig. 6).

6. *Single cording [half hitches]*

Worked over more than 2.5cm (1″) it makes an attractive spiral.

Joining

When making chains of flat [square] knots, the outer strands are often used up much more quickly than the centre ones and so either a knot can be introduced which uses only two strands or more strands can be added. Strands can be added at any time while making the fabric either to make a more complex design, to increase the size of the article or to replenish strands which have been used up.
To join new strands, overlap the ends of the old and new strands by 5cm (2″) and make 2 or 3 knots using both strands. Trim the ends close to the knots and continue knotting with the new strand. If possible, stagger the joining of the strands so that two are not joined in the same chain at the same time.

Hanging plant basket

To make a hanging basket 57cm (23″) long and 10cm (4″) diameter, to take a flower pot 12cm (5″) in diameter.
You will need:
18 strands of No. 2 unfinished cotton string, cut into 3.5m (10′) lengths, and a piece 28cm (11″) long.
6cm (2½″) diameter curtain ring.
Clear glue.
□ Mount the string on the curtain ring.
□ Overlap the ends of the 28cm (11″) length of string by 2cm (¾″) and secure them with sticky tape.
□ Hold the ring between your knees or tie it to an immovable object. Loop the circle of string over the ring and place it just below the knotting strands.
1st row. Make cording [double half hitches] over the knot bearer (fig.7).

2nd row. Arrange the pairs of strands into groups containing 4 strands (fig. 7). Make a chain of 4 flat [square] knots with each group.

7. *Cording over string knot bearer.*

3rd row. Take the 2 right strands from one group and the 2 left strands from the adjacent group and make a chain of 4 flat [square] knots with these. Regroup the remaining strnads and make 4 flat [square] knots with each group.
4th row. Regroup the strands and make 4 flat [square] knots with each.
□ Hold 2 chains of flat [square] knots and use all 8 strands to make 2 flat [square] knots, making each loop with 2 strands over 4 central strands.
□ Miss the next chain of flat [square] knots and work 2 large flat [square] knots with the next pair of flat [square] knot chains. Make a total of 3 pairs of flat [square] knots with 3 single flat [square] knot chains between them.
□ Working on the double flat [square] knot chains, divide each into the original groups of 4 strands and make 4 flat [square] knots. Using centre 2 strands, make a knotted chain (fig.5). Still working on the same strands, make an overhand knot 10cm (4″) from each end. Knot the other strands.
□ With the remaining 3 single flat [square] knot chains, make the handle.
To make a handle leave about 27cm (11″) of unworked string. Make 4 flat [square] knots with each group.
Using sticky tape bind all strands together for 5cm (2″) immediately above the flat [square] knots. Trim away all but 3 of the longest strands just above the sticky tape.
□ Use one strand to bind the other 2 strands with single cording [half hitches] (fig. 6) for a length of 13cm (5″) from the end of the sticky tape to make the handle. Loop the knotted strand and tape the ends of the two shortest ones to the taped section.
□ Using the remaining strand, make a single cording [half hitch] knot and wind it around until all the sticky tape is covered.
□ Make a single cording [half hitch] knot to secure the strand and trim, leaving a 2.5cm (1″) end. Dab glue on

8. *Completing the handle.*

the end and, using a hairpin [bobby pin], push the end inside the sticky tape. A handle can be made in this way with any number of strands as the core. When the glue has hardened, the basket is ready.

Hanging fruit basket

For a hanging basket 1m (3′) long and 25cm (10″) in diameter, to hold a 27cm (11″) bowl or basket up to 12cm (5″) deep. To adjust size add or subtract two extra strands.

You will need:
1 ball of parcel or gardening twine.
32 white rotelle beads.
18mm (¾″) curtain ring.
Clear glue.
☐ Cut the twine into 8 strands, each 3.5m (11′) long.
☐ Mount the yarn on the ring (fig. 1).
☐ Hold the ring between your knees or tie it to an immovable object.
1st row. Arrange the pairs of strands into groups containing 4 strands. Make 6 flat knots with each group (figs. 3 and 4).
2nd row. Take the 2 right strands from one group and the 2 left strands from the neighbouring group and make one flat [square] knot 5cm (2″) from the chain of flat [square] knots. Regroup the remaining strands, making one flat [square] knot with them 5cm (2″) from the flat [square] knot chains.
3rd row. Regroup the strands and make one flat [square] knot 7cm (3″) from the second row.
4th row. Regroup the strands again and make 2 flat [square] knots 10cm (4″) from the third row.
5th row. Regroup the strands and make 2 flat [square] knots 10cm (4″) from the fourth row.
☐ Thread a bead over the centre 2 strands of each group of flat square knots. If this is difficult, wrap sticky tape over the ends of the twine so they do not fray.
☐ Make half a flat [square] knot and thread another bead on the centre strands.
☐ Make 2 flat [square] knots with each group.
☐ Make a spiral using flat [square] knots, 17cm (7″) in length, or until the strands are about 2.5cm (1″) long. Using a long centre strand, cover the

other long strand and the short ends with single cording [half hitches] (fig.6) for 10cm (4″). Repeat with all other strands.
☐ Cut 4 more strands of twine each 1.5m (5′) long.
☐ Mount each strand on the top loop of the fourth row of flat [square] knots.
☐ Thread a bead on one strand and make 3 single cording [half hitch] knots with the same strand. Thread another bead on the other strand and make 3 single cording [half hitch] knots. Do this 3 more times using each strand alternately. Finish with a bead. Repeat with the other extra strands.
☐ Make a knotted chain (fig.5) with each pair of strands, 37cm (15″) long or until they are almost used up.
☐ Hold all the strands together that you used for making the spirals and allow the knotted chains to hang down.

Hanging plant basket, designed by Shelley Churchman, and fruit basket both save space and look attractive.

☐ Take one of the long strands that you are holding and cover all the strands for 10cm (4″) with single cording [half hitch] knots, pulling them very firmly.
☐ Position the knotted chains between the spirals and hold them just above the single cording [half hitches]. Use the same strand with which you were making single cording [half hitches] and make single cording knots over all the ends, catching the last knots of the knotted chains.
☐ Make single cording [half hitch] knots until the ends of the chains are covered.
☐ Make a handle in same way as for hanging plant basket.

Pegged rag rugs

A really economical method of making rugs is discussed here. It is the quick and simple pegged technique, also known as the proddy, clippy or—in northern Britain—the stobby technique.

The basic materials are the same as for hooked rugs: rags or yarn and a hessian [burlap] foundation. The difference lies in the way the rags are inserted to form the pile.

Hooked rugs are worked with the right side of the foundation facing up. The rags are cut into strips held below the fabric and a hook is then used to pull them through to the right side in loops which form the pile.

Pegged rugs are worked with the wrong side of the foundation facing up. The rag strips are cut into tabs— pieces about 5cm (2″) long—and the ends of the tabs are pushed or prodded through hessian [burlap] from the top to form a cut pile on the right side.

Hooked rugs are generally more hard wearing than pegged rugs, but pegging is less physically tiring and designs can be more intricate than is possible by hooking. The amounts of rags required are approximately the same for both methods.

Pegs. The implement used for prodding is a round, pointed peg, usually made from wood, about 10cm (4″) long and 1cm (⅜″) diameter. You can buy the pegs ready made or you could make your own by shaping the end of a piece of dowel rod with a file. (Years ago the small horn of an animal or a fragment of an antler might have been used to make a peg.)

Designs

Designs for pegged rugs can be quite ambitious because the tufts of pile are inserted individually, and it does not make much difference to the ease of working whether successive tufts are in the same or different fabrics. (With hooked rugs, designs have areas of one colour because a series of tufts is made from one fabric strip.)

You could adapt a design for a latch-hooked or needlepoint rug, you could make your own design, or you can sometimes buy hessian [burlap] specially printed with a design.

Cumbrian bull, designed by Denis Barker. The rug is made from rag strips which are prodded through a hessian [burlap] foundation with a wooden peg.

Your own design. The method you use for planning your own design depends on the type of design. Simple or pictorial designs can be sketched on to paper and then enlarged to scale on the hessian [burlap] foundation of the rug itself.

Use felt-tipped pen or chalk to draw the design on the hessian [burlap]. If you are including any lettering, this should be drawn in mirror image because the rug is worked with the reverse side facing up.

For intricate geometric and oriental-style designs you could work out the design on graph paper so that one square represents one double tuft of pile. On a double-pegged rug (the method which produces the closest pile—see box) each square would also represent two threads of the hessian [burlap]. On a single-pegged rug (the method which produces a looser pile) each square would represent four threads of hessian [burlap].

The paper design can then be used as a working chart because it would be too complicated and time-consuming to draw it on the foundation.

Preparing the tabs

Cut the fabric on the straight grain into strips about 1.2cm (½″) wide for double pegging or up to 2.5cm (1″) wide for single pegging, and as long as the available rags will allow.

To cut the strips into tabs, wind them round a piece of 12mm x 4cm (½″x1½″) grooved wood and cut along the grooved edge with a handyman's knife (fig.1a). Alternatively, fold a piece of strawboard to 6.5cm (2½″) wide and cut along the open side with shears.

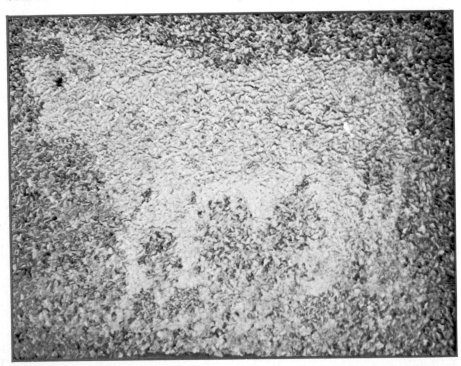

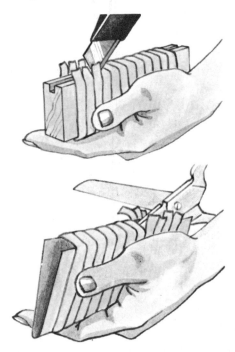

1a, b. *Cutting rag strips into tabs.*

Pegging the tabs

The hessian [burlap] should be mounted in a frame so the strips can be pegged through easily. If you are going to fold over the edges first, place the fabric in the frame with the raw edges of the hessian [burlap] facing up. There are two methods of pegging—double, which produces the most hard-wearing pile because the tabs are tightly packed, and single, which is quicker to do but less hard-wearing because the tabs are more widely spaced. Fig. 2 shows the two methods. Both forms of pegging are worked in rows across the width of the foundation to form an even close pile, changing colours as needed to fit the design.

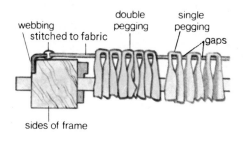

2. *Double and single pegging.*

Sheep in the snow, by Denis Barker, was inspired by English Cumbrian scenery.

Double pegging. Push the point of the peg through the fabric to make a hole in the position for the first tuft (fig. 3).

☐ Following fig. 4, fold the end of the first tab and push it through the hole with the peg. Use the fingers of your free hand to pull it half-way through.

☐ Make a second hole with the peg two threads of fabric along the row (fig. 5) and prod the other end of the tab through (fig. 6). Use the fingers of your free hand to pull the ends of the tab on the underside evenly into place.

☐ Prod the end of the next tab into the second hole (with the first tab) and pull halfway through (fig.7). Make a third hole two threads of fabric further on and prod through the other end of the second tab (fig.8). Continue in this way along the row.

☐ Work the next and subsequent rows in the same way, leaving two threads of hessian [burlap] between each row.

Single pegging. This gives a less dense and also less hard-wearing pile. The tabs can be up to 2.5cm (1″) wide.

☐ Insert the first tab as described for double pegging. Insert the following tab as for the first one, but leave two threads of hessian [burlap] between each tab.

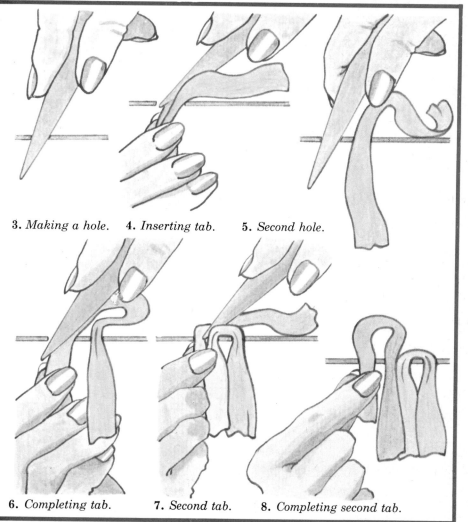

3. *Making a hole.*   4. *Inserting tab.*   5. *Second hole.*

6. *Completing tab.*   7. *Second tab.*   8. *Completing second tab.*

Pile rugs

Rugs made by the latch-hook method using Turkey wool are thick and hard-wearing.

A large rug need not take too long to make if two people work it simultaneously from opposite ends of the canvas, using both forms of the knot described on page 161.

Straight-sided rugs

Starting off. For a rug with straight sides, place the canvas on a table with the selvedges to your left and right and with the full length away from you.

As you progress, roll up the worked section so you do not have to lean over it to reach the row on which you are working.

To make a neat strong edge, turn up the cut end nearest you for about 5cm (2″) and fold it down so that the holes match the holes underneath exactly. Tack [baste] the edge in position. The first rows of knots are worked on the weft threads through double thickness. Leave the first two rows of holes in from the folded edge and one at each side of the canvas and work the first line of knots on the next weft thread from left to right (fig.1) or right to left if you are left-handed.

1. *Starting place for the first row of knots with a margin left for the edging.*

Work the second and subsequent rows on the following weft threads, leaving one hole at each selvedge, to within 5cm (2″) of the required length.

Finishing off. When the worked area of the rug is 5cm (2″) shorter than the required length, turn up the surplus canvas on to the right side and work the remaining rows of knots through the double thickness. Leave the last row of holes free for the edging.

Working the edging. To give a firm finish to the folded edges and to neaten the selvedge, a row of oversewing [overcasting] should be worked all round the edge of the rug. Use a carpet needle with a large eye and a skein of yarn in a colour to match or blend in with the colour used at the edge of the rug. The edging stitching is worked from left to right with the back of the rug facing up.

□ Hold the end of the yarn to the right so that it will be covered by the stitching, insert the needle into the first hole (it doesn't matter where you start) and work a few oversewing stitches over the outside thread of canvas to cover the yarn end.

□ Pull the needle through the same hole towards you, move to the fourth hole to the right, taking the yarn over the outside canvas thread and through the hole towards you (fig.2).

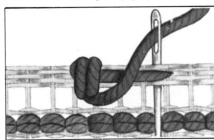

2. *Covering the tail of yarn.*

□ Take the yarn over the canvas thread at the top of the fourth hole, go back to the second hole and pull out the yarn towards you (fig.3).

3. *Starting the plaited edging.*

□ Take the yarn to the fifth hole, back to the third and so on in this way all round the edge.

Many attractive latch-hook rug designs, like this one by Rugplan, are inspired by classic Oriental patterns.

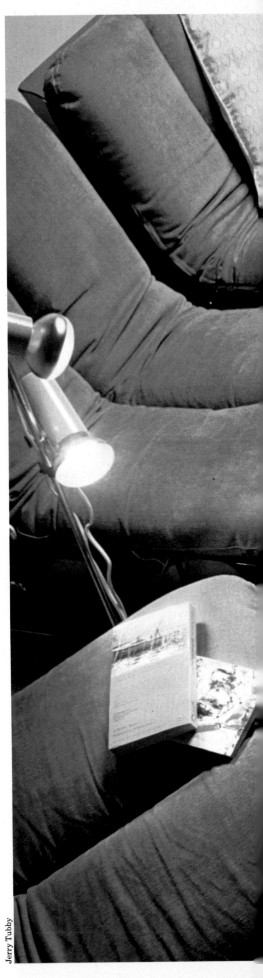

Barbara Firth

Jerry Tubby

154

Blue and yellow rug

Completed size: 90cm x 178cm (36″ x 70″).

You will need:

Canvas, 1.83m (2yd) of 90cm (36″) rug canvas, 10 holes per 7.5cm (3″).

Yarn, cut packs rug yarn (320 pieces per pack)—see chart.

2 skeins background colour for edging.

☐ Prepare the canvas as described overleaf, but turning up the cut edge for 2.5cm (1″) only.

Using the chart. The chart shows one quarter of the rug only, because the pattern is repeated on each of the remaining three quarters. Work the first row from left to right, following the chart and working the colours as shown in the key.

☐ When you reach the centre of the row complete it, still working from left to right but following the chart

Above: the back of the blue and gold rug showing how the pattern is repeated, in mirror image, on each quarter. When you have finished the rug, it is advisable to check from the back for missed knots and other mistakes.

Side edge

First knot first quarter

First knot second quarter

Centre

Colour	Symbol	No. of cut packs
Primrose yellow		2
Antique gold	○	24
Sun yellow	□	4
Dark blue	■	24
Mid blue	●	38

from right to left so that the mirror image is formed.

☐ When you have completed half the rug, turn the chart around.

Working from right to left, but following the same principle as before, repeat the last row worked. Work back to row one, working the last few rows through doubled canvas.

☐ Work round the rug in edging stitch.

Below: the chart for the blue and gold rug, showing a quarter of the design. To work the mirror image for the remaining quarter of the first half, work the knots from the centre outwards. For the second half turn the chart upside down and work as the first half.

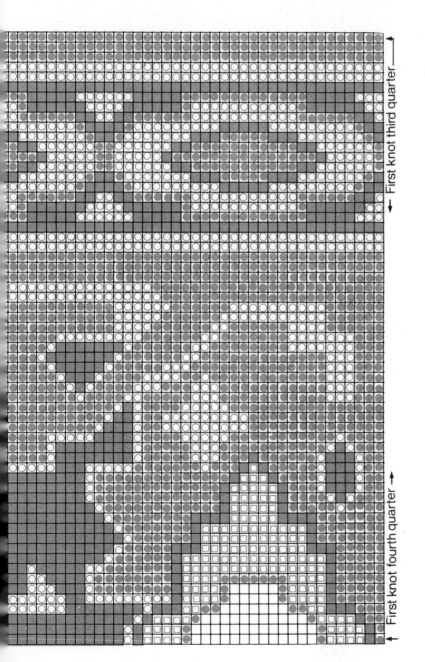

First knot third quarter →

First knot fourth quarter →

Round rugs

Starting off. Mark the area of the rug on the canvas in felt-tipped pen. Do not trim the canvas until the pile has been worked. Work the pile in straight rows across the marked area. None of the rows is worked through double thickness of canvas.

Semi-circular rugs. Mark the shape of the rug so that the straight edge lies along the selvedge of the canvas.

Finishing off. To make a neat, strong finish for round rugs (or for the curved edge of a semi-circular rug) you will need a length of carpet tape, 2.5cm (1″) wide, to fit the circumference plus 5cm (2″) for turnings [seam allowances]. The carpet tape is attached with strong sewing thread, such as linen carpet thread, and a large needle.

Trim spare canvas (fig.4a) to within 2.5cm (1″) of the pile. Fold under the unworked canvas on to the wrong side of the rug and pin on the carpet binding so that it is 6mm (¼″) in from fold (4b). Hem outer edge of the tape in place firmly using the strong thread. Pin the slight fullness which will have formed along the inner edge of the tape into darts and then hem the edge into place (fig.4c).

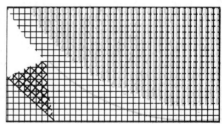

4a. *Trimming the surplus canvas to within 2.5cm (1″) of the knots.*

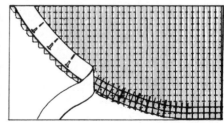

4b. *Pinning carpet tape to the folded edge of canvas.*

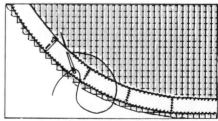

4c. *Hemming the inner edge of tape with the slight fullness formed into darts.*

Barbara Firth

157

Latch-hooked rugs

Rugs can be woven, knotted, hooked, stitched and even plaited, knitted and crocheted. With all the methods you can use new materials or you can recycle old fabrics and yarns to make hard-wearing and attractive floor coverings.

In one traditional method of rug-making the foundation is woven on a loom and the pile threads are knotted on to it by hand. A variation of this

method, which is simple to do at home, is to buy a woven canvas foundation and insert the pile into it with a latch-hook.

Equipment

Latch-hooks look like crochet hooks but have a wooden handle and a hinged latch which closes round the hook to prevent it from being caught in the canvas as the knot is formed. Latch-hooks are not expensive and can be bought from most handicraft shops. They are easy to use and once you get into a rhythm the rug grows quite quickly. For extra speed, you could buy a second hook so that two people can work on the rug at the same time, by working from opposite ends of the canvas.

The yarn. For making a short-pile rug you can buy a special coarse 6-ply rug wool—often called Turkey wool—or a 3-ply acrylic yarn. Both types of yarn are available in skeins which you cut to the length you want or they can be bought in packs of 320 pre-cut pieces, 7cm (2¾″) long. Each piece makes one knot with two strands of pile about 2cm (¾″) long and one pack of wool covers just over three 7.5cm (3″) square blocks on standard rug canvas.

The advantage of buying the cut packs is, of course, that you are saved the trouble of cutting the pieces yourself. On the other hand, you are restricted to the same length of pile throughout and some of the most unusual designs include areas of different pile height. You will in any case have to buy some skeins of uncut yarn in order to finish the edges of the canvas.

Cutting your own pile. When calculating the length of each strand, remember that each strand forms two lengths of pile and the knot uses up about 3cm (1¼″) of yarn. Therefore for a 5cm (2″) length of pile, for example, you should cut the pieces 13cm (5¼″) long.

To cut the pieces in this case, use a piece of firm cardboard 6.5cm (2⅝″) wide and wind the yarn round it. Cut yarn along one edge of the card.

Canvas with holes large enough to take the thick rug wool is often known as Turkey or Smyrna canvas. It is woven with double threads for strength and has 10 holes to 7.5cm (3″). It can be bought in different widths from 30.5cm-122cm (12″-48″).

To make counting individual squares easier, the canvas is divided into blocks of 7.5cm (3″), marked by different-coloured thread, usually red or brown. If you are making a rectangular or square rug you should buy the exact

Latch-hooking is a relaxing pastime and a quick and easy way of making fabric with a thick, hard-wearing pile, ideal for rugs and cushions.

width you want by 10cm (4″) longer than the required length. For round rugs and cushions of any shape you should buy an amount which is at least 10cm (4″) more than the required diameter.

Re-cycling materials. The latch-hook method can also be used for re-cycling strips of old fabrics and yarn. Before you start work you should experiment to see how wide the fabric strips should be cut or how many strands of yarn you would need in each knot in order to cover the canvas satisfactorily. With a double-knitting yarn, for example, you would probably need three or four strands in each knot.

The design

Short-pile, latch-hooked rugs lend themselves well to pictorial and oriental designs, and other attractive rugs can be based simply on geometric patterns or subtle blends of colour which may not form a definite pattern. In the same way as for needlepoint, it is possible to buy the canvas already printed with the design together with the necessary amount of yarn.

Alternatively you can choose a design printed on a chart or you could adapt a chart designed for needlepoint on a finer canvas, but you should avoid those with very fine detail as they lose their subtlety because of the thickness of the yarn and the pile. Or, if you are more ambitious, you could make up your own design.

Making your own design. Whether you choose an elaborate theme or prefer a more random effect it is advisable to work out your design to scale to give you the chance to adapt and improve your design before you start

Latch-hooking equipment—the latch-hook, Turkey canvas and cut yarn. The 7.5cm (3″) grid is marked by the coloured weft and warp threads which divide the canvas into 10-hole blocks.

work. You will also be able to work out how much of each colour yarn to buy, so that you do not run the risk of having to use yarn from different dye lots, and you will be able to work the knots across the rug in straight lines from one end of the canvas.

If instead you work areas of colour and then fill in the background, the result is likely to be uneven and you might miss squares because they are hidden by other knots. The exception to this is with geometric designs where you could work the basic outline first and then fill in the areas enclosed by it.

Transferring the design. Intricate designs can be transferred on to the canvas in various ways, such as by using paint to shade in the areas of colour. Or else, for less complicated designs which have bold outlines or large areas of one colour, you can trace the design on to the canvas with felt-tipped pen.

Calculating the amount of yarn. The only sure way of calculating the amount of yarn for each different colour in an intricate design is to count the number of knots to be worked. Draw out the design on graph paper and draw on your design to scale so that each square represents one hole on the canvas.

For less intricate designs where you are working large areas in one colour, it is normally possible to gauge the amount of yarn required by measuring each area.

Basic knots

Four-movement knot

The quickest knot consists of four movements.

Fig.1 Fold the cut length of wool in half and loop it round the neck of the hook below the crook and latch.

Fig.2 Holding the ends of the wool between the thumb and index finger of your left hand, insert the hook under the first of the weft threads (those running from left to right, across the canvas).

Fig.3 Turn the hook a little to the right, open the latch and place the ends of the wool into the hook.

Fig.4 Pull the hook under the thread and through the loop of wool. As you pull, the latch will close to prevent the hook from getting caught in the canvas.

Fig.5 Pull the ends of the wool tightly to make the knot firm.

Five-movement knot

When two people are working from opposite ends, one person should use the five-movement knot so the pile will lie in the same direction.

Fig.6 Insert the hook under the first weft thread. Fold the cut length of wool in half and, holding the ends between your thumb and index finger, loop it over the hook.

Cushions

The latch-hook method makes attractive and hard-wearing cushions, such as the floor cushion shown in the photograph. The pile can be worked on both sides of the cushion or, if you prefer, you could make the back of the cushion from fabric.

Starting and finishing. Because the raw edges are enclosed inside the finished cushion, you can leave an unworked margin of canvas for 2.5cm (1″) all round and use this for your turnings [seam allowances] when making up the cushion. Or, if the size of the cushion corresponds to the width of canvas available, work the knots up to the selvedges and use the selvedges as a narrow turning. Allow 2.5cm (1″) at each raw edge for turnings because the canvas may fray.

Sun floor cushion

These instructions are for a cushion 90cm (36″) square but they can be adapted for a smaller cushion by reducing the quantities proportionally.

You will need:

Canvas, 1 metre (39″) of 90cm (36″) rug canvas, 10 holes per 7.5cm (3″).

Rug yarn, (320 pieces per pack): 12 cut packs green; 10 cut packs yellow; 7 cut packs orange; 18 cut packs off-white.

Latch-hook.

Jerry Tubby

The simple sun motif makes a luxurious indoor or outdoor floor cushion: you can choose a colour for the border to tie in with your scheme. The yarn illustrated is Pingouin Tapis acrylic in green (shade 168), yellow (shade 161), orange (shade 152) and off-white (shade 105).

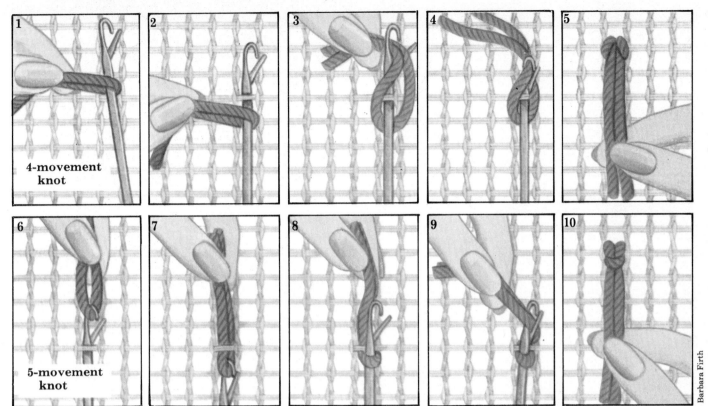

4-movement knot (panel 1)

5-movement knot (panel 6)

Barbara Firth

Fig.7 Pull the hook back through the canvas.
Fig.8 Push the hook through the loop of wool until the latch is clear and the loop is on the neck of the hook.
Fig.9 Place the cut ends of wool into the crook of the hook from below, so they are enclosed by the latch.
Pull the hook back firmly through the loop of wool until the ends are clear.
Fig.10 Pull the ends of the wool tightly to secure the knot.

Backing fabric, 1 metre (39″) square such as hessian [burlap] or velvet. Matching sewing thread, needle.
Felt-tipped pens in colours to match yarns.
Cushion pad, 90cm (36″) square.
☐ Enlarge the design of the sun (at the right) to scale and mark in its colours with felt-tip pens. Centre rug canvas over the design and trace the shapes of the areas in the appropriate colours. Leave the blank canvas at each edge for the turnings [seam allowances]
☐ Work the knots in straight rows across the canvas.
Making up. Stitch back of cushion to canvas, with right sides facing, by machining with a piping foot along the line of canvas nearest the first and last rows of knots and along the inside edge of one of the selvedges. Leave the remaining side open.
Trim the raw edges to within 1.5cm (½″) of the stitching. Do not trim the selvedges.
☐ Turn the cushion cover right side out and press the seams with your fingers.
☐ Insert the cushion pad, fold under turnings [seam allowances] along open side and slip stitch firmly.

Graph pattern for cushion. You will find that most rug canvas is woven with a 7.5cm (3″) grid line.

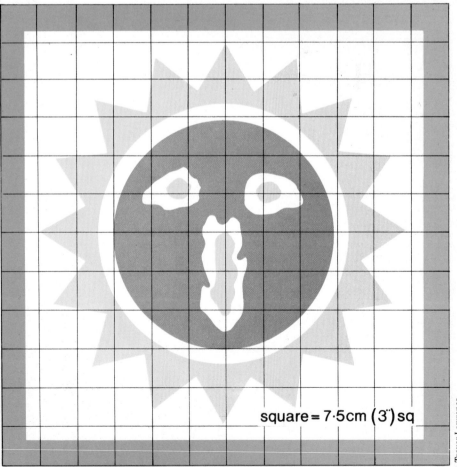

square = 7·5cm (3″)sq

Trevor Lawrence

Colourcrafts

Colour is fun, and a sense of colour is an invaluable skill
for all crafts. The following projects help you achieve
beautiful effects with dyes and paints.

Potato printing

Potato printing means, quite literally, using potatoes as printing blocks to stamp designs on to other surfaces. It is remarkably inexpensive and allows you a wide variety of designs that can be reproduced on paper, fabric, wood or even plastic.

Potatoes are an alternative to costly printing equipment and tools. Using only a kitchen knife you can cut motifs that can be stamped again and again. Moreover, designs do not have to be limited to the size of a potato since a larger design can be built up by repeating a single motif a number of times. Alternatively, a larger design can be made by using several different motifs together.

The low cost of materials make potato printing blocks suitable both for beginners and for people who want to experiment with designs. If one block doesn't work it is easy and cheap to make another one.

Making blocks

To make a printing block, wash, peel and cut a potato in half crosswise. Cut in a sawing motion to get a flat surface. This is the surface that will be used to print.

Cutting motifs

Motifs can be cut in several ways. So before you begin choose the one that best suits your design.

A motif can be incised into the potato by making V-shaped cuts with a knife

1. *Potatoes cut into geometric shapes.*

and gouging out the motif. Linoleum or woodcutting tools can also be used. If you use this method the surface that will receive colour is the area *surrounding* the design—the design itself is recessed.

The reverse of this method is also possible. By carving out the area surrounding the design, the motif you want to print will be left in high relief to receive colour.

Most potatoes are roughly egg-shaped. When cut in half an approximate circle is revealed which can be used to print similar rounded shapes like apples and plums, the sun and the centres of large flowers.

But the technique that gives the greatest scope for printing with potatoes involves cutting the whole piece into a geometric shape as in fig. 1. This way you get a number of forms—lines, squares, dots, triangles—that can be used repeatedly to produce a single larger shape or abstract design. By cutting the whole piece you also get a sharper printing edge and can see the rest of the design on the surface while you are printing. It is also easier to identify different blocks.

2. *These designs were made from one potato block (insert) printed in different directions. Top right: the block has been repeated several times in the same position. Far left: half the motifs are printed in as before and half are turned 90° to the left. The final design shows the block in four different angles.*

Opposite: potato printing gives a fresh simplicity to all sorts of objects as the stationery ideas show.

About paint

Any paint that mixes with water is suitable for potato printing. The potato itself contains water and, for this reason, oil-bound paints or printing inks cannot be used.

Watercolours, poster paints and tempera are all suitable for printing on paper and can be applied to the potato block with a brush or by using a piece of sponge as a stamping pad. To waterproof poster or watercolours on paper or card, spray with an artwork lacquer, obtainable at art shops.

Acrylic polymer paint is excellent for most surfaces, being naturally waterproof and hardwearing. It has to be applied with a brush as the paint dries too quickly to use the sponge method.

Fabric paste dyes are very satisfactory for printing on cloth, but bear in mind that these are dyes, not paints, and by printing one colour over another you will produce a third, since they will blend together. This method can be used successfully with a little foresight. Cold water dyes designed for use on natural fibres—cotton, wool, linen, silk—and on viscose rayon, should be used to get colour-fast results.

Apply the colour to the printing blocks with a paintbrush.

To print

Cover the surface of your printing block with colour and press it down firmly but gently on to the surface you wish to print.

If the motif is to be repeated, then recolour the block before you print again. This will ensure an even colour throughout. Alternatively, you can get variations in intensity by printing several times without recharging the block with colour.

As a general rule it is advisable to make a block for every colour you will need. Potatoes are fairly absorbent and the residue from the first colour may show through if another is used on the same block. If you are skilful, however, you can use two separate colours side by side on one block.

Always cut new blocks each day as potatoes tend to lose their firmness.

To make table mats

The table mats shown are made with a combination of simple printing methods, but primarily using potatoes. They are made in linen but cotton fabric of a similar weight will do.

You will need:
Sheet of drawing paper.
Black fibre pen.
Linen or cotton for mats.
Old newspaper.
Potatoes.
Carrots.
Fabric paste dyes.

☐ Trace the basic outlines of the mats you are going to print on to and enlarge them proportionately. Sketch the outline with a black pen.

☐ Put a magazine or pad of newspaper on your work table. Lay the outline on top of it and then put the linen mat over this. The heavy black outline can be seen through the linen and acts as a guide.

☐ To make the basket print rectangular and square shapes cut from potatoes and carrots.

☐ The peaches are simply potatoes cut in half and painted in two colours. The red and orange are merged slightly to get the special shading effects.

☐ To print the grapes use your finger to make finger prints.

☐ The leaves can be produced by painting in the leaf shape shown.

☐ When thoroughly dry, iron the mats according to the manufacturer's instructions to fix the dyes. Then work a line of stitching all around each mat and fray the fabric up to this line to make a fringe.

Janet Allen

3. *The designs on the left illustrate some of the great variety of patterns that can be produced from a single printing block. Like all designs in this chapter, they are by Janet Allen.*

Opposite: the vivid patterns on the mats are made from potatoes and carrots and from finger prints. The peaches are halves of potatoes, the grapes finger marks.

Block printing

Relief printing using fruit and vegetables is a basic printing technique, making use of the intrinsic designs of nature and simple printing procedures. Try your hand at relief printing with these glass mats which, together with the shopping bag overleaf, were designed by Janet Allen.

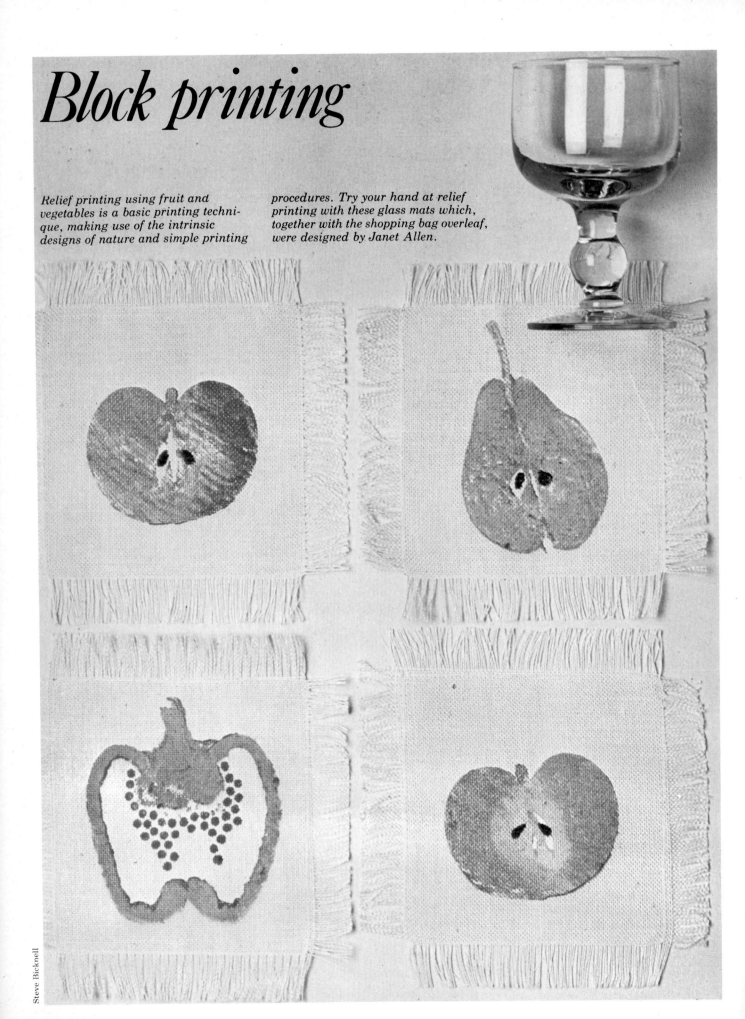

To put it at its simplest, relief printing usually involves applying colour to one surface and pressing the colour on to another surface. You can print on to all sorts of surfaces including paper, cloth and walls: the type of paint or ink you choose will depend on what you are printing.

Most relief printing methods involve the making of a printing block, but there are some objects—such as fruits—which in themselves are ready-made printing blocks.

Numerous fruits and vegetables have attractive shapes and inherent patterns. If, for example, you cut horizontally across an onion you reveal an eminently printable pattern of rings. Cut it vertically and you have another kind of pattern. The fruits or vegetables need to be fairly hard and firm—a tomato, for instance, is far too squashy—but apples, pears, cabbages, leeks and celery are a few of the suitable types.

Paints, inks and dyes

Water-solvent paints. For relief printing poster paint or powder colours should be of a thick consistency. Block printing watercolours may be used undiluted. You only require water for cleaning up afterwards. The colour can be applied with a stiff brush or you can use a sponge pad which is impregnated with colour and used as a stamping pad. These paints are not washable and are therefore really only suitable for paper. Paper printed with water-solvent colour may be varnished (when the print is absolutely dry) with paper varnish. This prolongs its life and makes it waterproof.

Oil-bound printing ink and fabric printing colours work best on fruit and vegetables if diluted with a very little white spirit. These inks are waterproof and fabric printing colours are washable. They require white spirit for cleaning up afterwards.

Fabric printing dyes are suitable for large, broad shapes but are slightly too liquid to pick up intricate patterns with this kind of printing. These dyes are washable and can be fixed by ironing the fabric. Use a temperature suitable for the type of fabric. Manufacturers give details of fixing procedures for their particular dyes.

Papers and fabrics

Do not use a non-absorbent, glossy paper because your printing object will tend to slide when you press it down. Newsprint is ideal for trial prints but it is inclined to become yellow within a short time and is easily torn. After first experimenting on cheap newsprint or newspaper, use a cartridge type of paper. Coloured papers can add interest to the design.

This method of relief printing requires the minimum of equipment.

Melvin Grey

The fabric printing colours and dyes work best on natural fibre fabrics. Some man-made fibre fabrics are not fast to washing or cleaning when printed. If in doubt, test a piece of printed fabric first. Cloth with a heavy starch dressing should first be washed and ironed before printing.

Preparing the fruit and vegetables

Have ready plenty of table space, a chopping board, a selection of sharp kitchen knives and some rags.

Experiment by cutting your fruits and vegetables in half, into quarters, diagonally across and at different points. Do not remove any peel or skin as it both defines the shape and helps to hold the cut piece together.

Most fruits and vegetables are rather wet when cut so it is advisable to dry them first gently with a rag.

To make the glass mats

You will need:

Firm pear and apple and a green pepper, all with good, clear shapes

Sharp knife

Fabric printing dyes

Stiff brush (eg small house-painting brush); small artist's paintbrush

Suitable fabric such as linen (enough for 4 squares, allowing an extra 5cm (2″) all round each one)

Scraps of fabric for trial prints

Rags and old blanket or piece of felt

Needle and thread

☐ Determine how large you want the mats to be and cut the linen into squares 5cm (2″) larger all round than final size—you will trim them down after printing. This makes it easier to centre the motif accurately. The mats shown here are 15cm (6″) square, including a 2cm (¾″) fringe.

☐ Place a piece of felt or blanket on a table to give some softness underneath the fabric being printed. Place your fabric on top of this.

☐ Slice the fruit or vegetable in half and carefully dry the cut surface.

☐ Apply the dye fairly liberally with the stiff brush and do a test print first on a scrap of fabric.

You may want to apply more than one colour, as shown on the apple prints. To do this, simply apply your chosen colours next to each other and gently blend the edges where they meet, using light, even strokes. The colours will merge into each other and you will ob-

tain the best results if you use colours which, when mixed, produce an intermediate colour which suits your print. For instance, on one of the apple prints red merges into orange via a reddish-orange. On the other apple print orange merges through yellow to green; both the mixture of orange and yellow and that of yellow and green produce acceptable intermediate colours. If you apply orange immediately next to green, the area where they mix will become brown and rather dark.

You can experiment with blending colour with dyes on paper. You may become interested in the whole fascinating subject of colour theory. If so, your local library should be able to provide some useful reading on the subject.

When printing, do not bang the fruit down as it may slide around, but carefully place it and apply gentle, even pressure. Some parts such as stalks will need to be pressed down with the end of a pencil. Lift the fruit away from the fabric very carefully.

☐ When you are confident of how much dye to apply and how hard to press to get an even print, go on to make your final prints.

☐ Paint the seeds in afterwards with a paintbrush or, as with the green pepper, with the end of a matchstick.

☐ When the prints are completely dry, iron the fabric to fix the dye.

☐ With a pencil dot at each corner mark the size of square required, excluding the fringe (11cm (4½″) square in the mats illustrated). You may find it

Eyecatching shopping bag—printed with halved fruits or vegetables—makes plain denim look really special.

easier to cut a square of cardboard to the size required: slide it under the fabric and centre your motif. Mark each corner of the square with a dot.

☐ Machine stitch from dot to dot, outlining the inner square.

☐ Mark another square, 2cm (¾″) larger all round, and cut the mats to this size.

☐ Now fray the cloth from the cut edge to the line of stitching to make a fringe all round.

To make a shopping bag
You will need:
53cm (21″) of 90cm (36″) wide denim,

170

linen, thick calico or other similar light-coloured material.

☐ Cut a piece of fabric 90cm x 45cm (36"x18") for the body of the bag and reserve the strip left over for the handles.

The selvedges or 45cm (18") edges form the top edges of the bag.

☐ To find the position for the base of the pears, measure 38cm (15") down from one top edge at each side and mark with a pin. As a guide line pin a strip of paper from side to side at position of pins, to mark the base line of the pears. There is no need for a pencil line which might be difficult to erase later. Print the pears as described for the glass mats.

☐ Mark a 10cm (4") turning along each top edge with a line of running stitches. Take the long strip of fabric and fold in half lengthwise, right sides together. Stitch down long edge, turn right side out and press. Topstitch along sides about 6mm (¼") in from the edge. Cut the strip in half.

☐ Stitch handles to bag as shown, turning raw ends under (fig.1).

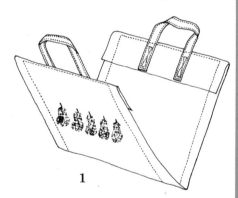

1

Work topstitching round edges of bag.

☐ Turn under top edges of bag along marked line. Pin in place and press along fold edge.

☐ Work lines of topstitching along the top of the bag edges close to the fold, and down the sides 2.5cm (1") in from the edge.

☐ Fold the bag in half, right sides together, and stitch sides closed taking a 12mm (½") seam allowance. Press seams open and turn right sides out.

Positioning prints with paper strip.

You can quite simply obtain beautiful printed patterns from most fruit and vegetables. Look closely at those you use everyday and, as you cut them up, think of how they would print and the way colour could be used to heighten the effect. The diagram below shows the various cuts and their respective printed effects, all from one leek. Try an onion cut across the middle or even walnut shells or mushrooms.

Cut 1: the tips of the leaves

Cut 2: across the middle

Cut 3: lengthwise

Cut 4: on the diagonal

Cut 5: across the base

Cut 5 printed side-by-side

Janet Allen

171

Simple marbling

Marbling is one of the simplest, most enjoyable and decorative methods of colouring surfaces. With the minimum of skill you can produce bright and lively patterns which are unobtainable by any other means.

Marbling is so called because the wavy and veined patterns which are often produced bear a resemblance to those of true marble. But this simulation is only one way of using the marbling technique because the swirling shapes and patterns you can produce are without limit.

As a general definition, marbling is the creation of designs or patterns on water which are transferred on to other materials. This description, however, leaves a lot unsaid as few other decorative processes give the user such a unique control of colours, yet allow such freedom of movement and creative arrangement of the pattern before the print is made. The final pattern is almost entirely dependent upon the taste and skill of the individual.

Origins of marbling

Marbling is one of the earliest forms of paper decoration and is thought to have originated in Turkey. The first examples imported into Europe were used to line boxes holding chessmen and dominoes. At one time the best marbled paper was produced in Holland and exported to England wrapped round small parcels of toys to enable it to pass free of duty. On arrival, it was carefully removed from the toys, flattened and sold, mainly to bookbinders for use in their finest bindings. Marbling is still associated with bookbinding and nearly everyone has seen the wonderfully coloured designs on the covers and end papers of old books. But the craft has a wealth of other purposes that have hardly been exploited. Not only paper can be marbled but also wood, plastic, cloth, leather, glass, metal, rubber and even wax. Totally original effects can be obtained by marbling leather handbags, silk scarves, cotton skirts, wooden boxes and lamp bases, plastic mats, glass

canisters—almost anything, in fact.

Methods of marbling

Different methods of marbling have long been used by different craftsmen, partly because the process was for a long time regarded as a secret art and practised behind locked doors. As might be expected, much traditional secrecy still persists and a number of variations on the basic techniques are still practised. But some of them are better than others for certain effects and surfaces.

Essentially, however, marbling relies upon the adage that oil and water will not mix and the earliest known method is simply this—to float oil colours on water. Later, vegetable colours were also used.

While other, more sophisticated, variations have developed, these two meth-

The variegated patterns of marbling are made basically by floating colours on water. Eggs from David Hicks.

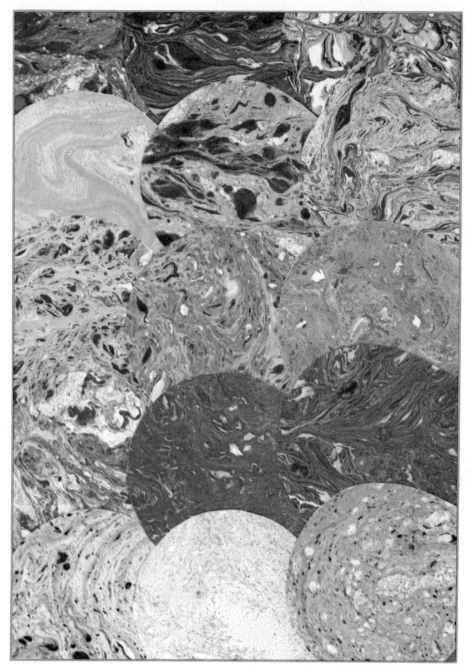

Typical patterns produced by the simple method of floating artists' oils.

Alasdair Ogilvie

ods are still two of the easiest to work with. Although they do not provide quite the control possible with more complex methods, they can be used on an incredibly wide range of surfaces, are successful with a minimum of practice and can be enjoyed by children and adults alike.

Using artists' oil colours

This method is particularly well-suited to marbling on paper but it can also be used on other materials.

Artists' oils also provide a splendid colour range to work with and patterns can be made using as many colours as you wish.

You will need:

Shallow, water-tight container such as a baking tin or photographic dish with minimum dimensions of 30cm x 38cm (12″x15″).

Packet of powdered gelatine size, available from hardware shops.

Artist's oil paints

Turpentine, or else you can use white spirit as a substitute.

Sharp instrument such as a knitting needle to swirl the colour

Paint brushes or small stirring sticks—one for each colour.

A few small jars or pots.

Old newspapers.

Sheets of paper.

Paper can be almost any sort but avoid those which are too soft, thin or porous. The best papers to use are white drawing paper, pastel paper and brown craft or other wrapping papers. The paper should be cut slightly smaller than the inside of the 'bath' or container.

Preparing the size. The solution for floating the colours, or size, as it is called, is made by dissolving one dessertspoonful of powdered gelatine size to 0.5lit (1pt) of water. To mix, place the gelatine in the container or tray and pour in a little boiling water, mixing well. When the size has completely dissolved, the remainder of the water can be added from the tap. Allow the prepared solution to stand and cool to normal room temperature.

The container should always be about three-quarters full.

Preparing the colours. Select two or three oil colours and squeeze about 13mm (½") from each tube into separate pots and dilute until runny with white spirit or turpentine. Put a brush or stick in each pot and keep the diluted colour well stirred.

Testing. Before proceeding it is important to test the colours and size to find their relative working strengths. Using the mixing stick or brush, drop a spot of each colour upon the surface of the size. Ideally, each spot should float on the surface and spread to form a circle of colour about 2.5cm-5cm (1"-2") in diameter.

Should the colour not expand sufficiently it is too thick and needs to be further diluted with white spirit or turpentine. If it spreads too much, more neat colour should be added to each diluted colour.

If the colour sinks straight to the bottom of the container this usually indicates that the size is too thick and needs to be thinned by adding more water.

Sometimes the spots of colour expand and then contract and this shows that either the size is the wrong temperature and should be allowed to cool or, if too cold, warmed slightly to normal room temperature. A little experimentation is necessary to find the right consistency and temperature. As soon as the colours and size are working satisfactorily you can begin marbling.

Marbling. To start, drop a few drops of each colour on to the surface of the size at regular intervals about 5cm-7.5cm (2"-3") apart.

The most enjoyable and creative stage has now been reached. The floating colours can be positioned by drawing a knitting needle or pointed stick across the surface of the size. The small blobs of colour can be teased, pushed and arranged in swirls, lines or any desired shape or pattern.

The size and water keep the colours from merging so that marvellous, variegated patterns and swirling rainbows of colour are possible.

If necessary, the pattern can be re-arranged many times until the desired result is obtained. At no time is it necessary to rush as the colours remain on the surface of the size for some time before sinking.

When you are satisfied with the design, carefully lower a sheet of paper on to the surface of the size, starting at one corner so that no bubbles of air are trapped underneath and no distortion of the colour pattern takes place.

When the entire surface of the paper has been in contact with the colour, lift the paper out with equal care, hold it over the container for a minute to drain and then place it, pattern upwards, on a sheet of old newspaper to dry.

You will soon find that the results will vary not only according to the patterns but also with how much paint is used,

the order in which the colours are applied and the colour of the paper.

After every print is made, skim the waste colour off the surface of the mixture by using old newspaper cut into strips about 7.5cm (3") wide and as long as the container is wide.

when you have finished, clean out the container with a piece of paper towel and white spirit or turpentine. The marbled paper, when fully dry, can be flattened if necessary by placing it under a light weight or smoothing it with a warm domestic iron.

Using vegetable oils

Another simple marbling technique involves the use of specially-produced colours, often with a banana oil base, which are sold specially for marbling. While the number of colours is limited

Artists' oils being floated on gelatine size. The size causes them to float.

Paper is lowered on to the surface of bath to collect the patterned colour.

After each item is marbled the bath must be cleaned by drawing paper across it.

the number of surfaces that can be marbled is enormous. Banana oil colours will marble paper, fabric, wood, glass, metal and wax. They can be managed by a child or used to produce more sophisticated effects, such as tortoise-shell, by experienced craftsmen.

The colours are floated on water and the procedure, with certain exceptions, is similar to that of using artists' oils. In the same way, vegetable oil-based colours will not mix when placed side by side in the bath, but different shades can be dropped on top of each other to mix.

The bath. To marble flat surfaces like cloth and paper, use a shallow tray; larger objects, such as wooden boxes, candles, or tins, require a container such as a bowl or bucket that is deep enough to immerse the object.

Vegetable oil-based colours are floated on water at room temperature, but if you live in a hard water area it may be necessary to add borax or a water softener if colours do not spread of their own accord. Add one heaped handful of borax per bucket of water.

Floating colours. Use only a few drops of colour, applied preferably with a dropper, and marble as soon as you have patterned the colours because they dry very quickly.

Marbling paper or cloth. Swirl your colours with a wire or stick, then lay the material carefully on the water, leave it for a moment then peel it off and allow to dry. Cloth is ready to be peeled off when the pattern shows through to the other side. This may also happen in lighter weights of paper. After 24 hours the colour will have set sufficiently to allow fabric to be washed. Use close-woven fabrics only, not wool. Leather can also be marbled in this way.

Marbling objects. Many objects, particularly metal and glass, should be given an undercoat of emulsion paint before marbling. Although white is probably best for showing colours, others can be used to give special contrast. If you wish glass to retain its transparency, then undercoat with gold size instead of paint. Gold size is available at art supply shops.

Candles should be marbled direct. Instead of laying objects on the surface of the water as with cloth or paper, dip them completely into it and they will collect the colour as they pass through the floating surface colours. Do not roll objects across the surface as they will collect too much pigment. If your container is big enough you can marble several items by dipping them in quick succession.

When taking objects out of the container, swirl the colour out of the way with a stick so the objects will not be

Table covered in marbled paper.

marbled twice.

It often requires some ingenuity to completely immerse an object and yet allow the entire surface to be exposed to colour. Candles can, of course, be held by their wicks. Round objects like wooden eggs will need a tiny screw in one end with a string attached. The hole can be filled with plastic wood or coloured later. Boxes can have tape attached to the inside of top and bottom and looped out to form a temporary 'handle', while dowel sticks and crumpled wire coat hangers inserted in bottles help to control them in the bath (fig.1).

To give greater durability and gloss after marbling, varnish items with at least two coats of clear polyurethane varnish, sanding between each coat.

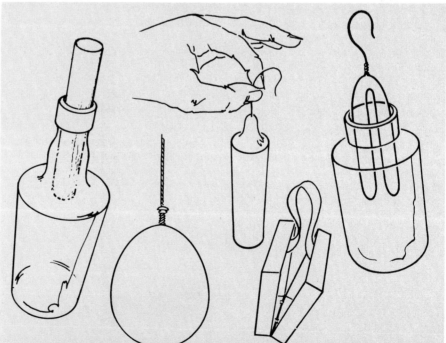

1. *Ways to hold different objects so they can be immersed in the marbling bath.*

175

Seaweed marbling

The art of marbling is enjoying an enthusiastic revival. The variety of the patterns and the vividness of the colours, the fact that almost any surface can be marbled and the sheer fun of doing it make it one of the most agreeable of occupations. Playing with floating marbling colours and teasing them into patterns is a fascinating process and once you start it is easy to get hooked.

There is an increasing demand for marbled goods but, because marbling cannot so far be practised on a large-scale commercial basis, demand still exceeds supply and if you become proficient you can make it pay.

Various methods of marbling exist. All are based on the principle of floating oil and vegetable colours on water or size. Some of these methods are faster and easier than others and produce both quick and colourful results, but for the finest control of patterns and the greatest beauty of colour a somewhat more complex method is necessary. Briefly, it involves using specially prepared colours from carrageen moss (Irish seaweed).

Seaweed marbling

Seaweed marbling produces colours that are unbelievably bright and vivid and, because the colours can be controlled so well, the patterns are especially easy to form. Any number can be produced and as your experience and confidence grow you will be able to swirl and comb the colours into finely regulated waves or twist them into delicate flower-like motifs.

Paper is the best thing to begin marbling on and marbled papers can be used in a wide variety of ways—as linings for drawers and boxes, coverings on notebooks and wastepaper baskets or to make a patchwork screen.

Lampshades can be cut from manilla paper and marbled to match your decor. You can marble papers for gift wrapping or, if you are more intrepid, you can marble your own wallpaper. Suitably covered and protected marbled paper can also be used on table mats, coffee tables and tray tops.

Equally wonderful effects can be got by marbling directly on to plastics, cloth and leather.

The materials and equipment for seaweed marbling take some effort to prepare but the result is well worth the trouble.

You will need:
Carrageen moss (Irish seaweed).
Formalin (formaldehyde).
Alum (sulphate of aluminium potassium).
Prepared marbling colours.
Oxgall.
Old newspapers.
Tray or trough for marbling.
Small sticks or brushes; eye dropper.
Pots or saucers for paints and one saucepan.
Material for marbling.
Knitting needle for swirling colours.
Fine sieve or old nylon stocking.

Carrageen moss can be obtained at health food shops, wine making suppliers and some pharmacies, while alum and formalin, a preservative, are both available at pharmacies.

Your tray or trough should be about 61cm x 30.5cm (24"x12") and deep enough to allow size solution to a depth of 2.5cm-5cm (1"-2"). The type of plastic tray used by butchers and bakers is suitable, or a photographic dish which is rather more expensive.

Colours for marbling can be bought specially prepared for this purpose, but if these are difficult to find at your art shop you can use solid poster colour pigments. These must be finely ground using a pestle and mortar and then mixed with water.

Preparation

To make the size put 28gm (1oz) of

Melvin Grey

A galaxy of floating, marbled colours; made by suspending specially prepared paint on an Irish seaweed size, this process makes infinitely subtle patterns. Wall paper is by Caroline Davis.

carrageen moss and 1.2lit (2pt) of water in a clean container such as a large saucepan and bring gradually to the boil over a low heat. Allow to boil for 3 or 4 minutes, stirring all the time. It is most important to take special care at this stage because success or failure could depend on it.

☐ Remove mixture from heat and stir in 1.2lit (2pt) of cold water, then 3 dessertspoonsful of formalin.

☐ Let the mixture stand for about 12 hours, overnight will do, in a cool place. It should set to form a jelly-like solution.

☐ Strain the size through a fine sieve or old nylon stocking. The formalin acts as a preserving agent and the size, if not used at once, can now be kept for several weeks.

To prepare colours with oxgall. Oxgall is usually obtained ready for use from art supply shops. If necessary, however, you can make your own but it is a slightly messy process. There is no synthetic substitute.

It is best to start by preparing and practising with only one or two colours, as it takes quite some time using oxgall to balance each colour and to get them to spread equally.

Pour 2 teaspoonsful of each colour into separate jars and initially add 6 drops oxgall to each. Stir thoroughly. Oxgall is added to colours to reduce surface tension and cause them to spread on the surface of the size.

Colours can be dropped on top of each other or side by side. Usually the second colour added to the tray needs more oxgall than the first. Try 10 drops, and continue adjusting the proportions until you have achieved the right consistency.

Oxgall is obtainable from a slaughterhouse. Add 1lit (1¾ pt) oxgall to 0.28lit (½pt) methylated spirits and mix well until the gall has dissolved. Put it in a bottle, seal and leave for about 24 hours so that the fatty sediment can settle to the bottom. Then decant the solution.

Paper. Cut old newspaper into 8cm (3″) strips and the same length as the width of the marbling trough. These will be used to skim the surface between each marbling.

If you are marbling paper, cut each sheet fractionally smaller than the trough. Most papers can be marbled—drawing paper, brown wrapping paper and manilla paper are all suitable.

Mordant. The material to be marbled must be mordanted first. A mordant, in this case alum, is a chemical which makes material and colour receptive to one another and improves colour tone and colour fastness.

To prepare mordant add 28g (1oz) of alum to 0.57lit (1pt) of hot water. Stir until crystals are dissolved.

Marbled papers were originally used for bookbinding, but they have a number of ingenious and practical uses as the photographs above and opposite show.

Testing

The colour and size must always be tested before beginning.

Skim the surface of the size first, then stir the colour and drop a speck on to the size with a brush or stick. It should expand evenly to a diameter of 5cm-7.5cm (2″-3″).

If colour does not spread, add two or more drops of oxgall, skim the size and test again. If it still does not spread, the size is probably too thick and needs to be thinned with cold water.

If the colour spreads and then shrinks, the size is probably colder than the colours and a little warm water should be mixed with the size.

The aim is to get the size to the correct viscosity so that it will hold the pattern after it has been drawn on its surface.

To marble

☐ Mordant material first; sponge the alum solution evenly over the surface to be marbled and for the best results, marble while still damp.

☐ Fill the tray to about 2.5cm (1″) with the marbling size and place it near a sink because you will need running water later on.

☐ Always start by skimming the surface of the size with old newspaper strips. Then stir up each colour and drop spots of colour over the entire surface, leaving enough room for each spot to spread properly.

☐ You are now ready to create your pattern. Using a knitting needle or other pointed instrument, swirl and pattern the colours by dragging it

To make a typical combed pattern, float colours as shown.

Draw a knitting needle through the colour crossways.

Then draw the needle lengthways through colours and finally, to get regulated waves, draw a comb across as shown below.

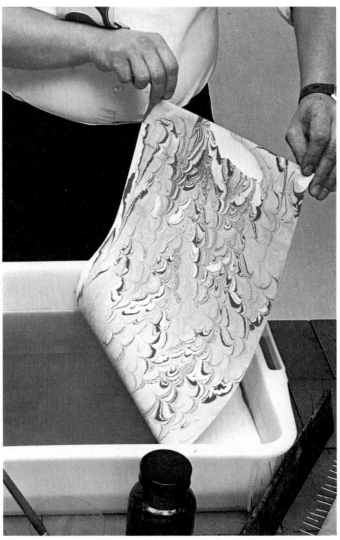

To print, lower paper on to the patterned colours and then lift it off carefully. Rinse and hang up to dry.

Dick Miller

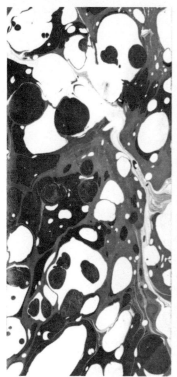

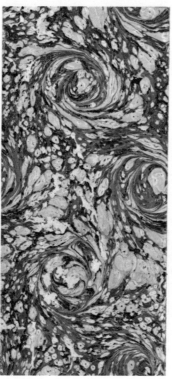

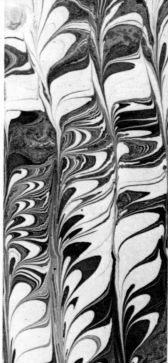

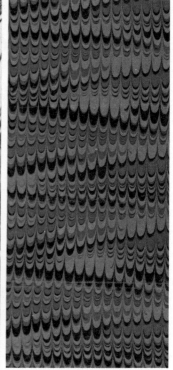

This pattern, called Turkish, is made by shaking colours on top of one another from a brush and then swirling until you like the result.

French curl is made by combing with ordinary marbling comb and then with wide-spaced comb in a circular motion.

Comb pattern is similar to that shown opposite and choice of colour is a big factor in its success. Three is a good number to work.

Nonpareil. This is the finest of combed patterns and shows careful control. Use a closely-spaced comb for miniature waves.

about through the colours. You can thus arrange and rearrange them until you like the result.

☐ When ready, carefully lower the paper or other material, alum side downwards, until it lies flat upon the surface of the size. Make sure you do not disturb the pattern or trap any air underneath the paper as this will prevent the sheet from touching the colour and leave blank spaces.

The material only needs to remain a few seconds. Then gently lift it out, lay it on a draining board, pattern side up, and pour water across the surface to remove surplus size and colour. Hang up to dry.

Special patterns

Over the many years that marbling has been practised in different parts of the world a number of standard patterns have been handed down from one marbler to another. These patterns have attractive names like Turkish, Italian, Snail, Nonpareil, some of which clearly have some connection with their country of origin.

Many of these traditional patterns are formed by drawing a comb evenly across the surface of the size. Two such patterns, Nonpareil and Comb, are illustrated.

To make a comb, cut two pieces of cardboard to a length slightly shorter than the width of the tray and about 5cm (2″) wide.

Accurately measure 12mm ($\frac{1}{2}$″) or 2.5cm (1″) segments along the length of one piece of cardboard. Notch the surface at each line, deep enough to embed a pin or needle, and make each notch 2.5cm (1″) long as illustrated (fig.1).

Now embed 5cm (2″) needles in the slots, sticking them firmly with contact adhesive.

Glue the second cardboard strip against the first, with the needles in between, and place under a weight to dry. The needles will protrude 2.5cm (1″) beyond the cardboard.

You will find it useful to have two such combs, one with the teeth 2.5cm (1″) apart and one with 12mm ($\frac{1}{2}$″) gaps. Remember when marbling not to be disheartened by failure as there are many things that can and do go wrong. Marbling is an art and although quick success can often be gained, it takes practice to really master it. It will help if all the apparatus used for marbling is kept perfectly clean, the seaweed size prepared with considerable care and the colours thoroughly mixed and tested before beginning.

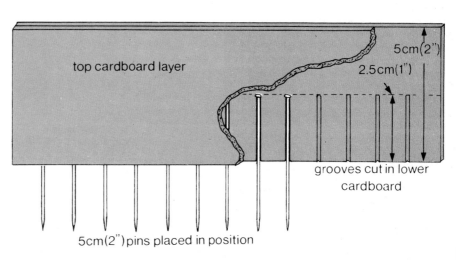

top cardboard layer

5cm(2″)

2.5cm(1″)

grooves cut in lower cardboard

5cm(2″)pins placed in position

1. *A marbling comb can be made at home using pins, cardboard and glue.*

Paul Williams

179

Tie-dyeing

Tie-dyeing is a way of decorating cloth by blocking out certain parts so that they do not 'take' the dye in which the cloth is dipped. This is done by knotting, folding, clipping, tying or binding the cloth so that the dye cannot penetrate these areas. All these ways of sealing off the fabric produce unusual and attractive results.

Using tie-dye methods, you can create an array of patterns that have an extraordinary illusory quality which is quite unlike anything else that printing or dyeing can produce. By planning which areas of the fabric you want to resist the dye, you can create repeated patterns or position a large motif, such as a flamboyant sunburst, in the centre of a garment or any other object.

Tie-dying is an age-old craft which originated in the East, probably in China, and spread along the ancient routes of the silk caravans to many other lands. Medieval Japanese nobles dressed in tie-dyed silks, and in India and Indonesia the craft became a highly developed and refined form of decoration. Examples of tie-dyeing have also been found in Pre-Columbian America, and it is still practised extensively in Africa where a distinctive style of wonderfully bold patterns has arisen, often using indigo dyes.

What will dye

Any fabric which is not too bulky can be tie-dyed as long as the fibre is receptive to dye. Silk is particularly beautiful when tie-dyed as its floating quality seems to lend itself to the radiant patterns which tie-dye produces. Cotton is perhaps the easiest fabric to work with because it takes dye extremely well and, being comparatively inexpensive, is a good choice for beginners.

Natural fibres (cotton, linen, silk, wool) and viscose rayon can be dyed with commercial cold water dyes. These are *fibre reactive* dyes, which means that the dye molecules form a bond with the fibre, rendering it colour fast.

Many synthetic fibres can be dyed with commercial hot water dyes and these come in a wide range of colours and shades. Unfortunately, these dyes are not colour fast and must always be washed separately.

Polyesters and fabrics with special finishes—to make them crease or stain-resistant, eg—cannot be dyed.

For more details about dyeing different fibres and fibre mixtures, and for using hot and cold water dyes, see Dyeing chapter 1, page 150.

Cloth that is going to be dyed must always be washed first to get rid of any dressing which may have been added by the manufacturer to give it 'body' and finish. Otherwise, the dressing will prevent dye penetrating the cloth.

Tying

Before you begin to tie the cloth it must be dry and free from creases.

It is wise to experiment with a few squares of inexpensive cotton or strips of old sheeting to find out about different effects, to try out different types of string and to see how tightly cloth should be bound.

String. All types of string will prevent penetration of the dye to some degree, but some strings will let dye penetrate more than others. Nylon string is totally resistant to cold water dyes.

Cotton thread is receptive to dyes of all kinds and is therefore not suitable unless your fabric is thickly bunched or folded. With thick bunching you can make graded patterns of colour because the inner sections of cloth will receive little or no dye while the outer layers may receive some colour through the thread.

Fishing line, plastic cord, rope and linen thread can all be used effectively.

Resist objects of all sorts can be used in tie-dyeing to give interesting and unusual patterns, and you will be able to find many ordinary household items to use. Paper clips, clothes pegs, bulldog clips, pipe cleaners—anything that grips the fabric, keeps dye out and is not itself harmed in the dyebath, will work and also will leave its own special mark or pattern.

Tie dyeing means binding parts of cloth with cords or other things, like the clothes pegs shown, and then dyeing it. The tied-off areas resist the dye and make the patterns. Opposite are some examples of different binding methods and resulting patterns.

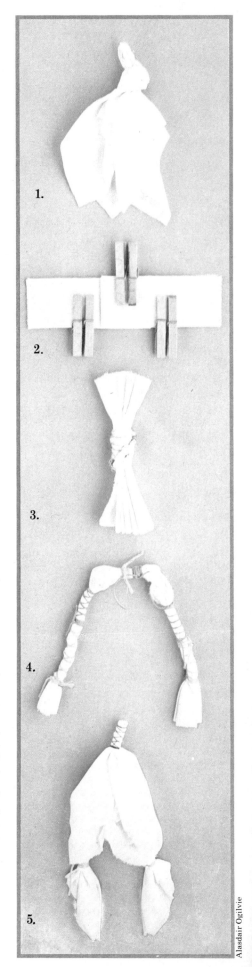

1.

2.

3.

4.

5.

Alasdair Ogilvie

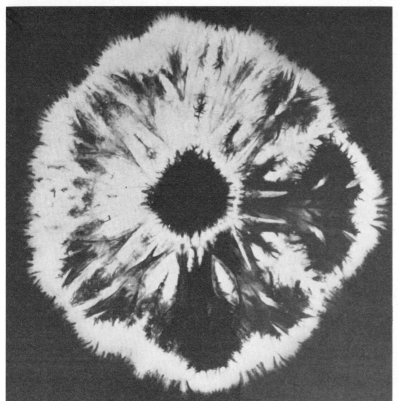

1. *The simplest tie of all is a knot and this can be in the centre or on the ends. For a regular effect make the knots equidistant.*

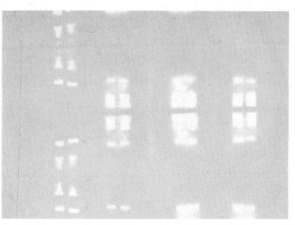

2. *Clothes pegs give interesting, blotted effects and cloth should be folded in accordion pleats first for a repeated effect. In the example shown the cloth has been pleated and then folded again in the middle.*

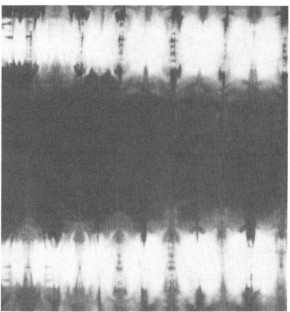

3. *This design is made by folding the piece of cloth in half, accordion pleating it and then binding with strong twine, as shown far left.*

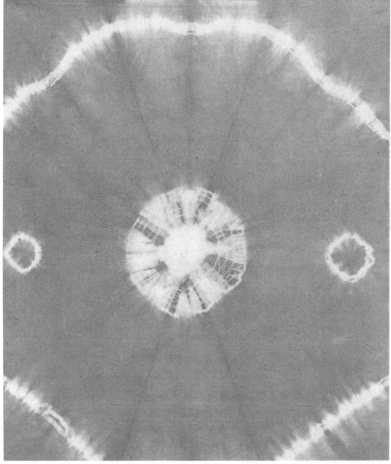

5. *These cobweb-like circles were made by picking up cloth centre with a needle, letting it fall in even folds, then binding the centre, inverting it and binding again in a lump below.*

4. *Cloth pleated and tied with spiral ties.*

Steve Bicknell

Rubber bands, wire, dental floss and masking tape are all useful substitutes for string and cord.

Several different objects can be combined to make a pattern on one piece of cloth and this is where your own ingenuity comes in. In the beginning you will have to test the result of each 'tie' before using it as a pattern, but as soon as you become familiar with the effects different 'ties' produce, you can then envisage a pattern and get on with it.

Always consider which 'ties' are most suitable for the type and weight of your material and for the use it will be put to. Fine cottons and silk, for instance, respond to fine threads and a close repetition of delicate ties, while fabrics of a looser weave need a large effect from knotting, pegging or heavy cord. Repeated patterns should be place-marked with a pencil before tying begins, so that you can be sure of a regular repeat.

All string, thread or cord must be tied very, very tightly and knotted firmly, so that it does not loosen in the dye-bath. If the string is unusually thick, or if for any reason there is a problem in getting the end of the string back to the beginning to make a knot, you can stitch the ends to the rest of the cord by using a large darning needle.

Dyeing

When your 'ties' are all securely tied or fastened, wet the cloth thoroughly and put it into the dyebath for the length of time stated in the manufacturer's instructions.

When the dye has taken, remove the fabric, leaving the ties intact, and rinse it thoroughly. If you have been using a hot water dye it is advisable to give it a good wash before untying to get rid of any excess dye. Do not undo the ties until the cloth has had time to dry thoroughly, or dye may seep into the white, unprotected areas. When undoing the ties it is very easy to nip the cloth accidentally with your scissors, so be very careful and insert the point of the scissors under the end, not the middle, of the tie.

Special effects can be created with dyes by dipping only part of the cloth into the dye—along the edges of accordion folds, for example.

Another fascinating effect that can be incorporated into tie-dying is using bleach on cloth you have dyed first, and then tied. This is a kind of reverse procedure because it is the dyed areas which make the pattern as the bleach removes the dye from the exposed areas.

By tying cloth with sewing thread or cord that has been dyed with a hot water dye you can make coloured lines on fabric where the dye from the cord

seeps through. Although it is much better to experiment on white cloth, you can begin with a light-coloured cloth, tie it, and dye a darker shade.

Multi-coloured tie-dyeing. Some marvellous colour combinations can be made by using more than one dyebath. In this way, the second colour can be applied either before or after you undo your first ties. If you make more ties in the same cloth, without untying the first ones, and then put the cloth in a second dyebath, your first ties will result in a white pattern, your second ties will have the colour of the first dyebath, and the cloth which was exposed throughout will either be the colour of the last dyebath or a blend of both colours.

When working with more than one colour it is important to remember that dyes blend. The blending action of dyes presents some exciting possibilities once the basic rules governing dyes and colours are understood. If you tie-dye white cloth light blue, add some more ties and then dye dark blue; in the end you will have white and light blue patterns where the respective ties have been, and the background will be dark blue. But if the second dyebath is yellow, then you will end up with white and light blue patterns on a green background, since the yellow and blue will blend to form green. In multi-coloured dyeing, the fabric must be thoroughly rinsed between each dyeing, and if the first ties are to be untied then the cloth must be allowed to dry thoroughly first.

Silk scarf was tied once and dyed yellow, then more ties were made.

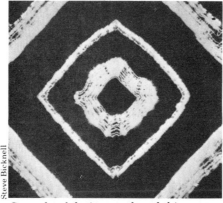

Second red dyeing produced this pattern

182

Cotton sheets and pillow cases were crumpled into sausages, tied at intervals and dyed in a washing machine.

Batik

The word batik (pronounced bateek) means 'wax writing' and this is basically what batik is. It is a way of decorating cloth by covering part of it with a coat of wax and then dyeing the cloth. The waxed area keeps its original colour and when the wax is removed the contrast between the dyed and undyed areas makes the pattern.

This chapter deals with the basic methods of the batik process, so that the beginner will be able to experiment later.

The exact origins of batik are unknown, but they are almost certainly in the Orient where the technique was used, long before printing, to enhance the appearance of fine garments. Batik became most deeply rooted in Indonesia, particularly the island of Java, where it was a highly developed art by the 13th century.

Batik was considered a fitting occupation for aristocratic ladies whose delicately painted designs, based on bird and flower motifs, were a sign of cultivation and refinement, just as fine needlework was for European ladies of a similar position.

Java is still famous for batik and the traditional patterns, developed over centuries, are still part of Javanese dress, although very few are made by the traditional method of wax painting. This, instead, has been rediscovered and put to use by craftsmen all over the world who find the freedom of working with liquid wax, and the control of colour possible through dyeing, makes batik an exciting and uniquely expressive medium to work in. Increasingly, the all-over patterns of Oriental batiks are being replaced by imaginative pictures and designs of all sorts, which are used to make wall hangings and soft sculpture as well as decorations for clothing and household items.

Part of the attraction of batik is its simplicity and the fact that you don't have to be artistic in the conventional sense to produce beautiful results. Some of the best effects in batik are in fact the work of chance. This is particularly true of the way in which the wax cracks to let small quantities of dye through, adding an unexpected and interesting effect to any design. This hairline detail, or 'crackling', is a special characteristic of most batik work.

Because batik wax is applied hot it is necessary to work fairly rapidly and this can produce a freedom (or loss of self-consciousness) that makes many people who think they cannot draw find, to their amazement, that they can. Of course, designs can be worked out beforehand and for many things, such as borders and trimmings, this is necessary; but designs drawn spontaneously in wax, or according to the briefest sketch, can bring surprising rewards.

Combined with the pleasure of drawing freehand is the fascination of working creatively with dyes—blending and mixing different colours—to get as vivid or as subtle a shade as you want.

Fabrics

Natural or vegetable fibre fabrics, such as cotton, linen and silk, are the ones to use for batik.

Viscose rayon can also be used, but avoid all synthetic fibres, no matter how closely they simulate natural fibres. Their true nature is revealed in the dyebath, by which time it is too late. They will not dye properly with cold dyes, which must necessarily be used for batik; otherwise the wax would melt in the dyebath.

To test fibres of which you are uncertain, try this quick test. Watch carefully as you hold a single fibre over a lighted match. The synthetic thread melts quickly into a hard residue. Organic fibres burn more slowly, and a soft ash is formed.

Silk is one of the best fabrics for batik —the finer woven the better—and a finer waxed line can be drawn on silk than on any other fabric. To start with, however, silk is far from necessary, and the expense may inhibit your inventiveness since you will be less willing to 'chance' a design.

Cotton is excellent, and some prefer it to silk on the grounds that the sheen of silk obscures the pattern.

In general, with coarser spun fabrics, more wax is absorbed and a fine sweeping line is harder to obtain, as the wax sinks rapidly into the cloth as it is applied. So, although you can batik canvas, calico and flannelette, these are only suitable for large, clear designs.

For intricate work and, in particular, pictures or wall hangings, fine linen or fine cotton is recommended. Especially delicate designs can be produced on batiste or cotton lawn—any thin cotton in fact which is not so transparent that your picture will look like an apparition.

Dye

Batik dye must be a cold dye since hot water would cause the hardened wax to melt in the dyebath. Ordinary cold water dyes are best for beginners and all contain instructions for their use; but after some experience you may prefer to use special, fast-acting cold dyes or vat dyes, which involve the use of additional chemicals but which 'take' a lot more quickly and, in the case of vat dyes, give exceptionally colourfast results.

Once you are used to working with wax you can begin to experiment more with mixing dyes, buying large amounts (less expensive) of the basic colours and making any others you need.

Wax

The ideal mixture for batik work is 30% beeswax to 70% paraffin wax, and to try it for the first time you can easily melt down candles. If, however, you decide to do more batik, it makes sense to get the wax from a craft supply house in bulk.

Beeswax adheres well to fabric, whereas paraffin wax is brittle, cracking easily. So how you mix the two determines how much crackling you get.

Crackling produces the fine lines that characterize most batik work. With pure paraffin wax there is the danger of it peeling off in the dyebath. A mixture of beeswax and paraffin wax therefore assures adherence, plus decorative crackling effects.

Beginner's equipment

The equipment you need to begin batik is fairly simple, and most of it can be found around the house.

Some old white sheets. Old, torn white cotton sheets have the advantage of being already free from chemical finishes (which would otherwise prevent the dye from penetrating).

Note: all new fabrics must be boiled to remove the finishing.

Candles (at least one containing beeswax).

Double saucepan, for melting wax.

Batik is a way of decorating cloth by painting with wax and then dyeing the cloth. The waxed areas keep the original colour. Examples shown were made in Sri Lanka (Ceylon).

Good quality artist's paintbrush.
Cold water dye and fixative.
Charcoal, or pencil, for making pre-liminary sketch.
Old picture frame. (Batik is normally worked on a special frame on which the cloth is tacked to keep it taut, but for beginners an old picture frame will serve just as well.)
You will also need to use the cooker, or (more convenient) a boiling ring or chafing dish (such as a fondue dish with candles beneath) to melt wax, and you will need access to a sink or a bowl for dyeing.

How to batik
Making the basic sketch. With a dark pencil or charcoal, begin to sketch your design on the cloth. It does not have to be elaborate—just a few guide-lines.
You can draw the first subject that comes to mind, or try the simple tree sketch in fig.1, which will give you some idea of the freedom of batik yet provide a basic guideline at the same time. The tree motif illustrates another useful principle in batik—that it is often a good idea to work the sur-rounding spaces with wax rather than the object which is being depicted. So, in the case of the tree, it is the sky or

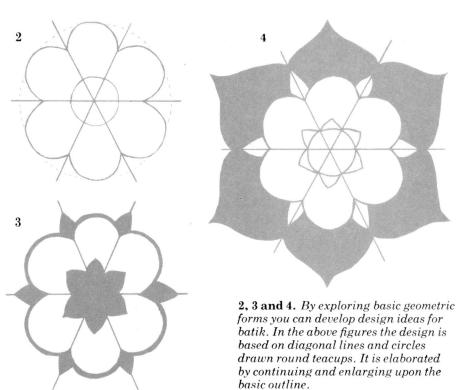

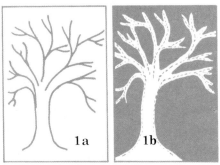

1. *Simple freehand sketches are the basis of many batik designs and often the surrounding areas are waxed rather than the image itself. In the tree sketch (b), blue indicates waxed area.*

2, 3 and 4. *By exploring basic geometric forms you can develop design ideas for batik. In the above figures the design is based on diagonal lines and circles drawn round teacups. It is elaborated by continuing and enlarging upon the basic outline.*

the space round the tree that matters. This can be a whole new way of looking at things.
Fig.2 shows a simple geometric design which can be made using round house-hold objects, like cups, to make the curves between the straight charcoal lines. You can add other shapes and innovations to this basic design as the illustrations show (figs.3,4).
Remember that you must always decide in your design whether you want the present colour of the cloth to be the background or the design itself, since this will determine where you apply the wax.
When you have made your sketch, stretch the cloth across the frame and fasten it with drawing pins. You can

A motif similar to the one explored above is painted in wax on to stretched cloth.

prop the frame up with a book to make it easier to work on.

To prepare wax, use either the cooker or a boiling ring. The latter is more useful since you can keep it beside you while you work. Otherwise, you will need to work beside the cooker.

Safety hints: hot wax is very inflammable so it is wise not to heat it directly. Insulate the wax pan by using a double boiler, or by putting it in a large pan with about 2.5cm (1″) water in the bottom. The water will need replacing as you work, so keep a jug nearby. Try to prevent the wax from reaching a temperature where it begins to smoke. As soon as the wax is bubbling gently, turn heat to low.

When the wax is hot enough to use it will penetrate a test piece of cloth, sealing it on both sides so that light readily shines through and the fabric has a wet look. If the wax looks whitish and opaque, it has probably not penetrated.

Place the wax beside you—to your right if you are right-handed, and to your left if left-handed—to avoid reaching over your work and possibly dripping wax on it unnecessarily.

Painting with wax. You will need to work quickly as the wax cools and dries rapidly on the brush. Stir the wax frequently with your brush, and let excess wax run off before removing the brush from the pan.

Fill in the design with wax, following your charcoal lines. Let the width of

After dyeing the waxed cloth opposite blue, the design is enlarged upon.

your brush determine the thickness of the line.

Do not go over the same place twice—this has no effect—but paint on boldly, continually renewing the flow of wax on your brush.

You can also make dots and lines by dripping wax directly on to the cloth from lighted candles, and this is often a good way to get your first sense of the wax technique since virtually no preparation is needed.

If the shape you have made suggests any further shapes to you, add them. (Figs.2-4 can be used, or merely act as suggestions to your own subconscious.)

Dyeing. When your sketch is finished in wax you are ready to dye. Unpin the cloth, crumple it a little to encourage the wax to vein and crack, and immerse the waxed cloth in the dyebath for the period of time recommended by the manufacturer.

When you remove the cloth from the dyebath, hang it up to drip, preferably over a bowl or sink. Do not rinse, wring or dry by artificial means—impatience at this point is only rewarded by pale and uneven dyeing. Leave the cloth to drip dry thoroughly. Remember that all dyes look several shades darker when wet, so don't worry if the fabric looks excessively dark when wet.

Multi-coloured dyeing. If you want to enlarge on the design by adding more colour, do not remove the wax. Instead, when dry, pin it to the frame again and wax any new areas. Bear in mind that these areas will retain the colour of the first dyebath, and that in the unwaxed areas the colour of the **second dye you have used will blend with that of the first by absorption into the pores of the material itself.** If you are dyeing the cloth the same colour the second time, remember that you can only dye to a darker shade— light blue to navy, for example.

To remove the wax. Iron it off between sheets of newspaper or boil it off in water. Wax can also be scraped off but this is not recommended for beginners since it is too easy to cut the cloth and ruin the whole thing.

After scraping, boiling or ironing, a small residue of wax will still remain on the cloth, giving it a wet look, which you may find desirable for wall hangings and other decorative devices, but for clothes and soft furnishings all traces of wax must be removed. This is done by dry cleaning or soaking cloth in strong detergent.

Cleaning up. It is worth being rigidly neat about putting away dyestuffs and cleaning up after you have finished work. Use a sieve to empty the dyebath, since wax would accumulate in the drain and cause a blockage.

Dick Miller

The finished design is made by dyeing the cloth red and removing the wax coating.

187

Colouring eggs

Starting at the beginning!

Eggs are universal symbols of creation and decorating them for gifts and festive occasions is an age-old pastime. In ancient China painted eggs were distributed as edible gifts by benevolent rulers and throughout the world they are still used in festivals and religious celebrations. In the Greek Orthodox church, for example, red eggs are handed out at Easter to symbolize the Resurrection, while in Mexico painted eggs are filled with confetti and used to celebrate the New Year.

The worldwide popularity of decorating eggs is not surprising, considering how much fun it is. The whole family can join in to make a collection and embellishments can be as simple or as elaborate as you wish. Souvenir eggs can commemorate a special day or event and gifts of decorated eggs can make positive expressions of friendship throughout the year. All can be used in a variety of ways to adorn a house or table, making lasting mementoes or momentary edible visions to delight children and grown-ups alike.

Preparing eggs

Before you begin, make sure the eggs are clean and free from grease. White eggs generally make better decorating surfaces than brown ones as they take colour in a purer form, but for special effects and for painting faces, brown eggs can be used very effectively. The brown simulates skin tones amazingly well.

Eggs may be decorated either hard-boiled or with the contents blown out. Blown eggs can be hung with string or wire and last longer, so are better suited for painstaking designs. But hard-boiled eggs are easier to do and are recommended for small children.

If you want a hardboiled egg to last a very long time, boil it slowly for half an hour.

To blow an egg place it in an eggcup, small end down, and with a large sewing or darning needle pierce a hole in the top. Then turn the egg upside down and repeat the process, this time making the hole slightly larger.

☐ Hold the egg over a bowl and, using a straw or placing your mouth against the smaller hole, blow the contents into the bowl. These may then be set aside for cooking. If the contents do not emerge easily, shake the egg or take a long needle and push it well into the hole to puncture the yolk.

When you have blown the egg, run water through it, shaking gently to clean.

It is advisable to place a drop of candle-wax over the holes before you begin to dye so the egg won't fill with the dye mixture.

Decorating techniques

Dyeing eggs. Use either vegetable food colouring (available in food stores

Draw on eggs with a wax crayon and dye; or paint with inks (centre egg).

and some pharmacies) or fabric dyes. Fabric dyes have the advantage of an enormous range of colours, producing rich or subtle tones, while food colouring tends to be limited to strong, often garish, hues.

Use the dye according to the directions on the packet, rolling the egg in the mixture with a spoon to get an even colour.

To dry eggs you can use either a rack or an eggcup but the best method is to hammer some nails into a board, sinking in only the tips. A blown egg can be placed on each nail to dry and there is no danger of the surface getting smeared (fig.1).

1

Boards for drying decorated eggs are easy to make using a plank and nails.

Painting eggs. This is one of the most popular forms of egg decoration and can be done in free form with a brush or by tracing a design on to the egg first.

For painting eggs poster paint, ink, felt-tipped pens and general purpose craft paints are all suitable. Egg decorating kits are also available and contain supplies for decorating and colouring eggs in a number of ways.

The kind of paint you use depends on your design; felt pens are excellent for line drawings and can be bought in several colours, while vivid poster paints give the intensity needed in motifs inspired by folk art.

A lustrous, pearl effect can be achieved by painting eggs with several coats of frosted nail varnish. Each coat should be left to dry before you apply the next one.

It is often useful when painting on eggs to steady them by placing in an eggcup and painting first one end and then the other.

Stick and paint techniques are intriguing to work with and can produce unusually delicate designs.

Take some small leaves, blades of grass, petals, or tiny, pressed flowers and dip them in vegetable oil so they will adhere to the surface of the egg.

Stick them on in whatever arrangement you choose and wrap the egg tightly in a piece of old nylon stocking, knotting it at either end of the egg.

Now dye the egg. Afterwards remove the casing and stuck-on objects—the fragile outline of the plants will be imprinted on the surface of the egg.

You can also use paper cut-outs for this technique.

Marbling. One of the most fascinating ways to get a marbled effect on eggs is also one of the oldest.

Wrap an egg in the papery outer skin of an onion and tie in place with some thread.

Tie the egg securely in an old nylon stocking or some cheesecloth and boil. The onion skin creates its own dye and design and when you remove it you will find a yellow, 'marbled' egg.

For a much greater variety of marbled tones, thread thin florist's wire or sewing thread through the holes in a blown egg. Fill a bowl ¾ full of water and drop one or more shades of oil-bound paint on the water. Swirl with a wire to mix the colours a bit and roll the egg lightly across the surface of the water so that it collects the paint floating on the top.

Dip each egg only once. The results are interesting and no two eggs the same.

Batik. This is an age-old form of painting on cloth with wax but is just as suitable for decorating eggs if a cold water dye is used.

Take a bit of candlewax or beeswax and melt it in a spoon over a candle. Using a fine brush or pointed stick, such as a cuticle stick, sketch a design on the egg.

To make dots, a dressmaking pin stuck in a cork can be used to drop the wax from the pin-head on to the egg.

When the wax has hardened, dye the egg and allow it to dry. Then remove the wax by holding the egg near a candle until the wax softens and can be absorbed into a paper towel or cloth.

For a more colourful result, instead of removing the wax after the first dyeing, apply more of it and dye the egg again in a different or darker shade than before. When all the wax is removed you will have three colours in the design instead of two.

Engraving techniques. These techniques produce attractive results but are not advisable for children to try. Always use hardboiled eggs for engraving since the pressure needed to cut the design could crack a blown egg.

There are several engraving techniques: one is to dye the egg first in a deep, rich colour, then take a sharp instrument, like a steel pen nib or a needle, and scratch your design on the egg, revealing the white surface beneath.

Another variation of this involves tracing the design on to the egg and then scratching it into the surface with a needle or some other sharp instrument. When the egg is dyed, the engraved lines take on a deeper colour than the rest of the surface.

Wax engraving can also be used on

Eggheads are fun to play with.

eggs. Heat some candlewax or beeswax in a double boiler and cover an egg with it by dipping first one end and then the other. Your design can then be engraved on the hardened wax so that, when the egg is dyed and the wax subsequently melted in hot water, the design appears on the egg like a line drawing.

To hang an egg

Fasten half a match-stick to some thread and insert it into the large hole in the top of a blown egg. The match will turn at an angle and anchor fast (fig.2). Wire can also be used in this

2

Decorated eggs can be hung up using a string and match-stick.

manner and the top bent conveniently into a hook.

Another alternative is to thread a string or ribbon through the egg and fix at the bottom by tying a bow or covering the hole with a bead.

Other ways with eggs

Apart from gifts and food, decorated eggs can be used in numerous ways: they make colourful 'drops' on mobiles or you can make an egg tree by suspending eggs from a tree limb.

Another idea is an egg paperweight: enlarge the bottom hole in a blown egg, fill the egg with plaster of Paris and decorate. Be sure the plaster is smooth at the bottom hole so the egg will stand upright on a desk.

Decorating eggs

Eggs are one of the most powerful and evocative of symbols, synonymous with fertility, birth and regeneration. Many ancient religious rites were held in the spring and this may well be the occasion when eggs were first painted. They still are in central Europe with religious figures, animals or plants. This tradition, although of pagan origin, is carried on throughout the world with the giving of Easter eggs.

The high point in the history of egg decoration was reached in Russia under the inspired hand of jeweller-artist Peter Carl Fabergé. He transformed the simple egg shape, encrusting it with jewels to make a fitting present for a tsar to give his tsarina.

Egg decoration is now enjoying a revival and as well as the attractive colouring processes which you can use to decorate eggs, they can also be trimmed with various appliqué materials and turned into delicately jewelled containers in the style created by Fabergé.

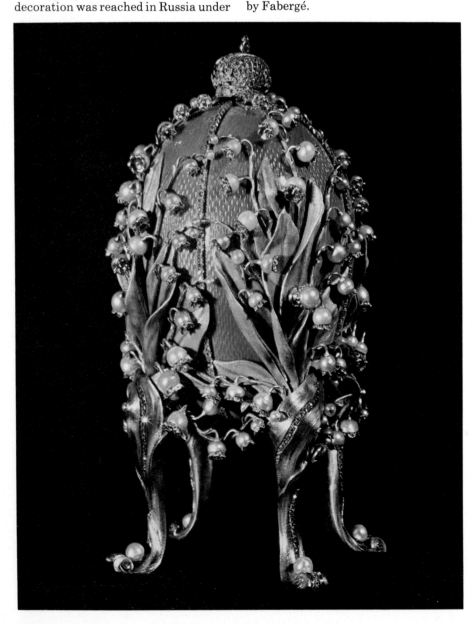

Applied decorations

Blown chicken eggs are the easiest to use for decoration of this kind since they are easily obtainable in large numbers. They should be cleaned, blown, dried and hung before decorating as described before. Fragile eggs should be hardened to avoid shattering; to do this paint on several coats of a PVA adhesive, such as Dufix, diluted with water.

Appliqué. Use the tiniest odds and ends, such as lace, braid or string from your work box, or cover with a miniature patchwork of fabric scraps. Add glitter with sequins and beads or make a topknot of feathers.

Peter Heinz

For an unusual but economical gift, appliqué a chicken egg with odds and ends from your work box.

Collage. Use bits of flocked foil or tissue paper coated with lacquer to finish, or brown paper which can look like leather when covered with shellac.

Découpage. For this technique (akin to collage) small magazine cut-outs or Victorian scrap designs are glued to the egg and then covered with several layers of lacquer.

Pressed flowers. Decorate eggs with little pressed flowers and leaves, keeping the scale small in proportion with the egg. Apply adhesive to the egg, never to the flowers, and finish with a spray of artists' fixative. PVA adhesive [wood glue] should be used with all these methods.

Paint. Eggs can be given a truly imperial look by covering with several coats of glossy paint. Stroke it on in one direction only and leave to dry between coats. A simple cord edging and one jewel perched on top are all that is needed for trimming.

Priceless gems were used by Fabergé to decorate the eggs he created for the Tsar. Here he used diamonds and pearls to represent lilies-of-the-valley.

Cut-out eggs

Eggs can be made even more intriguing by cutting 'windows' in their shells to display a tiny figure or scene inside. Miniature doors that open and close can also be cut so that the egg contains a surprise in the Russian manner. For this you can use toys, ornaments or models, in fact anything in scale that catches your eye.

Although it is possible to cut windows in chicken eggs using sharp pointed scissors, goose eggs are preferable, especially for the more elaborate cuts. Duck eggs are inclined to warp after a time and turkey eggs are rather fragile. Unfortunately, goose eggs are only obtainable during the laying season, so it is wise to empty and cut several and put them away as stock to be used later. Emu and ostrich eggs are magnificent but expensive and hard to find unless you happen to live near a safari park. Hard-shelled eggs such as these must, however, be cut with a power tool.

It takes a lot of practice to learn to cut a perfect oval, especially if you are using chicken eggs, so an appetite for omelettes is an advantage!

Basic cutting method

This is used for both windows and doors.

You will need:

Eggs and a bowl to hold their contents.
Sharp pointed scissors, razor blade or scalpel.
Small drill such as Griffin and Spalding multi-purpose tool (optional)
Adhesive [cellophane] tape, pencil.
Egg holder—use an empty egg box.

☐ Make sure the egg is absolutely clean. Dry the shell and leave the contents inside to support the egg while cutting, but have the bowl ready to catch the egg.

☐ Draw an oval on the side of the shell (fig.1a). It may help to make a pattern for this from a scrap of tissue.

☐ Cover the cutting line with transparent tape to reinforce it.

To cut a window. Using scissors make a hole in the centre of the area to be removed. Make sure that you only remove a small amount of shell with each cut as this will reduce chipping. Keep the scissor blades on the drawn outline when you reach it and try to make the cut as neat as possible. Remove the tape when completed. Any cracks can be covered with trimming later.

To cut a door. This is somewhat more difficult than cutting a window since the cut out area will be used as the door and so all mistakes made in cutting will be apparent. Use a razor blade or scalpel since this will assure a cleaner finish although it takes a little longer. As before, cover the cutting line with tape. Mark the cutting line with a groove by making repeated light strokes with the blade.

Alternatively, a small power drill, such as the battery-operated multi-purpose tool by Griffin and Spalding which can be fitted with fine cutting and drilling accessories, can be used. This is essential for working on harder shells and for more complicated cutting. Practice is needed to master the art of cutting without shattering the shell.

The smallest possible brass hinges about 1.25cm ($\frac{1}{2}$″) long (obtainable from DIY shops) firmly stuck with a contact adhesive such as Evo-stik Impact are used on these doors.

Cutting variations

Goose eggs are required for the majority of these and most of them should only be attempted after considerable practice.

The triptych. In this design (fig.1b) the vertical line that forms the central opening is cut *first*, before the door. It is possible, although extremely difficult, to use a chicken egg for this particular cut.

Top opening egg. This simple variation involves making a lid at the top instead of in the front of the egg. Always cut at the pointed end of the shell. A rubber band can be used to form a guideline which is then marked round with a pencil (fig.2).

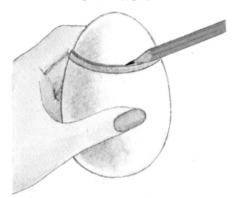

2. Cut made at pointed end of shell.

Tear shape. Draw an oval first, then shape the top into a point before cutting out, (fig.3).

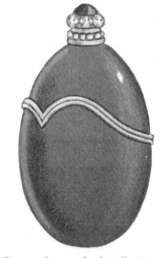

3. Tear shape: oval with pointed top.

The diagonal curve can look very effective, this comes round the upper part of the egg, rising upwards or dipping into a downwards point, (fig.4).

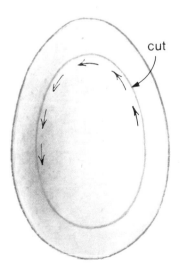

1a. Pencil oval shape on side of egg.

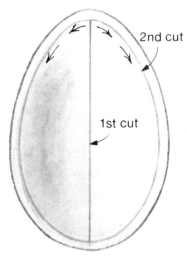

1b. Triptych: cut centre line first.

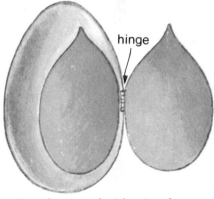

4. A diagonal curve looks effective.

191

The scallop. Four to six scallops can be made but more will weaken the shell. A small straight area must be left at the back for the hinge.

5. *Egg decorated with four scallops.*

Lattice egg. This is the most difficult of all to make. The shell is first cut in half and a hinge added. An oval shape is drawn on the lid section, this area is divided into a grid and the parts to be cut away are shaded with pencil (fig.6).

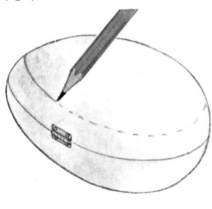

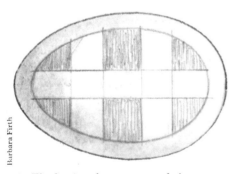

Barbara Firth

6. *The lattice: for experts only!*

Petal cuts. To mark the vertical divisions encircle the egg with rubber bands for a four-petalled egg or draw free-hand for a three-petalled version. Use a rubber band to mark the horizontal base line for the petals. Cut the vertical lines down from the top as far as the horizontal line, then cut along this to form the bases of the petals.

Mark petals and bases with corresponding numbers to match up when adding hinges, (fig.7).

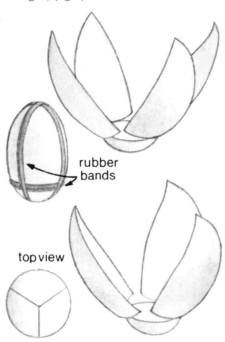

rubber bands

top view

7. *Both 3 and 4 petals are possible.*

Preparing for storage

If the cut egg is not to be immediately decorated, wash out the shell smoothing the membrane to remove air pockets. Remove the membrane if you are going to paint the interior.

Stick the door in position with sticky [cellophane] tape if you plan to trim the egg later (fig. 8).

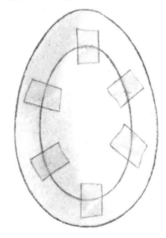

8. *Store egg with door in position.*

Ballast

Eggs that are intended to stand on a pedestal must be weighted at the base. For this you can use sand mixed with adhesive, ball bearings or lead dress weights, and cover with a tiny cardboard platform cut to fit the base of the egg. Figures inside the egg can be glued to the platform. Another idea is to fill the base of the egg with warm wax and sit figures on this. If working with

chicken eggs these bases are difficult to include as they take up too much of the total area.

Make sure you do not overcrowd your egg scene as the best eggs are often the simplest.

Hangers and pedestals

Eggs can be hung by a loop of ribbon glued lengthwise round the shell or you can stick them on a metal jewelry finding and hang from a nylon thread. Innumerable small decorative objects can be used as pedestals, from napkin rings, small lids and candle holders to pieces of driftwood. Attach the egg to the stand with contact adhesive.

Another attractive idea would be to construct an egg mobile. Suspend the eggs on varying lengths of thread or if the egg decoration is not too elaborate use coloured ribbons.

Bethlehem egg

The interior is painted with matt blue paint and covered with silver paper stars. The outside has several coats of blue nail polish. A tiny lamb is glued to a green fabric base with scraps of gold braid as straw. The bead and sequin trimming is stuck on with contact adhesive and the egg is finished with a blue ribbon bow.

It is important to keep the scene inside the egg in proportion to the egg itself, otherwise the overall appearance can be rather clumsy.

The imperial egg

This makes a glamorous jewelled box. Several coats of purple nail polish are used on both shell and door. The inside of the egg is trimmed with scraps of braid and sequins. Braid, pearls, sequins and beads are used to decorate the door (these are often easiest to apply if left on the strings on which they are supplied), a gap must be left where the hinge is to be positioned. An inexpensive cameo forms the centrepiece. The hinge is glued on last.

The triptych

Simply decorated but difficult to cut, it is glamorous enough to hold a piece of real jewelry. The outside of the shell and the doors are painted with black enamel. The edges are then trimmed with gold braid, leaving space for the hinges. The egg is then trimmed with diamanté and coral beads and gold sequins as illustrated, with a tiny fabric cushion inside the base.

It is hard to believe that these delicately jewelled containers by Stacey Carr started their lives as eggs. After some experience these designs could be within your scope. Braid and beads will take the place of Fabergé's real jewels.

194

Modelling crafts

There is immense satisfaction to be gained from the art of modelling. Creating attractive shapes from wax, plastic and clay provides all the basic skills you'll need.

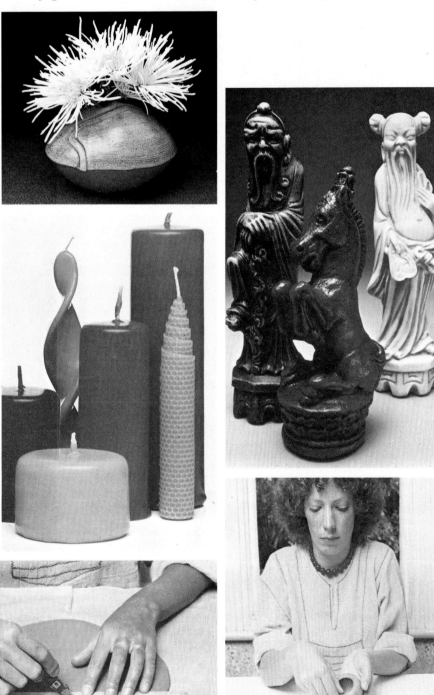

Simple candles

The very first candles probably consisted of pine branches, saturated either naturally or artificially with resin or fat. Sketches on prehistoric cave walls and ancient Egyptian tombs illustrate the use of candles and Pliny, in the first century AD, reported that in his time candles in Greece and Rome were made from flax threads coated with pitch and wax. During the Middle Ages the poorer folk burnt tallow, the rich—beeswax. The Roman Catholic churches actually demanded that their candles be made with a very large percentage of beeswax and even today they must still contain 25% beeswax.

As well as providing light, another primary use for candles was to act as a clock. King Alfred the Great and his subjects were able to tell the time of day from candles that burnt a certain, marked-off section in an hour. And right up until this century, bidding times at auctions were limited by means of a pin stuck into the side of a candle; proceedings stopped as soon as the pin fell out.

Beeswax and tallow were the only solid materials used in candlemaking until the end of the 18th century when the Sperm Oil Fishery began producing spermaceti, which yielded candles of great beauty, light—and expense! However, with the large-scale discovery of crude petroleum in 1859, paraffin wax emerged as a candle-making material and has prevailed ever since.

All the materials and equipment you will need to make the candles shown here are listed below. Collect together everything necessary before you start work. Some things you will already have around the house the rest are available from candlemakers' suppliers or pharmacists. Some suppliers produce a special beginner's kit to start you off.

Materials

Paraffin wax is available in solid blocks or in powdered form, ranging from pure white to cream. The grades vary widely but, for most candles, it is best to use a fully refined wax with a melting point of 57°C-60°C (135°F-140°F). The powdered paraffin wax is the simplest to use. You can also melt down old candle stubs and even your own failures. Plain-coloured pieces are easy to melt but if they are multi-coloured you will have to try to break up the component parts and melt them separately or you will end up with murky, brown candles.

Beeswax. You can buy this either in blocks or in honeycombed sheets of about 20cm x 40cm (8″x16″). Beeswax is expensive, so it's a luxury to use it alone—the best method is to add a little to paraffin wax. This will give your finished candle a superior gloss and will also make it burn longer.

The sheets come in natural and in several other colours and can be used alone to give rolled, honeycomb-effect candles. You will get about two large candles from each sheet. Any left-over scraps of beeswax sheet can be melted down and added to ordinary paraffin wax in the normal way.

Beekeepers, after they have removed their honey, can melt down the rest in boiling water. When it cools, the dross will have settled on the underside of the resulting cake of beeswax and can be scraped off so that the wax can be used.

Stearin. This is a white, flaky type of wax which helps dye to dissolve easily and completely. Stearin makes candles opaque (both pure white as well as coloured ones) and it is the stearin which causes the wax mixture to shrink a little and slip out of its mould easily. Use it in the proportion of 10% stearin to 90% wax.

Wax dyes. It is best to use these special dyes for candlemaking as opposed to any other kind of colouring. They are available in either powder or solid disc form and it is essential to take care when adding them to the wax —too much dye will mean that your candle will not glow.

Test the strength of the dye by taking a spoonful of the coloured candle wax and dropping it into cold water; as it sets, you will get an idea of the depth of the colour. So start with a little dye and build up the strength if necessary. For most colours a tiny pinch of powdered dye will colour 0.5lit (1pt) of liquid wax. The solid discs will each colour 2kg (about 4½lb) of wax to a pure, strong shade. If you want a lighter colour, cut the disc to size; if you want it darker, use more dye. You can also mix the colours so that you can choose from a much greater range. Powdered dye is cheaper but the discs give you a greater degree of accuracy.

Wicks. Candle wicks are made of bleached, woven linen thread and are usually sold in packs, sized according to the diameter of candle they will successfully burn. A 2.5cm (1″) wick will burn a paraffin wax candle 2.5cm (1″) in diameter. It will also burn a 2.5cm (1″) diameter hole in a larger candle so it is essential to choose the correct size, otherwise your wick could drown in a pool of molten wax. Likewise, a 5cm (2″) wick in a 2.5cm (1″) candle will burn down in no time.

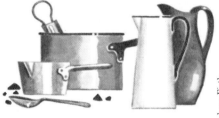

Barbara Firth

Equipment

Thermometer. A sugar thermometer with temperature readings up to 205°C (400°F) is essential. While there is very little danger of overheating wax to the point where it will burst into flames, it is impossible to judge when the wax is at the correct temperature without a thermometer. Also, each different type of candle—moulded, sand or dipped—requires a different working temperature.

Don't leave your thermometer in setting wax and, if any wax sets hard, don't try and pick it off—you will break the thermometer; dip it in hot water and melt the wax off.

Saucepans and jugs. Large saucepans are essential. Although you can manage with one by melting the stearin and dye first, then adding the wax, it is easier to dissolve the stearin and dye in one saucepan and melt the wax in another, especially if the wax is in block form and not powdered.

You need two tall jugs (enamel is best), a little deeper than the length of the

Dipping can produce candles of varying thickness—tapers to chunky candles. Those shown here are 25mm (1″) in diameter—the standard size for most candlesticks and holders. Designed by David Constable.

197

finished candle: one for dipping the candles and one for plunging them into cold water to harden.

Dipped candles

You will need:
1kg (2¼lb) paraffin wax
100gm (about ¼lb) stearin
Wax dye
Wick
Saucepan
2 tall jugs
Thermometer
Stick or pencil
☐ Melt 100gm (about ¼lb) stearin and

sprinkle a little powdered dye or scrape some solid dye on to it. Keep on a gentle heat and stir until all the dye is completely dissolved.
☐ In another saucepan melt 1kg (about 2¼lb) paraffin wax.
Never heat wax over a fierce flame and take care not to overheat, not to overfill the saucepan and not to splash hot wax on either yourself or the cooker [stove], since it will react like hot fat. In the very unlikely event of your managing to overheat the wax beyond its flash point, turn off the flame and try to cover the pan (with its lid if

The pear was made by dipping progressively less and less of the candle so that it became fuller towards the bottom. It was then moulded by hand when a little cooler and, when hard, the characteristic brown shading was painted on. All the other candles were overdipped to a different colour, then plunged into cold water for a glossy shine. Designed by David Constable.

possible)—don't attempt to carry it!
☐ Add the wax to the stearin/dye mixture and heat to 82°C (180F°).
☐ Fill a jug with wax. Tie one end of the

198

chosen wick length to a small stick or pencil and dip the wick into the wax. Remove it, pull it straight and hold it in the air for about 30 seconds until the wax hardens.

☐ Dip again and again until the candle is the right thickness for the wick (fig.1). Then hang it up to harden naturally.

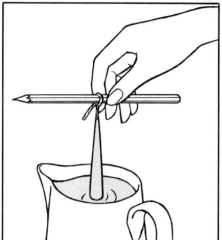

1. *Tie the end of the wick to a stick or pencil and dip it into the hot wax. Pull it so that the waxed wick hardens straight, then continue dipping until the candle is the required size.*

The wax in the jug may well cool before the desired thickness is reached; bubbles appearing on the surface of the wax or on the last layer on the candle show that the wax has cooled. When this happens, re-heat the wax to 82°C (180°F) before you dip again.

Depending on how wide a neck the jug has, you can dip more than one candle at the same time. Plunge the finished candle into a tall jug of cold water.

Variations

Shaping. Candles can be moulded to shape between dips. Build up the candle to about 12mm ($\frac{1}{2}$″) in diameter, then dip progressively less of the candle in the wax from a quarter of the way down the candle only, so that the lower part begins to thicken. At this stage roll the

Candle dipped in layers, hand-moulded into a ball and sections carved out.

candle between your hands to the shape you want. A pear-shaped candle can be made in this way.

Carving. By dipping a length of wick into a succession of different colours and building each one up to about 6mm ($\frac{1}{4}$″) thick, you can form multi-coloured layers. For this process, the wax must be very strongly dyed or the layers of colour will show through each other. When the candle is quite cold, carve patterns in the wax to reveal the underlying colours.

Twisting. To twist a dipped candle, take one that is still soft, lay it on a clean, smooth surface and flatten it slightly with a rolling pin. If it sticks, slide a knife under it and turn it over. Tap the base gently to square it off, then turn one end one way and the other end in the opposite direction at the same time to make the twist along the entire length of the candle. Cool it immediately in cold water.

Leave the candle in cold water until it is completely hard. Wax takes a long time to cool and if you take it out before it is really cold, the candle will distort.

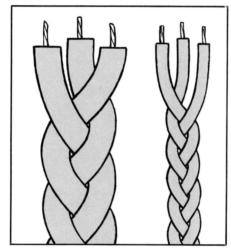

Plaiting a candle.

Plaiting. A plait of three different coloured dipped candles can be made very simply if you have someone to help you. Get them to hold the three ends as you plait while they are still soft and pliable. Cool at once in cold water.

Rolled beeswax

This traditional method of candle-making uses sheets of pure beeswax, honeycomb-textured and smelling delightfully of honey. As the sheets are usually workable at room temperature, you can roll a candle quite easily in a few minutes without heating. In colder weather you may have to soften the sheets slightly by warming them by a heater for a few minutes.

Choose a suitable wick for the finished diameter of the candle and cut it to the required candle length, plus a little

extra. Lay the wick along one edge of the sheet (fig.2) and fold the wax over

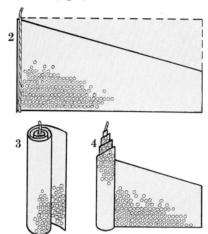

2,3,4. *Lay wick along one edge of beeswax sheet (the longer edge if you taper sheet) and roll up as shown.*

to cover it. Roll up the candles gently and evenly, making sure that the base of the candle is level (fig.3). Press the edge gently against the rolled candle to prevent it unrolling. Trim the wick to 6mm ($\frac{1}{4}$″) and dip the end of it in molten beeswax to prime it.

A variation can be made by trimming off the top end of the beeswax sheet at an angle (fig.2). Beginning at the longest side of the remaining section, lay the wick and roll up as before (fig.4).

Pieces of left-over beeswax can be used to decorate rolled candles. You can use two tapered sheets of different colours to give a two-tone effect.

Left to right: twisted dipped candle; squat bought candle, overdipped in yellow; red overdipped candle; brown overdipped candle; rolled beeswax.

199

Sand candles

Make evening garden parties glow with flares, stabbed firmly into grass or earth. They are made by building up a candle on a wick by pouring molten wax down the wick—the same process used for making long church candles.

To make a flare

For one flare
You will need:
A 45cm (18″) length of 2.5cm (1″) wick
200 gm (½lb) powdered paraffin wax
25 gm (1oz) stearin
A piece of cotton cloth, 50cm x 12.5 cm (20″x5″)
A 45cm (18″) length of bamboo cane, 1.25cm (½″) in diameter
Adhesive tape
Wax dye if required

☐ Melt stearin with dye (if you want a coloured candle) and add paraffin wax. When it has melted, put the wick into the molten wax, then remove it, allowing the drips to fall back into the pan. When the wick has cooled a little, pull it taut, allowing it to stiffen.

☐ Heat the wax to 71°C (160°F) then, using a tablespoon and holding the wick over the pan, spoon the molten wax down the wick. Don't have the wax too hot as it will re-melt the wax already built up on the candle and so will take longer to make.

☐ Spoon the wax around the wick about once a minute, rotating the wick between forefinger and thumb so that you get an even coat all over the wick. You may have to reheat the wax about every 10 minutes — remember to keep it on a low flame.

☐ You can run the candle under the cold tap to speed up the process but wipe the candle well with a tissue, as water trapped in the candle will make it splutter when burning.

☐ As the candle gets bigger it may require 3 or more spoonfuls in one go. Build it up to about 2cm (¾″) thick. If it is knobbly, lightly roll it out on a clean, smooth, cool surface while it is still warm to get rid of unevenness. Leave it flat to cool and harden.

☐ Split the bamboo into 4 for about 12cm (5″) down from one end. Holding it open, push the candle base in, taking care not to cut your hands on the sharp edges of the bamboo; stick the candle to the bamboo with adhesive tape.

☐ Put the cotton cloth into the remainder of the wax in the pot and heat slowly. When the cloth has absorbed the wax, unfold it over the pan, allowing the drips to fall back into the pan. When it has stopped dripping, wrap the cloth tightly around the candle, and lay it on its side to dry.

Flare candles on bamboo stalks to light gardens or patios. Designed by David Constable.

Like dipped candles and rolled beeswax candles, sand candles do not require a mould. All that's necessary is an object that can make a clear-cut hole in sand. An ash-tray, ornament, jelly mould, the bottom of a bottle, jar or bowl — any of these will do.

You will need:
Paraffin wax
Stearin
Dye (optional)
Thermometer
Sand
A bucket or box for the sand
An object to make the shape
Wick: choose one that leaves at least 2.5cm (1″) of wax unburned. For instance, if the candle is 7.5cm (3″) in diameter, put in a 5cm (2″) wick
A wicking needle: this is for making the hole for the wick through the partially set wax in the sand

☐ Fill a bucket or box with clean, damp sand and smooth off the surface to make it absolutely level without packing it down. Don't have a little bit of sand in the bottom of a deep box as you will not be able to impress the mould firmly enough.

☐ Dig a hole in the centre of the sand, push your mould into it, then remove the mould. If the sand is too wet the hole will not keep its shape, nor will enough sand cling to the wax.

Pushing the mould into the sand.

☐ Add stearin and dye to the paraffin wax and heat it in a saucepan to 250°F (121°C).

☐ Cut a length of wick to the depth of the candle; prime it by dipping it into the wax and pulling it straight.

☐ Pour the wax carefully into the shape in the sand. You may find it easier at first to pour the wax into a jug and from there into the hole. But remember that the hotter the wax the more sand is picked up; at 250°F (121°C) between 1.5cm (½″) and 2.5cm (1″) is picked up. If a thicker sand wall is required, the wax should be even hotter. As the wax cools, the level in the sand will drop; refill the hole as necessary, keeping the temperature of the new wax high.

Remove the mould carefully.

☐ Allow the sand candle to harden in a cold place for one or two hours. After this time, push the wicking needle down the centre and leave it standing upright.

Pouring the wax into the sand mould.

☐ Leave the candle overnight and dig it out the next day, loosening the sand around it carefully and brushing away any loose sand.

☐ Remove the needle and insert the already waxed wick into the hole.

☐ Top up around the wick hole with melted wax at 220°F (104°C) and allow it to set.

☐ Carve away areas of sand to make a design, taking care not to dig too deeply into the wax. If the right wick is chosen, the sand shell will remain intact after the candle has burned out and can be refilled with new wax.

Colourful sand candles have biscuit-like crusts. Designed by David Constable.

Clear casting with plastic

Plastic is a lightweight material and is easily worked. It comes in liquid form as a polyester resin or it can be a solid such as acrylic plastic. Therefore you either pour or cut it accordingly. Plastic is at its best when transparent or translucent. Unlike glass, it does not simply let light pass through it but diffuses it and carries it along its length, even around curves in a rod, to give the edge a fluorescent light. You can make all sorts of beautiful, modern designs in plastic, such as chess pieces, paper weights, jewelry, door knobs, magazine racks and trays.

If you think of plastic only as a substitute for materials such as glass, wood or metal, then you should reconsider. Plastic comes in an exciting variety of forms and colours and behaves in a completely different way from any other material.

Plastic is made up of chemicals derived from coal and petroleum and this chemical structure can be altered to suit different purposes.

Plastic is really a collective word for a number of materials, many quite unlike one another. However, they can be divided into two main groups.

Thermoplastics

These are plastics which are hard at normal temperatures but soften when heated. The temperature needs to be controlled to prevent the plastic from bubbling and therefore shrinking. The material can be shaped and moulded and will retain the new shape when it cools to its former solid mass. This process can be repeated a number of times before the material starts to break down. This means that if you make a mistake it can be corrected.

Acrylic in sheets or rods, celluloid, polystyrene and PVC are all examples of thermoplastics.

Thermosetting plastics

These are a group of materials that undergo a chemical change which is irreversible. They solidify in the presence of heat and, once shaped and cooled, they cannot be reworked. They can be reinforced with glass fibre which makes them strong enough to be used for structural purposes.

Polyester resins are thermosetting plastics. They have a syrup-like consistency and, when mixed with a catalyst—the hardener—they generate heat and then cool down to a solid. Resins are made for different applications so always make sure that the resin you use is suitable for the particular job you are doing. Resins for clear casting are especially made to remain clear with little or no optical distortion. They are also treated to avoid excessive shrinkage so that when a solid object is embedded in them they will not crack around the object. Polyester resin is easy to work with and is suitable for craft purposes in the home.

Terminology

A cast is the moulded resin.

Pigments are special dyes used to colour or tint the resins. They are either opaque or translucent.

Moulds specially made for casting resin are available from craft shops in any size and shape, but you can improvise: any glass or metal container with a smooth, highly polished surface is suitable. Plastic moulds or rubber moulds can also be used but as the resin will react with polystyrene, containers made from this material are unsuitable. Generally, soft plastic moulds such as polythene [polyethylene] are safe, but hard, brittle ones not.

Curing is the hardening of the resin. This process starts once the catalyst has been added to the resin and is complete when the cast has set to a solid. Heat is generated during this process. Air inhibits the curing of a pour so the exposed surface of the cast remains tacky. You can overcome this either by covering the pour to expel all air, which is difficult, or by removing the tacky surface with acetone.

The catalyst is a chemical, usually a peroxide solution, which reacts with the resin to turn it into a solid.

Gel is the stage where the resin is set but not hard. At this stage the surface will appear slightly rippled and is ready for a second pour.

These paper weights and pen-holder are exceptionally fine examples of resin casting. The piece on the left has a graphic design on the base which is optically very effective. Supplied by Barnabas (Covent Garden) Ltd.

Steve Bicknell

Clear cast embedding

Embedding is the process whereby an object is placed within a solid mass of resin. This is usually done in two layers for a single object, or in a number of layers, depending on the number of objects and the way they are spaced. Each layer is known as a pour. The first pour is to create the outer surface and to support the object. The second pour is to cover the object, thus embedding it.

There is no end to the things that can be embedded in resin. The casts you make can be varied not only by the

To make clear cast objects you will need wooden stirrers, moulds, paper cups, catalyst or hardener to mix with the resin, colour pigments to tint the cast and a measuring cup.

object you embed but also by the shape of the mould and the colour of the resin. You can tint the resin slightly for a special effect, or make the back or base of the mould an opaque colour as a background for the object.

You can make paper weights, buttons, door knobs, jewelry, key rings, picture mounts, chess and backgammon pieces —in fact you can apply this technique to most objects.

Experiment with embedding dried flowers and grasses, some of which are more suitable than others. The colour tends to fade—red more so than yellow —but everlasting flowers can be embedded successfully as they do not fade. You can embed coins, insects, colourful seeds, coloured glass chips, watch parts, unusual stamps, address cards and shells. You can also make large clear blocks to mount photographs or to set photographs in. Remember that whatever you embed must be free of moisture.

The process is easy and you do not require any special tools. The materials are easily available and for a high gloss finish the cast can be polished with a metal polish. Resins can be purchased from hobby shops or manu-

facturers in various quantities. Buy the appropriate catalyst at the same time. You can buy an embedding kit or you can buy the resin and catalyst separately.

To make a cast

For example, a paper weight.
You will need:
Clear cast resin and catalyst
Mould
Object to embed
Waxed paper cups
Measuring jug, wooden stirrers
Wax polish
Optional—colour pigment
Acetone is useful for cleaning, but it is highly inflammable so throw cleaning materials away.

Prepare your work area by covering the surface with paper.

Decide on the object you are going to embed, then select a mould suitable for the object's size and shape.

Measuring and preparing the mould. Some moulds are marked with their capacity; if not, fill the mould with water up to the level required for the first pour—usually $\frac{1}{2}$-$\frac{1}{3}$ the total depth of cast. Pour the water into a measuring jug to find the capacity.

If you do not want to mix the resin and catalyst in the measuring jug, pour the water into a paper cup and mark the water level. Dry the mould and the paper cup thoroughly before adding the resin.

Polish the mould with wax polish. Although this is not essential, depending on the type of mould you use, it does help to release the cast. If you want to make more than one cast prepare the moulds together.

Remember that the open end of the mould will usually be the back or bottom of the object you are making. The smooth inside surface of the mould will form the outside surface of the cast.

Measure out the resin and add the appropriate amount of catalyst. If you want to tint the cast, add the pigment before you add the catalyst and mix it well—stirring slowly to avoid trapping air bubbles.

☐ Once the catalyst has been added, stir the mixture slowly for a minute before pouring it into the mould.

☐ Set the mould aside on a level surface and cover it lightly with foil to prevent the surface from collecting dust. You can place the mould at an angle if you want a sloping surface.

Leave the cast for about three hours or until it has gelled. The length of time can vary depending on the amount of catalyst used.

Embedding an object

☐ Some objects are inclined to trap air when being embedded. If you are using a coin, prepare it by pouring a few

Once the casts have cured they can be finished by gluing a design to the tacky surface. You can then attach jeweller's findings to make brooches, earrings and key rings.

Glass beads were used to create this mosaic pattern.

It is difficult not to trap air bubbles when embedding intricate pieces.

Air bubbles between the photo and the cast spoil the effect of this piece.

Too much catalyst has been used in this cast, causing it to crack.

drops of resin mixed with catalyst on to the face. Leave to set and place this side down on the gel before the second pour.

Address cards can be treated in the same way. Dried flowers should be immersed in resin before being embedded.

☐ Place the object upside down on the tacky surface of the first pour. If the object is very light in weight you can coat it with a clear plastic adhesive to keep it in position. Once this has dried, make the second pour.

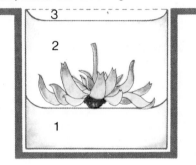

1. First pour 2. Object embedded in second pour 3. Resin or felt base.

☐ The tacky surface of the cast can be covered with a piece of felt or you can cover it with a thin layer of resin to which you have added more than the usual amount of catalyst. This will cure to a smooth finish.

The resin can take from 15 minutes to several hours to cure completely, depending on the brand of resin and the size of the cast.

Removing the cast. If a cast is difficult to remove from a mould, immerse it in cold water and bring to the boil. Then plunge it in cold water. If it still sticks repeat the process—it will work.

Polishing. Rub the cast down with a metal polish for a highly polished finish. You can also rub it down with a fine grade wet and dry paper and then use a metal polish, but this is difficult to do by hand and requires a lot of practice. If you do attempt it, try it out on a small test cast first.

Once you have made a few casts you will find it easy to make larger objects and to adapt the technique to a wide range of colourful articles.

Hints on embedding

Patience is essential for good results. Satisfy your initial enthusiasm by making small casts—larger casts take a long time to cure to obtain successful results. But even when making small casts, apply the following hints—they will improve your casts and make the whole process easier when you attempt larger pieces.

The object to be embedded must be dry and free of dust.

Avoid trapping air bubbles by stirring the resin slowly.

The percentage of catalyst used must be decreased as the amount of resin to be poured is increased. Too much catalyst will form cracks in the cast—although you might do this for special effects. The amount of heat generated is relative to the amount of catalyst used, so if an excessive amount of catalyst is used not only will it form cracks in the cast but it can also ruin the mould.

It is better to use too little catalyst than too much. The surface can always be cured artificially if necessary by applying a thin coat of resin to which a larger proportion of catalyst has been added. You can also use this method to glue a base to the tacky surface of the cast.

Store the resin containers in a cool, dark place and cover them so that they do not collect dust. Dust could fall into the resin when you pour it from the container, so work in a dust-free atmosphere and cover the casts while curing.

To avoid waste, always have a spare mould on hand in case you have any resin left over from a previous pour.

Safety hints

Take care: some plastics can be inflammable, some fumes can be toxic, and some may irritate the skin. However, they are perfectly safe to work with in the home if you take the following simple precautions.

Store all plastic materials in a cool, dark place.

The room in which you are working must be warm and well ventilated.

Do not smoke when working with plastics and do not work in a room where there is an open flame.

Keep materials away from food.

Avoid contact with the eyes.

If you find it difficult to work wearing rubber gloves use a barrier cream on the hands.

Work on a heat resistant surface that has been covered with tinfoil or waxed paper.

Use disposable containers for mixing resin in and do not throw away the excess until it has cooled down.

Wear old clothing and remove any spilt resin with acetone.

Should your skin come into contact with the resin wash it immediately with cold water.

Wipe up any spilt resin with a paper towel and dispose of it— do not use it a second time.

Dispose of all cleaning materials and waste as soon as you have finished working with the resin.

Modelling with plastic

When casting objects that do not need the optical clarity of, say clear-cast embedding, you can use ordinary casting resin. This can be coloured in any opaque colour or it can be finished and stained once the cast has cured. Depending on the object being cast and the required weight, the resin can be used either with a filler to give it weight or without if it does not need to be heavy.

Fillers

A filler is a material used to give a cast weight, to cut down on the amount of resin used, or to give it a metallic appearance. If the cast is to be opaque then a filler can be used, as no optical or translucent qualities are required. The filler can be up to 50% of the total volume to be cast.

You can use a metallic powder filler especially made for this purpose which gives the appearance of copper, iron or brass. Alternatively, you can use fine sand, flour, plaster of Paris, metal filings, glass fibres, talc, powdered slate or chalk. Different fillers will give you various textured finishes so you can experiment with small pieces until you get the particular results you want.

Colour pigments and stains

The cast can be coloured when you have mixed the resin and the filler but before you add the catalyst. Any of the colour pigments made for resin can be used. Black and ivory—which give a very natural colour—work particularly well. Once the casts have cured you can use any wood stain or household paint to 'antique' the cast. Cover the cast with the stain or paint and, while it is still wet, rub the paint from the more prominent surfaces and leave it to dry.

Manufactured moulds

Special-purpose moulds obtainable from craft suppliers generally come in four types.

Flexible moulds such as rubber moulds for candle-making, plaster casting or resin casting are probably the most versatile.

Semi-flexible moulds of polythene [polyethylene] are used for clear-cast resin and candles. You could cast plaster as well but the cast will not be interesting in itself unless the surface is decorated in some way.

Two-part moulds, usually produced by vacuum forming, are used for all types of materials but the range of available moulds is limited.

Rigid moulds such as ceramic, metal and glass offer a high degree of surface polish and therefore lend themselves especially well to resin casting.

Manufactured moulds can be bought from craft shops or manufacturers in many different forms. You can buy moulds to make chess pieces, candles, pendants and a variety of objects.

Although a bought mould will not give you an original design you can make it look different by giving it an antique appearance or by staining it. These moulds will give you some experience in casting more intricate pieces before you actually start making your own moulds.

The red and the green chessmen are coloured with pigment in the liquid resin. Like the white chess pieces they were then painted and rubbed to give them an antique appearance.

Supporting the mould

Once the moulds have been filled with resin they will have to be kept upright until they have cured. There are two ways in which to do this.

If the filler you have used is not heavy you can suspend the moulds in a piece of cardboard which has holes cut into it to fit the base of the mould. If the filler is heavy this might stretch the mould or pull it out of shape. To avoid this, hold the mould in a paper cup, slightly larger than the mould, and fill surrounding area with rice or fine sand.

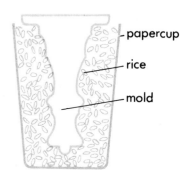

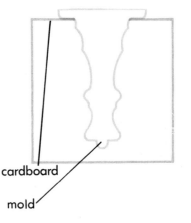

Once the moulds have been half filled with the resin mixture and it has been spread around the interior, they are suspended from cardboard or placed in rice and then filled with resin.

To make casts with filler

For example, a set of chessmen as illustrated.

You will need:
Casting resin
Filler
Colour pigment—optional
Catalyst or hardener
Moulds
Felt—optional, to attach to the base or bottom of the cast

☐ Prepare a working area in a well-ventilated room.

☐ Work out the quantity of resin and filler needed to fill various moulds. The instructions with a manufactured kit with resin, filler and moulds will usually include the capacity of the

moulds. Of the total quantity required, use about 60% resin and 40% filler.

☐ Mix the resin and the filler by stirring in small quantities of the filler until it has dispersed in the resin. The black and white chessmen illustrated have been made with a white filler—the black pieces were painted after curing.

☐ Add the colour pigment, if required, and thoroughly mix the resin. The red and green chessmen were coloured in this manner.

☐ Leave the resin mixture to stand for a few minutes so that any trapped air bubbles can rise to the surface.

☐ Add the catalyst or hardener to the mixture and stir it carefully to avoid making air bubbles.

☐ Half fill the mould and allow the mixture to flow around the entire surface of the mould by tilting and flexing the mould with thumb and fore-finger. This will ensure that all the detail in the mould is impressed and it also prevents trapping air.

☐ Suspend the mould from cardboard or pack it into a paper cup and fill the sides with rice.

☐ Fill the mould with the resin mix-ture and leave it to cure. Curing time will vary depending on room tempera-ture and the type of resin used.

☐ To remove the mould from the cured casting, wash it in warm soapy water and then gently peel back the mould. Do not rip the mould off as you can damage either it or the casting.

If there are small imperfections caused by air bubbles in the cast you can mix a small amount of resin and catalyst and use a matchstick to apply it to the cast. Once it is dry the appearance will be perfect.

These chessmen were made with a white filler. The white chessmen were stained and then rubbed down to leave the darker colour in the recesses, giving them an antique appearance. The black chessmen were painted.

Finishing

You can stain the piece or colour it, if you did not use the colour pigment. To give it an antique appearance rub off the stain or paint while it is still tacky. This will remove the stain or paint on the raised surfaces leaving the recesses darker. Rub the piece until you obtain the desired effect. Leave to dry.

☐ If you glue a piece of felt to the bottom of the cast then you will not have to worry about the tacky surface. Alternatively, sand down the cured cast with wet and dry paper.

Clay modelling

Clay is one of the most satisfying materials to work with. Even simple pinching and modelling with your fingers can produce exciting results and is a good way of becoming familiar with the texture and properties of clay. You can start working in a basic way without a kiln and, if your imagination is stimulated, then go on to use a potter's wheel and fire your own designs.

Natural clay. A lump of clay is made up of millions of tiny, plate-shaped particles. Water enables these flat particles to slide over each other without breaking up. When clay is dry, the particles will not move and if forced, will break. When only a small amount of water is present, movement is limited, and the clay is stiff to use. When the clay is about 25% water it

can be easily moulded and is ideal for modelling. More water turns the clay into a soft, formless mass.

Natural clay has the great advantage for the beginner of being an extremely cheap material. Two types of clay are commercially available: white clay is smooth, takes glaze well and is cleaner to use, whereas terracotta clay fires to a pleasant red colour at a fairly low temperature. Ready-to-use clay is available by post direct from the manufacturers, and usually contains about 25% water. It is polythene-wrapped in bags of various sizes, the 25kg (55lbs) weight being the most convenient for beginners. Store it in a cool place, carefully wrapped in polythene so that it does not dry out. When you have moulded the clay into a finished pot or model, the dried clay can be turned into a hard, permanent material by firing it in a pottery oven or kiln, a sawdust pit, or even a bonfire.

Self-hardening clays. For potters who do not have kilns, specially compounded clay mixtures are now available which, when exposed to the air for about 24-48 hours, become really hard and should not break or scratch. The self-hardening clays are clean to use, but are less satisfying to handle than natural clay. They are widely available from hobby shops, but are relatively expensive.

Pots made from self-hardening clay are not entirely durable, they cannot be glazed and they do not hold water. If you varnish them thoroughly first however, they can be made waterproof. Manufacturers supply varnishes intended for use with their clay products, and these can be applied over painted decorations. Some of the self-hardening clays can be fired, if you have access to a kiln, so that your most successful pieces can be made impervious.

Some of these manufactured products, like ColdClay, have an added advantage in that they are natural potting clay containing a hardening additive, rather than a synthetic substitute, so they handle like natural clay.

Handling qualities. Test the properties of your own clay; dry some pieces out and see how hard they become, wet other pieces and see how the amount of water present affects this quality of the clay, which is called plasticity. Pinching the clay and working it with a little water will quickly mix the two. A good test for judging the working qualities of the clay is to roll a piece between your hand into a coil which you wrap round your finger. If the coil bends without breaking, does not stick to your finger and retains its shape, then it is probably just right. If it cracks, it is too dry, and if it sticks and is floppy, it is too wet.

Testing the quality of the clay

Decorating unfired clay. If you are planning to work a design on the clay, press interesting shapes with snap fasteners, tiny buttons, or a pen-knife against the clay before it hardens.

Paint the clay only when it is completely dry. Several types of paint are useful for decorating. Poster paint used direct from the pot gives a strong opaque colour. Indian inks are waterproof and dry to give a semi-matt surface and subtle colours. Gouache colours are also excellent for decorating clay. For a shiny, durable finish, on painted patterns use a suitable clear varnish such as paper varnish or polyurethane lacquer.

Clay is one of the most beautiful and satisfying of natural materials. The textures and colours are infinite in their variety, and even the beginner can achieve splendid results.

The items shown here are made by advanced, professional craftsmen, and show a wide range of techniques. Try the projects in the following pages. They will provide a wonderful introduction to the craft.

Ceramic picture tiles

As well as being patted or sliced into a square block, clay can also be rolled out flat, rather like pastry. Clay sheets rolled out in this way are called slabs, and potters use them to build slab pots and dishes, to make sculptures and geometrical constructions.

The slab, because it is so easy to make, is an excellent form for the beginner to work with. Once rolled out to an even thickness, the clay can be cut into tiles with a sharp knife or scalpel, and other slabs of varying thickness can be trimmed and pressed on to the clay surface to give a relief effect. Like the block, the slab can be painted, impressed with objects or modelled upon.

Making a clay slab

Using a wooden rolling pin and a flat wooden surface such as a table top covered with hessian [burlap] or canvas, begin by flattening a ball of clay (fig.1) and rolling out so that it makes a rough oval (fig.2).

The clay can finally be rolled so that it is an even thickness all over by placing it between two flat strips of wood, each as thick as the required depth of the slab, and then rolling it with the ends of the rolling pin resting on the wooden strips (fig.3).

Two cheap wooden rulers glued together, for example, give a 6mm ($\frac{1}{4}''$) strip which is a useful thickness for tiles and similar shapes.

The resulting slab is now completely even, and the same thickness as the strips. Ease away the hessian [burlap] (fig. 4) as shown.

Relief modelling on a tile

The landscape tile shown here is a simple relief project that can be made in either natural or self-hardening clay. Follow these techniques to build up your own landscape, whether it is real or imagined.

To make a relief tile

You will need:
$\frac{3}{8}$kg ($\frac{3}{4}$lb) clay
Poster paints for decorating
Clear varnish, if required
Sharp knife; wooden ruler; rolling pin; 2 sticks about 6mm ($\frac{1}{4}''$) thick for rolling out clay; polythene sheeting.

☐ Roll out the clay evenly to a thickness of 6mm ($\frac{1}{4}''$) to accommodate your tile shape. Measure and mark out the tile on the rolled-out clay, using a torn-off corner of newspaper to give the right angles.

☐ To cut the tile lay the ruler along the edges of the tile and, using this and the newspaper as a guide, trim away the sides of the tile with the sharp knife (fig.5). To do this, slide the knife through the clay from one corner to half way along one edge of the clay then remove it. Then slide it again from the opposite corner. If you slice straight along the edge you will stretch the clay out of shape. Keep the trimmed off pieces to build up the picture.

☐ Cut out a series of curving shapes to represent mountain and valley formations.

☐ Build up the scene gradually, starting with the background masses and positioning more shapes on top of them so that the foreground is in the highest relief. Stick each land mass into place by teasing the back of it with an old toothbrush dipped in water. Tease the clay area on to which it is to be fixed in the same way and press the relief slab firmly into position with the fingertips.

☐ When the landscape is complete, place it on a sheet of newspaper, cover with a sheet of polythene and leave it to dry out slowly and thoroughly.

☐ When the tile is quite dry, paint it with poster colours. It is worth remembering that, unless you are a proficient painter, more striking effects are achieved with a few simple colours. As a general rule, paint the foreground high-reliefs in paler shades, toning down to dark colours in the distance. If desired, the completed tile can finally be painted with clear varnish or polyurethane lacquer to give it a glossy finish.

Right: landscape tile that makes an ideal first modelling project. Designed by Val Barry.

1. *Begin by flattening a square block of clay, using a wooden rolling pin.*

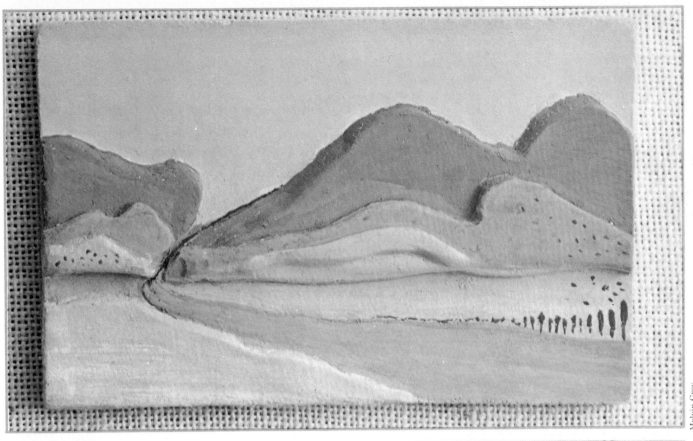

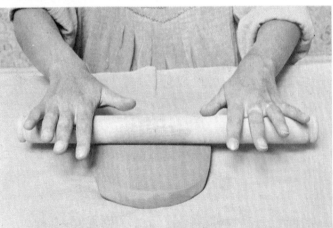

2. *First rolling—to flatten the clay into a rough oval.*

3. *Rolling in second direction to an even thickness, using two flat sticks as a guide.*

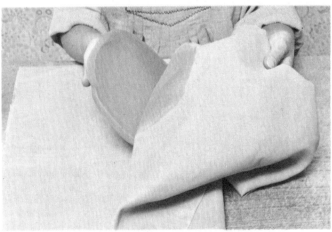

4. *Easing hessian [burlap] away from clay.*

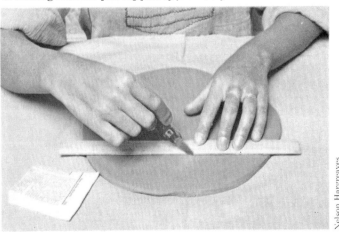

5. *Measuring out and cutting clay tile, using ruler as guide and a scrap of newspaper to give accurate right angles.*

To make the face tile

The relief modelled picture is one way in which the basic tile can be decorated. As another idea, try your own version of the stylized face picture shown here, or try making an abstract panel.

Coloured stains in the form of special coloured powders for staining clay or colouring glazes have been used. As the pigment is expensive, initial projects are best kept small—about 20cm x 30cm (8"x12")—as in the picture here. Choose 3 or 4 clay stains, remembering that fewer colours look more effective than a confusing variety, when combined with the texture of the clay.

Clay stained with coloured powders.

You will need:

1kg (2lb) clay
Coloured stains (coloured powders for staining clay or colouring glazes)
Flat wooden board or table; wooden rolling pin; 2 sticks about 6mm (¼") thick for rolling out clay; steel ruler; sharp knife; tracing paper; polythene sheeting; clear varnish, if required
Nails, screws and hairpins, or other small objects for texturing clay
Thin layer of sponge or foam, large enough to cover the picture
Heavy book, large enough to cover the picture

☐ Select one pale shade for the tile base, and mix about 4 teaspoons of powder with enough water to dissolve it completely. Work this mixture into a 700gm (1½lb) ball of clay until the colour is evenly spread.

☐ For the applied decorations prepare small quantities of clay about the size of a table tennis ball, in the same way. Keep the different coloured balls of clay separate, and make sure that the clay stays moist by covering it with sheets of polythene.

The face picture is built up from tiny balls of different coloured clays pressed on to the surface of the tile. The resulting technique is intricate and delicate. Designed by Zuzanna Kleczkowski.

Two mirrors in soft, terracotta coloured clay are another example of decorative slab work. The clay is sliced into attractive shapes, and a central portion is cut out so that the slab can be backed with mirror. Impressed and incised patterns complete the effect. Designed by The Birchwood Pottery.

☐ Trace off face shape shown opposite and then draw this carefully to scale, allowing yourself a margin of at least 5cm (2") all around the picture.

☐ Roll the base clay out to an even 6mm (¼") thickness. Patches of contrasting colour in the base clay are obtained by placing blobs of different colour on the tile, and rolling them in at the same time. It is best not to try to control where these areas merge but to let them find their own shape and position.

☐ Place the traced picture on the tile, and hold the corners in place with four small lumps of clay. Using a pencil, trace the design quickly on to the tile.

☐ Discard the paper and use a steel ruler and sharp knife to trim waste clay away from the picture.

☐ To apply the colour make clay beads by pinching off tiny pieces of clay in the different colours, and rolling them with the fingertips in the palm of your hand. It is easiest to build up the lines that form the picture first and then to fill in the areas of colour, so begin by pressing the beads in along the lines, and build up the solid areas gradually.

☐ Texture can be introduced after the beads have been applied with a pencil end, a matchstick, nail head or any other suitable shape.

☐ When the picture is finished, cover it with the foam and a heavy book, which will stop the clay warping as it dries out. When the picture is completely dry, finish it off with a coat of varnish.

☐ To hang the picture tile, screw a hook to a small square of wood and glue the wood to the tile with impact adhesive (fig.6).

6. *Attach the hook with a screw to a piece of wood about 2.5cm (1") square, 6mm (¼") thick.*

Simple pinch pots

Pinch pots or thumb pots are made by pushing the thumb into a ball of clay and gently squeezing the ball to hollow it out. Repeated squeezing or pinching turns the clay ball into a small bowl, which can then be manipulated with the fingers to give the shape you want. It is one of the simplest and most primitive ways to make a pot. Stone-Age Man made pots in this way for storing and cooking food, and primitive

peoples throughout the world still use this method for making domestic and decorative pots.

Modern potters also use the technique to make elaborate and delicate pots.

No tools are required; you simply work the clay in your hands so, for the beginner, it's a good way to become familiar with clay and what it will do. Because pinch pots are formed in the hands and fingers, they often have natural-looking, slightly irregular shapes that suggest organic forms. The delicate cream and grey pot shown here, for example, suggests a seed pod, and the thin and delicately textured bowl shown suggests an exotic flower.

To make a pinch pot

Choose clay which is soft but not too sticky. If the clay is hard it is difficult to work, and if it is sticky it will immediately collapse out of shape.

☐ Break the clay into pieces about the size of a tennis ball, and roll a piece between the palms of the hands until you have a smooth ball (fig.1).

☐ Hold the ball of clay in your left hand, balancing it so that it sits comfortably in the palm with the fingers curled loosely around it.

☐ Push the thumb of the right hand into the centre of the ball (fig.2), and go on pushing until you are about three quarters of the way down.

☐ Squeeze in a slow, spiralling movement, turning the ball evenly in the palm of the hand while you squeeze (fig.3).

You will find this squeezing and rotating process easier if you hold the ball of clay sideways in your palm. Keep the surface of the clay smooth, and follow the outside shape with your fingers as you squeeze.

If you remember that the outside and inside shape of a pot should always be the same, the walls of the pot should have a uniform thickness.

☐ Continue rotating and squeezing, working slowly up the walls of the pot and leaving the rim until last (fig.4). Aim to keep the opening of the pot as small as possible at first, or the pot will go out of control.

☐ Work the top of the pot last. Hold the pot sideways in the palm of the hand and gently squeeze the rim until round and even—the best way to do this is to reverse the position of the thumb and fingers so that the thumb controls the shape of the outer rim (fig.5).

☐ Use a finger to smooth out any cracks that may have appeared in the rim (fig.6).

Left: all these were made by pinching: bird shaped pot designed by Jane Gabbatiss; large pot by Deidre Burnett; fluted bowl by Elizabeth Duncombe.

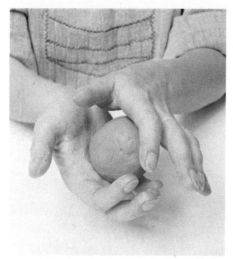

1. *Break the clay into pieces about the size of a tennis ball and roll each piece in the palms of the hands until it is completely smooth.*

2. *Hold the ball of clay loosely in the palm of the hand and begin to push the thumb of the other hand down into the centre of the ball.*

3. *With the thumb on the inside and the fingers on the outside, gently squeeze the clay. Hold the clay slightly sideways and rotate slowly.*

4. *Work from the bottom of the ball upwards, squeezing in a continuous, spiralling movement until the walls of the pot are about 6mm ($\frac{1}{4}$") thick.*

5. *To work the neck of the pot, reverse the position of thumb and fingers and gently squeeze the rim until it is round and even.*

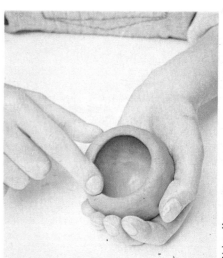

6. *Smooth away any cracks that may have appeared on the rim with a fingertip or, if it is too dry, use a slightly dampened sponge.*

215

☐ Work on several balls of clay at one time, allowing them to stiffen in the intervals of being worked. Pinch the clay until it is about 2.5cm (1″) thick, then stand it upside down on the rim to stiffen. Do not stand it on the base or it will sag and spoil the smooth inside curve.

Once the pot has stiffened slightly you will be able to pinch it thinner and still keep a good shape.

If your pot goes wrong. With practice, small bowls and vases can be made in about ten minutes, but never try to hurry a pot. Do not work the clay for too long either, or it will dry and split from the warmth of your hands. If it does crack, you may be working with clay that is too hard. Smooth the cracks away with a fingertip, but do not try to wet the clay or it will collapse. If you find that it is too dry to work with comfortably, moisten your hands very slightly.

Developing different shapes. If you are working with real clay and intend at a later stage to fire your pot, be careful not to fold the clay. Folding traps air inside the clay, which will cause the clay to crack or even explode when you come to fire it.

Begin by making a few simple bowls and see how thin you can pinch them. When you have mastered this, try making different shapes—some round and some oval.

Once you are familiar with the process, the first simple bowl and vase shapes can be developed into delicately controlled organic shapes. They can also be placed rim to rim to make a rounded shape, oval or flattened, which is called a pebble pot.

To make a pebble pot

Pinch two bowls with same size rims.
☐ Score the rims with an old toothbrush dipped in water and press them firmly together. The air trapped inside supports the shape while the pot is being worked.
☐ Seal the join by rolling out a small coil of clay, a little thinner than a

pencil for a pot about 10cm (4″) in diameter, and pressing it round the join. Smooth this with the fingers until the surface of the pot is smooth and the join invisible.

Put the pot on one side to allow the join to dry out.

A pebble pot can be left as a smoothly rounded sphere or oval shape, or it can be tapped with a flat piece of wood to give an angled, textured form.

Cutting holes. If the pot is to be fired, it must be pierced so that the air trapped in the pot will not expand with the heat and crack the pot.

When the pot is dry, cut a hole in the surface as with the interesting oval pot shown here.

Pebble pots made in self-hardening clay, however, do not need to be fired and so the clay can be left solid.

Joining pinch pots

Another idea is to join together a group of small pinch pots to form a cluster that could be used as a cruet, a tiny pot-pourri, or a place to store rings, pins and beads. Use the same method to join the pots—score both surfaces with a moistened toothbrush and press them firmly together.

Decorating pinch pots

Pinch pots made in self-hardening clay can be painted with poster colours, Indian inks or gouache. The pots in the group shown here were decorated in geometric patterns in colours similar to natural earth colours, to emphasize the pleasing simplicity of their shapes. Self-hardening clay pots can also be decorated by impressing shapes into them at the semi-dry stage, to give a textured effect, or they can be varnished for a plain, shiny look.

If you are working with real clay, however, and the pot is to be fired, there is a variety of interesting decorative possibilities that do not involve the use of glaze.

The pot can be impressed when it is semi-dry, or it can be left until it is bone-dry and then incised.

This form of incised decoration is done by scratching the surface of the bone-dry clay with a fine pin or knife point. Designs can be geometric or flowing, and can look particularly intricate and delicate.

Whichever form of decoration you choose, aim to accentuate the basic shape of the pot by relating your design to it. Decoration should always compliment the pot and add extra interest.

Right: simple pinch pots, decorated with poster paints, make attractive containers. Designed by Shirley Brown. Textured pot with impressed pattern designed by Val Barry.

Alasdair Ogilvie

Fine example of an oval pebble pot, designed by Jane Gabbatiss.

Melvin Grey

Papercrafts

You'll be amazed at the variety of projects for working in paper. Make fantasy flowers, exotic oriental kites, papier maché models, plus wonderful collage pictures.

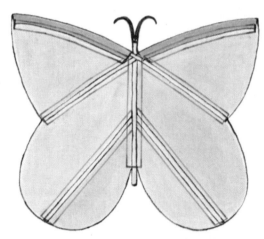

Simple kites

No one knows who flew the first kite or why. According to tradition, kites were invented by the Greek scientist Archytas of Tarentum about 400BC, but they are known to have been flown in China some 600 years earlier. Since then, kite flying has become a national pastime in Korea, Malaya, China and Japan, and it is from these countries that the prettiest designs have come.

Probably the easiest shape for the beginner to start with is the cutter kite, an elongated diamond shape with a tail. It can be made in under an hour and decorated in many different ways.

Choosing the materials

Surprisingly, there is no need to bother unduly about the weight of a kite unless it is to be flown in very light winds. Choose any paper you like for the cover—heavy papers such as cartridge or wallpaper; medium weights such as decorative wrapping papers, posters or shelf paper; or light-weight papers such as tissue. Crepe is probably the only unsuitable paper because of its tendency to stretch.

The sticks for the frame can be garden canes, balsa or pine battens, dowels or even twigs. Split thicker, heavier sticks lengthwise with a sharp kitchen knife to make them lighter.

Balance is more important than weight, so shave off any knots or thicker sections. To test for balance, mark the middle of the stick and balance it across the back of the knife blade. If one end dips, shave a little off it.

Making and decorating cutter kites is only part of the enjoyment—flying them will amuse the children for days.

Cutter kite

Scale the size of this kite up or down as you wish, according to the size required. The important part is the proportionate length of the sticks; *the longer stick should be half as long again as the shorter one.*

You will need:
Two sticks, one 61cm (24″) long and the other 91cm (36″) long.
Large sheet of paper for the cover.
Small ball of thin string or strong thread.
Glue or sticky tape.

Scissors and craft knife.
Pencil and ruler.
Curtain ring.
Poster paint and brush (optional).
Scraps of coloured paper or streamers for the tail.
Flying line and reel.

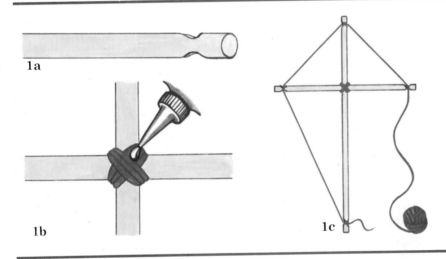

The frame. First cut two small notches, each about 6mm ($\frac{1}{4}$″) in from each end of both sticks (fig.1a).

☐ Make a mark at the centre of the shorter stick and a mark one third of the way along the longer one.

☐ Lay the sticks across each other at right angles, the marks touching, and bind the join tightly with thread.

☐ Put a dab of glue on the join for extra strength (fig.1b).

☐ Tie a piece of thread to the notched end of one of the sticks and take it across to the other sticks in turn, winding it tightly around each notch two or three times (fig.1c).

☐ Tie the ends to complete the frame.

The cover. Lay the frame on the wrong side of the sheet of paper and cut round it, cutting about 2.5cm (1″) outside the string (fig.2).

☐ Trim off the corners of the paper (see fig.2).

☐ Fold the edges of the paper up over the string and stick them down with glue or sticky tape.

Decoration. Turn the kite face up, with the frame underneath, and decorate the front by painting it or by pasting on paper shapes.

Keep the design simple and the colours bold, because details will be lost when the kite is in the sky. A bold motif cut from a poster, or even the poster itself, would make an 'instant' decoration.

Coral Mula

Bridle. This is the name for the strings which hold the kite at the correct angle to the wind and to which the towing line is attached. The cutter kite has two pieces of string or thread making a double bridle.

☐ Lay the kite on the table, decorated side uppermost.

☐ Take a piece of thread long enough to reach round one short and one long side of the kite with just a little to spare. Tie the ends to the notched ends of the vertical stick where they jut out beyond the cover (fig.3a).

☐ Tie the second bridle to each end of the horizontal stick. This time the piece of thread should be twice the length of one of the short sides of the kite, with a little to spare (fig.3b).

☐ Loop the curtain ring on to the long bridle (fig.4) about one third of the way down it, and then on to the centre of the short bridle.

☐ Test the balance of the kite by holding it above the table by the ring. The two sides should be equidistant from the table and the kite itself should hang at an angle of about 45° to it. If necessary, adjust the angles slightly by slipping the ring along the bridles.

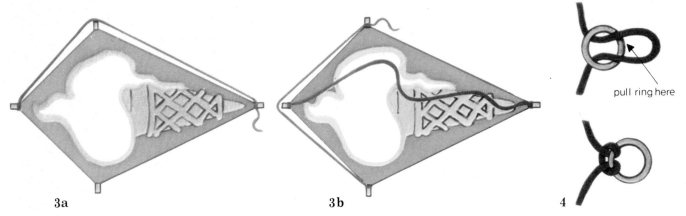

pull ring here

3a   3b   4

Tail. Some kites will fly well without any kind of tail, but the cutter kite needs one at least three times its own length. Make it from long paper streamers, or make the traditional kind of tail by knotting rectangles of paper on to a length of string.

☐ For a traditional tail, use pieces of paper about 15cm x 6cm (6"x 2½") and set them about 8cm (3") apart along the length of string. Attach them by means of a slip knot.

☐ To do this, wind the string over your hand to form a loop (fig.5).

☐ Make a twist in the centre of one of the pieces of paper and then insert it

through the loop.

☐ Pull the ends of the thread tight.

☐ Repeat along the length of the string to form the tail.

☐ Tie the tail to the stick at the bottom of the kite.

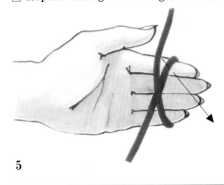

5

Flying-line and reel. Before you can fly the kite you need a flying-line and reel which can be bought quite cheaply from toy shops or some sports equipment shops.

To make your own flying-line, use about 60 metres of light nylon, Terylene cord or fishing-line and wind it on to a length of strong cardboard tube to act as a reel.

If, on the other hand, you want to make your own reel, you will need two rectangles of plywood, about 15cm x 5cm (6"x 2"), two pieces of dowelling about 15cm (6") long, a drill and strong glue. Drill two holes in each of the two pieces of plywood, to the same diameter as the dowels, and assemble the reel as shown in fig.6, gluing each dowel into place.

Tie the end of the line firmly to the reel and wind it on tightly. The other end of the line should be tied to the kite's bridle or towing-ring.

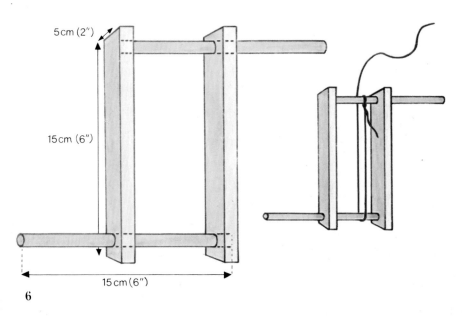

5cm (2")

15cm (6")

15cm (6")

6

Coral Mula.

Flying a kite

Do not assume that you need to wait for a really windy day in order to try out your kite. On the contrary, a gentle but steady breeze is all you need, and too much wind can damage a kite. If the tree tops are bending, then the wind is too strong for kite flying.

Always take a pair of gloves with you to stop the line cutting into your hands.

Where to fly a kite. Choose a large open space, such as a field or park, and keep well away from trees or telegraph poles.

It is not at all necessary to fly a kite from a hill, but if you wish to do so, stand on the windward side about 20 metres (just over 20 yards) from the top so as to take full advantage of the steady updraught. If you stand right on the summit the kit will be caught in the turbulence of conflicting air streams and will be more difficult to fly.

Launching and landing. Stand with your back to the wind and hold the kite by the towing-ring at arm's length. Have the reel on the ground at your feet.

☐ Wait until the wind lifts the kite and then release it, letting the line slip out through your fingers.

☐ If you have a helper, ask him to stand a little way in front of you holding the kite tilted slightly forwards until the wind lifts it out of his hands. Do not let him throw it into the air and do not try to run with it yourself. Neither will help to set it aloft. Make the kite rise by pulling on the line.

☐ Grip the line at arm's length and bend your forearm right back at the elbow, still gripping the line.

☐ Straighten your arm again slowly, letting the line slip through your fingers as you do so.

☐ Continue pulling and letting out the line until the kite is high in the sky.

☐ Land the kite simply by winding in the line.

☐ If it is pulling strongly, walk towards it as you wind.

☐ If you have a helper, he can put his hand over the line and walk towards the kite, pulling it down gradually while you wind in the line.

Watch out for any spectators appearing in front of you, as a kite may often crash as it comes in low and could be dangerous.

Repair kit. It is a good idea to take along with you a shoulder bag or satchel to carry a small repair kit made up of a reel of sticky tape for mending torn paper, several sewing needles that can be taped to broken struts to act as splints, and a pair of scissors for cutting tangles out of the line. Take an extra piece of tail as well.

The sky's the limit but the pleasure is inexhaustible.

Jerry Tubby

Correcting faults

There are several common faults, which are easy to correct, thus making all the difference to successful flying.

If the kite will not rise, it is probably flying too flat to the wind. Move the towing-ring a little higher. If the tail is hanging down rather than streaming out behind, then shortening the tail may help the kite to rise.

Fluttering and dipping. The kite may be flying too close to the wind. Move the towing-ring down a little.

Spinning, diving and looping the loop. The kite needs a longer or heavier tail. This is a common fault.

Falling consistently to one side. Tape a small weight—a tiny piece of twig, perhaps—to the back of the kite on the opposite side.

Safety note

Believe it or not, kite flying can be dangerous. Be sure to remember these two important points.

Kites can act as lightning conductors, so never fly a kite in stormy weather, or with a wire line, or with a wet line of any description.

Kites can be a real hazard to aircraft. By law you must be at least 5km (4 miles) away from the nearest airfield and you may not fly the kite higher than 60 metres (200ft).

Other kite shapes: X marks bridle position on sticks. Pierce paper to bring bridle to right side.

Oriental kites

In Asia kite-flying is far from being a game for children. It is a serious national pastime for adults and the calendar is filled with festivals and tournaments, many of them with religious significance. Kites can take the form of fabulous birds or beasts which are then imbued with evil spirits in order to float away the harm that may otherwise attack the owner's family. Others are used for fighting, their lines covered with glue and then dipped in powdered glass so as to sever an opponent's line. In Japan one village will often vie with another to make an enormous kite which takes several people to fly it, each controlling an individual guide-line.

Fish, birds and insects are characteristic subjects for Oriental kites. Most have a special symbolic or religious meaning but all have the ability to inspire wonder and the sheer joy of aerial spectacles which is the essence of kite flying.

Jerry Tubby

225

Carp

This fish shape, which is shown on the previous page, is the simplest of all the Japanese kite designs. On the boys' festival on May 5th a carp is flown for every male child in the household in the hope that the boy will emulate the character of this fish which swims upstream, overcoming all difficulties. The kite is tubular, rather like a wind-sock, with a hole at each end. Make it any size that you like, provided that the hole at the mouth is larger than the one at the tail so that the wind will inflate the body.

You will need:
Two large sheets of tissue or other light-weight paper.
Poster paints or scraps of coloured paper.
Medium gauge wire.
Short length of thread or twine.

Pencil, scissors and glue.
☐ Draw the carp shape freehand on the paper and cut it out, cutting through two thicknesses at once.
☐ Glue the pieces together along the top and bottom edges. Fold the seam over and glue down.
☐ Paint the carp or, if you have used tissue, decorate it with paper shapes.
☐ Bend the wire into a loop to fit the carp's mouth and glue it in place, folding the edges of the paper over it.
☐ Tie the ends of the thread or twine to the wire at either side of the carp's mouth. The flying-line can be attached to this loop.
Although very decorative, this kite is not a good flyer and will only rise if there is a very strong updraught.

Butterfly

This is a popular design, perhaps because the fluttering of a kite tends to resemble a butterfly.

You will need:
3 pieces of bamboo garden cane about 60cm (24″) long.
Sheet of strong paper, such as cartridge paper about 60cm (24″) square
Adhesive [cellophane] tape
Curtain ring to act as towing-ring
Twine or strong thread.
Scissors and craft knife.
Pencil.
Poster paints and brush.
☐ Fold the paper in half and draw a half butterfly shape on it so that the fold is along the butterfly's spine. Draw the largest shape possible and cut out.
☐ Open the paper out flat and paint it with any design you choose.
☐ While the paint is drying, split the cane lengthwise with the knife.
You will need firm, rigid pieces for the butterfly's spine and lower wing supports and thin, pliable pieces for the upper wing supports: 30cm (12″) for the spine, two pieces 30cm (12″) for the lower wings and two pieces 60cm (24″) for the upper wings.
☐ Mark the position of the supports on the back of the butterfly, making sure that one side is the exact mirror image of the other for perfect balance. Follow fig. 1.
Now enlist the help of a friend. One pair of hands is needed to hold each support in place while the other tapes it in position.
☐ Fix the supports in this order: spine, lower supports, lower half of upper supports.
☐ Fold the top edge of the paper over the remaining half of the upper supports and tape them (see fig. 1).
☐ Tape two thin bamboo antennae to the top of the spine.
☐ With the right side of the kite facing you, make tiny holes in the kite and tie a piece of thread through them on to the frame at each of the three points marked **x** in fig. 1.
☐ Attach threads to each end of the horizontal stick and attach the tow-rope so the kite hangs at a 45° angle. This kite, which does not need a tail, will fly even better if it offers a convex surface to the wind.
☐ To curve the kite, tie a piece of thread to one upper wing tip, stretch it across behind the kite, and tie it to the opposte wing tip, pulling it so tight that the kite is bowed.

Butterfly variations

When you have made a simple butterfly you may like to go on to a more complex design.

The dragonfly kite, a typical Eastern design, has a comic character which is exhibited both in its vivid colouring and its ridiculous expression.

You will need:
Materials as for the simple butterfly, this time using tissue paper for the cover and decorating it with torn tissue paper shapes.
The kites in figs.2 and 3 have rigid spines and pliable wing supports bowed into shape with thread.
Figs.4 and 5 show the design of the frames, heavy lines representing the canes and dotted lines the threads.
☐ Follow the usual procedure of notching the canes, binding them where they cross and fitting the paper cover in the normal way.
When making the double butterfly (see fig.5), bow the four wing supports into arcs and bind the sticks where they cross.
☐ Add extra thread supports (shown in green) before removing the two longer bow strings (shown in red).

☐ Attach a single bridle to the points marked X in fig. 5 and then add a flying-line as required.

Bird

The body of this kite (shown on page 225) is built on a bamboo framework rather like the ribs of a rowing boat and the head is a thin hollow shell of papier mâché.

You will need:
Bamboo cane.
Medium weight white paper, such as shelf paper.
Absorbent paper for papier mâché, such as newspaper.
Plasticine [modelling clay].
Flour and water paste.
Glue.
Water-colour paints.
Brush.
Thread or thin twine.

Knife and razor blade.
☐ Begin by splitting a number of pieces of cane to build the body.
☐ Construct a framework and bind the pieces where they overlap (fig.6a). Try to match the two halves perfectly with joins in exactly the same places.
☐ Following fig.6b construct the front of the body with a series of curved canes to form the ribs.
☐ Spread glue on the curved ribs.
☐ Cover the sections of the ribbed framework with strips of paper.
☐ Use a razor blade to trim the paper where it overlaps to form a butt joint.
☐ Trim off surplus paper.
☐ Now shape the head in plasticine [modelling clay] and cover it with a thin layer of papier mâché.
☐ When the head is dry, dig out the plasticine [modelling clay] and glue the head to the body.

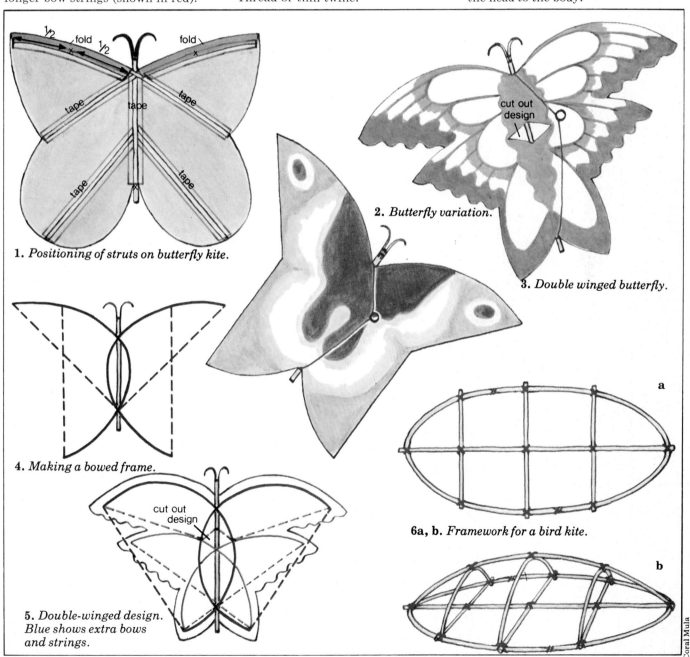

1. *Positioning of struts on butterfly kite.*

2. *Butterfly variation.*

3. *Double winged butterfly.*

4. *Making a bowed frame.*

5. *Double-winged design. Blue shows extra bows and strings.*

6a, b. *Framework for a bird kite.*

Coral Mula

☐ Make two separate wings and join them together (fig. 7).

The wings have bamboo along two sides and a thread (dotted line) to bow the tops of shape. These threads may be removed later if wished.

☐ Bind and glue the finished wings on to the back of the body.

☐ Cut out a tail shape in paper and reinforce the top by gluing on a piece of thin card.

☐ Attach the tail to the bird with loops of thread.

☐ Tie a single bridle to the body framework at the neck and three-quarters of the way down its body.

Dragonfly

Make this as for the bird, but build up the tail sections on flat bamboo frameworks. Tie the sections loosely together with thread.

Giant kite

There is no limit to the size and complexity of the kites you can make. The giant kite illustrated is built up on a rectangle of thin plywood with a decorative lantern set in the middle. The fabulous birds and beasts perched round the frame are all made on the same principle as the bird already described and you can let your imagination run riot on the tassels, lanterns and slogans that act as the tail.

Remember that the two sides of the kite must balance each other exactly in weight and shape.

Right: a fanciful, fabulous kite composed of bird-like demons round a lantern.

Below: the decorative potential of Oriental kites makes them as popular for wall hangings as for flying.

7. *Bamboo struts for bird kite wings. Dotted lines show position of strings.*

Coral Mula

Camera Press

229

Paper collage

Collages of coloured tissue paper are
great fun and easy to make: children
as well as adults will derive pleasure
from this form of picture making, since
little skill at handicrafts is needed to

*Well-placed overlapping of straight-
edged tissue papers of various colours
produces a picture representing a city
skyline. Its dramatic effect is heightened
by the area of white round the picture.*

Jerry Tubby

make a pleasing design. The basic method involves gluing down layers of torn or cut tissue paper of different shapes and colours, some overlapping and some not, on to a surface such as a piece of hardboard [plywood]. Even a first attempt can have very rewarding results. Tissue paper, one of the most popular of decorative papers, has many artistic possibilities because its delicacy and translucency allows for a subtle blending of colour and a variety of shapes.

Pictures may be abstract, representational, with or without a definite structure, according to your personal taste. You will become more skilled with practice and will eventually find that you know how to achieve a desired result, rather than laying down the paper in a haphazard way. Many famous painters, such as Matisse and Picasso, have turned to collage with tissue paper as another form of expression, with beautiful results.

Materials

The materials needed are inexpensive and widely available from stationers and art shops.

Tissue paper in various colours.

Non-toxic white glue such as Evo-stik or UHU, thoroughly mixed with the same amount of water.

Hardboard [plywood] is the best kind of wood to use if the work is intended to be permanent. It is lightweight but rigid, and does not buckle or warp on contact with water. White canvas board, illustration board, or stiff card [cardboard] are also suitable. In fact the technique may be used on any surface to which the glue and water solution will adhere: glass, plastic, wood and metal can all be used as well as hardboard or canvas board.

A primer or sealer for applying to porous surfaces before you start, so that they will take the glue.

Cloth or soft tissues for blotting excess glue.

25mm (1″) wide flat acrylic fibre brush.
Pencil.

Scissors and ruler (optional).

Clear polyurethane varnish and paintbrush (optional).

Shape and colour

Often the most interesting shapes can be obtained by tearing rather than cutting the tissue paper. Jagged mountain peaks, stormy seascapes and cloud effects can all be produced by tearing the paper carefully. The tearing method is, however, only suitable if your design is composed of fairly large pieces of paper. Smaller pieces are better cut, especially if you wish to use geometric shapes or if your design requires straight edges for its effect— for example if you are producing a

picture of a building. The jungle scene illustrated here is made from cut papers and the result is more detailed than it could be if only torn papers were used. You can use co-ordinating or contrasting colours for your picture, depending on the subject. It is a good idea to experiment with the material before embarking on a picture. Tear small pieces of paper and stick them down on a small piece of white card. Overlap

some of the pieces to see the changes in colour. Well-placed overlapping of papers helps to create the design and gives a feeling of depth to the picture. Using tissue papers in light colours

'Jungle scene' by Alisdair Ogilvie uses many layers of paper in small cut pieces, creating a richness of colour which vividly conveys the lushness and depth of jungle vegetation.

Alisdair Ogilvie

231

will impart a mood of lightness and delicacy. The more layers you overlap, the deeper and richer the colour will become. If you use dark-coloured papers they will appear black when overlapped. Use the collages shown here simply as a guide when making your own: do not try to copy them too closely as it would be extremely difficult to reproduce them exactly.

Gluing the papers

The tissue paper is glued to the chosen surface with white glue which will not show through the tissue. A solution of half glue and half water is used: a strong adhesive is not necessary to stick down such light papers.

'Johnny Appleseed' by American collagist David Bruce Fanger uses torn and wrinkled papers of different sizes. The papers have been 'bled' where a blending of the colours was required.

The procedure for gluing is always the same. Having torn or cut your first piece of paper to the size and shape

232

you require, place it in position on the board. Lightly mark its position with a pencil to indicate the area of the board over which to spread the glue. Remove the tissue paper and brush on the glue. While the surface of the board is still wet, place the tissue in position, gently pressing it in place; then brush more glue over the surface of the tissue to coat it with a protective film, removing any air bubbles as you work. Do not remove small wrinkles in the paper as these will add texture to the design. Continue to add pieces of tissue paper in this way until your design is complete. (You can begin by covering the entire board with an uncut sheet of tissue paper, if you wish. This will have the effect of making the particular colour occur in different hues throughout the picture.)

To ensure that no part of the board is visible, take the tissue paper beyond the edges of the board and glue it down round the sides and to the back.

The water in the glue solution will not make the colour come out of the paper and bleed on to the adjacent paper. However, if you want to encourage the colour to bleed, creating interesting effects, dip the glue brush in a little more water and apply to the edges of the glued paper.

When the picture is finished and the glue is dry, apply another coat of glue to the entire surface of the picture, as

'L'Escargot' (*The Snail*) *by Matisse (1869-1954). He used tissue paper instead of paint when he was too ill to paint.*

a protective covering. When this coating of glue is dry, place the picture (unless it is on hardboard) under a weight overnight, in order to flatten it. (The water in the glue solution may have buckled the board slightly.) If the board is still not flat, glue a sheet of paper all over the back of the board to straighten it.

If a more permanent protective covering is desired, use a clear polyurethane varnish to coat the surface. This has the advantage of preventing fading.

233

Japanese papers

Japanese hand-made art papers are among the most beautiful made today. They range from fibrous textured papers with strong, natural colours, to the most fragile 'lacy' papers which look like delicate lace. The papers are made either from wood pulp or cotton fibres and are therefore of a high quality. Japanese craftsmen guard the secret of the lacy paper formula so that this paper is relatively rare.

Sometimes extra fibres, dried leaves and flowers, pieces of gold leaf and butterflies are embedded in the pulp. These are usually translucent and are shown to best advantage when light shows through them, as in mobiles, screens, lampshades and window decorations. Some papers have such wonderful variations in fibre colours that definite designs such as apples, fish and dragons can be identified in the fibre dyes.

These papers can be bought from specialist art shops and some handi-craft shops and stationers. They are sold by the sheet—measuring about 1m by 65cm (39″x 26″). As they are often quite fragile they should be stored flat or carefully rolled between protective layers of other paper to prevent tearing or creasing. If creases occur, iron gently with a cool iron.

As you might imagine, the names of the various Japanese papers are as exotic as the papers themselves—the lily candle holder was made with Koto Buki, and the mobile with natural Ogura. Other lacy types include Rakasi Hana-Asa and Rakasui, while a simple brown textured paper is called Sugi Kawa.

Making a mobile

A disc mobile is an excellent first project for using Japanese hand-made papers. It is quite simple to make and shows off the full beauty of the paper.

You will need:
1 sheet white Japanese paper such as Ogura.
1 sheet coloured Japanese paper such as Sugi Kawa.
2 strips natural wood shavings.
A piece of bamboo about 30cm (12″) long.
8.5kg (19 lb) nylon fishing line, 2m (6′) long.
A piece of string, about 60cm (24″) long.
Clear adhesive, such as UHU.
Paperclips, ruler.
A darning needle.
Stanley knife or a pair of scissors.
Strips of wood shavings, natural or coloured—usually about 4cm (1½″) wide and 80cm (31″) long—can be bought from many craft and DIY shops.

Geoffrey Frosh

Left: some samples of Japanese paper. **A.** *Yamato Chiri;* **B.** *'Scallops';* **C.** *'Stars';* **D.** *'Net';* **E.** *'Daisies'.*

Bamboo is available from the same sources, and reels of nylon fishing line can be bought from sports shops and some handicraft shops.

☐ Soak the wood shavings in water for about 30-40 minutes or until quite supple.

☐ Using a Stanley knife against a ruler, cut the shavings into strips of varying lengths—from about 10cm-30cm (4″-12″) but about 2cm (¾″) wide in every case. The mobile in the photograph is made up of 26 circles, although of course you can make as many as you like.

☐ Curve each strip into a ring. Secure each overlap seam with a paperclip, lay it on its rim and leave to dry.

☐ Remove the paperclips and stick the seam of each wood shaving ring with adhesive.

☐ Using the point of a darning needle make small holes on opposite sides of each ring. The holes should be just large enough to be able to thread the fishing line easily.

☐ Place blotting paper or old newspapers on a firm flat surface and place a sheet of the Japanese paper on top.

☐ Spread a little adhesive along one rim of each wood shaving ring and stick down on to the Japanese paper. Place the rings close enough to each other to avoid wasting too much paper. Allow sufficient space between them to enable you to cut them out easily afterwards.

☐ When the adhesive is thoroughly dry, cut away surplus paper with small scissors so that the paper discs fit the rings exactly.

☐ Cut the fishing line into four pieces of differing or equal length according to your taste.

☐ Tie a knot at the end of one piece of fishing line. Put a tiny dab of glue on the knot. Thread one of the discs on to the line and push it down gently until the wood shaving rests against the knot.

☐ Thread the remaining discs on to the fishing line, placing them at intervals and in colour patterns of your choice. Always stick the discs on to glued knots.

☐ Tie the loose end of each piece of fishing line on the bamboo, again securing the knots with adhesive.

☐ Tie ends of string to each end of bamboo stick, tie and hang up in a light place.

A disc mobile shows off the airy quality of Japanese paper; its place in a window where the light shows through it accentuates its translucency.

Geoffrey Frosh

□ Continue making loops at regular intervals the whole length of the milliner's wire without ever cutting it, and securing each loop with a short length of binding wire.

□ Cut the paper to the approximate shape of the loops.

□ Spread a little adhesive around one rim of each loop and stick the paper to it.

□ When completely dry, trim the paper neatly to size. Spray the paper with flameproofing spray.

□ At this stage the loops are still loose and the next process is to straighten them.

Coax the strip into a spiral allowing ample space in the centre to stand the candle.

□ Use binding wire to secure the spiral in two or three places and use your hands to gently cup the flower petals into a pretty shape. The number of turns in the spiral will of course depend on the size of candle used. A fat candle, as shown in the photograph, standing alone or on a saucer of the same diameter will be encircled by three layers of petals—a total of about forty petals.

Left: a water-lily candle holder makes an elegant table decoration. Below: dragonfly mobile uses woodshaving frames to display Japanese paper wings. Doubled milliner's wire was used to thread the wooden beads for the body.

Water-lily candle holder

Milliner's wire is another material which makes an excellent frame to support delicate light-weight papers and this decorative candle holder is not difficult to make. For safety's sake, however, it is essential that—either before or after making up—the paper is sprayed with flameproofing spray.

Milliner's wire is obtainable from haberdashers [notion departments] and binding wire from florists.

You will need:

1 sheet Japanese lacy paper.
1 roll milliner's wire, about 14m (15yd) long.
Binding wire.
Wire cutters or combination pliers.
Clear adhesive, such as UHU.
Flameproofing aerosol spray.

□ Unwind about 30cm (12") of milliner's wire. Curve it so the loose end touches the 30cm (12") mark and cross the wires at this point to make a loop.

□ Secure the loop with a twist of binding wire but do not cut the milliner's wire.

□ Unwind another 2.5cm (1") of milliner's wire before making a second loop the same way and the same size as before (fig.1). Secure the loop with binding wire as before.

Butterfly lampshade

Artificial light is also very effective for showing off the special qualities of Japanese papers, and the iridescent colours of butterflies' wings glow prettily at night in this lampshade. Choose a very low watt (not more than 60w), pearlized bulb and a simple lamp base which does not overpower or distract the eye from the delicate tracery of the paper shade.

You will need:

1 sheet Japanese lacy paper, preferably embedded with butterflies or dried flowers.

A straight-sided lampshade frame with four panels.

Scissors, pencil and ruler.

Newspaper or other rough paper.

White enamel paint and brush.

Clear adhesive, such as UHU.

Velvet ribbon long enough to go round the top and bottom rings allowing for seam overlaps.

☐ Paint the lampshade frame with the gloss paint and leave to dry. (If the frame is already white this is, of course, unnecessary.)

☐ Measure the four oblong panels that go to make up the lampshade frame and

Right: this lampshade is made of Japanese paper with leaves and butterflies embedded in it. Below: stylized bouquet has lacy paper petals, made in the same way as those for the candle holder; leaves are textured paper.

Tony Page

Geoffrey Frosh

cut a pattern for each in newspaper or other rough paper.

☐ Hold these patterns against the lampshade frame to test they are the correct size and then use them as templates to cut out your Japanese paper. Cut on the generous side to avoid the possibility of any unsightly gaps at the side struts. A small overlap of paper panels is a good idea and you will need a little extra length for pulling taut. Any real surplus can be trimmed to size once the paper is stuck to the frame.

☐ Spread a thin line of glue down the two side struts and those parts of the top and bottom ring that go to make up one panel.

☐ Carefully position the appropriate piece of Japanese paper and stick it on the frame. Attach at the top first, then the sides, gently pulling the sheet taut from the bottom, and finally affixing the bottom.

☐ Trim off surplus, and repeat the process for the remaining three panels of the lampshade.

☐ When quite dry, spread a thin band of adhesive on the outside of the paper shade close to the top ring of the frame and gently press the velvet ribbon trim into position; similarly attach ribbon to the bottom of the shade.

Papier mâché

Papier mâché is a modelling material consisting of pieces of paper used with paste or glue and moulded round a shape to make functional and decorative objects. It is a cheap and easy material to use and has the advantage of drying naturally to a hard and durable substance, without having to be baked like clay.

The craft of making objects from papier mâché is an ancient one. Soon after the Chinese discovered how to make paper, about 2000 years ago, they began to experiment with ways of moulding it by tearing it into pieces, mixing it with glue, and shaping it into useful and attractive objects. The interest in this craft declined for hundreds of years until the French revived it in the 18th century. They called it papier mâché, meaning literally 'chewed-up paper'. They used it to make trays, boxes and even furniture (particularly chairs) which were often inlaid with mother of pearl.

All these colourful objects are made of papier mâché, using moulds ranging from clay to bottles and bowls.

Uses for papier mâché were far more limited then than they are today, since the invention of epoxy resin which makes the papier mâché object much stronger and more durable than traditional water-soluble glues and pastes. Epoxy resin can also be used as a surface finish.

Materials

Most of the materials needed to make papier mâché objects can be found at home.

Paper. The main item is of course paper; old newspapers will probably be your chief source. You can also use paper towels, soft tissues or white

Melvin Grey

tissue paper. It is worth experimenting, too, with other types of paper such as rag paper, which is stronger than ordinary paper because its ingredients include cotton or linen rags as well as wood pulp. Sources of rag paper include used fine stationery, pages from old ledgers and old damaged books, and drawing papers.

You can also use paper to decorate an object built up from several layers of papier mâché, if you wish. Gift wrapping paper, wallpaper, coloured tissue paper and coloured magazine pictures are all suitable. In fact, almost any kind of paper may be used.

Pastes and glues. You will also need some kind of paste or glue for binding the paper together to make papier mâché. The one traditionally used for the purpose is a paste made from flour and water which is stirred over a low heat until enough water has been added to make it smooth and creamy. Wallpaper paste such as Polycell, mixed with water according to the manufacturer's instructions, also makes a strong glue.

However, epoxy resin, such as Aral-

The duck and hens were all moulded on plasticine and painted in bright colours. Designed by Ruth Beard.

dite, is the strongest type of glue to use. It will make papier mâché objects virtually unbreakable, waterproof, flame-proof and dirt-proof. It should always be used for large or complex objects without a base support, since they might otherwise buckle.

Using epoxy resin simply as a surface finish for a smaller piece means that the object will not only be protected as if a varnish were used, but it will also be strengthened as the epoxy penetrates the papier mâché itself.

Moulds. Some sort of mould will also be required to support the papier mâché object while it is being made. It can either be removed after the papier mâché has dried, or integrated into the piece for added strength. The mould can be either a rigid shape (a plastic bottle, tin can, cardboard cylinder, a glass or china dish or bowl, fruit or vegetables, or even a balloon) or it can be flexible (chicken wire, crumpled newspaper, clay or plasticine).

239

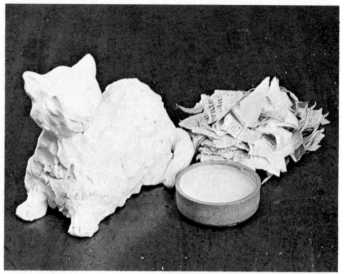

Methods

There are three basic ways of making papier mâché. The most common is to cut or tear the paper into small strips or squares and glue them on to a base or mould. Tearing rather than cutting the paper means that it will have rough edges which will give a smoother surface than straight edges when glued down in layers. Paper may be torn against a ruler to make fairly uniform strips.

Another method, called lamination, consists of gluing together several sheets of paper to make one strong flexible sheet. This can then be shaped over a base or cut into strips before it is applied.

The third method involves breaking down small pieces of paper into a mash or pulp by soaking them in water for several hours. The water is then squeezed out of the paper until it becomes a pulp, and glue is added to make it bind together. Paper mash is often used to add texture and strength to an object moulded from strips of papier mâché, but can also be moulded like clay.

There are several commercial mixes available for making 'instant' paper mash, for example Letracraft Instant Papier Mâché, to which only water has to be added. These are easy to use and can be bought from art and craft shops.

Modelling on plasticine

Plasticine [modelling clay] is a medium flexible enough to mould into complex shapes yet strong enough to also stay firm while the papier mâché is applied to it.

The charming papier mâché birds and animals shown on these pages are not at all difficult to make, using the most common method of applying the paper —the strip method.

You will need:

Plasticine [modelling clay] (about 450gm (1 lb) for a papier mâché model animal or bird 7.5cm (3″) high).
Newspaper or magazine paper, and soft tissues.
Epoxy resin such as Araldite, or wallpaper paste such as Polycell, or flour-and-water paste, or liquid starch to which two tablespoons of salt or sand are added per litre (quart) for extra strength.
Vaseline.
Kitchen knife, waxed paper, coarse and fine glasspaper [sandpaper].
White emulsion paint.
Brushes and poster or acrylic paints.
Two 2.5cm (1″) household paintbrushes.
Glass eyes (those used in soft toy making are suitable).
General-purpose glue such as Bostik 1.
Small bell (for the cat).
12.5cm (5″) length of thin string (from which to hang the cat's bell).
Lengths of raffia measuring about 8.5m (9yd) long altogether, for the large hen's nest.
Clear polyurethane varnish.

☐ Mould the shape of the animal or bird in plasticine, omitting details such as beaks and ears. Keep the basic shapes simple and sloping gently out towards the base, without undercuts, so that the plasticine is easily removed when the papier mâché is hard. Smooth the plasticine, using a knife or a ruler if necessary.

☐ Place the mould on a sheet of waxed paper and coat the mould with Vaseline. This prevents the papier mâché from sticking to the mould.

☐ Tear newspaper or magazine paper into very small pieces, not more than about 2.5cm x 1.25cm (1″x ½″), and smaller still for the neck and tail areas.

☐ Moisten each piece with a small amount of the prepared glue or paste and place it on the mould. (Adhesives should be applied sparingly so that the pieces will dry quickly and evenly.) Each piece should slightly overlap the previous one. When the entire mould is covered in this way, smooth the paper down with a household paintbrush and fingers making sure there are no gaps.

☐ Repeat until about eight coats of paper have been applied, except when covering the small cat's mould. In order to fix the bell on the cat, cover this mould with the first four or five layers of paper only, then thread the bell on to a length of string. Tie the string round the neck of the cat over the paper layers, with the bell in position in the front. Cover the mould with the last three or four layers of paper so that the surface is smooth and the string does not show as a ridge in the paper. It is a good idea to use paper of different colours or types for different coats, to help check that each layer is completely and evenly covered.

☐ Model the beak, ears and other details on the covered moulds with shredded soft tissues mixed with paste or glue.

☐ Set the model aside to dry in a warm place such as in an airing cupboard, near a radiator, or out in the sun, keeping it on the sheet of waxed paper. Allow the model to dry for at least a day.

☐ With the tip of a kitchen knife, ease out the plasticine. This is a great deal easier to do if the knife is warm.
Note: you could also remove the mould by sawing all round the model and removing the laminated cast in two halves. The two halves, however, would then have to be stuck together again with two or three more layers of paper, which would take much longer.

☐ Any rough edges on the model should now be sanded lightly with coarse and then fine glasspaper [sandpaper] until smooth.

☐ You could apply a layer of epoxy resin to the model, for extra strength.

☐ Apply two coats of white emulsion paint to the model with a household paintbrush. This gives a uniformly coloured surface to decorate.

☐ When the paint is dry, apply general-

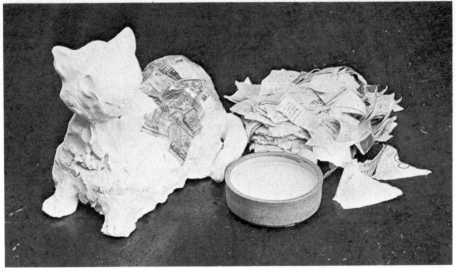

To make the large cat, model the shape in plasticine over a base of boxes, to avoid using a huge amount of plasticine. When you are satisfied with the shape, moisten the paper strips with glue or paste and stick down.

the score lines with a knife to remove the two halves from the mould. Stick them together again with more damp papier mâché, at the same time applying it to any cracks or bumps.

☐ Let this dry—if it is put in a warm oven with the door open at this stage (110°C (225°F), gas mark ¼), it will quickly become very hard indeed. Sand down, paint and finish as for the first method described.

Mixed instant papier mâché can be stored in a plastic bag in a refrigerator for about a week.

This cat, like the larger cat behind it (designed by Lorraine Johnson), makes a charming shelf decoration.

purpose glue to the backs of the glass eyes and stick them in position.

☐ With the large water-colour brush, paint the background colour of the animal or bird with poster or acrylic paint. With the smaller brush, paint features, spots, feathers, whiskers, or whatever you think is suitable or amusing.

☐ When the paint is dry, apply two coats of clear polyurethane varnish to the object.

☐ For the larger hen's nest, plait the lengths of raffia and sew them together with smaller pieces of raffia into a nest shape.

Using instant papier mâché. For an easier and quicker way to make a bird or animal like those illustrated, use instant papier mâché, which is a pulp. As well as the materials already described, you will need two plastic bags, a rolling pin or milk bottle, and instant paper pulp such as that made by Letracraft.

☐ Make up the papier mâché according to the manufacturer's instructions.

☐ Mould plasticine [modelling clay] and coat with Vaseline.

☐ Roll out the instant papier mâché between two plastic bags to a thickness of 6mm (¼″).

☐ Remove the top bag and, keeping the rolled-out papier mâché on the bag below it, apply to the mould, smoothing down round the mould with the plastic bag. Remove the bag and smooth the papier mâché into its final shape with a damp knife.

☐ While the papier mâché is still damp, score a line with the knife round the centre of the model, dividing it into two identical halves.

Note: removing the cast in two pieces and joining them again can be done easily with instant paper mash. Do not remove the cast from the mould at this stage.

☐ Leave the model to dry. Instant papier mâché will dry at room tempera-

ture but for faster drying, put it in a warm place as described for conventional papier mâché.

☐ When the model is dry, cut along

Melvin Grey

241

Tissue paper flowers

Artificial flowers are not new; the beauty of real flowers has always been a source of fascination and attempts to copy them over the years have been ingenious and varied. All sorts of different materials have been used, including wax, shells, glass, china, wood, felt, wool and many different kinds of fabric and paper.

Artificial flowers are now most commonly made in paper—they are easy to make and have great decorative appeal, and there is still scope for those with a serious interest in flowers to achieve accurate results.

Look at a real flower

Before beginning to make flowers, it is important to know how real ones are constructed. For a cross-section of the components of a flower, showing the main parts together with their proper names, see fig.1.

Although you can make satisfactory and decorative flowers by learning some useful papercraft techniques, you may wish to go a stage further and make some that are closely copied from nature. It is then important to know exactly how a flower is formed by taking it apart and noting the exact number of petals and where they are

placed, the shape of the calyx and the distribution of the stamens. Whatever kind of flower you are making, it is a good idea to incorporate some accurate botanical details—they make the flower more interesting and subtle.

Tissue paper

Tissue is ideal for the beginner. It gives good results without requiring a great deal of expertise in handling, and the colours available are pretty enough to give the flowers the glow and fragility of real ones. A 'rainbow' variety is also available which gives an attractive effect to flower petals. The quality of tissue paper varies from flimsy to firm: it is worth buying the best available because it gives better, more long-lasting results. Tissue paper does have certain disadvantages, however, in comparison with the initially more difficult to handle crepe paper. It cannot be shaped in the same way, and if it becomes over-handled or crumpled it may lose its bright crispness. It also fades rather quickly when exposed to sunlight, so arrange the completed flowers in an attractive container placed well back from the window, and direct some lamplight through them in the evening. Take care not to get tissue paper wet; even a few spots of water can cause the dye to run and spoil the paper.

Flower-making equipment

The only other materials required are wire and stem covering. Florists' wire is a very fine wire used for securing the flower to the stem, and galvanized wire in various thicknesses is used for stems. Wire stems can be covered with strips of green crepe paper, but rubberized garden tape can also be used.

Only the most basic equipment is necessary—a pair of good quality sharp, pointed scissors with a blade

Add a splash of colour to dark walls with pompon paper flowers. Fill a jug with flowers on covered stems and place against a contrasting background. While making the flowers, pin individual blooms directly to a wall to prevent them getting crumpled. From a kit designed by Priscilla Lobley.

petal
stamen
anther
filament
pistil
stigma
style
ovary
calyx (sepals)

Barbara Firth

Melvin Grey

1. *Cross section through a composite flower, showing the main parts.*

about 6cm (2½″) long, a pair of wire cutters—the type used for electrical repairs—and a wood glue or paste

To make tissue peonies

Peonies are large, striking flowers that vary in colour from yellow, white and magenta to all shades of pink and red. The dark red varieties are the most familiar, but there are delicate two-shaded flowers in tones of white and gold, pink and cream and pale and deep pink that look particularly subtle made up in tissue paper.

You will need:

For 2 flowers you will need 2 sheets of tissue paper, each in a different shade, such as magenta and lemon or pink and cream.

25cm-35cm (10″-15″) of 1.25mm (18 Gauge) galvanized wire.

Florists' wire or green plastic-covered wire. Green crêpe paper.

Wood glue or paste.

☐ Cut off the required number of galvanized wire lengths for stems and straighten them out.

☐ Each sheet of tissue paper measures about 50cm x 74cm (20″x30″). Divide each sheet into 6 equal squares by folding the paper in half and then into 3 (fig.1a). For each flower you will need 3 squares of one shade for the centre petals and 3 squares of the other colour for the outer petals.

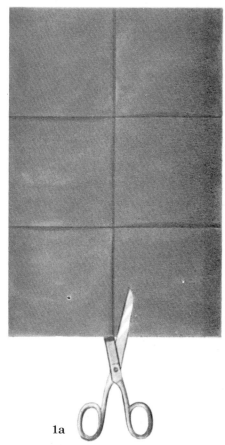

1a. *Dividing a whole sheet of tissue paper into six equal squares.*

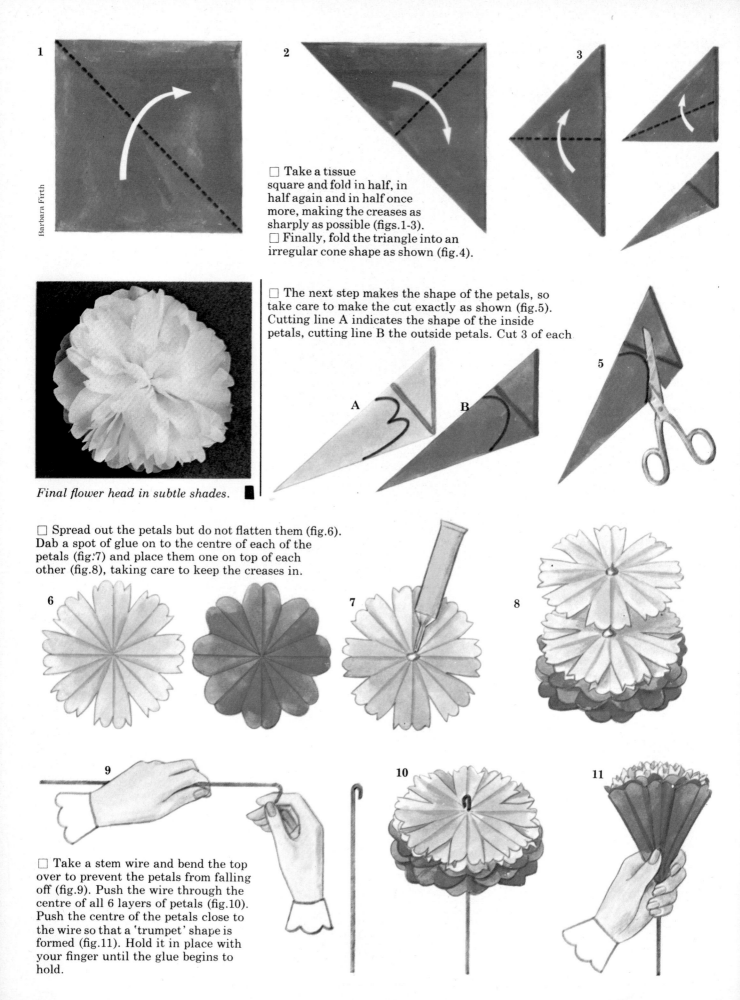

1

2

☐ Take a tissue square and fold in half, in half again and in half once more, making the creases as sharply as possible (figs.1-3).
☐ Finally, fold the triangle into an irregular cone shape as shown (fig.4).

3

☐ The next step makes the shape of the petals, so take care to make the cut exactly as shown (fig.5). Cutting line A indicates the shape of the inside petals, cutting line B the outside petals. Cut 3 of each.

A   B   **5**

Final flower head in subtle shades.

☐ Spread out the petals but do not flatten them (fig.6). Dab a spot of glue on to the centre of each of the petals (fig.7) and place them one on top of each other (fig.8), taking care to keep the creases in.

6   **7**   **8**

9

☐ Take a stem wire and bend the top over to prevent the petals from falling off (fig.9). Push the wire through the centre of all 6 layers of petals (fig.10). Push the centre of the petals close to the wire so that a 'trumpet' shape is formed (fig.11). Hold it in place with your finger until the glue begins to hold.

10   **11**

☐ Secure base of flower by binding tightly with Florists' or green plastic-covered wire (fig.12). Shape the flower by gently separating each of the layers of outer petals and turning them downwards, and by separating the inner petals and leaving them standing vertically (fig.13).

12

13

☐ Cover the stem wire by cutting a strip of green crepe paper about 2.5cm (1″) wide and wrapping it very tightly round the base of the flower. A dab of glue on the end of the paper may help to hold it in position (fig.14).

14

☐ Rotate the wire, and wrap paper strip in a bandaging movement down to the bottom of the wire (fig.15). Break off the paper and secure the end with a spot of glue (fig.16).

15

16

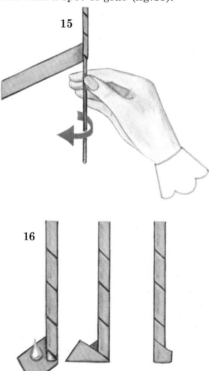

Delicate tissue paper peonies designed by Priscilla Lobley.

Ribbon and tissue flowers

A cluster of enchanting small flowers, made from strips of tissue, crepe paper or self-stick paper-backed ribbon, turns any gift parcel into a more personal and original gift.

You could also make some to stand in a small pot on a table for festive occasions; sew some on to velvet for a pretty headband or attach them to hairpins stuck in a polystyrene ball on a length of dowelling to make a tiny ornamental tree. Stand it in a small plastic pot and set in a cellulose filler such as Polyfilla or fill the pot with pebbles to make it stand firmly.

Tissue roses

You will need:

1 sheet of red, pink or yellow tissue paper. (Each sheet will make about 16 small roses.)
1 sheet of green tissue paper.
Paste.

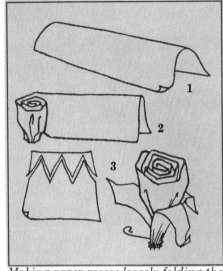

Making paper roses: loosely folding the tissue, winding it into a rose shape, and a rose with its leaf.

☐ For a rose 4cm (1½″) high, cut a piece of tissue 9cm (3½″) wide and 25cm (10″) long. Fuller roses can be 9cm (3½″) wide and 51cm (20″) long.

☐ Fold in half lengthways but don't crease (fig.1).

☐ Following fig.2, roll and bunch up the tissue, squeezing it together at the bottom until the rose is formed. Roll the centre tightly; vary the squeezes and folds by bunching more in some places than others. Secure with paste.

☐ Cut a 5cm (2″) square of green tissue for leaves and cut into shape (fig.3). Roll round the bottom of the rose and stick in place or tie with matching sewing thread.

Ribbon roses

You will need:

2.5cm (1″) wide Hallmark or other self-stick, gift-wrap ribbon in colours of your choice and green for leaves.

☐ Cut a 51cm (20″) strip of ribbon.

☐ Holding it in the left hand, 2.5cm (1″) from the end, roll the ribbon inwards to form a tight core—approximately 6 turns (fig.4).

☐ Fold the ribbon at a right angle towards the core, forming a diagonal edge (fig.5). Crease the fold from A to B.

☐ Rotate the core, keeping points A and B level with the top of the core (fig.6).

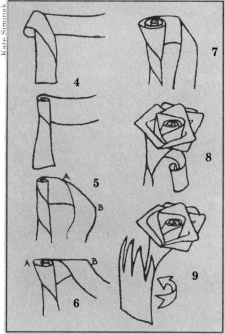

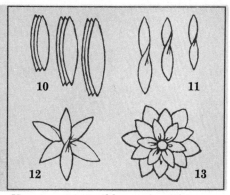

How to cut out ribbon poinsettias.

Follow these steps for ribbon roses.

☐ At the end of each crease, fold again at a right angle, crease again and rotate core (fig.7). Repeat until the rose is the desired size.

☐ Moisten the end and wrap round the core to fasten (fig.8).

☐ Cut some leaves from green ribbon (fig.9). Moisten and wrap round the base for a stem.

Ribbon poinsettia

You will need:

2.5cm (1″) wide Hallmark or other self-stick, gift-wrap ribbon in red or yellow.

☐ Cut 3 strips of ribbon in each of these lengths: 15.5cm (6″), 12.5cm (5″), and 10cm (4″). Cut both ends of each piece to a sharp point (fig.10).

☐ Moisten the centres and twist the centre of each strip to form two petals (fig.11).

☐ Moisten the centres of the medium-size petals and join them together. Repeat with the larger and smaller petals (fig.12).

☐ Moisten the centres of the medium-size petals and join them to the largest petals. Add the smallest petals.

☐ Add a circle of coloured ribbon to the centre (fig.13).

A small posy of yellow ribbon roses. Below: a group of exciting-looking parcels decorated with an assortment of ribbon and tissue paper flowers.

Flowercrafts

Everyone loves flowers, and the following projects show just
how much scope there is in preserving and drying them.
Dry herbs too, and plant a pretty bottle garden.

Preserving flowers

There are three basic ways of preserving plant material such as flowers, foliage, seed heads, leaves and grasses. Try them all if you can. If you can't, choose the method most suited to the facilities that you have available.

Air-drying. If, for example, you have an airy space with room for hooks or a line to hang the flowers on, then try the air-drying method.

Dessicant powder. Flowers dried out by the second method in a dessicant powder such as borax or silica gel may be easier for some in that the only space required is a large box to hold the powder and the flowers.

Glycerine. Plant material can be preserved with glycerine; the main requirements are some jars, bottles and the space to store them upright.

Details for each of these methods are given below, but before you begin preserving flowers you must know when to pick them so they will be in the best possible condition to give the best results. Also, some plants are more suited to one method of preservation than to others.

Gathering flowers

Try to cut the flowers on a dry, warm day when there will be a minimum of moisture on the plant surface. Never pick material when it is raining or when dew is forming. As a general rule, choose flowers just before they come into full bloom. Fully open blossoms, or flowers that have already begun to set seed, will merely shed petals and seeds as you attempt to preserve them.

Air drying

Pick the material and remove the leaves from the stems. Leaves that are left on will simply wither and tangle in the stems as they are drying.

If the flowers are fairly small, put them into small bunches and tie them with string or plastic ties, leaving a loop to slide on to a line or hook.

If you have chosen material with large flower heads, try to hang them separately. There is nothing more frustrating than to dry flowers perfectly and then to damage them in trying to disentangle the florets. As the material dries it will tend to shrink, so you may need to tighten the ties to hold the stems securely.

The bunches must be hung, well apart, on a line or on hooks in a cool, dry, airy and dark place. Too much light and warmth tend to make the material brittle and faded, and flowers become mildewed in damp surroundings.

Flowers with heavy or fragile heads can be dried by standing them upright

Many flowers can be preserved by simply hanging them upside down in a cool, dry dark place such as a cupboard.

in a jar. For this method make sure that the plant has a strong stem and that the head does not tend to droop. If the stems are very short, cut down to about 2.5cm (1″) from the head and push a length of 0.9mm (19-20 gauge) florists' wire up the stem and into the flower head and push the end of the wire into a bed of sand or a piece of plastic foam. Leave the flowers to dry in this position.

The length of drying time necessary varies enormously. Delicate material such as grasses may only take a week, but heavier flowers, containing more moisture, may need three weeks or more.

The material should be checked to see if it feels quite dry and dehydrated before removing it for storage.

Hydrangea and molucella, both very popular in dried flower arrangements, require a little extra attention. The plants should be cut and stripped of leaves as usual. The stems should then be placed in about 5cm (2″) of water and left in a warm room. When all the water has gone the stems should be tied, hung and left to dry as usual. (Cut hydrangeas on a new stem if possible.)

Material to choose for air drying. This list of plants is very far from being complete, but it is a guide to suitable material. If you would like to try drying a flower that is not included then there is nothing to lose in experimenting to see if it will work.

Rounded shapes. The following three flowers are often used in dried arrangements and are called everlastings: *ammobium alatum grandiflorum* (everlasting sand flower) has silvery-white petals and a domed yellow centre. It grows to about 0.6m (2′) tall but the stems are short in proportion to the flower heads, so you may need to lengthen them when you come to arrange them; *anaphalis* (pearl everlasting) which has a grey leaf and a white flower and *helichrysum bracteatum* (straw flower) which has flowers rather like those of a stiff, shiny-petalled double daisy in an assortment of colours. This must be cut before the flowers are fully open.

Other rounded shapes are *achillea filipendulina* (garden yarrow)—dry by standing in an empty jar to avoid damaging the large flower heads; and *catananche coerulea* (cupid's dart).

Spiky shapes which can be air dried are *acanthus spinosus* (bear's breeches), useful for large arrangements; delphinium (pick as soon as the top floret opens, and dry hanging upside down), and *limonium sinuatum* (sea lavender).

Silica gel crystals preserve delicate blossoms and help retain vivid colours too. Preserved with Lasting Flower.

Clusters which are effective in dried arrangements are *acacia dealbata* (mimosa)—the little yellow balls remain and hold some of their perfume; *eryngium* (sea holly)—cut before the seedheads mature; and *gypsophila elegans* (baby's breath).

Leaves and grasses include *aspidistra* (parlour palm); *briza maxima* (pearl grass) and *lagurus ovatus* (hare's tail).

Seedheads include *alliums* (dry upside down if possible); *aquilegia* (columbine); *dipsacus fullonium* (teasels); and *lunaria* (honesty).

Fruits and cones can be opened by drying in a cool oven while *cucurbita* (gourds) should be ripened by hanging them up by the stems or by placing them on a tray and turning frequently.

Drying flowers in powder

The powders used in this method are borax, silica gel crystals, or sand, and of these silica gel is probably the best. It dries flowers efficiently and the crystals are very light and therefore

less likely to crush delicate blossoms. Furthermore, silica gel crystals can be dried out in a warm oven after use and then used again. Both silica gel and borax can be bought in pharmacies.

The advantage of drying in powder is that flowers preserved by this method retain much of their original colour. Some silica gel preparations on the market, such as Lasting Flower, have additional chemicals which help retain vivid hues to a truly amazing degree. But these flowers are susceptible to damp and if your room is not fairly dry they should be kept under glass.

Before beginning to use a dessicant

powder, the flowers must be dry and in good condition. Any of the powders may be used, although sand tends to be rather heavy for delicate petals.

Cover the bottom of a box or biscuit tin with the powder, carefully lay the flowers on this and pour over more powder (fig.1) so they are completely covered. Take care that there is plenty of powder between the petals and stamens. Leave them, and the powder will draw the moisture from the petals. Make sure that you do not add any moisture to the mixture by putting the box in a damp place. The box should be kept in a warm, dry place.

The length of time it takes to dry the

With a dessicant powder, floral wire, tape and foam you can make beautiful life-like arrangements.

flowers again varies. To test, gently scrape off powder from a petal; if any trace of moisture remains, re-cover and leave. Most flowers take about two days to dry completely.

When they are dry, remove and store them in a dark place. You could store them in a box, adding a few crystals of silica gel to absorb any moisture.

Florists' wire to support the stems can be added before or after drying and is essential for flowers used in formal bouquets, posies and head-dresses.

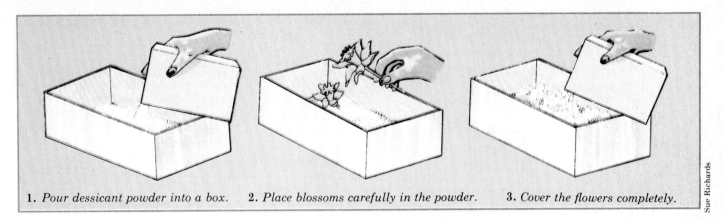

1. *Pour dessicant powder into a box.* **2.** *Place blossoms carefully in the powder.* **3.** *Cover the flowers completely.*

Material to choose for powder drying. This method is more suited to flowers than foliage. The more simple and open-faced flowers are best—anemones, marigolds, daisies and cornflowers, for example. Small roses can be very successful if you make quite sure that the powder is well distributed among the petals. Larger specimens tend to work less well.

Preserving in glycerine

This process replaces the water in the plant with glycerine, giving a supple and quite lasting result. Glycerine looks like a clear, syrupy liquid.

Stems should be placed in water for a few hours before putting them in the glycerine. Make sure that the material is in good condition before you begin—attempting to preserve damaged leaves is a waste of effort. Woody stems should be split to make sure that the glycerine can travel up them.

Make a mixture of two-parts water to one-part glycerine and place the stems in about 10cm (4″) of the liquid. Leave for about two or three weeks when the leaves should become supple and change colour. Remove from the glycerine mixture and, if the leaves begin to droop, hang them upside down for a few days to make sure that the glycerine reaches to the top.

Plant material to be preserved by this method should be gathered before the dying autumn colours begin to show—if you leave it too late, the plant loses its power to absorb liquid.

Material to choose for preserving in glycerine include *clematis vitalba* (wild clematis)—the flower heads do not disintegrate and the leaves turn deep bronze; *hydrangea; molucella laevis* (bells of Ireland)—preserve these in a dry place to avoid mould. The mixture may not be able to reach the upper flowers, so it is helpful to remove a few top flowers before you begin; *polygonatum multiflorum* (Solomon's seal).

The glycerine method is particularly

Leaves and foliage can be preserved by standing in one part glycerine, two parts water. They often change colour.

suitable for leaves—here is a brief list of some of the possibilities: *Aspidistra lurida* (parlour palm)—process may take up to six months; *convallaria majalis* (lily of the valley)—leaves may be completely submerged in the mix-ture; *fagus sylvatica* (beech)—pick while still green and fresh. Beech nuts left on the branch will also be preserved; *helleborus* (Christmas rose); *magnolia grandiflora* (magnolia); *quercus* (oak); and *rhododendron*.

253

Drying herbs

The fragrances of sweet smelling herbs, spices and flowers can be captured all year round in pot-pourri and sachets. Rooms, cupboards, household and personal linen can be kept fragrant and fresh with all the varieties of aromatic plants. You can give each drawer or cupboard a distinctive scent—sweet, spicy, delicate or intoxicating—making it both a special pleasure to open it and the contents delightful to wear or use in the home.

Fragrant herbs and flowers grow everywhere. They can be gathered and dried or they can be bought already dried at herbalist shops and mixed at home with essential oils and fixatives to give them scent. It is in the subtle blending of these fragrances and, in pot-pourri, of colour, too, that herbal art lies.

Harvesting herbs and flowers

Spring and summer are the seasons to harvest herbs and flowers for sweet-smelling pot-pourri, sachets and herb pillows, for once winter comes most of the herbs vanish from sight.

You must harvest herbs when their aromatic oils are most powerful, so pick them just before they flower, in the early morning when the dew has dried and before the sun is hot. Pick flowers when they are just open and absolutely unblemished, even though it seems hard to plunder them at that moment.

Harvest seeds when they are ready to fall, and roots at the end of the season. Pick only enough to lightly cover whatever drying shelves you have arranged and let the leaves remain on the stem. Separate any petals you want. Handle both leaves and flowers very gently to prevent bruising. As you pick herbs or flowers lay them one-deep on a tray or flat box.

Drying herbs and flowers

Your aim is to dry the herbs quite quickly with an even, low warmth—not less than 70°F (21°C) or more than 100°F (38°C). A good, even ventilation is just as important as the heat to carry away the humidity of the drying plants. Too much heat or too sunny or light a place will brown the leaves or, at least, dissipate the aromatic properties you

are trying to conserve. So you want a dark place with little or no dust, but warmth and plenty of air.

Possible drying places are an airing cupboard or a clothes drying cupboard; a plate-warming compartment of an oven; a darkened, warm, well-ventilated room, passage or cupboard where you could set up a small fan heater; an attic, garage or darkened green-house; a dry, well-aired cellar, perhaps near a boiler.

The shelves must be well separated so

A beautiful container adds another sensual dimension to pot-pourri.

that air can pass freely between them. You could use muslin attached to a wooden framework, hessian [burlap] or open weave cloth stretched over dowels or framing, or the flat bottoms of cardboard boxes which have been perforated to let air through, but do not use wire mesh.

If you can alter and regulate the heat, one method is to begin drying with a temperature of about 90°F (32°C) for one day and then reduce the heat to 70°F (21°C) until the drying process is finished.

The drying space should only faintly smell of herbs; a strong smell means there is too much heat and escaping aromas. Don't add a fresh batch of

herbs until the first batch is dry or you will add more humidity to the air. Turn the herbs as they are drying from time to time.

Experiment with drying until you get the fullest colour and smell in the herbs. It takes from four to fourteen days or more to dry herbs and flowers. Some flowers, such as rosemary flowers, are better dried slowly at a lower temperature than herbs.

Leaves are dry when they are brittle but will not shatter. Flower petals should feel dry and slightly crisp. Roots should dry right through with no soft centre.

Store all dried plants in airtight containers in a cool, dark place.

Air drying. Tying a bunch of herbs and flowers and hanging them upside down in a dry, airy space is an old method of drying herbs, and more satisfactory in a dry climate than in a humid one. Air drying is likely to retain less colour and scent but needs no special arrangements.

Pot-pourri

Pot-pourri can be made of all scented plants—flowers, fruits, herbs, barks, spices—and it is the blending of these that produces the dimly fragrant, sometimes mysterious, aromas.

Choose a main scent—it is often rose petals in a pot-pourri, lavender in a sachet—then add others to give the mixture fleeting undertones. You can also add drops of essential oils bought from a herb stockist. A fixative, such as orris root, is needed to hold the perfumes longer than the flowers and leaves can on their own.

Choose a beautiful container—an apothecary jar, open-work silver or ceramic pot, china or porcelain box or urn. If the pot-pourri is to be seen, arrange it with leaves of elusive greens, small rosebuds, marigolds, pressed violets, pansies and everlasting flowers. Some of these do not hold their scent as well as, say, roses, tuberoses and lavender, but they give perfect shape and delicate colour.

Experiment with scents because they vary from garden to garden and overlap from plant to plant. For example, neroli is a scented substance in fragrant roses which is also in geraniums, jasmine, orange blossom and wall-flowers. Citronellol is in roses, geraniums and eucalyptus, and eugenol is in bay, cloves, hyacinths and tuberoses. The choice of scent is infinite—violet, jonquil, narcissus, lilac, honeysuckle, lily of the valley, the mints, rose geranium, rosemary, and in warmer climates, oleander, magnolia, lotus, jasmine, gardenia, orange blossom, acacia or wattles.

Also consider using these—cloves, nutmeg, cinnamon, mace, vanilla pod

Bill McLaughlin

from the Mexican creeper, woodruff, tonquin beans, sandalwood, cedar and sassafras, eucalyptus leaves and citrus peel.

Floral pot-pourri

There are dozens of combinations to experiment with, but this one is simple.
1 lit (2pt) rose petals.
0.5 lit (1pt) rose geranium leaves.
0.5 lit (1pt) lavender flowers.
1 cup rosemary needles.
2 tablespoons each of ground cloves, cinnamon, allspice.
3 tablespoons crushed orris root and powdered gum benzoin.
20 drops essential oil of rose.
5 drops essential oil of sandalwood or citrus.

Jasmine pot-pourri

0.5 lit (1pt) jasmine flowers.
0.3lit ($\frac{1}{2}$pt) orange blossoms and gardenias.
0.3 lit ($\frac{1}{2}$pt) geranium leaves, including the lemon, peppermint and rose-scented ones.
57gm (2 oz) cassia.
57gm (2 oz) gum benzoin.
A vanilla pod or drops of vanilla oil.

Herbal pot-pourri

Choose the leaves from angelica, basil, bay, rose geranium, bergamot, borage, lemon balm, lemon verbena, thyme or lemon thyme, lovage, marjoram, mint, rosemary, sage, sweet cicely, tarragon and eucalyptus.
Choose flowers from borage, camomile, elder, lavender, lime, cowslips, cornflowers, clover, marigolds, nasturtiums, rose petals, wallflowers and violets.
Choose spices from ground cardamon, cinnamon, cloves, nutmeg, citrus peel and coriander,

To make a pot-pourri

Add drops of oils to dried flowers and fixatives, then put flowers, leaves and spices in layers in the container. Use small, whole flowers and leaves to decorate the top layer. Place mixture in airtight container and leave jar for six weeks, turning the ingredients weekly.

Herb pillows

For dreams of summer, put a herb pillow in your pillow case. Herbs to soothe the insomniac include angelica, woodruff, sage, hops, dill, camomile, bergamot, lavender, valerian (a rather unpleasant smell), lemon balm, lemon verbena, tarragon, elder flowers and borage.
The herbs that were used for strewing on bare floors in the Middle Ages are also good for herb pillows—thyme, mint, basil, hyssop, marjoram and rosemary.
Make a cotton or muslin bag to any

size you want, to hold the herbs, and then make a cover for it that can be laundered—in sprigged cotton or perhaps white embroidery on white cotton. Mix together equal parts of lavender, lemon verbena and mint, and add small quantities of any of the herbs listed above.
Or mix equal parts of rosemary blossoms, rosemary needles, pine needles, rose geranium leaves and lemon balm. Or mix equal parts of rose petals and lavender, and add small amounts of woodruff, camomile, dill, sage, bergamot and tarragon.
Or use hops only. Many people feel a hop pillow is best for insomnia.

Sachets

Hang these on hangers; put them in drawers, linen cupboards and under

Presentation is part of the delight of herbs. While the delicate colouring of pot-pourri should be visible, the fragrance of herbal pillows is emphasized by floral-printed casing, and a bit of lace adds freshness to sachets.

cushions. Try a half-and-half mixture of lavender and lemon verbena; or southernwood, bergamot and lemon balm with twice as many rose petals and lavender.
If you wish, add to any of these mixtures some spices—coriander seeds, cloves or cinnamon.
Sachets can be made of small squares of silk, cotton print or organdie, and treated as miniature pillows, or they can be gathered across the top and secured with a ribbon. This method means that they can be refilled later on.

Dyeing flowers

256

The colours of natural plant materials, whether leaves, flowers or seed heads, cannot be surpassed. However, there are times when unnatural colour combinations are required to change or emphasize existing colours. Rich, fanciful arrangements or gentle, more subtle ones are the results.

Plant colour can be changed by dyeing, bleaching or painting. The methods of each are simple and the choice you adopt is largely governed by the plant material you have selected.

Dip-dyeing

Flowers with dried stems such as grasses–hare's-tail, cat's-tail–teazels, glixias, bleached dried leaves, alliums, helichrysum, maize, honesty, love-in-a-mist seeds and agapanthus seed heads can all be dip-dyed.

You will need:
Hot water fabric dye.
Saucepan.
Jam jars tall enough to support plant material.
Kettle. Fan heater.
Absorbent dried plant material as described above.

☐ Mix a solution of the powdered dye and water according to the instructions on the packet but use boiling water from a kettle instead of heating the mixture on a cooker.

☐ Swirl the plants gently in the dye solution until the proper shade is reached or, if necessary, immerse them entirely. Remember that the colour will dry a lighter shade.

To dry, stand the material in the jars. Place the jars on layers of newspaper and blow dry with a fan heater.

If the stems bend over too much because of excessive water intake, lay them on the newspaper until they are half dry, then stand them upright and blow dry.

(All plant material will dry more quickly in front of a fan heater and the action of the fan tends to fluff them up again.)

Painting dried material

Dried plants which are not too delicate or feathery can be spray-painted and this is especially useful for decorating fir cones, and similar material which can be used for Christmas or other festive decorations. Gold or silver can also be painted on in this way.

Nuts, lotus seeds, verbascum, wheat, barley, poppy seeds and laurel, ivy or holly leaves can all be spray painted.

To spray cones and other materials which have no stem, put them in a flat open box. This confines the spray and avoids the necessity of handling the

Fantasy colours can be produced; natural colours emphasized with dye and paint.

objects. Shake the box from time to time to jostle the cones so that their entire surface is sprayed.

For long-stemmed plants, hold and spray several at a time to catch any drifting paint. Drying takes only a few minutes.

Varnish can be sprayed on in the same fashion.

Bleaching

Tough wood and bark material like cones and teazels can be bleached and, while this is a simple process, it is important to work in rubber gloves and preferably outdoors—the fumes of the bleach are very strong.

Use household bleach but buy the strongest brand you can and use it full strength. Put the plant material into the bleach and leave it for a few minutes. If the bleach is strong enough the change in colour will be immediate. When the material is as light as you wish, remove it and rinse thoroughly in water.

Blow dry in front of a fan heater, otherwise seedheads such as fir cones tend to close up.

Colouring live flowers

Many white or pale flowers, like carnations or chrysanthemums, can be dyed to produce unusual colours by allowing the flowers literally to drink the dye.

You will need:
Cold water dye such as Dylon.
Glycerine.
Warm water.
Container.

☐ Mix cold water dye with glycerine and add warm water according to instructions on dye packet. For example, using a tin of Dylon cold water dye, add 2 teaspoons of glycerine and .5 litre (½pt) warm water.

☐ When the mixture has cooled, place the flower stems in the dye solution. Colour begins to appear after about an hour but the final depth of shade will depend upon the length of time the flowers are left in the dye.

This in no way harms the flowers which can then be transferred to a vase or bowl.

Some fresh flowers will drink colour.

Floral decorations

Using floral foam and material which you may have air dried or powder dried at home yourself—or that you might have bought from florists or herbalists—you can create a number of floral decorations that will add a festive note to your home and can then be stored away and used again when you feel like it. To get a more fanciful or unusual effect you may prefer to dye some of the material. Other effects can be achieved by bleaching or painting dried flowers and plants.

Hanging flower balls

These elegant decorations can be made very simply and the type of flowers and colours you choose will lend a mood to each. Masses of tiny flower heads are usually used for this kind of arrangement in order to keep the ball as round as possible in shape. Some flowers which are suitable are everlasting flowers like *ammobium alatum grandiflorum* (sand flower), *anaphalis* (pearl), *helichrysum* (straw flower), and *lunaria annua* (honesty); also sea lavender, *nigella* (love-in-a-mist), *astrantia* (masterwort) and *catananche* (cupid's dart).

You will need:
Ball of dry florists' foam (Oasis), 5cm (2") in diameter, available from florists.
Kitchen foil (optional).

2 knitting needles, a thick and a very thin one (or similar long pointed tools).
Ribbon: about 1m (1yd) of very narrow ribbon, and a length of wider ribbon twice the diameter of the ball plus enough to make a long loop.
10 large pearl beads.
Fine wire for binding.
Selection of dried material: in this case straw flower and honesty.
General-purpose glue (optional).

☐ Take a ball of dry florists' foam and cover it with kitchen foil. The foil is not absolutely necessary, but it helps to seal the foam and so prevent it from crumbling.

☐ Using a thick knitting needle, push a hole through the centre of the ball and work both ends of the wider ribbon down through the hole by poking them with the smaller knitting needle. Knot the two ribbon ends together when they emerge at the base. The loop at the top is used to hang the flower ball (fig.1).

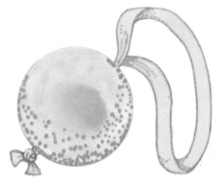

Lesley Fox

1. *Insert ribbon through floral foam.*

☐ Cover the surface of the ball with dried material which has had the stems cut to 2.5cm (1") or less. You can use the same flowers throughout or work according to a predetermined plan or design using, for example, a geometric arrangement. If the stems are delicate, make a hole with the fine knitting needle before pushing the stems in to prevent them breaking. In which case, you might even add a dab of glue to make sure they stay in the pierced holes.

☐ Thread each pearl on wire, twisting the ends together to form stems (fig.2), to add in a similar way.

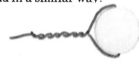

2. *Thread beads on wire and twist.*

☐ Tie the narrow ribbon into small bows, put a pin through the centre and stick it into the ball.

Elegant flower ball suggests a jewelled pomander and is made on a base of floral foam. By Pamela Woods.

Tony Page

Cone tree

Cone-shaped trees are made with floral foam which can often be purchased already in cone shape from florists' shops. A base can be made with an upturned egg-cup with the foam shape glued on top. If you choose a wooden base, it can be dyed with fabric dye along with dried plant material to complement your colour scheme (fig.3). Add the dried material starting from the base. Put the largest shapes at the bottom and add smaller and smaller pieces as you get to the top.

3. *Foam glued to upturned wooden eggcup, dyed to match dried plant materials.*

For a first attempt it is a good idea to use dried leaves around the base and build up the design with seed heads, beech nuts, berries and perhaps some of the everlasting flower heads such as straw flower or sand flower. As you get to the top, keep the shapes as neat and rounded as possible to avoid throwing the cone shape off balance.

The poppy seeds in the cone tree shown provide a dramatic contrast to the tiny dried flowers, and the quaking grasses which shake with the slightest disturbance give a shimmering effect.

Tony Page

Alternative spiral design

Step one: start by building up one basic spiral outline.

Step two: after basic outline, start at base.

Step three: Fill in remaining gaps.

Sue Richards

'Whispering cone' tree whose fragile grasses shiver at the slightest disturbance, giving a shimmering, life-like effect.

Large-sized cone trees. For really large dried material—big cones, Chinese lanterns, whole clusters of hydrangea and berries—you may need to make your own base from wire mesh.

To make a mesh base you will need:
Newspaper or other paper for pattern.
Wire mesh with 1.2cm (½″) holes for cone.
Wire cutters or floral scissors.
Fine wire or twine for binding edges together.
Crumbled florists' foam.
Masking or adhesive tape.

☐ Make a pattern from a piece of paper by folding a square shape in half to make a triangle (fig.4).

☐ Join the two short sides with a piece of tape so that they form a cone shape, and trim the base evenly so it can stand upright (fig.5). Then cut the tape and stretch out pattern over wire mesh.

☐ Cut round the pattern with shears and join the edges of the wire by binding them with fine wire or twine (fig.6).

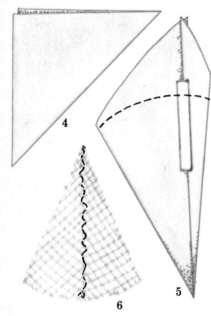

Pattern for mesh base used for large cone trees. **4.** *Fold square in half on the diagonal.* **5.** *Tape sides together and trim edge to make it even.* **6.** *Cut out pattern in wire mesh and bind edges together with fine wire.*

☐ Line the inside of the cone with the newspaper pattern and fill the interior with crumbled foam, packing it tightly.

☐ Seal off the base of the cone by putting overlapping strips of tape across it, preferably making two layers —the second at right angles to the first. This completes the cone shape which can now be decorated in the same manner as for Hanging flower balls.

Fir cone tree made of natural and bleached fir cones is a handsome year-round arrangement. Pamela Woods.

'Bay' trees

Round bay trees standing on thin stalks in their tubs look like fantasies from Alice in Wonderland, yet they can be carried to even more imaginative dimensions using floral foam and dried materials—and they can be made any size from miniature to 'life'.

You must of course find a pot or tub the right size to 'plant' your tree in. This can be any size of plastic pot, or a wooden tub or paint tin. Plant by sticking the ball of floral foam on top of a rod and securing it in the pot. To prevent your tree from being top-heavy you can weight your container by filling it with sand or small stones.

Remember, these trees can be made in any size. If you can get a huge pot and a big enough pole you can make a really large one to stand in a hall. If you cannot get a large enough piece of foam, you can often have one cut by a floral supplier, or you can use styrofoam. Ask your florist for the supplier nearest to you.

You will need:

Flower pot, tin or tub.

Enough sand or stones to fill the container if it is a large one.

Cellulose filler [Spackle], plaster of Paris or cement, available from hardware stores.

Thin metal rod or wooden dowelling.

Ball of floral foam such as Oasis.

String.

Dried flower material.

Artificial fruit (optional).

Ribbon and paint can be used according to personal choice.

☐ Put a few heavy pebbles in the bottom of the pot and then, if it is a large pot, fill to about 2.5cm (1″) below the rim with stones or sand, and cover with plaster [Spackle] or cement.

☐ Place a thin rod in the centre and let it set in the plaster [Spackle]. The length of the rod should be in proportion to the size of the pot, and this is a matter of personal taste. (Make sure the rod stays vertical while the filler dries and prop it up if necessary.)

☐ Take a ball of foam and push it down over the rod until it is embedded about half way. The size of the ball will depend on the size of the pot, or vice versa, and as a general rule estimate that the size of the covered ball will be about twice that of the pot.

☐ Wind a piece of string tightly around the rod at the base of the ball to prevent the foam slipping any further down the rod. The string will be concealed by the dried material—or it can be disguised by tying a strip of ribbon over it.

At this point it is a good idea to paint the rod and pot to harmonize with the arrangement and if you plan to do so, try a vivid Chinese red as long as it will not overpower the arrangement,

Melvin Grey

or a softer gold or bronze paint. Alternatively you could paint the tub one colour, bright green for instance, and give the rod a coat of bark-like brown enamel. Another decorative solution is to wrap the rod in a colourful ribbon or crepe paper, but this should be done later.

☐ Add the material to the ball at the top in much the same way as for the cone tree previously described.

Keep all dried material to a stem length if not more than 5cm (2″) and, if necessary mount on special wire

Delicate little 'bay' tree by Pamela Woods is an example of the fanciful trees in all sizes that can be made by sticking materials into a foam ball.

known as stubb wire (obtainable from florists) and cut wire to this length. Use your largest material first, pushing it closely into the surface before adding the smaller flowers and grasses. An interesting outline can be achieved by varying the length of visible stems.

To disguise cement or plaster in the pot you can use pebbles or paint it.

Bottle decorations

Bottle gardens are virtually self-contained worlds needing little attention once they are planted and in the case of air-tight versions, called terrariums, they are entirely self-perpetuating. This is because moisture collects on the interior walls of the bottle and 'rains' on the miniature garden below. Also the life cycle continues unimpeded since plants both make and use oxygen and carbon dioxide.

Many delicate plants normally difficult to grow in homes flourish particularly well in bottle gardens because they are protected from draughts and, if moist enough, enjoy perfect greenhouse conditions.

Bottles

A sizeable glass container is required for a bottle garden, preferably one with a glass lid or sides that curve over the garden so that condensed moisture can collect and water the plants. The glass can be slightly tinted but it must be borne in mind that tinted glass reduces the penetration of light. In some exposed conditions, however, this may be desirable.

Large wine jars or demijohns, and bulbous carboys used for storing acid and chemicals are particularly suitable. Another possibility is to turn a large jar on its side so that one side becomes 'earth' and the opposite is 'sky'.

One of the attractions of bottle gardens—as with ships in bottles—is their improbable appearance and the

narrower the neck the more effective is the result in this respect. However, the neck of any bottle destined to become a garden must be wide enough to get small plants through and also provide enough room to manipulate the tools with which the garden is planted.

Tools
Tools must be improvised.
Old forks and teaspoons make useful rakes and trowels when lashed to a slender stick or piece of dowelling. If they are in throw-away condition a dab of glue to bind the implement to the stick is advisable before lashing the two together.

A cotton reel with a dowel stuck firmly through the centre hole, makes a useful rammer for packing down soil.
Maintenance tools if required can consist of a razor blade glued to a stick for pruning, and 'chopsticks' made of two extra-long sticks for collecting bits and pieces.

Suitable plants for bottle gardens

Asplenium nidus
Begonia
Cryptanthus
Chlorophytum
Fittonia
Ficus pumila
Hedera (Ivy)
Kalanchoe
Maranta (arrowroot)
Peperomia
Pilea
Pellaea (cliff-brake)
Sanseveria (snake plant or leopard lily)
Spathiphyllum

Planting a garden
Clean the bottle well with detergent and water and line the bottom of the container with pebbles or bits of crockery for drainage.
Potting medium is then added. This should be a sterilized form of potting

Part of the enjoyment of creating bottle gardens is 'landscaping', since each garden must suit the size and shape of its container. Gardens shown are by Selwyn Davidson.

David Levin

1. *'Landscape' your garden on a plate before beginning to plant it.*

2. *Pour in compost over drainage pebbles.*

3. *Push each tiny plant gently through the neck of the bottle.*

4. *By tilting the bottle plants can be dropped more easily into place.*

Melvin Grey

5. *Use improvised tools to manipulate plants and arrange compost in the bottle.*

6. *Final decorations such as pebbles can be added using a 'funnel' to complete the garden. Designed by Selwyn Davidson.*

David Levin

medium and when you are inserting it, a funnel will protect the glass sides of the container from becoming soiled. Arrange the compost to suit your planting scheme using the fork or spoon to make any undulations and the rammer to pack the soil.

Arranging the plants. Because of the difficulties of re-arranging plants in the bottle it is advisable to lay out the garden first on a dish or platter. The chart on page 263 gives a list of the recommended plants for bottle gardens. When a suitable arrangement has been made plants can be transferred one at a time into position in the bottle.

Planting. Use the trowel to make a little hole for the plant. Put in the plant and fill in the hole round it by jiggling soil about with the trowel. If you are not very successful at this

do not worry—the plants will root themselves when they have been watered. Sometimes the bottle can be tipped to facilitate dropping the plant into a corner. On other occasions the long-handled implements can be used as 'chopsticks' to manipulate plants.

It is better to start planting from the outside of the bottle, and work inwards towards the centre. Do not press the plants against the sides of the container although it is permissible to allow some of the leaves to touch the sides.

Ornaments. Both natural ornaments and artifacts can be added for texture and decoration: moss, bark, rocks, toadstools, even a snail will flourish in this moist clime. Alternatively, a miniature bridge or house in keeping with the overall scale could be included.

The finished garden is a world of its own, requiring little attention and providing hothouse growing conditions.

Clean the sides of the container if necessary with a piece of plastic sponge which has been tied to a long wire made from a straightened out coat-hanger.

Watering can be accomplished with a small spray. If the bottle is then corked it will cloud up, but only temporarily. Bottle gardens never need watering as often as ordinary house plants and if the bottle is corked then you may not have to add any water for months. It is advisable, however, to watch the garden fairly closely at first to make sure it does not dry up and to give it time to establish itself as a microcosm or world of its own.

Jewelcrafts

Baubles bangles and beads are expensive to buy. Here are
some really ingenious ideas for making your own jewelry.
You can choose from several marvellous techniques.

Bead jewelry

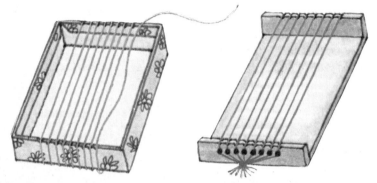

1a. *Simple cardboard loom with notches.*   **1b.** *Wood loom with nails.*

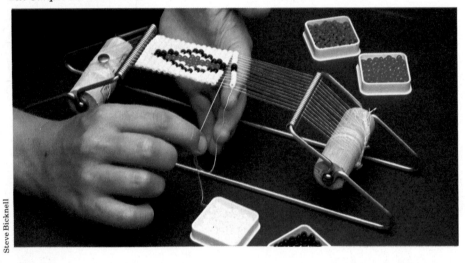

Metal loom with separators for warp threads and rollers for winding work.

Weaving beads on a loom is similar to fabric weaving. The warp threads, ie the ones going lengthwise, are stretched on to the loom and the weft, ie the threads going from side to side, are threaded in and out of the warp.

One bead is caught up between each warp thread to produce flat strips of beadwork with the beads lying in parallel rows. On the finished work, none of the warp or weft threads are visible between the beads.

The loom

Bead weaving looms can be made at home from a cardboard box with cut notches or wood and nails (fig.1) and these are perfectly adequate for weaving small pieces of beadwork.

If you want to weave long pieces it is necessary to buy a loom which enables you to wind the work on as it progresses. There are two types available: a wooden loom and a metal loom. The metal loom has rollers at each end which enable you to wind the work backwards and forwards quite easily. On a wooden loom the work can be wound on, but not as easily as on a metal loom. The instructions given in this chapter apply to a metal loom.

Setting up. Each warp thread should be 45cm (18″) longer than the finished work is to be. The number of warp threads should be one more than the number of beads which will be on each row. A piece that is nine beads wide will need ten warp threads.

First the warp threads are placed side by side and joined together at each end with a knot. One end is secured in the rivet on one of the rollers, and the warp threads are wound on to this roller until the knot at that end can be attached to the roller at the other end.

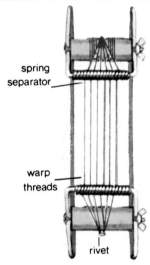

spring separator

warp threads

rivet

2. *Details of a metal bead loom.*

The threads are then spaced out over the separator, one thread in each groove. The knot is secured to roller rivet (fig.2).

The width of the bead loom obviously limits the width of the beadwork that can be made on the loom. The metal loom has separators for 35 threads which means that 34 beads is the maximum width that can be made. Many strips of 34 beads wide could be made and sewn together side by side to provide a wider strip. Very long pieces can be made by winding the work on to the rollers, and by joining strips end to end there is really no limit to how long a piece can be made. The warp on a home-made loom can be set up as shown in fig.1.

When the warp is on the loom, the weaving can start. A beading needle is threaded and the thread knotted to the outside warp thread on the left-hand side. The number of beads required for the first row is threaded on to the weft thread and passed underneath the warp threads.

With the other hand, one bead is pushed up between each warp thread and the needle is passed back through the beads, over the top of the warp threads, thereby securing them to the

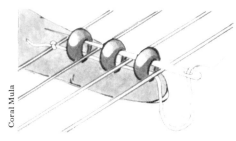

3. Passing the needle round the end warp thread and back through the beads.

warp (fig.3).

To wind the work on as it progresses, the screw at the side of the roller is loosened and the roller turned. The warp does not have to be slotted into the separator again as the beadwork already woven will space the warp correctly.

Woven bead necklaces, inspired by patterns of American Indians.

Indian necklace

Bead weaving is a traditional craft of the American Indians. This necklace is based on the colours and designs used by them for centuries to make jewelry and other decorative objects.

You will need:
Beeswax.
Beading thread such as Drima made by Coats.
2 beading needles.
Bead loom.
Glass beads size 10 (about 1mm ($\frac{1}{16}$") diameter) in the following colours and

amounts:
57gm (2oz) white.
28gm (1oz) black.
14gm ($\frac{1}{2}$oz) red.
14gm ($\frac{1}{2}$oz) dark blue.
14gm ($\frac{1}{2}$oz) yellow.
14gm ($\frac{1}{2}$oz) light blue.
14gm ($\frac{1}{2}$oz) brown.
In the instructions **w** = white, **r** = red **b** = dark blue.
☐ Thread the loom with 32 warp

Work the Indian necklace from this detailed photograph.

threads 81cm (32″) long as explained earlier.

☐ Thread the needle with a long thread, double it and rub with beeswax.

☐ Tie it to the sixteenth warp thread from the left-hand side. This is where the weaving starts to create the V shape at the bottom of the necklace. (The fringe is made later.)

☐ Following the photograph thread one **w** bead on to the warp thread.

☐ Pass the thread down between warp threads 15 and 16 and up between threads 17 and 18 (counting from the left-hand side).

☐ Push the **w** bead up between threads 16 and 17 and thread the needle through it.

☐ Thread 3**w** beads, pass the needle down between threads 14 and 15 and up between threads 18 and 19, push the beads up between the warp threads and pass the needle back through them.

☐ Continue in this way following the pattern in the photograph.

☐ Wind on the work when necessary. To divide the threads after row 59 has been worked, move 16 warp threads along the comb at the top which separates the warp threads and continue weaving up one section.

☐ When you have finished one side, start the other side using a new weft thread tied to the 17th warp thread.

☐ When the necklace narrows, move the surplus warp threads slightly away from the weaving by hooking over the spring separator and continue the pattern. The warp threads will later be fastened into the beadwork.

The fringe. When you have completed the bead weaving, roll the beadwork back on to the top roller until the beginning of the necklace is sitting between the separators.

☐ Cut the first warp thread as close to the knot as possible and thread it on to the needle.

☐ Thread 8**w**, 8**b**, 8**r**, 3**w**. Pass the needle back through 8**r**, 8**b**, 8**w**.

☐ Pass the needle through a few beads on row 15 and finish off the Indian necklace with a slip knot tied between two beads.

☐ Repeat this with each warp thread.

Finishing off. There are two methods of joining up the two ends. The first method involves weaving each warp thread into the other side of the necklace and securing with slip knots. This gives a very neat reversible finish. The second method is easier but not neat on both sides.

☐ Ask someone to hold the two ends of the necklace together while you tie one warp thread from each side together to form a row of knots. Dab each row with colourless nail varnish.

☐ Glue a piece of suede or felt to the row of knots to cover them up and strengthen the join.

270

Steve Bicknell

Blue and white necklace

This is made from three solid pieces of bead weaving held together with strings of beads.

You will need:
Bead loom.
Beading needle.
Beeswax.
Beading thread such as Drima made by Coats.
Glass beads size 10 (about 1mm ($\frac{1}{16}$″) diameter) in the following colours and amounts:
85gm (3oz) dark blue.
28gm (1oz) white.
14gm ($\frac{1}{2}$oz) green.
14gm ($\frac{1}{2}$oz) light blue.
In the instructions **d** = dark blue, **g** = green, **w** = white.

☐ Thread the warp on the loom as

Work the blue and white necklace from this photograph by counting the beads and rows. Designer Marjory Murphy.

described earlier. You will need 31 warp threads each 81cm (32″) long.

☐ Wind 25cm (10″) of the warp threads on to the bottom roller before starting to weave—this will be used later for the fringing.

☐ Thread a needle with a long double thread, rub it with beeswax and tie to the 15th warp thread counting from the left-hand side.

☐ For the point, thread 2**g** beads and push the needle down between the 14th space from the left and up through the 17th. Push the beads up between the warp threads and thread the needle back through them.

☐ Thread one **g** bead and pass the needle down through the 14th space and up through the 13th space. Hold the bead between the 14th and 15th warp threads and pass the needle back through the bead. This bead is now the first on the second row.

☐ Thread the remaining beads of the second row, ie 2**w** and 1**g**, and secure between the warp threads in the usual way, passing the needle through all four beads.

☐ Continue weaving following pattern shown in photograph opposite. Complete 32 rows.

☐ To decrease for row 33, pass the needle back through the first **g** bead of row 32. Now move the outer warp threads slightly away from the main body of the work and weave as before on fewer warp threads. As fewer beads are threaded for each row the work will decrease on both sides.

☐ Repeat this method for decreasing for each row.

☐ When you have finished row 46, fasten off the thread in the row before by making slip knots.

☐ Remove the top of the warp threads from the loom and on to each pair of warp threads starting from the left or right-hand side thread **d** beads in the following order and amounts: 48, 44, 41, 39, 38, 34, 32, 30 (on to one warp thread), 30, 32, 34, 38, 39, 41, 44, 48. This makes sixteen ropes altogether.

☐ Replace the warp on to the loom.

☐ Thread a needle and tie the thread to the 15th and 16th warp threads. Weave the square on the left of the necklace following the pattern. Use warp threads 15 and 16 as one.

This tight-fitting, striking bracelet can be made on a warp of shirring elastic so that no fastening is needed.

☐ Weave the square on the right-hand side on the remaining 15 warp threads.

For the fringing roll the beadwork back on to the top roller until the end of the necklace is sitting between the separators.

☐ Release one warp thread at a time from the knot and thread on to this warp thread 16**d** and 3**w** beads.

☐ Pass the needle back through the 16**d** beads and fasten the thread by making a series of slip knots into the beadwork.

☐ Repeat this for each warp thread.

To finish off. Remove the necklace from the loom, and on to each pair of warp threads put sufficient **d** beads for the required length. Tie the matching warp threads together and dab the knots with colourless nail varnish.

☐ Thread the ends through a few beads and trim.

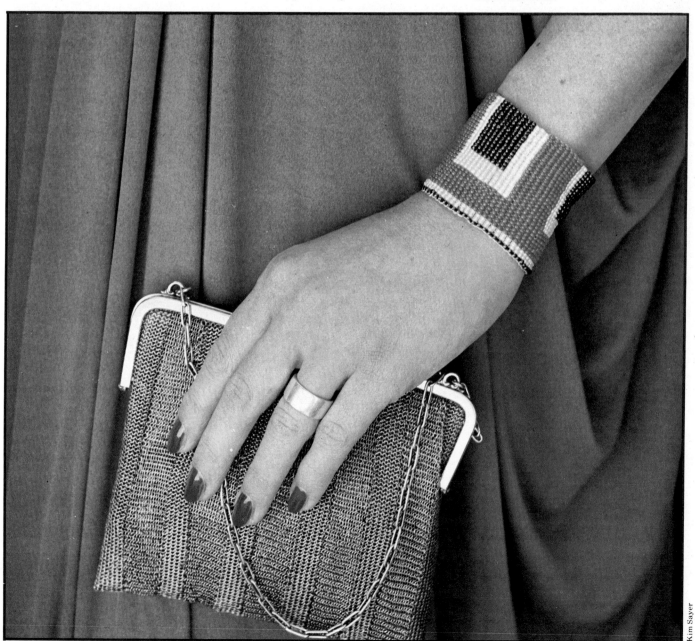

Polished stone jewelry

Tumbling is the process that smoothes and polishes pebbles and stones so that they are ready for use as jewelry or any other decoration. It is done with a tumbling machine, which runs from an ordinary power point in the home. This machine can take any potentially attractive pebble or small stone and smooth it till it has a permanent shine. You can tumble pebbles picked up from the beach or stones you have found in the countryside. Or, if you are not satisfied with what you have collected or want greater variety, you can buy rough pieces of stone from lapidary shops and polish them. The smoother the stone you start with, the shorter the process; but even rough pieces can be polished successfully. And the results are stones of beauty and fascination that you can use in all sorts of different ways.

Choosing a tumbler

A simple tumbling machine consists of a small barrel, which is turned by rollers, powered through a pully or gear system by an electric motor. The stones are placed inside the barrel with just enough water to cover them and a small quantity of very hard grit, called silicon carbide. They then tumble on top of each other till they are smoothed down. Coarse grit is used at first, then finer grits and lastly a polishing agent.

There are tumbling kits available which usually include a machine, the necessary grits and polishing agents, a batch of stones, epoxy resin glue and a selection of findings or jewelry mounts, to which you attach your polished stones. Any shop specializing in lapidary will stock all the equipment you need—they are quite used to giving guidance to beginners so don't be put off by the fact that they also deal in finished stones and supplies for experts.

Tumbling machines are available in a variety of sizes and with one or more barrels. Most small machines run at one speed only but some offer variable speeds.

Machines with two or more barrels are very useful, since you can tumble different sets of stones at the same time. This avoids the bother of having to wait till one cycle is completed before starting another. It is ideal, too, if you can keep one barrel exclusively for the final polish since, for this, the barrel must be completely free of grit. In small barrels you can only tumble stones up to about 40mm (1½″), therefore a larger barrel means that you can tumble larger stones.

With a variable-speed machine you can shorten the first, rough tumbling stage by using the high speed. The low speed (standard for one-speed machines) is used for the later stages, when fast tumbling will cause cracking and unsatisfactory results.

The disadvantage of larger or more complicated machines is that they cost more. If you intend to make jewelry in commercial quantities they are well worth the extra cost, but the beginner will probably be satisfied with a small machine.

Small, one-speed machines usually have a capacity of 0.675kg (1½lb) to 1.35kg (3lb) and are able to tumble 100-200 pebbles at a time, from the size of a pea up to roughly the size of the top joint of your thumb. With the larger machines you can tumble slightly larger stones.

The smoothing grits used in tumbling machines are made of silicon carbide. This is much harder than any pebble, with a hardness of 9½ on Mohs' scale, and makes an excellent abrasive for smoothing pebbles.

The grits are distinguished by grade numbers — the higher the grade number, the finer the grit. '60 grade' grit, which is commonly used for grinding the rough edges off pebbles, will pass through a screen with 60 meshes per 2.5cm (1″). Grits from 60 grade to 600 grade, which roughly correspond to the difference between coarse sandpaper and fine glasspaper,

Tumbled jasper pebbles have been carefully matched to make up this necklace. The stones are glued into bell caps.

Sandra Lousada

STONES FOR TUMBLING
grouped according to Mohs' scale

Below is a list of the stones most commonly available through rock shops which are suitable for tumbling.

You will notice that some stones range over two or three numbers, such as Serpentine 2½-4. This is because some stones have different hardness values, depending on what part of the world they come from. Always test them before mixing with other stones in your tumbler. Add to this list the Mohs' scale number of other stones you find or buy.

8	Beryl 8 Chrysoberyl 8½	Topaz 8
7	Most Agates 7½ Agatized Coral 7½ Amethyst 7 Bloodstone 7 Chalcedony 7½ Crocidolite (Tiger Eye) 7 Cornelian 7½ Chrysoprase 7 Citrine 7 Chalcedony Onyx 7 Flint 7½ Garnet 7½ Green Garnet 7 Green Chalcedony 7½ Iolite 7	Jadeite 6½-7 Jasper 6-7 Mookaite 7½ Moroccan Beans 7½ Petrified Wood 7 Petrified Bone 7 Pink Botswana 7½ Quartz Crystal 7 Rock Crystal 7 Rose Quartz 7 Rutilated Quartz 7 Smoky Quartz 7 Tourmaline 7½ Turitella Agate 6-7 Zircon 7½
6	Amazonite 6 Aventurine 6-6½ Black Jade 6½ Bruneau Jasper 6½ Chrysocolla 5-7½ Green Jade 6½ Hematite 5½ Jadeite 6½-7 Jasper 6-7 Labradorite 6	Magnetite 6 Opal 6 Prehnite 6-6½ Pyrite 6 Rhodonite 5½-6½ Rutile 6-6½ Sodalite 6 Sunstone 6 Turitella Agate 6-7 Turquoise 4-6
5	Apatite 5 Brazilianite 5½ Chrysocolla 5-7½ Moonstone 5	Nephrite 5½ Obsidian 5 Rhyolite 5-6 Turquoise 4-6
4	Bowenite 4 Fluorite 4	Serpentine 2½-4 Turquoise 4-6
3	Aragonite 3 Calcite Onyx 3½ Coral 3½ Jet 3	Limestone 3 Malachite 3½ Marble 3-3½ Serpentine 2½-4
2	Alabaster 2 Amber 2-2½	Serpentine 2½-4

are available at any rock shop.

Polishing agents are used in the final tumbling stage. These are either tin oxide or cerium oxide and are used to add the polish when a stone is already smooth.

Running a tumbler

When your tumbling machine is operating, it will run 24 hours a day for up to three weeks at a time—and it will be very noisy. Therefore you must put it somewhere where it will not be in the way and where there is a power point. The stones tumbling over each other make a continuous swishing noise, so the tumbler should not be located where noise will be a nuisance. A workshop in the garden is ideal but a little-used corner away from bedrooms will do.

If you put the machine on top of several layers of newspaper, this will help to deaden the sound and also to catch any dirt that may spill when you load or unload the machine. A strong cardboard box, with one end open for ventilation, also acts as an effective sound barrier.

Operating the tumbler. Before you load the machine, check the pebbles you are going to use—they should be of varying sizes and of similar hardness like those listed in the chart of Mohs' scale numbers on the left.

The smaller stones 'fit in' to the angles of the larger ones, so that more of their surface is being rubbed at any one time. Softer stones will rapidly be worn away by the harder ones, become ruined and clog up the whole process. Try to make a batch of pebbles in a similar condition—if there are some which are much more pitted than others, they will inevitably need more rough tumbling.

Load the barrel three-quarters full of appropriate pebbles. Pour in water till it just covers them. Add coarse silicon carbide grit according to the manufacturer's instructions—a tablespoonful of 60 grade grit is about right for a 0.675kg (1½lb) barrel.

Make sure that the lid of the barrel fits tightly, place the barrel on the rollers and switch on the motor. The barrel should turn smoothly at about 40 revolutions per minute and the sound of the pebbles should be an even, swishing rumble.

If the sound is uneven and clicking noises can be heard, check your load. You may have too few pebbles, or some that are too large; if it sounds as if there is little movement going on, you may have too many. In time, you will know immediately by the sound coming from the tumbler if the operation is going well.

The first rough-grind stage will continue for 5-7 days; exactly how long depends on the hardness and initial smoothness of the pebbles. The rough-grind cycle is finished when the grit has been completely worn into clay. Inspect the load daily. You will not see too much difference in the first day or two, so replace any stones you took out, seal the lid and continue tumbling. Many stones contain small quantities of gas, which are released as the surfaces of the stones are ground away. These small quantities may build up if you do not remove the lid once in every 24 hours.

When the grit has been worn away, empty the whole load through a sieve into a bucket half filled with water. Let the sludge sink to the bottom and then wash as much grit as possible off the pebbles by dunking the sieve in the water at the top of the bucket. Finally, rinse the pebbles in running water and let them dry on a soft cloth.

If there is clean water at the top of the bucket, you may pour it off but do *not* let any of the sludge go down the drain—you will block it. The sludge dries like cement. Empty the sludge into a plastic bag, which can be sealed and thrown in the dustbin.

The second rough-grind cycle. If you are working with rounded beach pebbles, already partly smoothed by

A tumbling machine, together with a second barrel. This machine is constructed so that the second barrel, which is sold separately, runs from the same motor as the first and can be geared to run at high speed for rough tumbling or at low speed for polishing.

wave action, the rough-grind stage may only need one cycle. However, if you are using jagged, broken gem-stones from a rock face, you may need three complete rough-grind cycles to achieve a good shape. In that case, repeat the operation with clean barrel, water and grit.

Eventually, the surface roughness will have been worn away, at least from most of the batch. At this stage sort the stones. Any that are still badly marked should be held back for re-tumbling with your next batch. The stones that are ready for the next stage will have an opaque look when dry but should be free of rough edges or obvious imperfections.

Second stage tumbling. Rinse the barrel thoroughly. Any particles of grit that remain will interfere with the finer grinding to come.

Replace the pebbles. If you have had to discard many, you may have to rough-grind another load before moving on to this stage. The barrel should be more than two-thirds full and, once again, too few pebbles will give a bad result. Load the barrel as before, using a finer grit (200 grade) and repeat the procedure, inspecting daily until the grit is worn away. This stage should remove the roughness left after the first stage.

When this is done, after a few days' tumbling, clean the barrel and pebbles as before, using the sludge-collecting method described in the first stage to avoid blocking the drains.

Fine grinding. Re-load and repeat the

operation, using very fine silicon carbide grit (600 grade). Tumble for 5—7 days. Keep checking the load daily, until the surface of the pebbles is perfectly smooth and has a semi-gloss finish.

It is essential at this stage that you clean everything thoroughly—the pebbles, the barrel and the lid. If there are any grains of grit left, you will fail to achieve a high polish. Check the stones again and reject any that are cracked. Be absolutely ruthless about this; cracked stones will cause scratches on the others. Re-tumble them with your next load before polishing them.

The final polish. Put the selected pebbles back into the clean barrel carefully, so they do not chip each other as they fall. Add clean water to cover them. Add polishing powder, according to the manufacturer's instructions —a teaspoonful of tin oxide or cerium oxide should be right for a 0.675kg (1½lb) machine.

If, when you start tumbling, sharp noises indicate that the pebbles are rattling unevenly against each other, you may add a teaspoonful of wall-paper glue to thicken the mixture, but do not use too much. Clean plastic pellets, which are available at rock-shops, make a good filler if you do not have quite a full load.

Check the pebbles daily, as before. It will probably be about four days before they show a good gleam but keep going until there is no noticeable improvement on the day before. There is a perfect polish when the pebbles shine as brilliantly when they are dry as when they are wet.

Clean the barrel and rinse off the stones. Sometimes, the polish can be improved by tumbling for a few hours with a few drops of detergent in water. Be careful not to use too much detergent, or the bubbles will force the lid off. Finally, rinse and dry the stones. They should now have a sparkle which they will never lose.

General hints

It is a good idea to keep a record of exactly how long you have taken over each stage and exactly what materials and quantities you have used. Keep a couple of stones untumbled from each batch, so you can compare them with the final result and refer to them later, when you have a similar batch to work with.

Don't be afraid to experiment with different grades of grit or varying lengths of time—different stones will need slightly different procedures and even the experts are continually experimenting! You should be able to get an impressive result first time but, as always, there is no substitute for practical experience.

Making jewelry

Once you have polished stones, the next step is to use them. Stones can be made very simply into attractive—and unique—pieces of jewelry by using commercially available mountings, which are called 'findings'.

Findings are sold in lapidary shops and many craft shops which also sell polished stones, if you want to make jewelry but are not interested in polishing stones yourself.

Findings are made in various metals, at varying prices—the beginner is wise to start with cheap metal ones but, when you have made a few pieces, you may want to set a special stone in silver or gold. This is no more difficult, but do remember that the beauty of the stones is usually best shown off by simple settings.

Essentially, jewelry is made by gluing the stones to findings. There are three basic types of jewelry findings—flat pads, to which stones with flat bases are glued; bell caps which are bent over an end of a stone (usually a pear-shaped one); and claw settings where you glue a stone to a base and bend adjustable 'claws' round the stone to hold it in position.

These three types cover the findings you glue to the stone. Other findings include jump rings which are used to connect one section (notably, bell caps) to another. You can buy bracelets or necklets which may have flat pads or claws, others may need jump rings and bell caps to attach the stones. In general, you can buy findings for use as ear-rings, pendants, brooches, cuff-links, key rings—almost any piece of jewelry you may want to make—using one or other of the three methods.

The right finding for each stone. What finding you use depends on the stone and what you intend to do with it. Stones that taper to a point are most suitable for bell caps and for use as pendants, key rings or anywhere they can dangle. Stones with a flat side can be used on flat-based findings for rings and brooches. Round stones are generally best in 'claw' settings which can be adjusted to fit them.

To make jewelry

You will need:

Polished stones.
Findings.
Epoxy resin adhesive.
Saucer for mixing adhesive.
Match-sticks for applying adhesive.
Jewelry pliers or tweezers.
Spirit.
Clean rags.
Shallow tray or tin.
Salt or sand.

Preparing stones and findings. Wash the stones and findings in warm water and detergent, to remove all traces of

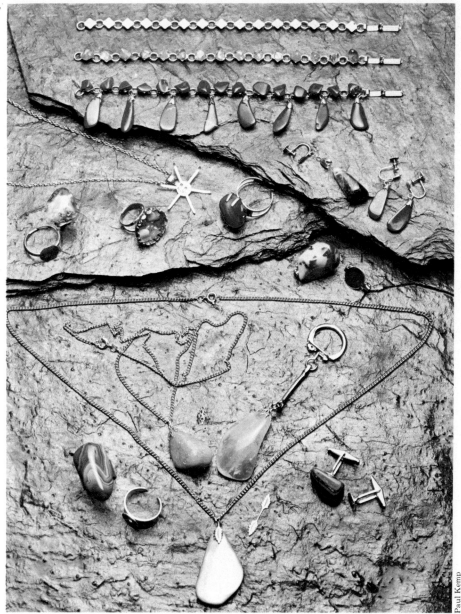

Paul Kemp

Jewelry findings, showing which types of finding are most appropriate to various shapes of tumbled stones.

dirt and grease. Rinse and dry them thoroughly. Even the natural oils from fingers may affect adhesion, so a final wipe over with spirit is a good idea.

☐ Mix the epoxy resin, according to the manufacturer's instructions. Epoxy resin has the advantage of being extremely strong when it is set; but it is correspondingly difficult to remove, so be careful not to let any unwanted traces go hard.

☐ Since the resin takes time to set (up to three days for complete hardening), you may have to hold the stone and finding in position. To do this, pour a quantity of salt, sand or rice into a tray or tin and support them with this. Push the band of a ring or back of a brooch into the sand, so that the surface to be glued stays clear and level. If you are applying a bell cap to a stone, push the stone in and set the bell cap on it.

☐ Apply the resin with a match-stick to both the finding and the stone. Wipe off any unwanted blobs of glue with a clean rag.

☐ **With a 'claw' mount** bend the claws into position with jewelry pliers (tweezers may do) before inserting the stone. Pull them out of place as little as possible when inserting the stone and then bend them firmly over it.

☐ **With a bell cap** be careful to position the cap, by watching the position of the eyelet at the top of the cap, so that the face of the stone that you prefer will face outwards when it hangs.

☐ When the glue is dry, brush off any particles of salt or sand from the finding and stone. If the piece needs to be connected to a chain or bracelet do this with a jump ring. Jewelry pliers will open these and twist them shut.

Wire jewelry

Because most people tend to think that working with metal involves using heavy machinery, it is rather neglected as a craft material. But primitive man did marvellous things with the minimum of tools and now modern, small-scale aids make it possible for anyone to take up a wide variety of metal-working techniques at home. And since metal is so versatile the creative design possibilities are endless, once the basic techniques are mastered.

Jewelry made with these basic metal working techniques can be extremely attractive and easy to make.

Wire

Many early pieces of jewelry were based on patterns created with wire which had been made by hand. As an introduction to the possibilities of working with metal, interesting jewelry can be made from various types of wire. The techniques can be developed to form very intricate pieces and wire combines well with other materials, like leather and all kinds of stones. Economically, it is a good idea to start with copper, brass or silver-plated wire. Once you acquire the knack of bending the wire in various ways you can graduate to fine silver wire.

Care. Keep stocks of wire labelled with their thickness or gauge number until you have learnt to recognize the various sizes. Wrap the wire up in plastic bags to prevent discolouration when you are not working with it. Always keep wire as straight as possible. If the wire has been kept in a large coil it can be straightened by lightly smoothing it with the fingers.

Polish and finishing. Clean the completed pieces by immersing them in a liquid silver cleaner. Wash in soapy luke-warm water and dry. To prevent future discolouration, spray with a metal or clear varnish. If the silver is being used with other materials, clean it thoroughly first.

Joins. Note how joined pieces hang. The pieces do not stay flat but alternate – one flat and the other at right angles to it (fig.1). Designs must follow this pattern otherwise the piece of jewelry will not hang in the correct way. A piece of work will never appear the

1

same when lying on the work bench as when it is suspended, so always hold your work up to look at it.

It is difficult to correct or straighten a piece of wire without it looking untidy and overworked so, if a mistake is made, it is better to start again with a new piece of wire.

You can use the discarded pieces for making jump rings.

Tools

Round-nosed pliers do not have to be expensive but check that the jaws make contact along their entire length. The inside of the jaw should be smooth otherwise it will damage the surface of the wire. If they are not smooth, cover the jaws with sticking plaster, although this does make it slightly more difficult to grip heavy wire firmly. All-in-one pliers that cut and bend round and square lines are only suitable in the early stages. Once more

This intricate sunray necklace is not nearly as difficult to make as it looks.

Steve Bicknell

276

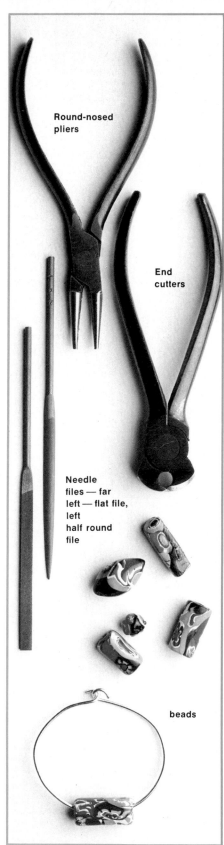

Round-nosed pliers

End cutters

Needle files — far left — flat file, left half round file

beads

Basic jewelry-making tools and silver-plated wire bracelet with bead.

progressive techniques are reached a higher quality of tool is required.

Curling with round-nosed pliers. The size of the curl depends on the position of the wire in the jaws of the pliers. A small curl is made with the wire at the front of the pliers and a large one with it at the back.

The end of the wire in the jaws should not stick out beyond the pliers. Grip the pliers firmly and turn in a clockwise direction using the thumb of the other hand to apply pressure to the wire close to the jaws. You can work in an anti-clockwise direction if you find it easier but whichever way you do, make it a habit to work in the same direction. Try to complete a curl without having to regrip the wire.

Diagonal wire cutters or end cutters. It is easier to cut jump rings with the diagonal wire cutters, but either these or end cutters will do.

Metal file. You can use a medium sized metal file or you can buy a selection of Swiss or needle files. You will not need all the files to make the pieces shown here, but it is economical to buy a set of about 6 as they will be useful later.

It is sensible to spend as much as you can afford on tools, all of which can be bought from a hardware store.

Bracelet with bead
You will need:
18cm (7″) of 1.5mm (gauge 15) silver-plated wire
One bead that will fit onto wire
☐File ends of wire and thread the bead. Shape with fingers and make a curl at either end to hook together.

Earrings
You will need:
31cm (12″) of 1.5mm (gauge 15) silver-plated wire
A pair of earring findings, clip-on or screw type, available from craft shops, haberdashers [notion departments] or jewellers. Ensure they have a hook or eye for attaching a jump ring.
Jump rings are used to attach and assemble jewelry. Make 2 jump rings by placing the end of the wire halfway down the jaws and working it around until you have 2 complete circles (fig.2).
☐Line up the end cutters with the end of the wire and cut through both coils (fig.3).

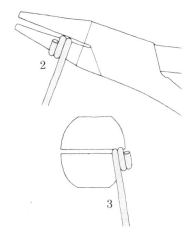

2

3

☐File ends of rings flat and smooth.
☐To make a larger number of jump rings coil the wire around any cylindrical shape of the right size (fig.4).

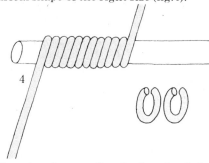

4

Hanging drops. Cut 2 of each of the lengths shown in fig.5 and file ends.

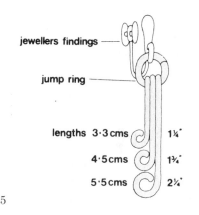

jewellers findings

jump ring

lengths	3·3 cms	1¼″
4·5cms	1¾″
5·5cms	2¼″

5

☐Make a small loop at one end of each piece of wire (fig. 6). These will thread onto the jump rings.

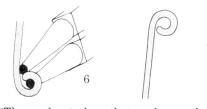

6

Victoria Drew

☐The curls at the other end must be made at right angles to the loop. You must curve 3 pieces in a clockwise direction and 3 in an anti-clockwise direction. To do this divide the lengths of wire into 2 equal groups so that you have the same number of equal lengths in each pile.
Working from one pile, hold the loop to curve away from yourself and make a curl at the other end so that it is in a vertical position when the loop is in a horizontal one.
Make a small curl for the short piece of wire and increase to larger curls for the other 2 pieces, the longest piece having the largest curl.
☐Repeat with the other 3 pieces but hold the loop so that it curves towards you. Assemble the pieces with the jump rings and findings as illustrated. Close the jump rings using the pliers. When doing this do not hold the earring in such a way as to bend any of the pieces.

The curvy bracelet

You will need:

38cm (15″) of 1.5mm (gauge 15) silver-plated wire

☐At the centre of the wire make a large curl with the pliers to let the wire cross about 2.5cm (1″) from the curve. Bend as shown in fig. 7.

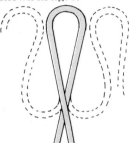

☐Make the next curve where the wire crosses and continue to form the pattern illustrated.

☐Bend the wire with your fingers so that it fits round the wrist. The bracelet is not circular but elliptical.

☐Bend each end into a U-shape so that they hook into one another.

The size of the bracelet can be varied by opening or closing the angles of the curves.

The pendant

You will need:

91cm (37″) of 1.5mm (gauge 15) silver-plated wire

45cm (18″) of 0.6mm (gauge 23) silver-plated wire for the thong

Leather thong 56cm (22″) long, about 5mm (¼″) in diameter

☐The 6 suspended pieces on the inside of the horseshoe (fig.8) are made in the same way as the 6 earring pieces.

☐Make the horseshoe with 16cm (7″) of wire. File the ends and fold the wire around a cylindrical object of 3cm (1¼″) diameter. Do this by holding the

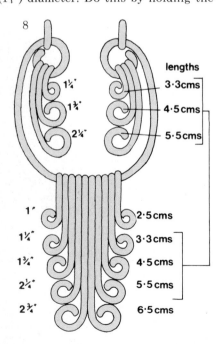

8

lengths

1¼″ 3·3cms
1¾″ 4·5cms
2¼″ 5·5cms

1″   2·5cms
1¼″   3·3cms
1¾″   4·5cms
2¼″   5·5cms
2¾″   6·5cms

halfway point of the wire to the cylinder with one hand using the thumb to keep the wire firmly in position. With the other hand work the wire around the cylinder, starting by applying pressure to the wire closest to the thumb of the other hand. Bend the wire until the ends meet (fig.9).

☐To make the 10 suspended pieces at

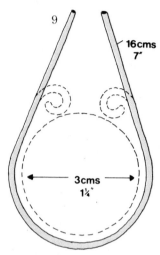

9

16cms
7″

3cms
1¼″

the bottom of the horseshoe cut 2 each of the following lengths:

2.5cm (1″), 3.3cm (1¼″), 4.5cm (1¾″), 5.5cm (2¼″), 6.5cm (2¾″).

☐File the ends and make a small loop at one end of each piece. Divide the pieces into 2 groups and proceed as for the earrings. The 3 shorter pieces from one pile are made with small curls, the next piece is slightly larger and the longest piece has the largest curve.

☐Thread the pieces on to the horseshoe to form the pattern illustrated.

☐Make a large curl at either end of the horseshoe but do not close them completely. Thread the 6 pieces and close the open ends.

☐Make any adjustments to the pieces to even out the pattern.

☐Make 2 jump rings and hook them through the 2 curls on the horseshoe. Close the jump rings and thread the leather thong through them.

Hook and eye closure. For the thong use the 0.6mm (gauge 23) wire.

☐For the eye use 20cm (8″) of wire and make a loop 3cm (1½″) from the end of the wire (fig.10).

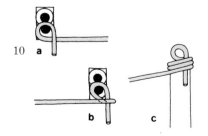

10 a

b   c

☐Wind the long end of the wire around the thong 4 times. You may find it easier to do this if you start a short distance from the end of the thong and trim it when you have finished.

☐Cut off the short end of the wire and continue winding the wire to the end. Press the end firmly into the thong with the pliers, without damaging the coils.

☐To make the hook use the remaining wire and make a U-shape 5cm (2″)

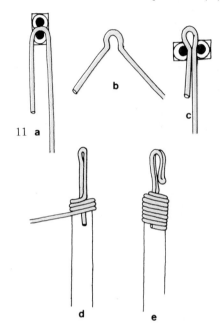

11 a

b

c

d   e

from the end (fig.11). Start winding the wire around the thong 2.5cm (1″) from the end of the U-shape and proceed as before.

☐Bend the end around to form a hook and make any adjustment necessary so that it fits the eye.

Preparing designs

Once you have a working knowledge of different wires you can design your own jewelry. Always start by drawing a full-scale, linear diagram with a felt-tipped pen to the same thickness as the wire you intend to use. Make your motifs according to this diagram or a prototype made from it.

It is difficult to make every section identical, but by using the diagram you can retain the scale, which gives an overall unity to the design. The discrepancies between the various sections give the piece its original appearance, impossible to achieve when similar articles are mass produced.

The sunray necklace

You will need:

3m (10′) of 1.5mm (gauge 15) silver-plated wire

The individual pieces must be made as near identical as possible otherwise they will not hang evenly when linked together. The pieces are joined together by 2 equal loops made at right angles to one another and interlinked.

☐Cut a 6.5cm (2½″) piece of wire.

☐Use this for measuring and cut another 43 pieces of the same length.

☐File one end of each piece flat.

☐Cut 8cm (3″) of wire and file one end. Make a large loop for the eye at the filed end by putting the wire right

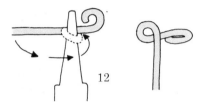

into the jaws of the pliers. Make the 2nd loop using the pliers about 5mm (¼″) from the front (fig.12). The loops for all the following pieces, except the last one, must be made in exactly the same position.

☐Working from the pile and using the pliers in the same position throughout, make an open loop at the filed end to form a hook shape. Insert this through the 2nd loop of the previous piece and

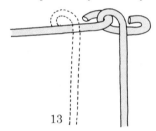

close the hook (fig.13).

☐Hold the 2nd piece in the position used in fig.1 and curl the wire around to complete the pattern.

☐Repeat for all the pieces of wire.

☐To make the hook cut a 12cm (4½″) piece of wire and file one end. Make a hook and insert it through the 2nd curl of the previous piece and close the hook. Make a U-shape 2.5cm (1″) from this curl (fig.14). Fold the end over

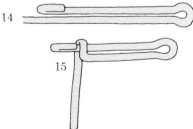

near the first curl and complete the pattern (fig.15). Fold the length of U-shape in half to complete the hook. Suspend the piece over an upturned mixing bowl. Make any adjustment necessary so the hook and eye fit.

☐Trim the individual pieces so that they are all of the same length. File the ends and make any adjustment necessary to let the pieces hang at the same angle.

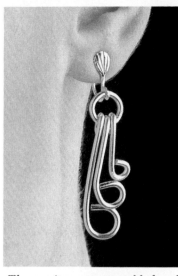

The earrings are assembled and attached to jump rings

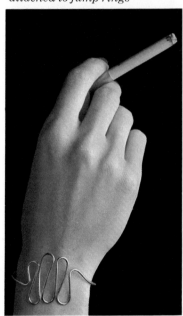

Steve Bicknell

A series of curls form the curvy bracelet, left. The pendant above develops into a large necklace, below left. Hang the completed necklace over an upturned mixing bowl and make adjustments to it so that it hangs evenly. If you make the sunray necklace, below right from silver wire, first use cheaper wire to practise making the two pieces at the ends.

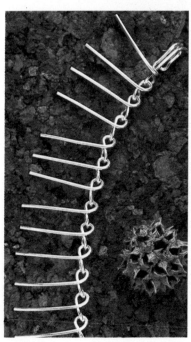

Metalcrafts&Glass

These unusual projects are a wonderful introduction to working with glass and metal. Etching and stained glass are described, as well as simple metal decoration.

Etching on glass

Glass is a familiar material which we use every day—for storage, drinking out of, to let light into our homes and to look through; it can be stained, coloured, etched or engraved and craftsmen have produced exquisitely decorated pieces of glassware. As a material, it has the unique property of rigid transparency. Yet very few people attempt to work with it to produce decorative effects of their own. Reluctance to try handling glass may be explained by the mystique it has developed over the years—master craftsmen spend so long studying and learning how to make glass, to blow shapes and to master the arts of firing and annealing (the process of toughening glass). But there is no need to be overawed—with modern materials to help, you can easily learn how to create decorative effects and to build up designs and structures in glass.

Acid etching

Etching on glass, by allowing controlled amounts of acid to eat away selected parts of the top layer of the glass to make a design, is an old-established craft. It dates from the discovery in 1771 of hydrofluoric acid. This acid is used in various solutions, the purest of which will dissolve glass but leave the remaining surface clear when the acid is poured off. If the acid is combined with an alkali to produce sodium or ammonium bifluoride, known as 'white acid', the remaining effect will be frosted.

Perhaps the most common example of acid-etched glass is the frosted light bulb. When these are made, a solution of white acid is poured into the bulb and then drained off, leaving a rough internal surface which blocks out much of the light. Then a milder solution is applied which removes most of the rough edges and lets the light through again, with the familiar frosted effect.

What acid should you use? Commercial etching is done with powerful solutions of hydrofluoric acid, which should only be used in carefully controlled, well-ventilated conditions. Now, however, commercial etching fluid is available, which is much milder and, given reasonable care, quite safe. This fluid produces a frosted effect. It can be bought as part of a kit, which includes all you need to start decorative etching—gum-backed stencils, applicators and tweezers as well as etching fluid. The individual components are also available separately at craft shops.

What glass should you use? You can use any glass. The finest decorative work is usually done on lead glass, which was developed in the seventeenth century and was the chosen material of the great Dutch engravers, because it is relatively soft and very clear. It is expensive, because lead is an ingredient—the highest quality, Full Lead Crystal Glass, has a minimum of 30% lead content while the next grade, Lead Crystal, which includes most Waterford Glass, has a minimum of 24% lead content.

By using stencils you can etch labels on jars. Designed by Jennifer Grant.

Most glass in the home is likely to be a variety of soda-lime-silica glass which, as the name implies, is largely made of these three constituents—silica sand, soda ash and limestone. This glass has a tendency to be greenish, like old bottles, and small quantities of other chemicals are usually added to reduce this.

There is no need to insist on using lead glass for your decorations—you will be much better advised to use objects you can find around the home or buy cheaply. You can create delightful effects on old jam jars or coffee containers, easily bought spice jars or cheap wine glasses. All of these will probably be made of soda-lime-silica glass.

Within this broad category, there are hundreds of different types of glass, with slightly different constituents and properties. Etching fluid will react slightly differently on each of them, so you will have to experiment, particularly with the length of time you allow it to work. It is advisable, also, to make your first attempts at decoration on a waste piece of glass, until you are confident in your own ability.

Controlling the acid

To achieve a good pattern it is absolutely essential that you control the application of the acid carefully and accurately. You do this by 'stopping-out'. There are a variety of materials you can use for this which will prevent the acid from reaching the areas you want to remain unaffected.

In traditional acid etching, the whole object on which a design is to be etched is immersed in a bath of acid, so very thorough stopping out is needed. This is usually done by covering the surface with Brunswick Black, which is a thick, acid-resistant varnish; at the edges of the design, thin lead foil is often glued on with a beeswax-tallow mixture to give a sharp edge.

For our purposes, such elaborate protection will not be necessary. A glass-etching kit will supply gum-backed stencils or you could use glue and paper, but the best material is a contact plastic like Fablon or ConTac. It is essential that the material should be resistant to the acid and that there should be no bubbles or unglued parts along the edge under which the acid can seep, to spoil the line. When you have stuck the material down, rub over it with the back of a spoon or, better still, with a small roller to smooth down the edge.

Making a pattern. If you are using ready-made, gum-backed stencils, then this will be no problem. Simply cut the appropriate section from a stencil sheet, peel off the backing and stick it on. If you are using several pieces—

as for lettering—then be careful to align them properly.

If you are not using ready-made stencils, you will have to cut the design out of the stop-out material. It is easiest to work if you can fit the design on to one piece of stop-out material, so that it can be cut and handled as one piece. This is possible if you are working on flat glass or straight-sided tumblers or jars. In this case you can draw the design on to the material and cut it out before attaching it to the glass (fig.1). You can use ordinary stencils, or trace a design you like, or draw your own—until you cut

Jerry Tubby

To make a pretty, frosted window, cut a design from contact plastic, stick it to the glass and start etching.

the design out, you can keep altering and improving it.

A word of warning: with some patterns and letters, you will have to stop-out the inside as well as the outside of the shape, although they do not connect. For example, to etch the letter 'O', it is important that the centre piece of stop-out material be positioned exactly in the middle of the shape. In such cases, it is best to stick a solid piece of material on the glass,

1a. *When working on a straight-sided glass or jar, cut the design out of the stop-out material before sticking it on the glass.*

Victoria Drew

1b. *When the stop-out material is stuck on to the glass, the area to be etched is left uncovered.*

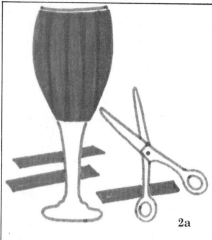

2a. *To cover a curved surface with stop-out material, cut the material into strips and lay them down so that all the glass is covered; the strips overlap at the narrower top and bottom.*

2b. *Draw the design on to the material after you stick it down.*

2c. *Cut the design out and peel off the areas you want to etch.*

with the letter drawn on it. Cut out and lift off the area you want to etch, using either a scalpel or a sharp knife and tweezers.

If you are working with glass that is curved in two directions—like a wine glass, as opposed to a straight-sided tumbler—you will not be able to lay a flat sheet on it without it creasing, unless you are going to etch only a very small area. To overcome this problem cut the material into strips before

drawing the design. After preparing the glass (see Etching method, below), stick the strips on to the glass to cover the area to be etched (fig.2). Draw the design in pencil. When you are satisfied with it, cut the material carefully with a scalpel or sharp knife and lift off the parts covering the areas you want to etch.

Etching method
You will need:
Glass
Etching fluid
Stop-out material
Brush, or cotton bud on stick [Q-tip]
Tweezers
Spoon or small roller
Detergent, soft cloth
Running water

☐ Clean the glass on which you will be etching by washing it with detergent to remove all the grease from the surface. This is essential as the fluid will not act properly on a greasy surface. Be careful not to get finger-marks on the clean glass. Handle it only by areas that will not be etched. Dry the glass with a clean, soft cloth and make sure it is thoroughly dry before putting on the stop-out material.

☐ Prepare your stop-out stencil. Using tweezers to avoid finger-marks, put the stencil in position on the glass. If you are working on curved glass, now is the time to cut the stencil. If you are using more than one piece of stop-out material, then be careful to line them up accurately. Smooth the material down with a spoon or small roller to make sure that the edges are solid. This is particularly important if you have overlapping pieces, for the join may be a vulnerable point.

☐ It is advisable to leave the stop-out stencils for an hour or two after they are stuck down, to set firmer. It is much more important to get a good edge than to be able to peel the material off easily. Most adhesives, even contact adhesives, set harder if left for a while and so will resist the acid better.

☐ Make sure the surface to be etched is horizontal, as the etching fluid will run down a slope.

If you are working on a curved surface, such as a jar or drinking glass, you will have to etch it a bit at a time. Keep the part you are etching horizontal by holding it in place with bookends, paperweights or anything to stop it rolling.

☐ Take the container of etching fluid and check the manufacturer's instructions. They will probably tell you to shake it vigorously to dispel any sediment that may have gathered, which would leave a diluted and ineffective solution at the top. Use a small brush or a bud of cotton wool on the end of

a toothpick to paint the fluid on to the glass. Put it on as thick as you can without spilling it.

Leave the fluid on the glass for 5 to 10 minutes. The exact length of time needed for the fluid to work will depend on the glass: experience is the only real guide.

☐ Wash off the fluid with warm running water. Do this quickly and carefully to avoid dislodging the stop-out material. Dab the glass dry with a

clean cloth and take a good look at it. If there are any patchy areas where the fluid has not worked properly, make sure the glass is completely dry and re-apply the fluid.

If you are working on a curved surface and the section you have been working on is completed, turn the glass, prop it up again and apply the fluid to the next area.

☐ When all the unmasked areas in your design have been frosted, peel off the stencils. If they are stuck very hard, try soaking them in warm water. In really intractable cases, try using lighter fluid to loosen the glue.

Safety hints

Commercial etching fluid is specially designed to be as safe as possible. But you are working with an acid, however mild it is, and it can burn. You should be careful, particularly if there are children about. Never let the fluid

Anything made of glass can be decorated by etching—give a new sparkle to wine glasses or add a motif to a simple glass bowl.

get in the eyes, on spectacles, or on clothes. Never drink it or lick the applicators, like pencils. If any spills, dilute it with plenty of water and make sure it is washed off completely. If you act promptly, it will not cause severe burns even if spilt on skin.

Stained glass effects

The most attractive thing about the use of glass as a medium for artistic expression is its transparent quality—it is even more exciting to use if the glass is coloured. Stained glass has been employed for centuries to create lovely effects such as light shining through different colours of glass to point out a design or to make a bright shaft of colour in a room.

Traditional stained glass work involves using small pieces of differently coloured glass and joining them together with strips of lead to form designs. But now that there are several transparent glass paints available you can create the effect of stained glass without the expense and difficulty of both cutting and leading glass. There are also materials which simulate the effect of traditional leading. So you can decorate a flat piece of glass to make a panel, a chopped bottle for a candle-holder, a large beaker for a flower vase or any glass object which you want to enrich. With these new materials stained glass work has become a craft which everybody can learn.

Materials for painting

The essential materials for creating stained glass effects are the paints and the 'leading'. These can be bought from craft shops, either separately or together in kit form.

Paints made by the same manufacturer can usually be mixed together, but do check this before buying them. If they can be mixed you may prefer to buy the primary colours (red, yellow and blue) and make different hues yourself. The essential property of these paints is that they are transparent and will adhere to glass.

Artificial leading. One type is in tube form, like an oil paint, which is squeezed out where the lines are needed, and takes an hour or so to harden. This gives a very dark effect, as illustrated on the right.

There is another type of artificial leading which is like a putty and comes separately in two constituents which have to be mixed together. In order to apply this putty, you must mix it into a ball, roll it out into a long, thin tube and place it in position. It hardens in about three hours. Brush lampblack over the putty to darken it to the colour of lead. (Lampblack is available at most hardware stores.) The final result is very impressive, almost indistinguishable from traditional lead, but it requires more effort than the 'tube' type and is not so widely available.

Steve Bicknell

Paint a round glass lampshade and introduce soft, moody lighting into your living room or any other room in the house. Designed by Karina Sterry.

Above: paint your candle holders or table lanterns for a colourful display.

Below: draw a design on paper, place under the glass and trace with 'leading'.

This design, suitable for glass painting can be enlarged on graph paper.

Whichever materials you use, do practise on some scrap glass first—a jam-jar or a small piece of window pane glass will do. Once you have mastered the technique you can start putting your own ideas into effect.

To paint a glass surface

You will need:
Glass paints and glass.
Leading.
Small brush and paper for design.
Polyurethane varnish (optional).

☐ Draw the design you want to paint on a piece of paper, the same size as the finished object. You can make up your own design or copy one from elsewhere, but the most effective designs are usually made up of small segments. Too large an area of one colour means that you run the risk of the colour being uneven, although as you become more experienced, you may want to create a mottled effect.

☐ Thoroughly clean the glass to be decorated with warm water and detergent. If there is any grease on the surface the paint will not adhere properly. Rinse and dry the glass, taking care not to touch with your fingers the surface to be painted.

Decorate a glass panel with this cheerful fish or paint a complete aquarium. Designed by Reeves Ltd.

☐ Tape the piece of paper with the design drawn on it to the back of the glass, so that you can see the design through the glass. Lay the glass on a flat surface.

☐ Check the manufacturer's instructions for the 'tube' leading, which comes with a nozzle at the end of the tube. Cut the nozzle at different places to give different thicknesses—the nearer to the base the nozzle is cut, the wider the hole will be and the thicker the line of leading. Make the first cut near the top of the nozzle; you can always cut again for a thicker line.

☐ Trace the lines of the design with the leading. Hold the tube at a slight angle to the glass, with the nozzle lightly touching the glass, and squeeze gently and regularly as you draw the nozzle along the glass. Avoid resting your hand on the glass. If necessary, wear cotton gloves or put a piece of clean fabric under your hand to avoid getting grease from your skin on to the surface.

☐ After each line has been drawn, clean the nozzle with a pin before starting a new line. Be sure that the leading is free of holes and gaps and that it touches the glass wherever you intend it to.

☐ If you want the leading to lie flat, smooth it down gently with your fingers before it is quite dry—about 15

minutes after application. At this stage you can use a match-stick or spoon handle to push the leading over the glass to even out any irregularities.

☐ If you want to thicken the line without cutting the nozzle further, hold the tube in a vertical position and squeeze slightly harder, but still with even pressure. This will increase the flow and thicken the line.

☐ Leave the leading to dry for an hour before starting to paint.

☐ Take the sheet of paper away from the glass. When painting it is important to be able to see right through the glass or it is impossible to judge how transparent the colours will look. So put some white paper down on your working surface, to give a reflective background, and raise the glass about 15mm ($\frac{1}{2}$″) above the paper by resting it on small blocks. Keep the surface of the glass as level as possible to reduce the risk of the paint running.

☐ Mix the paint according to the manufacturer's instructions—some paints may only need to be shaken before application, others need to be shaken and then diluted with one part of water to two parts of paint. If the paint has to be mixed, be sure to get the proportions right—if the paint is too thick, it will be difficult to cover the glass evenly; if the paint is runny, it will tend to pull away from the leading

and concentrate in the centre of each area of paint.

☐ Apply the paint by letting it flow from the brush, rather than using vigorous brush strokes. If the paint is of the right consistency, it should level itself off into a smooth coat. The more paint you put on the deeper the colour will be because less light is allowed through.

Let the paint dry for at least three hours before handling it, or before putting another coat over it if you feel the colour needs to be deeper.

You can experiment to get a rippled effect by putting on a very thin coat and waiting until it is tacky. Then dab on little dots of colour to give deliberately uneven colour.

☐ Clean brushes thoroughly with warm water and detergent immediately after use. Rinse them in cold water.

Finishing. Paints sold for painting on glass are usually water-resistant, so that the painted surface can be cleaned *gently* with cold water. But for a more durable finish, especially if the glass will be in a steamy atmosphere, such as a kitchen or bathroom, coat the surface with a polyurethane-based clear varnish. Make sure the paint is completely dry before you apply this. The varnish will probably add a yellow tinge to the colours, so test it on a scrap piece before using it.

Above: hang a painted window in front of a plain one, and change your view. Designed by Craft Materials Supplies.

Below: glass paints are very versatile— go abstract with a brightly lit panel. Designed by Reeves Ltd.

Recycling tin cans

Apart from paper, tin cans are probably the greatest throw-away items in any dustbin. They come in a variety of shapes and sizes, from ordinary round cans to the more unusual shapes often used for pâtés. Some cans incorporate a corrugated design in the curved surface. The catering trade buys fruit juices in large tin cans which invariably end up on the rubbish heap in just the same way as the cans which we buy and take home.

The natural resources of the earth are dwindling away and, although it is impossible to replace them, everyone can certainly attempt to conserve and make better use of them.

A tin can, once empty, has served its obvious purpose but, instead of throwing it away, why not spend a little time punching a design in the tin and then using it as a candle-holder or a receptacle for pot plants?

You can attach pieces of wire to the tin cans, fill them with trailing plants and suspend them from the ceiling. You can also use them for candle-holders, letting the holes in the tin form an intricate pattern of light spots around the room.

Position for punching cans.

Designs

You may feel that there is a limited number of things to do with tin cans, but you can make them more interesting by working out designs for them rather than punching holes at random. To do this cut a piece of plain paper to fit around a tin can (fig.1).

The punched tin cans make attractive holders. Designed by Tony Wilson.

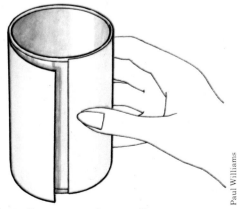

1. *Cut paper to fit around can.*

Open the piece of paper to a flat surface and divide it into a number of sections of equal size. You can measure the sections to make them exactly the same or you can judge the size by eye (fig.2). The number of sections does

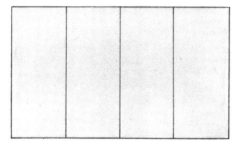

2. *Divide paper into sections.*

not matter, but the larger the tin can the more sections you should make. In each section draw circles to the size you want to punch the holes and repeat pattern in each section (fig.3). Or you can reverse them in alternate sections (fig.4). Use a ruler or tape measure to help you with straight lines and a cup or saucer for curved lines.

3. *Draw the pattern on to the paper indicating the size and shape of the holes you wish to punch.*

4. *The designs are easy to change. Any one design can be varied by reversing the pattern in alternate sections.*

You can make very intricate designs and you can also vary the shape of the holes by using different implements as your punching tools.

Tools

You will need:
Hammer.
Nail-punch or large nail for round holes. An old screwdriver will make elongated holes—the larger the screwdriver the closer to a straight line the hole will be. You will damage a good

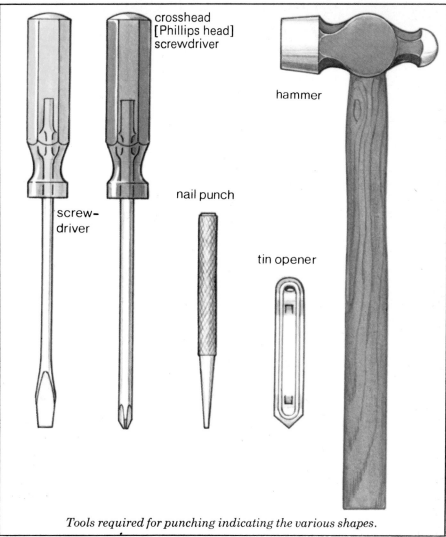

Tools required for punching indicating the various shapes.

screwdriver if you use it for punching tins, so use an old one.
Tin opener (of the type used for soft drinks or beer cans) will make triangular-shaped holes.
A piece of wood or dowel large enough to fit neatly inside the cans.

Punching

Prepare the tin cans by cleaning them and removing the labels. If there are any sharp edges around the lip of the cans use the hammer to flatten them and smooth the surface.
To punch. If you punch holes from the bottom towards the open end, the can will dent and lose its shape. To avoid this the can should be supported from the inside. Any piece of wood or dowel can be used for this purpose. Insert a block inside the tin can where you are about to punch holes (fig.5). Or slide a length of thick dowel into the can (fig.6).
Wrap the design around the tin can and secure it by taping the ends together. Use the nail-punch and hammer to make holes at the required spots. If you want to re-use the design make very light indents in the tin can and remove the paper design before

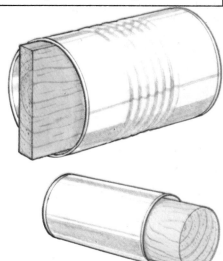

5, 6. *To prevent can from buckling while being punched insert a piece of wood to support the can.*

actually punching the holes in the can. Alternatively, trace the design before attaching and punching the holes.
If you use the tin cans for plant pots, paint or varnish them to prevent them from rusting.

291

Modelling sheet copper

Modelling thin copper sheet is an ancient oriental craft. For centuries copper has been used to decorate surfaces—even covering whole walls. Pictures, wall panels, fire screens and jewel boxes can be decorated with copper. The completed items look very solid but in fact a very thin sheet of copper is used and then mounted on to a base board.

The effects can be varied, for example you may cover a cigar box and oxidize the copper to give it an antique finish or, for a wall panel, you can leave it fairly bright. Another idea is to use metal blanks (as for the blanks used in enamelling), and cover them with the modelled copper to form jewelry. You can make labels for decanters similarly. The technique does not involve hammers at all. The design is traced on to the face of the copper and then modelled from the back. The indentations are then filled and the facing surface is polished to complete the object. No anvils are required and it can be done on any firm flat surface—the kitchen table will do.

The copper sheeting can be obtained in various sizes. Craft stores will be able to supply the necessary tools. You can use a kit if you prefer or buy only what you need if you already have some equipment.

The copper sheet is very thin and fairly soft so do not be misled by the solid metallic appearance. Be careful when handling the copper as it creases and dents very easily. The marks are impossible to remove and will spoil the end result.

A dead ball point pen or a knitting needle, with not too sharp a point, is used to trace the outline of the design on to the face of the copper.

The copper is placed on the work table on a soft surface such as a folded towel, an old bath mat or piece of foam rubber of similar thickness.

The modelling is done from the back of the copper with various spatulas or modelling tools. Here you can improvise; the handle of a teaspoon or knife can be used but the disadvantage is that the grip is not comfortable unless you wrap the tool with a piece of cloth and masking tape so that it fits comfortably in your hand—it is held like a pencil but requires more pressure.

A filler is used in the indentations so that the copper will not dent once the design has been completed. There is a variety of suitable fillers. Use whatever you have to hand or what is economical; candle wax, beeswax, wall filler and clear-cast embedding resin with hardener are all suitable fillers. Any of these can be used for flat surfaces but if a slightly curved surface, such as a label for a decanter, is being made use beeswax as it will not crack or break when curved. It is melted and poured into the indentations before the metal is curved. Once the wax has set the label can be curved gently with the fingers.

Oxidizing. The copper can be given an antique appearance by applying an oxidizing agent sometimes called copper patina. You can buy it from craft stores or mix your own by adding six parts of water to one part of potassium sulphide from chemists.

Technique. Practise on a piece of scrap copper before actually making up a design. On a small piece of copper draw a circle with a dead ball point pen. Turn the copper over and draw another line as close as possible to, and within, the circle.

Place the copper on a towel or old bath mat with the second line you drew facing upwards. Use a modelling tool and push it gently backwards and forwards using short strokes within the circle. Turn the copper over and check your results. Do it evenly so that the surface does not have bumps or mounds. You can continue until the copper becomes thin. You will soon get the 'feel' of it and if the copper does tear it will give you a guide as to how much you can force the copper out and will prevent you from doing it when making up a design.

Designs. Any picture will do—from vintage cars to abstract motifs of your own choice. Draw full size designs on to paper (or trace them) and mark in any necessary detail.

A wall panel

The panel is 20cm x 15cm (8"x6") and mounted on a base. The frame is optional.

You will need:

Suitable design on tracing paper.
Dead ball point pen or knitting needle.
Modelling tools.
Copper sheet .13mm (gauge No.35), 22cm x 17cm (8¾"x6¾")—any copper around this thickness will do. Craft stores often refer to it as .0056".
Masking tape or equivalent.
Filler—any of the above mentioned will do.
Base board such as chipboard [particle board] 20cm×15cm (8"×6"), 6mm (¼") thick. The copper is larger than the base board so that the sides can be folded around the base board to hide it.
Potassium sulphide—optional—to give the copper an antique appearance
Methylated spirit [de-natured alcohol]
All-purpose adhesive.
Lacquer or clear varnish—optional—to seal the copper surface and prevent

Louis Jordaan

The fire screen is made from a thin sheet of copper which has been tooled and mounted on to a hardboard base.

Above: trace pattern used for making one of the soldiers illustrated.
Right: the completed copper panels make attractive wall decorations.
Below: the first step in making the panel is transferring the design.

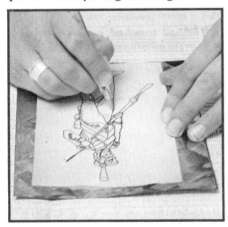

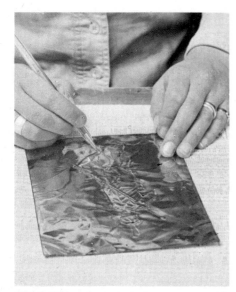

The outline is repeated on wrong side of copper just inside original design.

The modelling or tooling is done from the back using a wooden spatula.

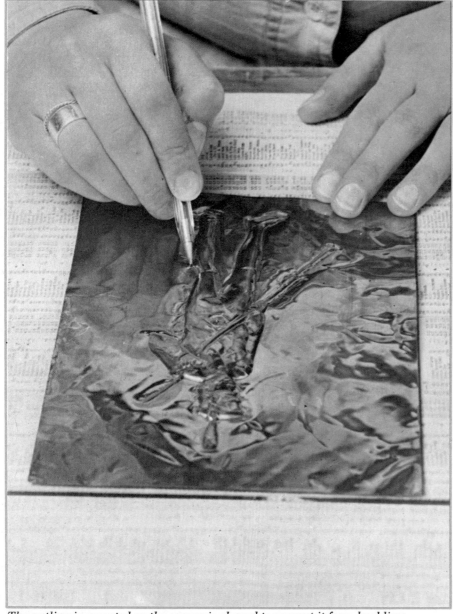

The outline is repeated as the copper is shaped to prevent it from buckling.

it from discolouring. Metal polish. Piece of glass or old tile to work on.

☐ Cover the work surface with paper. Place the more attractive surface of the copper facing upwards. Use masking tape to hold the design on the copper in position.

☐ Using the dead ball point pen trace over the design. Keep the pressure even and make sure to go over all the lines making up the design.

☐ Lift the copper and look at the back of it to see that the design is complete and that the lines are even.

☐ Remove the design from the copper and lay the copper face downwards. Now draw the design on the wrong side just inside the lines of the design, but around the main outline only. Look at the facing side of the copper and you will see that the design is now slightly raised.

☐ Place the copper, face downwards on a soft surface, such as a folded towel or a bath mat. Use a modelling tool and start to press the copper down with firm strokes, moving the tool backwards and forwards. Work evenly all over the design but within the sections of the pattern.

Some parts need to be pushed out more than others. Turn the copper over and check your results. Continue until you get the desired effect. You will develop a 'feel' for the copper and know when it is getting thin—do not push it out too much or the copper will tear. Once the copper has been pushed out, it is impossible to push it back so try not to make any mistakes. Work in stages and check your results as you progress.

☐ Turn the completed design face upwards on your working surface without the towel. Go over the exact outline firmly with the ball point pen. (This will prevent the metal from buckling and keep the design flat.) Do this carefully turning the copper as required so that you can reach the outline without putting any pressure on the shaped copper. Make sure the surface on which you are working is quite flat. (A piece of glass or an old tile is ideal for this.)

☐ Add more detail, if necessary by working on the towel again. Once you have finished go over the outline as before. This is important as it keeps the work absolutely flat which is necessary to mount the copper on to the base.

☐ Once the design is complete the indentations must be filled to protect them from possible dents. Use a filler of your choice.

If you are using wax melt it and then carefully pour it into the recesses. Once it has hardened you can scrape off any excess or spilt wax with a knife.

If you are using another type of filler, work neatly and make sure there is no filler spilt on the copper outside the design as it will show on the completed outside surface. Resin takes a while to set hard but the results are excellent—so place it in an airing cupboard and be patient until it is absolutely hard.

The tacky resin surface is also a good adhesive when you mount the copper.

☐ Once the filler is dry spread glue over the entire back surface of the copper—including the filler. Apply glue to one side of the base board.

☐ Place the copper on to the glued surface of the base board. Make sure it is in the correct position and gently push the copper down. Work from the area around the design towards the outer edges of the copper.

☐ Go over the outline again to make sure that it is quite flat. Using scissors cut the corners of the copper where it overhangs the base board and fold the copper down as close to the edge of the base board as possible.

☐ You can leave the background as it is or use a metal knitting needle to make indentations, at random, all over or starting from the design and decreasing the texturing as you work away from it. Another method of decorating the background is to use the round head of a hammer and to lightly beat the metal. Be very careful when doing this so that you do not damage any of the raised surfaces.

☐ Clean the surface with metal polish. Do this a number of times if necessary until the metal is very shiny.

☐ To darken the copper—for an antique appearance—use the potassium sulphide. Mix 1 teaspoon of potassium sulphide with 6 tablespoons of water. This mixture is hard on the hands so protect them with rubber gloves.

The copper surface must be free of grease to make this successful so wipe surface with methylated spirits [denatured alcohol] before applying patina.

☐ Apply the mixture to tne copper with a piece of cottonwool. Do it evenly until the copper is completely black. Wipe off any excess liquid.

☐ Use a small amount of metal polish and start polishing the surface concentrating on the pushed out parts of the copper. This will highlight the design. The copper will start returning to its original colour. Continue this polishing until only the recessed parts are left dark.

If you are not happy with your result you can darken the surface again and start over until the right effect is achieved.

☐ To protect the surface and to prevent it from discolouring apply a coat of lacquer or varnish to the design. If you do not do this the copper will discolour and need repolishing.

The design can now be framed, or hung as it is if the sides have been neatly folded back.

To prevent the shaped copper from being damaged a filler is used to fill the recessed areas at the back. The back must be flat when completed.

Once the filler is dry the entire back of copper is glued and placed on base.

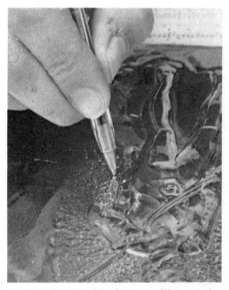

The background is decorated by a series of random dots around the design.

Oxidizing agent blackens the copper.

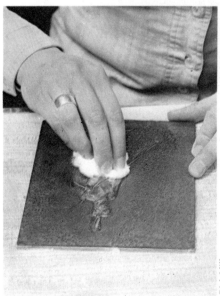

Metal polish highlights raised areas.

Index